TO BE
DISPOSED
BY
AUTHORITY

Policies for a small planet

Policies for a small planet

From the International Institute for
Environment and Development

Edited by Johan Holmberg

Foreword by Sir Crispin Tickell

Publications Ltd   London

First published 1992 by
Earthscan Publications Limited
120 Pentonville Road, London N1 9JN

British Library Cataloguing in Publication Data
A catalogue record for this book is available from the British Library
ISBN 1–85383–132–8

Typeset by Saxon Printing Ltd, Derby
Printed by Biddles Ltd, Guildford and Kings Lynn

Earthscan Publications Ltd is an editorially independent subsidiary of Kogan
Page Limited and publishes in association with the International Institute for
Environment and Development and the World Wide Fund for Nature (UK).

Contents

Contributors

Bruce Aylward, a development/environmental economist, works with the IIED/UCL London Environmental Economics Centre, which he joined in 1990.

Edward Barbier, an environmental economist, joined IIED in 1986 and since 1990 has been director of the London Environmental Economics Centre.

Stephen Bass, a forester/agriculturalist, joined IIED in 1990 and is associate director of its Forestry and Land Use Programme.

Joshua Bishop, an environmental economist, has worked with the London Environmental Economics Centre since 1991.

Joanne Burgess, an environmental economist, has worked with the London Environmental Economics Centre since 1988.

Irene Guijt, an irrigation engineer, has worked with the IIED Sustainable Agriculture Programme since 1990.

Jorge Hardoy, an architect and urban planner, is director of IIED–America Latina in Buenos Aires and co-director of the IIED Human Settlements Programme.

Johan Holmberg, an economist, is director of the IIED programme of support to the preparations for UNCED and is on leave of absence from the Swedish International Development Authority.

Gregory Kats, an energy specialist, works as a freelance consultant.

Diana Mitlin, an economist, has been working with the IIED Human Settlements Programme since 1989.

Jules Pretty, an agricultural ecologist, joined IIED in 1986 and is director of its Sustainable Agriculture Programme.

Nick Robins, a specialist on industry and environment issues, is currently working with the XIth Directorate-General on the European Commission's preparations for UNCED.

John Rowley is assistant director of Public Affairs at the International Planned Parenthood Federation in London and editor of *People and the Planet*.

Richard Sandbrook, a biologist and chartered accountant, joined IIED in 1976 and has been its executive director since 1989.

Caroline Sargent, a plant ecologist/forester, joined IIED in 1988 and is director of its Forestry and Land Use Programme.

David Satterthwaite, a development planner, is co-director of the IIED Human Settlements Programme.

Ian Scoones, an ecologist, joined IIED in 1988 and is working for both the Drylands Programme and the Sustainable Agriculture Programme.

Robin Sharp, a development writer and NGO specialist, headed the IIED Southern Networks Programme during 1986–92 and is now working free-lance.

John Thompson, a resource geographer, has worked with the IIED Sustainable Agriculture Programme since 1990.

Camilla Toulmin, an economist, joined IIED in 1987 and is director of its Drylands Programme.

Alex Trisoglio, a specialist on industry and environment issues, manages business and industry programmes at the International Academy of Environment in Geneva.

Foreword

Sustainable development can mean different things to different people, but it still represents a most productive way of thinking. Long before the Brundtland Commission report on environment and development gave the idea its blessing, the IIED had been using it as an indispensable instrument of policy analysis. For it to be understood and made fully effective, we have to look at certain cherished assumptions and habits of thought, and create new and more realistic values.

That means:

- We need to recast our vocabulary. Words are not only a means of expression but also the building blocks of thought. The instruments of economic analysis are blunt and rusty. Such words as 'growth', 'development', 'cost-benefit analysis', even 'gross national product', are used in such a misleading way that they are more than ripe for redefinition.
- We need to realize that conventional wisdom is sometimes a contradiction in terms. Some trends, for example consumption of non-renewable resources, are going in the wrong direction; and sometimes we make renewable resources non-renewable. Unfortunately, as René Dubos pointed out, people can adapt themselves to almost anything: for example, not to mind car exhausts, urban sprawl, 'starless skies, treeless avenues, shapeless buildings, tasteless bread, joyless celebrations'.
- We need to change the culture. Many have lamented the division between the cultures of science and the arts. They are right to do so. But neither is now in charge. Our real bosses are the business managers. It was Edmund Burke who feared that the age of 'sophisters, economists and calculators' had come. Their calculations are strictly short term.
- We need to recast parts of our educational systems to promote better understanding of the environment. In some countries this has begun

11

already, and in others it was always there. In general I have found the young more in tune with nature than their teachers.

- We need a value system which enshrines the principle of sustainability over generations. Here the Brundtland Report has made a beginning, with its definition of sustainable development as 'development that meets the needs of the present without compromising the ability of future generations to meet their own needs'. But we have far to go. The proposed Earth Charter for the Summit in June 1992 is the first test.

The present book is an attempt to pull the arguments together, and to give them practical shape. It comes at a critical time. I wish it all success.

Sir Crispin Tickell
Chairman, IIED Board of Directors

Preface

The 1992 United Nations Conference on Environment and Development, variously referred to as the Earth Summit or Eco '92 or simply by the acronym UNCED, is the major event on the world environment agenda as the end of the twentieth century approaches. During 1991, preparations for the conference increasingly captured the attention of the community of institutions and individuals directly concerned with protecting the environment, and gradually the media have also taken an interest. In the months leading up to the event itself in Rio de Janeiro, Brazil, in June 1992, there is no doubt that UNCED will also have the attention of world leaders and feature in political discussions within and between nations.

For twenty years, the International Institute for Environment and Development (IIED) has been at the forefront of the debate about the relationship between environment and development. UNCED marks the end of the beginning of that debate and the first time that environment and development issues will be reviewed together in a global setting. As planning for UNCED got under way in 1989, it was therefore natural that IIED would also plan for its involvement in the preparations for this major event. The IIED 1992 Programme was started in 1990, and this volume was written as part of that activity.

Work on the book has been a collaborative effort within the Institute, involving all in-house research programmes and a few outsiders collaborating with us. It is an attempt to spell out what we mean by sustainable development in our fields of interest, given the current and mostly distressing trends. In keeping with the advocacy role of the Institute, we have focused on policy prescriptives for governments, development agencies and others active in formulating the sustainable development agenda.

IIED is a small institute that cannot cover all aspects and specialized fields pertinent to sustainable development. The book therefore reflects the collective expertise within the Institute and does not purport to provide complete coverage. Our remit is to work with developing countries, and we have therefore not, in the main, concerned ourselves with issues of sustainability in the industrialized countries.

The IIED 1992 Programme is being financed by contributions from the governments of Denmark, the Netherlands, Norway, Sweden and the UK. This book would not have been written without their generous support, and we are grateful to them all. Special thanks are due to Vinetta Holness, who helped me edit the copious manuscripts.

Johan Holmberg
London, December 1991

Abbreviations and Acronyms

ACORD	Agency for Co-operation and Research in Development
ACTS	African Centre for Technology Studies
ADR	Average disparity ratio
CAMPFIRE	Communal Area Management Programme for Indigenous Resource Exploitation
CBO	Congressional Budget Office
CFCs	Chlorofluorocarbons
CMC	Cercle Modial du Consensus
CMIE	Centre for Monitoring Indian Economy
CONAMUP	National Co-ordinating Body of Mexico's Urban Popular Movement
CSE	Centre for Science and Environment
CWS	Church World Service
DAC	Development Assistance Committee of the OECD
DANIDA	Danish International Development Agency
DFI	Direct foreign investment
EC	European Community
ECLAC	Economic Commission for Latin America and the Caribbean
EDR	Extreme disparity ratio
EPA	Environmental Protection Agency
FAO	Food and Agriculture Organization of the United Nations
FINNIDA	Finnish International Development Agency
GATT	General Agreement on Tariffs and Trade
GDP	Gross domestic product
GEF	Global Environment Facility
GNP	Gross national product
GRET	Groupe de Recherche et d'Echanges Technologiques

HEI	High external input (system of agriculture)
ICC	International Chamber of Commerce
IEA	International Energy Agency
IFAD	International Fund for Agricultural Development
IIASA	International Institute for Applied Systems Analysis
IIED	International Institute for Environment and Development
ILO	International Labour Organization
IMF	International Monetary Fund
IPCC	Intergovernmental Panel on Climate Change
IPM	Integrated pest management
IPPF	International Planned Parenthood Federation
IRRI	International Rice Research Institute
IUCN	International Union for the Conservation of Nature and Natural Resources
LEEC	London Environmental Economics Centre
LEI	Low external input (system of agriculture)
LWR	Lutheran World Relief
MIT	Massachusetts Institute of Technology
MITI	Ministry for International Trade and Industry
MV	Modern (seed) variety
NANGO	National Association of NGOs
NCS	National conservation strategy
NGO	Non-governmental organization
NIA	National Irrigation Authority
NIC	Newly industrializing country
NORAD	Norwegian Agency for Development
NRC	National Research Council
NTFPs	Non-timber forest products
ODA	Official development assistance
ODA	Overseas Development Administration
ODF	Official development finance
ODI	Overseas Development Institute
OECD	Organization for Economic Co-operation and Development
OTA	Office of Technology Assessment
PEC	Primary environmental care
PV	Photovoltaic
R & D	Research and development
RRA	Rapid rural appraisal
Rs	Rupees

SADCC	Southern Africa Development Co-ordination Conference
SARA	Superfund Amendment and Reauthorization Act
SIDA	Swedish International Development Authority
SINA	Settlements Information Network Africa
SPARC	Society for Promotion of Area Resource Centres
T & D	Transmission and distribution
T & V	Training and visit
TFAP	Tropical Forest Action Programme
TRI	US Toxics Release Inventory
TUC	Trades Union Congress
UCL	University College London
UNCED	United Nations Conference on Environment and Development
UNCHS	United Nations Centre for Human Settlements
UNCOD	United Nations Conference on Desertification
UNCTAD	United Nations Conference on Trade and Development
UNCTC	United Nations Centre on Transnational Corporations
UNDP	United Nations Development Programme
UNEP	United Nations Environment Programme
UNESCO	United Nations Educational, Scientific and Cultural Organization
UNFPA	United Nations Population Fund
UNICEF	United Nations Children's Fund
UNIDO	United Nations Industrial Development Organization
USAID	United States Agency for International Development
US DOE	United States Department of Energy
WCED	World Commission on Environment and Development
WHO	World Health Organization
WICEM	World Industry Conference on Environmental Management
WIDER	World Institute for Development Economics Research
WWF	World Wide Fund for Nature/World Wildlife Fund

1 Sustainable Development: What Is to Be Done?

Johan Holmberg and Richard Sandbrook

INTRODUCTION

Uncertainty characterizes the world at the beginning of the 1990s. It is difficult to have a vision of the future. Following the break-up of the Soviet Union, the world political scene is changing quickly and dramatically. European nations are increasingly acting as a monolithic bloc; the United States is becoming inward-looking; and all the while the poorest nations are falling yet further behind in world development. These and other trends provide the setting for the 1992 UN Conference on Environment and Development (UNCED). They will, until the end of the century, affect the prospects for protection of the environment and for development.

During its twenty years of existence IIED has been promoting a vision encapsulated in the term 'sustainable development'. The founder of IIED, Barbara Ward, first used the term in the mid-1970s to make the point that environmental protection and development are linked (Ward and Dubos, 1972). The Institute can claim some credit in making the term as broadly used as it is today. IIED is now gradually moving beyond conceptualizing sustainable development towards putting it into operation. It is in that context that this book should be read.

In a manner, what we have done in this book is to call our own bluff, spelling out our vision of a sustainable future and the steps necessary to get there. In the principal area of interest to us, namely the less developed Third World, we have asked ourselves the question: what does a sustainable future look like and what will be required to achieve it? For example, how can the world's forests be made sustainable, given current deforestation trends? What can be done to make the burgeoning Third World cities sustainable for the majority of their inhabitants? What does sustainable agriculture mean? How can the African drylands be made sustainable? What about industry and energy in the emerging economies?

A certain humility is required, given the political uncertainty. Unforeseen developments may soon render our visions invalid. However, there are a number of global trends that are certain. These include the widening income disparities between and within nations, the increasing marginalization of the poor and the high rates of population growth putting further strain on the economies of the developing world. The accompanying destruction of the natural resource base and the environment in these same countries, through complex interactions between poverty, population growth and fragile ecosystems, further adds to their instability. Using such trends as points of departure, we have set out to suggest a policy agenda for sustainable development: policies for a small planet.

This book is mostly concerned with the developing countries. We address ourselves to those interested in Third World development: governments, aid agencies, NGOs, students of development and others. We do not pretend to provide a complete picture; we view the developing world through the prism of our experiences and knowledge, as we are a small institute we cannot pretend to cover all aspects. We appreciate the limits of this approach; after all, some 20 per cent of the world's people consume 80 per cent of its resources, and they do not live in the Third World. Making the industrial world sustainable is a challenge no less important. But that is not what this book is about.

THE CONCEPT OF SUSTAINABLE DEVELOPMENT

The use of the concept

The concept of sustainable development has a complex pedigree. It came to fame when the World Commission on Environment and Development (WCED, also known as the Brundtland Commission) reported in 1987 (WCED, 1987). Others point out that it was first promoted in the *World Conservation Strategy* in 1980 (IUCN, 1980). A few, not least the sponsors of this book, used it long before to stress the links between environment and development needs. Whatever the origins, the Brundtland Commission was the political turning-point, making the concept one of geopolitical significance and the catchphrase it has become today. Since 1987, all manner of political leaders have talked about sustainable development, and reams of paper have been published on the subject; some seventy definitions are in circulation. Sustainable development as a concept has become devalued to the point where, to some, it is now just a cliché.

If a phrase becomes all things to all people, it is soon of no value to any. Catchphrases have come and gone before, one example being 'appropriate technology'. The original assumption by Schumacher and others was that some technologies are inappropriate while others fit (Schumacher, 1974). But that, of course, depends on who is judging, and as more and more interests claimed the phrase for their own it gradually became redundant. Certainly authors such as Redclift have already arrived at the conclusion that sustainable development is a truism or, more negatively according to O'Riordan, a contradiction in terms (see O'Riordan, 1985; Redclift, 1987). Many environmentalists hate the term with a passion, since it appears to license economic growth. Sadly it is often interchanged with 'sustainable growth', which is dangerously simplistic. The conflicts between states of ecological equilibrium and economic development in the long term are still not answered. Equally, there are no straightforward links between the state of economic welfare (or the lack thereof) and environmental degradation.

Another muddle in the literature occurs between what sustainable development fundamentally involves and what is desirable in the pursuit of it. For example, participation in decision-making is held to be important in achieving sustainable development, and yet, as we all know, democracy is hardly the most efficient – albeit in the long run arguably the most equitable – mechanism for allocating scarce resources. Some suggest that this politically expedient fuzziness will have to be overcome in favour of intellectual clarity and rigour, if the concept of sustainable development is to be of fundamental importance (see e.g. Lele, 1989).

However, such critiques miss a major point. The basic implication of the concept of sustainable development, as embraced by the Brundtland Commission and others, is that we should leave to the next generation a stock of 'quality of life' assets no less than those we have inherited (Pearce, Markandya and Barbier, 1989). It is a political goal. But this can be interpreted in three ways:

- that the next generation should inherit such a stock of wealth, comprising man-made assets and environmental assets;
- or that the next generation should inherit a stock of environmental assets no less than that inherited by the previous generation;
- or that the inherited stock should comprise man-made assets, natural assets and 'human capital'.

The first interpretation stresses all capital assets, man-made and 'natural'. The second emphasizes 'natural capital' only. The third includes cultural and other human inheritances. Throughout recent history, human development has followed the pattern of the first interpretation. But as the world is becoming 'full', and human perturbations of ecological functions are straining them to their breaking-point, so our concept of 'stock' should mature. Furthermore, the condition of 'human capital' – that is, society and its cultural inheritance – is also at risk and must be built into any desirable concept of development. The distinctions between economic growth, sustainable growth and sustainable development are made in Box 1.1.

Box 1.1: Sustainable growth and sustainable development

Economic growth means that real GNP per capita is increasing over time. But observation of such a trend does *not* mean that growth is 'sustainable'.

Sustainable economic growth means that real GNP per capita is increasing over time *and* the increase is not threatened by 'feedback' either from biophysical impacts (pollution, resource problems) or from social impacts (poverty, social disruption).

Sustainable development means *either* that per capita utility or well-being is increasing over time with free exchange or substitution between natural and man-made capital *or* that per capita utility or well-being is increasing over time subject to non-declining natural wealth.

There are several reasons why the second and more narrow focus is justified, including:

- non-substitutability between environmental assets (the ozone layer cannot be recreated);
- uncertainty (our limited understanding of the life-supporting functions of many environmental assets dictates that they be preserved for the future);
- irreversibility (once lost, no species can be recreated);
- and equity (the poor are usually more affected by bad environments than the rich).

Source: adapted from Pearce, Markandya and Barbier (1989).

The defence of sustainable development can be conducted on two levels. The first is that of the pragmatist, the second that of the academic. For the latter, the question is, does the concept have within it, or the potential to have within it, any useful insights that would allow the world to progress with more clarity and understanding than before? For some of us, the academic discussion is best left to those better able to conduct it. The argument here is based principally on expediency and pragmatism. The vagueness of the term is no real drawback. The powerful intuitive idea underlying the concept is that of *intergenerational equity*: our development is sustainable only to the extent that we can meet our needs without prejudice to those of future generations. This is similar in its intuitive appeal, although perhaps less emotionally charged, to concepts such as 'freedom' and 'justice'. While there is broad general agreement around the world about what such terms mean, the actual achievement of human freedom, justice and sustainable development will be specific to local conditions and possibilities (Holmberg, Bass and Timberlake, 1991).

In any event, the practice of development that can be called sustainable on any basis is far behind the rhetoric. There is not enough empirical evidence or experience on which to base a solid definition. The meaning is itself evolving. Sustainable development is the intuitively solid 'handrail that guides us along as we proceed toward development' (Tickell, 1991). Development that does not meet the intergenerational equity criterion simply must be bad development, as common sense would (should) tell us.

Towards an IIED definition

Partly for the above cited reasons, there is no such thing as a universally agreed definition of sustainable development within IIED. There has never been in our group a felt need for a rigorous, theoretically consistent definition beyond the notional 'handrail'. But there have been attempts to formulate an analytical approach based on the concept of sustainable development in practice.

The most adventurous attempt arose from a meeting in September 1986 in which all sides put their own interpretations on the table and Ed Barbier sought the reconciliation (Barbier, 1987). It starts from the premise that development intrinsically involves trade-offs between conflicting goals, such as between economic growth and environmental conservation, introducing modern technology and preserving traditional culture, or reconciling growth with improved social equity. Given that many of the qualitatitive dimensions of the trade-offs cannot be accurately measured, the process inevitably becomes subject to judgement based on prevailing values and ethical norms. The process is dynamic with regard to space and time, and the trade-offs will differ between locations and time scales.

Barbier identified three systems as basic to any process of development: the biological or ecological resource system, the economic system and the social system. Human society applies a set of goals to each system, each with its own hierarchy of sub-goals and targets. The objective of sustainable development will then be to maximize goal achievement across these three systems at one and the same time through an adaptive process of trade-offs. It will not be possible to maximize all goals all the time, and there may be conflict among intra-system goals. Choices must therefore be made as to which goals should receive greater priority. Different development strategies will assign different priorities.

System goals could include the following:

Biological system goals

- Genetic diversity.
- Resilience.
- Biological productivity.

Economic system goals

- Increasing production of goods and services.
- Satisfying basic needs or reducing poverty.
- Improving equity.

Social system goals

- Cultural diversity.
- Social justice.
- Gender equality.
- Participation.

Figure 1.1 illustrates how these three systems converge, as develop-ment becomes increasingly sustainable and system goals overlap. In an unsustainable development process, maximum production of goods and services, for example, is attempted with no regard to biological resilience, genetic diversity, social justice or participation, just to name a few goals deemed to have low priority. The three systems are then separate and goals are maximized with no regard for the trade-offs involved. For example, maintaining wildlife habitats to preserve genetic diversity by forcibly keeping away poor people, without providing them with alternative livelihood opportunities, would be one such case. But as the circles become increasingly concentric, serious trade-offs begin, and development with respect to all three systems becomes more sustainable.

Figure 1.1: Sustainable Development as a Process of Trade-Offs

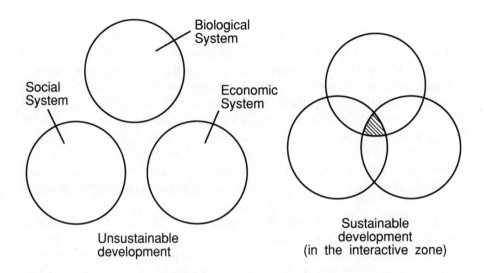

Source: Barbier (1987).

Given the need for trade-offs between (and within) systems in the interest of the greater whole, disciplined and consistent choices must be made as to which goals should receive priority in the development strategy. But the process of trade-offs among goals must be adaptive, for as individual preferences, social norms, ecological conditions, and so on, change over time, so must the relative priorities or weights assigned to various goals (Barbier, 1987). Early on in the development process, conservation of the environment will mean protecting the natural resource base on which the economy depends, and this will require a set of policies and actions. Later on in that process, the priorities for environmental conservation will be different and place more emphasis on minimizing the detritus of the industrialized society, again with different policies and actions.

Interactions among the different system goals change as the scale or hierarchy of the systems is extended from the local to the regional, and thence to the national and even global level. As systems theory holds that the behaviour of higher systems in such a hierarchy is not readily discovered from study of lower systems, and vice versa, the choice of sustainable development goals to be pursued at, say, national level may differ from those advocated at the local level. In all humility, no one in IIED has gone very far in reconciling sustainability up and down the hierarchy. Describing sustainable development for a Pacific island is much easier than for all of Western Europe.

None the less, this text has essentially placed sustainable development within the context of a nation state. This is limited, for in an increasingly interrelated world no nation is able to develop in a vacuum. Technical innovations in communications, where everyone's news is readily available everywhere, in commerce, where economies of scale require elimination of trade barriers for the common good of all, and in capital markets, where huge amounts move instantly across the globe, mean that no country can insulate itself against events in others. In the environmental sphere, where the ultimate impacts on systems are global, all nations are similarly connected together in an interdependent world.

This book does not attempt a description of a sustainable global system. But a few international issues are important for sustainable development on the national and even on the local level. First, it may be trite to say that peace is an essential but insufficient condition. The relaxation of superpower tensions in recent years has already meant an end to many 'small' wars in the Third World (El Salvador, Nicaragua, Afghanistan, Cambodia, Angola, Ethiopia, to mention some) and been conducive to development. Long may that last. Second, it is obvious that countries using a major share, perhaps most, of their export revenue to service foreign debt will never be able to develop sustainably in the absence of international initiatives to write off that debt. Third, better terms of trade for their exports, mainly primary commodities and to a large extent agricultural produce, will be supportive of sustainable development in poor countries. Fourth, while foreign aid will not be a decisive factor, more aid on more liberal (less tied) terms will clearly help.

But these taken together are not sufficient conditions for sustainable development. We do not subscribe to the view often heard from Southern representatives that the underlying causes of underdevelopment, poverty and environmental destruction in developing countries can be traced to the North. Many arguably can, at least on a historical basis, but in our view people and their governments have to assume responsibility for their own development, including their role as actors on the international scene. There is ample evidence to show that national economic and social policies make all the difference with regard to the course, content and speed of development.

The concept of sustainable development at a national and local level is already proving its utility in so far as it provokes groups to set a wide spectrum of goals and then to reconcile them. A good example is the record of the International Union for the Conservation of Nature (IUCN) Conference on Conservation and Development held in Ottawa in 1986. This diverse group from over fifty countries made up of natural and social scientists, politicians, industrialists and activists concluded that

> Sustainable development seeks . . . to respond to five broad requirements: (1) integration of conservation and development, (2) satisfaction of basic human needs, (3) achievement of equity and social justice, (4) provision of social self-determination and cultural diversity, and (5) maintenance of ecological integrity.
>
> (Jacobs and Munroe,1987).

It is inconceivable that such a diverse set of conditions would have occurred even five years previously. It is precisely this attention to the reconciliation or trade-offs implicit in sustainable development that has inspired much useful work since the early 1980s. The results amount to a new renaissance in thinking on social welfare and development issues.

Four dilemmas

But this enthusiasm should not hide real disagreements for which no resolution has yet been found; four of them will be discussed here. *First* on the list is the argument that the world cannot go on making economic growth, as conventionally perceived and measured, the unquestioned objective of development policy. This case is convincingly argued by Goodland and others in a recent volume (1991). They make the point that by definition growth means *more*: more throughput and also, at a given level of technology, more inputs and more wastes. We are already in a full world that cannot absorb much more. The signs are plentiful: human activity has been said to use, directly and indirectly, about 40 per cent of the net primary product of land-based photosynthesis; there is much evidence to suggest that the build-up of carbon dioxide and other heat-trapping gases in the atmosphere has reached such levels that we are inexorably entering a phase of global warming; the rupture of the ozone shield is already such that the world seems set for a billion additional skin cancers, many of them fatal, among people alive today; and the rates of biological species extinction are the fastest they have ever been in recorded history and are accelerating.

As Goodland *et al*. point out, we can quibble about whether 40 per cent of land-based photosynthesis is too much; there is, after all, 60 per cent left. But with the world population set to double within forty years or so, humanity will within one generation be using 80 per cent of terrestrial photosynthesis unless the efficiency of use improves. It is impossible to deny that such a harvest would tax many ecological systems to their limits, and that the world is indeed 'full'. In a 'full world' era, natural capital is becoming the limiting factor for productive activity, and the objective of economic policy should therefore be to increase the productivity of natural capital, the scarcest production factor. It is no longer the availability of resources that sets limits to growth but the availability of sink functions, such as the atmosphere, the oceans and the forests that absorb such wastes as greenhouse gases. These open-access resources are grossly misused. In a 'full world', economic growth, as conventionally defined, should increasingly be limited to the purposes of poverty alleviation in developing countries, whereas the rich countries cannot go on raising their physical output and must concentrate on raising their efficiency in resource use. Such a conclusion as this flies in the face of the prevailing economic and business ethic, and remains a debate that is far from resolved (ibid.).

The *second* dilemma relates to the measurement of progress in holistic and not just in economic terms. It is precisely because of the change in emphasis from quantitative economic aspects of development (per capita income, per capita consumption, and so on) towards other, qualitative measures that those who attempt to define the term 'growth' get into trouble. The factors that make up sustainable development differ from those involved in conventional economic development. There is a need for a completely new set of growth indicators and a set of methodologies for obtaining them. While the quantitative dimensions of sustainability (such as food intake, real income and life expectancy) can be captured by some 'basic needs' index, it is much more difficult to quantify the more qualitative dimensions (such as cultural diversity, social cohesion and environmental quality improvements). A rigorous exploration of such indices has yet to be made, but attempts in that direction have begun (see e.g. Daly and Cobb, 1989; UNDP, 1990 and 1991).

The matter is compounded further by the continuous and dynamic process of trade-offs referred to earlier. This means that measurements of success in making trade-off configurations will differ with regard to location and to time, and hence that measures of well-being will not be comparable. To illustrate: building the first new road through an African desert is hardly the same as building the last road in south-east

England. There is room for innovation and research to make sustainable development as unambiguously measurable as economic growth is said to be.

The *third* dilemma relates to the trade-offs that are intrinsic to our definition of sustainable development (Figure 1.1). We may intuitively agree that these trade-offs will have to entail, for example, less emphasis on an economic goal such as 'exports' in order to allow measures to protect the environment to keep abreast of the 'exporting' economic activity. A contemporary example is that the exploitation of existing forests should only proceed at a rate commensurate with reforestation. We may also agree that economic growth should not take place at the expense of increasing marginalization of the poor, if we are concerned about the social dimension to sustainable development. Such trade-offs can in practice be very difficult to make and are the stock-in-trade of policy-makers and politicians.

Thus far, the tools involved are underdeveloped. Environmental economics is attempting to find a common currency for them by ascribing values to the different systems, costs and benefits, but the art form is not without controversy. In particular, the dilemma arises in the trade-offs between potentially conflicting environmental goals. Future generations will need ample supplies of topsoil, timber and water. But what supplies of currently endangered species like elephants and lions will they need? What value do they have? What about preserving one species, like elephants, and not another, like lions, and which one is more important anyway? In the debates on preservation of the rainforests in the Amazon, Brazilian representatives can often be heard to ask angrily whether it is the people or the animals that are more important. For whom is development, and what is to be conserved by making it sustainable?

This can pit those interested primarily in development for people against those for whom conservation of the environment has top priority. Both want to see sustainable development, both will say that the environment will need to be preserved for future generations, but they may differ strongly on the means and the methods for bringing this about. They certainly do not readily accept the economists' calculus. In circumstances of poverty, it is easy to adopt the Third World perspective that says human needs are paramount. But such an approach does not reconcile with the definition of sustainable development that includes stable levels of natural capital (Box 1.1). Simply saying that sustainable development cannot be all things to all people all the time – it is a goal, an attitude, a broad guiding principle rather than a precise methodology – is a cop-out. But is it a necessary one in a complex and unequal world?

The *fourth* dilemma involves the relationship between sustainable development and democratic government. Key to the concept of sustainable development is the time dimension, the notion that future generations should not be worse off because of today's needs. But modern democratic governments appeal to the voters alive today. They are in the business of getting elected and staying in power. To do so they work hard to convince the voters that their priorities provide the most benefits for the most people. It is hardly surprising that they borrow resources from future generations to meet present aspirations, and that they have difficulties in convincing voters to forgo current aspirations for the sake of generations unborn. Similarly, politicians do not win elections by promising voters a better deal for citizens in other countries, even if this improves the overall chances of a sustainable world order. Issues such as foreign aid, debt or cross-border pollution are rarely electoral issues anywhere (Holmberg, Bass and Timberlake, 1991).

It is easy to blame the politicians for the lack of sustainable development that we see in the world today. One suspects that many are well aware of what needs to be done, and yet nobody (almost) seems able to act consistently. Some sympathy for politicians facing the dilemma is needed. Contrary to a common view, they seldom lead, but follow what they perceive to be the prevailing public opinion. Polls repeatedly reveal a strong concern for the environment until the sacrifice is made plain. Politicians know that concern is seldom strong enough for a radical path to be possible. In the 1988 parliamentary election in Sweden, the environment was a big issue: the effects of the Chernobyl disaster were still felt in many parts of the country; a multitude of dead seals (killed by a virus, it turned out later) mysteriously floated ashore along the Swedish coasts; and the voters sent the environmentalist Green Party to Parliament for the first time ever. In the subsequent 1991 election, both Chernobyl and the seals had long been forgotten; increasing unemployment and reform of the welfare state were the major issues; and the Greens were promptly ejected from Parliament. Despite all the talk about global environmental issues, like global warming, during the intervening years, the environment was barely mentioned in the 1991 election. Thus the narrow time and distance horizons of democratic governments collide with the concept of sustainable development. (To avoid misunderstanding, it is worth stressing that the horizons of non-democratic governments tend to be even more limited.)

The industrialized Northern countries are the main contributors to global environmental problems, but changing their polluting ways is proving a slow process, far too slow to impact significantly on the problems. The European Community countries' commitment to roll back emissions of greenhouse gases to 1990 levels by the year 2000, while significant and far beyond what the USA has been prepared to commit itself to so far, is still only 60 per cent of what would be required to stabilize concentrations of greenhouse gases in the atmosphere. The main reason, of course, is the limited time horizons of the governments involved, rendering it difficult for them to take the broader view. On a global level, sustainable development will, largely for this reason alone, remain elusive for some time yet.

All this leads to the conclusion that there is no short cut. It is necessary to build patterns of sustainable development from the bottom up, showing by example what can be acheived at local levels and then working to disseminate positive experiences. When local progress is constrained by factors beyond the control of the community concerned, public pressure will grow to amend the national and eventually also the international context. IIED has most experience at this local level, and so it is to that agenda that we now turn.

MAKING DEVELOPMENT SUSTAINABLE: PRIMARY ENVIRONMENTAL CARE

We use the term 'primary environmental care' (PEC) to describe the process for progress towards sustainability at the 'grass roots'. It groups approaches that have been shown to work at the community or neighbourhood level. It was first amplified at a workshop in Siena, Italy, in 1990 hosted by the Italian aid agency with IIED participation, and it has since then been widely used not only by IIED but also, for example, by aid agencies like Oxfam and the United Nations Children's Fund (UNICEF). Primary environmental care is the essence of most of the recommendations made in many of the subsequent chapters in this book (Borrini, 1990; Pretty and Sandbrook, 1991).

Effectively, PEC is the umbrella term for development approaches in the interactive zone between economic, environmental and social systems (Figure 1.1). It builds directly on the debate on rural development that originated in the 1970s, with which it has in common the objective of raising the productivity and welfare of the poor but with an added concern for protection of their environment. It includes processes by which local groups or communities, not necessarily in rural areas, organize themselves with varying degrees of outside support to apply their skills and knowledge for the care of their natural resources and environment while satisfying livelihood needs. It is equally valid in poor as in rich countries, although this discussion has poor, developing countries primarily in mind.

PEC has three integral elements:

- meeting and satisfying of basic needs – the economic goal;
- protection and optimal utilization of the environment – the environmental goal;
- and empowering of groups and communities – the social goal.

The basic ideas behind PEC are not new and have been endorsed by governments, NGOs and donor agencies for years. What is new is the increasing consensus that the three sets of goals should be considered together and that success of PEC will depend on:

- local groups and communities that are permitted to organize, participate and influence development priorities;
- local groups and communities that are permitted access to natural and financial resources;
- local groups and communities that select and help to develop productive and environmentally sensitive technologies;
- outside institutions that empower the local community by way of political support and open access to information, and that take an adaptive and flexible approach if they provide resources.

None of this is inconsistent with what is familiar in domestic situations in the North. But it is quite evident that time after time it is forgotten in the 'development aid' business and by governments wishing to short-cut the development process. There are exceptions. A recent review of eighty bilateral and multilateral projects carried out by IIED suggests that there are common elements essential to success of PEC and hence to the trade-offs that make for sustainable development (see Pretty and Sandbrook, 1991, where a bibliography on PEC is provided). One such element is building on local knowledge, including management systems and technical solutions. The livelihoods of poor households are usually diverse, in rural areas depending on a mix of agricultural produce, wild plants and animals, remittances and trading. Decision-making is complex, and it is difficult for outsiders to predict needs and preferences with accuracy. Local management systems developed over generations are tuned to the needs of local people and the characteristics of available resources. Another element involves building on existing social structures. In successful examples, outsiders play the role of bringing interested groups together and facilitating the process of information exchange and decision-making. Techniques and approaches are all designed to motivate people to care for their place of living while meeting their livelihood needs. PEC approaches typically begin small and do not over-innovate. They are typically flexible in their design and of medium- to long-term duration (five to ten or more years). Successfully introduced technologies are commonly low risk, easy to teach and demonstrate, and tested locally, and they offer prospects of clear on-site benefits in the coming season or year. External inputs are small and focus on catalytic functions.

It would be wrong to suggest that PEC approaches are the only answer to sustainable development. Primary environmental care by definition does not address what needs to be done when communities interact. People can help to bring about sustainable development only if the local, regional and national government policy framework is propitious to that end. But the reverse is equally true: sustainable development will not come about without active involvement of the people concerned. Perhaps one of the major lessons from the last two decades of development work in the Third World, from the last two centuries of development worldwide and also from the experiences emerging from Eastern Europe and the former Soviet Union, is that development, to be sustainable, requires the active involvement of people, the beneficiaries themselves, in the design and implementation of activities intended to improve their welfare. Empowerment of people to take increasing charge of their own development is the key ingredient, combined with a clear knowledge of environmental constraints and of requirements to meet basic needs.

OUTLINE OF THE REST OF THIS BOOK

Most of the chapters to follow have the primary environmental care thesis as their common denominator. However, sustainable development clearly requires more than what can reasonably be included under the PEC umbrella. It will require policies for many sectors beyond the community level. It will require financial resources. It will require national and global institutions and a political culture.

In Chapter 2, 'Organizing for Change', we discuss the prerequisites for empowerment. People can only exercise their right to participate in their own development if governments guarantee civil and political rights, including freedom of association and of information, and an independent judiciary. Participation can then lead to real empowerment through education, awareness raising and skills training. This will presuppose scope for democratic processes from village to global level. But these processes can be diverse, and it would be a mistake to take the Western democratic model for granted. Institutions are not neutral factors in development and have often been exploitative of the poor. More fundamental than their efficiency are issues concerning their scale, orientation, relevance and values in relation to economic and social needs. In particular, sustainable development calls for more coherent efforts to strengthen the quality, representativeness and resources of local government. Given the chance, people can make direct democracy work powerfully in favour of sustainable development.

In Chapter 3, 'Economic Policy and Sustainable Natural Resource Management', we argue the importance of economic policy. Improved economic analysis of both the impacts and the causes underlying environmental degradation will become crucial in the years ahead. Once major macro-economic distortions are corrected, as is happening in increasing numbers of developing countries, there will need to be more widespread use of techniques which focus more closely on the adjustments necessary to overcome market and policy failures that cause environmental degradation. The long-term contribution of environmental economics is to elucidate the trade-offs discussed earlier (Figure 1.1).

Drawing on the experience of the IIED Sustainable Agriculture Programme in Chapter 4, 'Regenerating Agriculture', we suggest that agricultural systems characterized by low external inputs can raise yields by 50 per cent or more. Such systems build on farmers' traditional knowledge, maximizing the use of renewable resources internal to the farm. The chapter argues that there are low-external input technologies available that achieve permanent improvements in agricultural production. Selection of the elements appropriate to local livelihoods has been shown to produce highly effective and sustainable solutions. These are generally on a small scale but can be made more widespread by governments through appropriate institutional and legal frameworks and economic incentives.

Discussing a vision of the future city in Chapter 5, 'The Future City', we point out that urban centres in the Third World generate lower levels of resource use and waste per person than those in industrialized countries. However, other indicators are far worse, such as health and employment. Again it will be necessary to make more use of the knowledge, ingenuity and organizational capacity of citizens themselves. The chapter stresses the question of entitlements; if governments no longer treated as illegal a vast array of individual, household and community-based actions, they would release the most dynamic force available within cities. Governments need to provide essential resources – land sites, technical advice, infrastructure and basic services – as well as a legal framework to protect individuals from industrial pollution and from economic exploitation.

In Chapter 6, 'Restructuring Industry for Sustainable Development', the considerable opportunities for large-scale changes in favour of an eco-industrial revolution are reviewed. The industrial 'business-as-usual' scenario is already causing major environmental problems in developing countries. Governments should avoid the large-scale interventions of the past and concentrate on what they do best: providing strategic direction, overcoming sectional interests, preventing market failures and stimulating those responsible for environmental problems, whether producers or consumers, to take action themselves.

Chapter 7, 'The Future Shape of Forests', is concerned with sustainable forestry. In many countries, particularly in the tropics, natural forests are continually being cut back in favour of non-forest uses. The boundary between forest and non-forest is an unstable 'frontier' that must be managed. This involves establishing a stable forest continuum which can accommodate changing circumstances. It would comprise a system of interlinked forest types, subject to various degrees of human intervention, ranging from protected forest in its natural state to plantation forestry. Current forestry policies are often outdated, having been formulated decades ago with economic and strategic needs paramount. A new framework for sustainable forestry development is suggested, based upon the primacy of maintaining forest ecological processes and biological diversity, while building on the way of life and aspirations of the specific groups of people who determine what happens in the forests.

Chapter 8, 'The Future of Africa's Drylands', examines examples of successful development in the African drylands and argues, consistently with the other chapters, that the transfer of rights and responsibilities to local user groups to manage natural resources is a necessary condition for more sustainable development in these regions. There are other conditions, too, such as the availability of financial and human resources. These resources need not be very substantial but should be of longer-term duration and of higher quality than is often the case today. The political will of governments to decentralize and vest increased authority in local community institutions is essential. New approaches are advocated to agricultural research, training and extension, involving the farmers themselves, along with policy changes at national and international levels to give farmers better economic returns.

The patterns of energy use in the developing world are wasteful as a consequence of poor policies and self-serving foreign aid. Developing countries have often failed to share in the large gains in energy efficiency enjoyed by industrialized nations in recent decades. Chapter 9, 'Achieving Sustainability in Energy Use in Developing Countries', suggests that over-investment in expanding production and a lack of investment in cutting waste mean that much energy is wasted. Existing energy policies discriminate against renewable energy technologies. A shift of energy investment towards an emphasis on energy efficiency is necessary, financially and environmentally, and the outline of a strategy to that end is provided.

In Chapter 10, 'Financing Sustainable Development', we make the point that nothing in the previous chapters suggests that sustainable development necessarily requires the huge incremental financial resource flows sometimes suggested. Nevertheless, the severity of global environmental problems and poverty in large parts of the world, the rapidly increasing development needs in the former Soviet bloc and domestic needs in many donor countries will combine to cause capital shortages that may constrain development in the Third World during the 1990s. The application of economic incentive mechanisms, like carbon taxes, for purposes of environmental management is indicated. Some of these also have considerable potential for raising revenue, suggesting the possibility of their wider application to meet the twin objectives of raising finance for sustainable development while reducing pollution in keeping with the 'polluter pays' principle.

Finally, in Chapter 11, 'Living in a Sustainable World', we review life in a sustainable world from the perspectives of population policy in the South and patterns of consumption in the North. In a 'full world', it becomes essential to slow down population growth and reduce profligate consumption. Examples are cited to show that primary environmental care, with an added focus on empowerment of women, can be a successful approach to promote family planning. To change consumption patterns in the North, it is suggested that a new ethic or morality of consumption must emerge. This can be encouraged by governments helping to make prices reflect full environmental costs and providing increased incentives for the development of environmentally benign technologies.

CONCLUSIONS

This is a book about visions for a sustainable developing world and the policies required to get there. We refrain from a rigorous definition and argue that sustainable development is an intuitively powerful concept that, as commonly understood, provides a useful guide for development practitioners. It involves trade-offs between biological, economic and social systems and is found in the interactive zone between these systems. There are a number of international factors that may be necessary, but insufficient, conditions for sustainable development on a national level, including peace, debt reduction, more propitious terms of trade and non-declining foreign aid. There are also several dilemmas related to the concept, including the role of growth as the unquestioned objective of economic policy, techniques for measuring sustainable development, the trade-offs between conflicting environmental goals and the limited time and distance horizons of elected politicians. These dilemmas will only be resolved as experience is gained and thinking evolves.

It is essential to focus on the grass roots or community level when making sustainable development operational. Processes that meet basic needs, while protecting the environment and empowering the poor, thus internalizing the necessary trade-offs, have been labelled 'primary environmental care', similar in many respects to primary health care. Primary environmental care is as little able to solve all environmental and poverty problems in a country or region as primary health care can solve all health-related problems; but there is ample experience that sustainable development will not be possible in the absence of the involvement and empowerment of the intended beneficiaries of the development process.

Much of the remainder of this book sets out approaches to primary environmental care by sector and case. It suggests policy options, reflecting the gradual move in IIED's work from conceptualizing to operationalizing sustainable development. There is, of course, no escape from the conclusion that sustainable development, as with so much else in life, boils down to political commitment and able leadership. The means required in financial terms are not necessarily very large, but the shifts in political power and patronage, and into forgoing achievable consumption, amount to a sacrifice in favour of an uncertain future. We would like to be optimistic, despite much of the evidence, and say that the political will to bring about sustainable development in the Third World is at hand. What we can say with some confidence is that, if and when the policy-makers are ready, the requisite knowledge is available.

REFERENCES AND BIBLIOGRAPHY

Barbier, Edward B., 1987. 'The concept of sustainable economic development', *Environmental Conservation*, 14, 2, Summer, pp. 101–10.

Borrini, Grazia (ed.), 1990. *Lessons Learned in Community-Based Environmental Management: Proceedings of the 1990 Primary Environmental Care Workshop*, Istituto Superiore di Sanità, Directorate-General for Development Co-operation, Ministry of Foreign Affairs, Rome.

Daly, Herman E. and Cobb, John B., 1989. *For the Common Good*, Beacon Press, Boston, Mass.

Goodland, Robert, Daly, Herman, El Serafy, Salah and Droste, Bernd von (eds.), 1991. *Environmentally Sustainable Economic Development: Building on Brundtland*, UNESCO, Paris.

Holmberg, Johan, Bass, Stephen and Timberlake, Lloyd, 1991. *Defending the Future – a Guide to Sustainable Development*. Earthscan, London.

IUCN, 1980. *World Conservation Strategy: Living Resource Conservation for Sustainable Development*, IUCN, UNEP and WWF, Gland, Switzerland.

Jacobs, P. and Munroe, D. (eds.), 1987. *Conservation with Equity: Strategies for Sustainable Development*, proceedings of the Conference on Conservation and Development: Implementing the World Conservation Strategy, Ottawa, Canada, 31 May–5 June 1986, IUCN, Gland, Switzerland.

Lele, Scharachchandra M., 1989. 'Sustainable development: a critical review', *World Development*.

O'Riordan, T., 1985. 'Future directions in environmental policy', *Journal of Environmental Planning*, 17, pp. 1431–46.

Pearce, David, Markandya, Anil and Barbier, Edward B., 1989. *Blueprint for a Green Economy*, Earthscan, London.

Pretty, Jules and Sandbrook, Richard, 1991. 'Operationalizing sustainable development at the community level: primary environmental care', paper for members of the DAC Working Party on Development Assistance and the Environment, IIED, London, October.

Redclift, M., 1987. *Sustainable Development: Exploring the Contradictions*, Methuen, New York.

Schumacher, E. F., 1974. *Small Is Beautiful: A Study of Economics as if People Mattered*, Abacus, London.

Tickell, Crispin, 1991. Speech to UNEP-UK seminar, London, 9 October.

UNDP, 1990. *Human Development Report 1990*, Oxford University Press, Oxford.

UNDP, 1991. *Human Development Report 1991*, Oxford University Press, Oxford.

Ward, Barbara and Dubos, René, 1972. *Only One Earth – the Care and Maintenance of a Small Planet*, Deutsch, London.

WCED, 1987. *Our Common Future* (Brundtland Report), Oxford University Press, Oxford.

2 Organizing for Change: People-Power and the Role of Institutions

Robin Sharp

INTRODUCTION

The nature and the scale of changes needed in all countries to achieve sustainable human development are increasingly well documented and understood. Many of these changes – political, technical and social – are spelled out in other chapters of this book. Critical to any chances of success in implementing them, however, is the complex chain of organizational mechanisms through which both the broad objectives and the specific planning targets must be articulated.

While they are in principle convergent, the pathways to sustainable development start from many points of the compass, often unconnected and mutually invisible. To be clear where they should take us, it is essential to understand the processes and the different levels of institutional machinery on which progress will depend.

This chapter therefore seeks to identify some criteria for a systems approach to sustainability. We ask what is meant by and what can be achieved through people's participation, how it grows out of democratic processes, how those processes in turn depend on a strong and appropriate structure of institutions, and how those institutions grow from and are supported by a root system of human resources.

The questions we shall discuss here are (1) how participatory decision-making and representative institutions can best be established in countries of the South with very diverse political and social traditions, and (2) whether the current approaches of international agencies and donors are moving in the right direction. Some of the issues raised are not equally applicable to all regions; particular weight has been given to the situation of sub-Saharan Africa, bearing in mind the current wave of political change in that region and the concentration there of foreign advice and interventions. Many of these issues, nevertheless, are of relevance to people and institutions in all countries.

SUSTAINABLE DEVELOPMENT: THE PEOPLE'S ROLE

The concept of sustainable development embodies a belief that people should be able to alter and improve their lives in accordance with criteria which take account of the needs of others and which protect the planet and future generations. Thus people's rights and responsibilities form the crux of any discussion of sustainability.

People's movements in many countries have assumed the responsibility for challenging unsustainable systems or practices – the rape of tropical rainforests, industrial pollution, high-cost technologies for poor people or inequities in the distribution of wealth and resources. Where people have become aware of threats to their own or the world's future, these movements have accepted the responsibility of mobilizing to oppose them – sometimes even at the risk of their lives.

As for people's rights, the commitment of governments and development agencies to 'popular participation' as a necessary ingredient of sustainable development has been enshrined in the Arusha Declaration on Popular Participation in Development (1990) and the Manila Declaration on People's Participation and Sustainable Development (1989). In one sense, this assertion of the right to participation does no more than reiterate a citizen's entitlement as set forth in the Universal Declaration of Human Rights, adopted by the UN General Assembly in 1948. However, its progressive elevation to a place of prominence on the development agenda reflects two more empirical factors.

The most recent impetus has been the upsurge of public demands for democracy in many countries and the consequent demise of repressive regimes. Second, and over a longer period, a wealth of evidence has been accumulated that development projects designed and implemented without the full involvement of the intended beneficiaries have had a high rate of failure – and conversely, that projects planned with them from the outset, on an appropriate scale and using their skills and resources, have had a relatively high rate of success.

Aid agencies have drawn the lessons from this experience and sought to incorporate participatory principles into their projects. While this is undoubtedly an advance, it is not yet sufficient evidence that aid interventions are enabling the people they mobilize to engage in a genuinely sustainable process of self-improvement. Sometimes a project is described as 'sustainable' on the grounds simply of its survival beyond the phase of external support; but neither this, nor even its 'success' measured by limited project goals, necessarily implies true sustainability.

Over and above these factors, there are two more fundamental arguments for people now to be demanding their voice in the future. Both have to do with the physical limits to expansionism, which has historically been at the core of the human experiment and which has provided an escape-valve when pressures have threatened to explode a society's stability.

One is that humanity's room for spatial expansion, hitherto taken for granted, has come to an end. Among other things, this means that the poorest of the world's people, who could previously as a last resort distance themselves from the powerful minorities seeking to exploit them or their resources, now have nowhere left to go. They must stand their ground or lose the struggle for survival, as the plight of indigenous peoples in many countries bleakly testifies.

The other argument concerns the limits of life support available from the biosphere. It challenges, on scientific grounds, the implicit assumption that development can mean a steady growth in material living standards for four-fifths of the world's people without curbing the consumption of the rest. While this analysis is not uncontested, its proponents insist that 'sustainable development must be development without growth – but with population control and wealth redistribution – if it is to be a serious attack on poverty' (Daly, 1991).

Faced with these actual or anticipated limits, many of those concerned to achieve sustainable management of our 'global village' have come to believe that democratic processes are essential for change, given that privileged minorities controlling power – nationally and internationally – will seldom if ever countenance the needed reforms.

The failure to institute such reforms up to now has left many governments in the South largely unaccountable for their actions, especially their massive accumulation of international debt, which is a principal reason for millions of people continuing to die of hunger and for the net flow of funds from South to North having reached US$50 billion a year. And if the borrowers are to blame, where is the accountability of the Northern and international lending agencies, who have been accessories – wittingly or otherwise – to massive misappropriation of their funds? More effective people's participation is necessary at both ends of the North–South axis if the costs of adjustment to a sustainable society are to be equitably shared and not simply loaded on to those least able to bear the burden.

For all the benefits they can induce, however, participatory systems are not a panacea. Consultations among NGOs in advance of the 1992 UNCED have led to their identifying a list of five criteria for sustainable development: Who initiates? Who decides? Who participates? Who benefits? And who controls? A report on the consultations added: 'If the answer to all these questions is "the people", then *projects* can be assured of sustainability' (*Ecoforum*, 1991; emphasis added). This underlines an important distinction to be made between project-level participation – on a scale where direct democracy is often possible – and that in wider political fora, where the same cannot apply. Confusion frequently arises from use of the same term to mean different things (CWS and LWF, 1991). Participatory systems have up to now worked best at community or project level, where there are bonds of solidarity among the people and where, in the best cases, the five NGO criteria cited above can be met. But where they are introduced at a higher (for example, national) level to replace a rigid centralized authority, such systems – which are then necessarily representative, not direct – may unleash suppressed tensions and wreck the equilibrium previously maintained between rival social groups.

Whether at community or national level, for people to participate actively and without reward in public affairs costs them time and effort. In some cases it may well also entail financial or physical risk for those who find themselves in opposition to the majority. It is therefore not surprising if most people prefer to leave the business to others. Even in established democracies, the majority of citizens will only participate on a given issue when it directly affects their personal interests or seriously affronts their sense of justice. When we speak of participation, then, what we should mean is the *opportunity* to participate.

This, in turn, raises the awkward question of what conditions constitute adequate opportunity. Many of these are culture- or subject-specific, but the most obvious include:

- full access to information on policy issues and development plans;
- freedom of association to permit the discussion of issues by all interested groups within the community;
- regular meetings at which elected officials or the representatives of official agencies can receive and respond to the views of the community and be held accountable for the actions taken on its behalf (Gran, 1983).

These conditions, it goes without saying, will need to be realized in a wide variety of institutional forms, allowing for the forms themselves to change.

In looking to the future, there is a temptation to seek scenarios that describe a stable-state sustainable society, not least in respect of the institutions which we believe would be necessary to maintain it. However, sustainable development cannot be a fixed destination; rather it is a process, as part of which our institutions and human resources can be moulded to meet the perceived priorities of the time. Those priorities will also change, depending partly on the extent to which they prove achievable and partly on the emergence of others which may seem more urgent.

In the end, the opportunity for people's participation in any society is determined by the quality of civil and political rights that they are accorded: in a word, political freedom. It is thus significant that the United Nations Development Programme's *Human Development Report*, in its initial work to construct an index of freedoms by country, detects a high correlation between human development and human freedom (UNDP, 1991).

PARTICIPATION AND EMPOWERMENT

When it is decided by the power brokers – usually governments or large donor agencies – that the people must be given a say in projects that affect them, their first step has often been to devise a process of consultation. The people are told what is to be done and their views are invited, but they are given no access to the decision-making process. When this is found inadequate, they are offered participation – a place, but often little real influence – in the policy-making or planning committees.

For the people to take charge of their own destiny, therefore, something more than participation is required. To encompass that 'something more', the development community has adopted the term *empowerment*.

Empowerment literally means the granting of power to an individual or group for a specified purpose. But where is this power supposed to come from? The usual assumption is that it has to be transferred from a controlling authority, which implies a zero-sum transaction. And since those who hold power are seldom ready to relinquish it, some commentators suggest that 'empowerment' may need to mean the struggle of the disadvantaged to achieve it (Hasan, 1991).

But there is also another kind of power that can be created where there was none before. This is empowerment through ideas, through education or, more specifically, through a process such as 'education for consciousness', the method developed and spread in the 1970s by the Brazilian educator Paulo Freire (Freire, 1970 and 1973). Here, empowerment is a positive-sum game, enabling people to understand not only why they are poor or disenfranchised but also what they can do about it – without waiting for concessions from authority.

This kind of empowerment is also frequently stimulated through participatory appraisal exercises at community level, giving villagers a clear sense of how they can improve their lives in practical ways. Much can be done to raise the consciousness of the poor and to help them understand the systems that restrict or oppress them, so that a confrontation with authority, if and when necessary, is more likely to yield benefits.

THE DEMOCRATIC IMPERATIVE

At the beginning of the 1990s, capitalist democracy appears to have emerged the victor from more than four decades of global confrontation with socialist central planning. Authoritarian regimes in many countries have suddenly found themselves facing a tidal wave of demands for civil liberties and a multi-party political system. A number have already gone under, and others seem certain to succumb. An era of rigid, autocratic governments in Eastern Europe, much of Africa and other Third World countries appears to be coming to an end. Jubilant crowds in capitals from Bucharest to Bamako (Mali) have celebrated the demise of entrenched dictatorships.

Thus for many countries deprived of them hitherto, some measure of democracy and popular participation may now be on the way. But is it time yet to rejoice? As the nations of Eastern Europe have quickly discovered, freedom from tyranny is no panacea for social and economic ills. The lesson will be much harder for emerging democracies in the South, especially those in Africa with scant resources to manage the transition. Therefore, if participatory systems are an essential underpinning for sustainable development, an assessment of the prospects for progress must begin with a review of what participation-in-development has meant and accomplished up to now.

Democracy as a system of government has had a chequered history. Following its codification by the city-states of ancient Greece, government by the people was subsequently forgotten in Europe for the best part of 2,000 years, though it found expression in different forms in pre-colonial cultures as far apart as India and North America. From the sixteenth century and earlier, many Indian villages were self-sufficient and autonomous, governed by an unofficial council of elders and a number of village functionaries (Banuri, 1991).

When revived in a modified form in Europe and North America in the nineteenth and twentieth centuries, the democratic principles of the colonial powers were not generally extended to the governance of their territories in the Southern hemisphere. So when these colonies in Asia and Africa gained their political independence after the Second World War – nearly a century and a half after most of South America – many gravitated towards the alternative model of the socialist bloc, which at the time seemed to offer many social and political benefits.

By the mid-1970s, halfway through the United Nations' Second Development Decade, many leading development thinkers had become aware that the conventional strategies propounded up to that time were not addressing the real problems. In 1975 an international team produced the outlines for what they called 'another development' – needs-oriented, endogenous, self-reliant, ecologically sound and based on structural transformations. For this kind of development, it was stressed, 'whether governments are enlightened or not, there is no substitute for the people's own, truly democratic organization' (Dag Hammarskjold Foundation, 1975).

In fact, for the next fifteen years, virtually until 1990, the international development community chose to turn a blind eye to the undemocratic nature of many governments in the South; indeed, the superpowers and some other Northern governments competed to support them for reasons of geopolitical or commercial interest. One result was that people's participation – and the development of indigenous institutions on which it depends – was in many countries conceivable only in the context of individual programmes or projects. Another was that independent groups embraced the idea of networking as a means of enabling people to participate in development planning and activities without being confined by the bureaucratic straitjacket of more formal institutions. National and international networks sprang up in many regions, providing an alternative institutional model for development promotion.

Over the past decade this commitment to participatory development has made significant progress, most notably in the practical work of non-governmental agencies and in methodologies devised by the more progressive research institutes. For many of the former it is now standard practice to try to involve the intended beneficiaries in the design, planning and management of projects, while the latter have developed a range of user-friendly techniques for participatory planning, such as farmer participatory research and rapid rural appraisal (RRA) (see e.g. McCracken, Pretty and Conway, 1988).

The hallmark of RRA is its reliance on simple techniques which can be understood and used by villagers themselves and which do not depend on literacy. They include the drawing of resource maps, seasonal calendars and diagrams to illustrate intra-village relationships, the ranking of people's priorities and preferences, and the use of folklore, songs and poetry, which can reveal much about the community's history, values and customs. Use of these techniques has spread with remarkable speed over the past five years, and nowhere more dramatically than in India (Pretty and Sandbrook, 1991).

These techniques represent an important advance. A difficult question, however, concerns the extent to which participatory development projects will be tolerated – or can retain their integrity – within a non-participatory political system. There are many countries where such projects have thrived at community level even though the national government has been anti-democratic; examples include countries as diverse as Kenya, Pakistan and Indonesia. Participatory projects have spread not only in the rural areas, where the governments in question could perhaps afford to ignore them, but also in urban areas, taking up problems such as housing and health care, water and sanitation.

Many centralist governments have not stood in the way of small-scale participatory initiatives, but there is a variable borderline beyond which such projects will find themselves in conflict with the government's assertion of its prerogative in policy-making. The viability of local-level participation in the absence of a positive enabling environment can only be measured on a case-by-case basis, but it will depend significantly on the spread of similar initiatives (strength in numbers) and the level up to which participation is permitted in the pyramid of social organizations.

In government-to-government aid programmes, with some honourable exceptions, the approach to people's participation has generally been to add on a token consultation process. The affected populations are then invited to give their views on a project already decided and about which they usually have little information. Some donor agencies are now moving this consultative process up to the preliminary planning phase, so the people's views may be taken into account; but consultation (an interview, a questionnaire) is not participation. The World Bank recently produced detailed guidelines for its staff on how to involve NGOs and community organizations in assessing the environmental impact of its projects (World Bank, 1991). The guidelines were presented as a recipe for the 'participation' of these groups; but while they reflected much thought and sensitivity on appropriate methods of consultation they stopped well short of suggesting any direct involvement for such groups in project decision-making.

WHO DEFINES DEMOCRACY?

In Africa, the 'lost decade' of the 1980s has been described as synonymous with the failure of the state, which in its current form 'has not managed to promote either development or popular participation' (ACORD, 1990). But the start of the 1990s has seen dramatic changes. Apart from the demise of nearly a dozen dictators, giving a new lease of life to the domino theory, potentially the most far-reaching change has been the decision of several major aid-giving nations to make their development assistance conditional on the recipient countries' progress towards democracy.

This new conditionality has been made possible by the end of the cold war, removing much of the rationale for shoring up unconstitutional client regimes. Whether or not such political conditionality is considered to infringe a country's sovereignty, the pragmatic question is what kind of democracy it demands. Will the conditions imposed by the aid-givers really promote the empowerment of the people? Will they provide a basis for more just and efficient government? The omens so far are not altogether encouraging.

To put first things first, there is now an authentic democratic groundswell of public opinion in many of the countries of the South themselves. For much of Africa, in particular, this opens up radical possibilities of renewal from within: the first chance, it could be argued, for the people of that region to redefine the parameters of their political organization since the pre-colonial era.

This process of renewal already has its own dynamic, independent of external pressures which may seek to reinforce it. These pressures may be helpful, where their purpose is to open up the range of available options. A measure of conditionality attached to human rights, for example, may be needed to deter governments from using political repression to protect themselves from the consequences of economic liberalization.

But pressure by Northern donors may equally prove counter-productive if they attempt to go beyond this to prescribe specific solutions, and this is what is happening at the present time. Furthermore, as commentators in the United States have noted, there is an assumption – central to the discussions of democratization among

47

Northern policy-makers – that democracy and a free market are structurally linked (CWS and LWR, 1991). This again poses the question: are we all talking about the same thing?

For policy-makers brought up under a Western parliamentary form of government, the need for more than one political party to provide the checks and balances of a democratic system appears self-evident. Though the semblance is often greater that the reality, it seems to be the essential ingredient for public choice. As such, some Northern development agencies have adopted an almost evangelical fervour in urging multi-party democracy upon Southern countries looking for a new way forward. One is reminded of the words of Aldous Huxley more than sixty years ago when he observed: 'For vast numbers of people the idea of democracy has become a religious idea, which it is a duty to try to carry into practice in all circumstances, regardless of the practical requirements of each particular case.'

In the context of Africa today, one knowledgeable observer notes that 'blanket demands for the rapid introduction of multi-party systems along Western lines do not always do justice to the complexity of the situation' (Hofmeier, 1991). That complexity includes several socio-political factors which differentiate the African from the Western reality. In particular, there is the risk of ethnic and/or religious antagonisms being manipulated and sharpened by the creation of competing political parties. Although various African leaders have found it convenient to invoke this as a justification of one-party rule, the danger of factional conflict is in many cases real – as, for example, in the case of Mali, where the overthrow of dictatorship has led to the creation of more than forty political parties and aggravated hostility between the majority Bambara and the nomadic Tuareg of the north.

Quite apart from such inherent obstacles to political transformation, there is evidence that external pressures which stress form (e.g. multi-partyism) rather than substance make it fairly easy for autocratic rulers to construct a deceptive façade of democracy to satisfy them. Free elections present no problem; gerrymandering can ensure the desired result. Decentralization is easy; power is devolved to those who will do what they are told. And as Julius Nyerere has noted, corrupt governments can fearlessly assign their friends as puppeteers to run pseudo-independent political parties. In short, the forms of democratic practice are easily fudged. Even a genuine commitment to multi-party politics may only have the effect of segmenting the existing ruling class. Without a range of other measures, there is no guarantee that it will do anything to empower the people as a whole.

A further thorny question for those carrying the banner of sustainable development is whether governments introducing democratic systems will be more or less able to commit themselves to the kind of long-term development strategies their countries need. As in the West, short-term electoral opportunism can be expected to come to the fore, offsetting in varying degrees the gains of a more open and participatory system. With a time horizon of five years or less, elected governments face the inexorable logic that jam today will buy more votes than ovens for bread tomorrow. The nation's long-term economic health and the rights of future generations are not seen as the issues for a winning political manifesto.

The conclusion may be drawn that while sustainable development requires a participatory political process, the imposition of unfamiliar democratic forms without the necessary checks and balances in place is liable to prove socially divisive and counter-productive. What is needed, then, from the external supporters of political renewal in the South is less emphasis on form and more thoughtful attention to substance – that is, practical efforts to lay the groundwork for a pluralist society. As one distinguished African commentator has noted: 'The needed transformation in the political process goes beyond multi-partyism or concessions granted by the government. It is necessary to strengthen civil society at all levels including peasants, workers and student movements, NGOs, professional associations, academic groups, etc.' (Damiba, 1991).

A first appropriate step for external agencies in this process would be a constant and thorough monitoring of the observance of human rights. Related areas of attention should cover

> many different freedoms and institutions, such as the maintenance of the rule of law, the compulsory accountability of government bodies, the prevention of uncontrolled nepotism and other patronage, permission of a true pluralism of ideas, the unimpeded existence of different associations, interest groups and a free press, and finally as much separation as possible between parties (or the party) and the state or between the political and economic spheres.
>
> (Hofmeier, 1991)

To these could be added a campaign of public information and education, needed in many countries to raise people's awareness of the implications of an evolving democratic process and to give them the basic conceptual tools for participation.

THE 'GOVERNANCE' DEBATE

Along with the new donor commitment to democracy in development has come a critical spotlight on the structure and efficiency of institutions in the developing world which are needed to support it. This debate on 'good governance' was initiated by the World Bank in its long-term perspective study of sub-Saharan Africa (World Bank, 1989). While provoking controversy – and with good reason – it has done much to generate awareness that the best-laid plans for sustainable development will go nowhere without adequate institutional mechanisms to formulate policies and implement them.

At one level, the World Bank's concerns can be seen to focus primarily on the efficiency of economic management. In its long-term study emphasis is placed on the need for a 'leaner, better disciplined, better trained and more motivated public service', public enterprises with managerial autonomy and monitorable performance indicators, and a greater role for local government. At another level, however, behind the assertion that 'better governance requires political renewal', the Bank's analysis is seen by some critics as highly ideological, suggesting that Western liberal democracy is the only path to development.

Put simply, an equation can be formulated to show that good governance = good decision-makers + good decisions + good implementation. And few would argue with the Bank's general contention that the requirements include the rule of law, public accountability and the free flow of information. But beyond this, critics detect a tendency to write one blanket prescription for all countries – the same failure to disaggregate according to national and local conditions which they consider a principal flaw of the structural adjustment programmes of the 1980s.

So far the debate on governance has raised more questions than it has answered. For instance, harsh economic reforms demanded by the International Monetary Fund (IMF) and the World Bank in Africa have been more easily and effectively undertaken by authoritarian regimes, which have frequently imposed even more stringent controls to push the policies through. Furthermore, the budget cuts introduced with these reforms have often resulted in near-impossible working conditions in government, leading to a 'brain drain' and yet lower performance by the very institutions on which the eventual outcome of the reforms depends. And Northern agencies have so far failed to come forward with offers of special help for governments prepared to initiate democratic reforms in difficult economic conditions.

ORGANIZATIONAL FRAMEWORKS

On the basis of the foregoing analysis, we should now look at the organizational framework or structures which are needed if sustainable development policies are to work in practice. There are two fundamental questions to be asked about the direction of institutional change in the context of sustainability:

- What kind of democratic processes and machinery are necessary to unshackle the productive energies of the Third World populations and to convince them that new efforts will be for their own benefit?
- What are the conditions required to make such processes work?

What processes?

People's participation is a multiform and dynamic process; it is not something that can be instituted simply by legislation, even though this will in most cases be a necessary condition. To have democratic rights on paper in no way guarantees the ability to exercise them. The process is multiform in the sense that it cannot be initiated from a single starting-point and achieved by a linear progression. An NGO in Borneo, Burundi or Brazil may want to operate in a participatory manner, but it will be blocked at the start if its project beneficiaries at community level are subject to cultural, political or economic domination by traditional chiefs, politicians or merchants – or if the central government denies the NGO access to information and refuses collaboration with its own extension services. Based on a case study from Peru, one analysis of citizen participation emphasizes that it must be understood in the context of political and governmental institutions which are complex and shifting, in which strange alliances abound and in which the motives to participate are conflicting (Peattie, 1990). Despite the complexities, democratic processes for sustainable development must *start from where the people are*, in terms of both place and socio-cultural environment. That this basic condition remains a dead letter in many parts of the world (and is broken by a good number of the model Western democracies) can be attributed essentially to two factors:

- over-concentration of political, commercial or social power in the hands of small minorities; and
- the resultant giantism of centralized institutions and top-heavy bureaucracies unable to respond either to needs or to opportunities.

However, cracks have recently been appearing in many of the monolithic national structures that control people's development in the

South. Some interpret them as signs of a global trend towards decentralization and people power: perhaps even the 'paradigm shift' for which some of the more progressive development thinkers have long been scanning the horizon.

Decentralization is said to be an idea whose time has come (Banuri, 1991). But how widespread is the empirical evidence for change in this direction? Without doubt, the strongest single impulse during the 1980s was provided by the structural adjustment programmes requiring many Southern governments to cut back social services and to divest themselves of unprofitable enterprises. Some cuts left a vacuum; others led to a delegation of responsibilities to provincial and local levels of government but gave them little room to be more than executing agencies for the centre. Very few provided for a real transfer of power to the local agencies best placed to fill the gap, whether governmental or other.

Meanwhile, as illustrated by many examples in the present volume, a mass of evidence has been accumulated to show that decentralized development schemes are almost invariably those with the best track record. In most cases, though, these are schemes initiated at community or project level, and there is still little conclusive evidence that power relinquished by central governments will percolate to the grass roots.

Advocates of decentralization also have to overcome a number of objections from different quarters – for example, that it may encourage anarchy, that co-ordination between agencies and the enforcement of rules or laws will be more difficult, and that the rights of individuals or smaller groups will be hard to protect (ibid.). These are not concerns to be minimized, but assuming they can be satisfactorily resolved, action will be needed at various levels to promote a decentralized development model. More research is needed to define appropriate policies for international agencies and national governments. Better training is required for extension workers to develop strategies and programmes with the people, and for officials at national, intermediate and local levels to prepare and engage them in new ways of working and new inter-level relationships.

One important consequence of a shift in rights and responsibilities from central government to the local level should be an improvement in the management of resources – human, physical and financial. But for the system to work in this way, a local community must be able to obtain decision-making power over its own affairs. In other words, there must be an enabling environment – in particular, a framework of law and an organizational infrastructure through which representative bodies at community level can inform themselves on issues of the day and then transmit their views or decisions both to other communities and to the higher authorities.

For this infrastructure to be effective, three essential requirements must be borne in mind:

- *transparency*, which means that the processes of decision-making must be open to public view and thus be seen to be free of interference from special interests;
- *accountability*, not only in the financial sense to guard against the poor management or misappropriation of funds, but also politically to ensure that agreed policies and programmes are carried through; and
- *freedom of information*, which requires independence for the press and other news media so that the people's right to participate in public affairs is backed up by the right to know.

What conditions?

To make the necessary provision for these rights and responsibilities, governments must demonstrate their commitment to popular participation on a number of fronts:

- by establishing a proper legislative framework to give their commitment the force of law and by strengthening the integrity and powers of the judiciary in whatever ways are required to ensure compliance;
- by issuing instructions to public agencies and employees to ensure that legislation is respected, by providing any resources needed to reform existing institutions and practices, and by monitoring progress and publishing regular reports to highlight areas of success and/ or difficulty;
- by providing education and skills training at the community, district and provincial levels to produce an adequate cadre of trained and well-motivated people who will understand the values of, and be competent to manage, a participatory system.

The term 'multi-partyism' is often used to imply that a political system which freely allows the establishment of political parties will, by definition, be democratic. This is a dangerous over-simplification. A multi-party system provides better protection for freedom of the individual, but it is not in itself enough. Just as important are the strength, orientation and credibility of the organizations which stand between the ordinary citizen and the state: the village committee, the rural workers' association, the schoolteachers' union, the handicrafts co-operative, the federation of women's groups, the national NGO consortium and many more.

It goes without saying that if these intermediate organizations are weak they will be poorly placed to represent the interests of those they speak for in any participatory system; indeed, for their constituents the system will not function. They must be strong in order to command credibility with their members/supporters and also with the higher organs of government that they deal with.

A good example is the NGO consortium of Zimbabwe, VOICE, which grew out of a pre-independence welfare organization and until recently experienced declining support among its members. Many felt that VOICE was unable to represent their interests effectively and that this restricted their scope for participation in development policy issues at national level. Under a recent restructuring and with a new name – the National Association of NGOs (NANGO) – the consortium has adopted a new constitution and a decentralized management structure, providing for more effective involvement of its members at all levels. A renewed sense of optimism and commitment is already evident.

Even with far greater human and technical resources, many social institutions considered to be the backbone of democracy in the North fail to meet the criteria of real participation. In countries of the South newly embarking on a democratic course, few of the pre-conditions exist for participation at the national level; there may nevertheless be room to build on traditional forms of collective decision-making at community level, which have the advantage of being established and well understood.

THE ROLE OF INSTITUTIONS

People in the environment/development business are good at inventing the kind of magic passwords – such as 'participatory appraisal', 'good governance' and 'sustainability' itself – which punctuate this chapter. Though reality lags behind, they give us a comforting sense of being on the right track. But what is needed to achieve the kind of harmonious balance implied by this occult vocabulary?

First and foremost, most analysts agree, is the need for effective machinery to carry and convert the sustainable development model from theory to practice. In simple terms, what is required is an interlocking network of institutions capable of acting as a power grid to harness and distribute a nation's human energy. Without such a matrix to articulate and give coherence to people's aspirations and efforts, no development can be built to last.

Scarcely more than a generation ago, India epitomized the misery of the Third World with widespread hunger and seemingly irreversible poverty. Today, more than 300 million Indians are still extremely poor, but the country has become the world's eighth largest industrial power, due in significant measure to its highly developed organizational infrastructure, which includes, from village level upwards, several thousand non-governmental groups active in every field of social and economic concern.

In other countries, however, and most notably in Africa, the development of formal institutions has until recently been confined to organs of central government and the ruling party. In the past, institution-building projects in the South by large aid agencies have also frequently been too short in duration and too narrow in their objectives.

A World Bank publication, acknowledging that institutional development is a slow process, says that the Bank's most successful attempts have been over long periods, 'usually several decades'. Institutional projects, which at first concentrated on only one or two issues, were found not to work very well; however, even when introduced into integrated rural or urban programmes they have still tended to produce poor results. Significantly, the most progress has been made in sectors of 'high specificity' – such as finance, industry and advance technology, where standards and performance can be measured with precision – and the least in social or 'people-oriented' activities such as rural development and health care (Israel, 1987).

This account of the World Bank's experience starts from a rather narrow definition of institutional development as being 'the process of improving the ability of institutions to make effective use of the human and financial resources available'. Arguably it should have the more fundamental purpose of evaluating the relevance of institutions – both severally and in relation to others – in addressing economic or social needs. Only with such terms of reference will institutions be identified which have outlived their purpose or which, perhaps, had doubtful reasons to exist in the first place. The point is important because institutions are not a neutral factor in the development process; they represent values, which in turn represent the interests of some political or social group. As a consequence they can be highly exploitative. One school of thought maintains that in today's institutionalized society, health, learning, dignity, independence and creative endeavour are defined as little more than the performance of the institutions which claim to serve these ends (Illich, 1970).

In seeking to strengthen the institutional base for sustainable development, therefore, care must first be taken to ensure that the values are right and that both the scale and the orientation of any institution are appropriate. Only then is it time to address the technical questions about effective use of resources – and here again it must be remembered that the transfer of scientific, technical or managerial expertise to a given organization will not be enough to enhance its performance if constraints on its operation (upstream) or its outputs (downstream) remain unchanged.

So how should we visualize the kinds of institution that will support sustainable patterns of development?

THE MICRO LEVEL

At community level, a viable institution will be one that represents people's ideas, interests and/or needs, which has their confidence and the power to communicate their views effectively in dealings with higher authorities. This presupposes a degree of decentralization of decision-making, and it assumes a capacity of both leaders and members of the community to take advantage of their rights. It requires that local institutions have access to information about national development and resource-use policies, plus the skills to interpret this information in order to formulate realistically their own expectations.

Local organizations must be the bedrock of any participatory development process. As well as giving people some say in the policy decisions that affect them, they can mobilize local resources, give better representation to women and adapt externally designed programmes to local conditions. Whether urban or rural, formal or informal, local organizations are among the most important and active in shaping their environment and can be crucial for sustainable resource use (Pretty and Sandbrook, 1991).

What, then, is needed to promote the development of institutions at the micro level and to facilitate their work? Before anything else, the right to organize. On this point one commentator has stressed that for the people to be empowered, the people must be 'created' through institutions or collective organization. Others cite needs for co-operation with government agencies and technical assistance, while a study of housing and health in Third World cities lists four conditions for promoting community participation: representative governments at all levels; local government support; the adoption of a more community-based approach by government programmes; and the introduction of 'community facilitators' to liaise with the government and other agencies.

THE MESO LEVEL

At the intermediate levels of social, economic and political organization
– that wide stratum sandwiched between government and the grass
roots – a more complex mix of technical, managerial and information-
handling skills is needed to make the institutional machinery effective.
In between the macro and the micro, this *meso* level of institutions
includes provincial and district authorities, co-operatives, research and
training institutes, the small-scale private sector, trade unions, religious
groups and a range of independent, non-profit organizations. For this
sector to function effectively in the national interest, it must cultivate
the ability to face both ways: to interpret the grass roots to the centre
and vice versa. This role is well established in certain countries of the
South, but it is something new in those where the transmission of power
has hitherto been unidirectional. It therefore calls for many new skills
on the part of those who should provide a key interface between policy-
makers and the mass of the people.

Three important elements in the meso-level infrastructure are
federations of community groups and local government, both of which
may straddle the micro–meso line, and NGOs. National and provincial
federations of poor farmers or community organizations have
developed in many countries. They range from the Fédération des
Groupements Naam, supporting as many as 200,000 peasant members
in Burkina Faso, to the National Co-ordinating Body of Mexico's
Urban Popular Movement (CONAMUP), an umbrella for dozens of
urban groups throughout the country. Such federations can have a key
role in mobilizing and sharing resources available within the movement,
as well as providing an effective front for interaction and negotiation
with government and external research or aid agencies (Bebbington,
1991).

A recurrent message of this book is that sustainable practices require
a transfer of power and responsibility from central government to the
local level. Given the importance that this attaches to the functions of
local government, much will need to be done before most city, town and
village administrations in the South are equipped for the task.

As pointed out earlier, decentralization has most often meant
increased responsibilities for local government without any increase in
its already inadequate financial resources or decision-making authority.
In most urban centres, government already has no more than a minor
role in housing construction, water supply, road building or other basic
services – and in worst-case situations local government can have a

negative influence, repressing community organizations and favouring investments that benefit a small élite (see Chapter 5).

Improving the quality and resources of local government should thus be a priority in any sustainable development strategy. Quality means that such authorities must be elected and accountable to the community, having well-defined powers commensurate with their responsibility for community affairs. To ensure an adequate degree of autonomy, local governments must also have access to independent sources of revenue – something that many national governments, and not only those in the South, do their best to resist.

Across most countries of Latin America, Asia and Africa, NGOs – either foreign or indigenous – have over the past two decades become principal actors in development at the meso level. At best they have proved more flexible, more innovative and more ready to introduce participatory approaches than official organizations. They have also successfully challenged many large-scale official development schemes which threatened the rights or resources of the poor.

For this reason NGOs are regarded with ambivalence if not suspicion by many governments. Given their control of substantial Northern funds, governments have been obliged to recognize them as partners in the development process. But for this partnership to have real meaning, NGOs and other organizations representing the people's interests must gain access to the policy-making process. In practice, they will only be accorded a meaningful role in policy formulation when they are able to demonstrate a thorough understanding of the technical and political constraints prevailing in any given sector. Even if nominally granted, access to the policy arena will be meaningless for people's organizations unless they are equipped to take advantage of it.

The policy role of Southern NGOs is actually or potentially one of their most important functions. This has been demonstrated in the past ten years by numerous groups in Asia and Latin America, which have formed networks and coalitions to campaign on issues of concern to their constituencies. In Africa, however, only a tiny handful of non-governmental groups have so far been able to develop anything like a policy platform. Some are now making new efforts in this direction, beginning with the skills required to underpin policy formulation.

Much more cross-fertilization and networking between meso-level institutions is needed to develop the consensus on strategies which must support participatory development goals. Among other things it demands a good degree of institutional flexibility, as noted in Chapter 4.

THE MACRO LEVEL

For a number of national governments, the last decade of the twentieth century has begun with a profound – and in some cases traumatic – reappraisal of the role of the state. The dismantling of the public sector in many Third World countries during the 1980s, under pressure from the IMF, was presented as an objective economic necessity. However, the institutional restructuring which this divestiture will entail for many countries of the South in the 1990s is being tied to an overtly political agenda. Some of this – the emphasis on democratic systems and people's participation – should help to cement the foundations for sustainable development. But there is a real danger that the demise of autocratic regimes will be taken as evidence that the South now needs carbon copies of Western institutions to make democracy work. The already evident tendency of some donor countries to equate democracy with multi-party politics and free-market principles is a case in point.

The institutions of government in low-income countries vary so widely in both scope and quality that it is impossible to generalize about their needs. Some have efficient and well-staffed ministries working on clearly defined policies to promote sustainable development as far as their means allow. Others have little or no effective infrastructure and, in the case of the poorest countries of sub-Saharan Africa, few human resources or other means to start building it.

What can be said is that most countries should be seeking to strengthen their capacities in policy-making and in socio-economic and technical research, with three objectives in view:

- to enhance their economic independence by acquiring greater negotiating parity with Northern agencies on finance, aid and trade;
- to upgrade national research inputs to policy-making, thus reducing their dependence on external advice which can seldom take full account of the critical indigenous factors of cultural and social relations;
- to facilitate the process of institutional restructuring below govern-ment level by assisting in the identification of mechanisms and linkages required between the macro, meso and micro levels.

INSTITUTIONS IN THE NORTH

In countries of the North, meanwhile, a crescendo of voices urging environmental protection and 'green' policies has brought a rapid growth of institutions committed to sustainable development over the past decade. Governments have set up new ministries of the environment and campaigns by non-governmental agencies have mobilized wide public support on many issues.

But popular support for sustainable development tends to stop short of policy areas where people perceive their own interests to be at stake. This means there is little or no public pressure for changes in international terms of trade or in resource-intensive consumerist lifestyles. To deal with these issues, Northern countries need more independent organizations able to analyse the costs and benefits of various policy options.

Internationally, much attention has been given in recent times to ways of reforming the institutions of global governance: the United Nations system, the World Bank and the IMF. In April 1991, a meeting of thirty world leaders convened in Stockholm by the Swedish Prime Minister, Ingvar Carlsson, concluded that the United Nations 'is today not strong enough to deal with the tasks that face it . . . needs to be modernized and its organization updated'. In particular, their statement said, the UN needed to be able to handle the security dimension of economic and ecological issues at the Security Council level. Pointing out that the IMF and World Bank had expanded their activities beyond those originally intended, the meeting called for a world summit on global governance to review these and related issues.

HUMAN RESOURCES

To achieve sustainable development, people must be able to participate in decisions that affect their lives. To provide for this participation requires a democratic political process with effective and accountable institutions at all levels. And institutions, to be effective, must be able to count on a supply of competent, well-motivated people to run them.

For countries of the South, therefore, the path to a sustainable future has to start with programmes of human resource development. Many in Asia and Latin America are already some way down this road; other countries – including most of Africa – have made little progress in recent years, and not a few are losing ground. The World Bank's long-term study of sub-Saharan Africa (World Bank, 1989) judged the quality of primary and secondary education in the region to be 'low and declining', while higher education revealed an inappropriate mix of outputs, over-production of poor-quality graduates and high costs.

At one end of the educational spectrum, learning to read and write can empower the poor by enabling them to gain greater awareness of circumstances and changes that could improve their lives. At the other, Southern nations need highly trained specialists for policy-making, research, planning and management. In some countries, unbalanced spending on higher education has produced a surfeit of graduates in certain fields and a shortfall in others. Shortages of trained personnel have been exacerbated by the continuing 'brain drain' of talent to the North, in some cases to jobs for the very aid agencies which affect to deplore it. There are estimated to be well over 100,000 trained Africans currently living in Europe and North America.

Setting out a strategic agenda for Africa in the 1990s, the World Bank suggested that, whatever the political vantage-points of different governments or organizations, there was 'broad understanding, in particular, on the absolute priority to be given to human resource and institutional development' (World Bank, 1989). This is where any sustainable development must have its roots.

CONCLUSIONS

From this review of the structural elements of sustainability, two kinds of conclusion can be drawn: those of principle (what ought to be done, as change allows), and those of pragmatism (what can and cannot be done within existing constraints). But there is no fixed boundary between them. What is a distant ideal for one country may already be the accepted wisdom in another; what was unthinkable last year may be within reach today. Hence it would be invidious to attempt a demarcation between the two categories.

This chapter has sought to show that organizing for change towards a sustainable global future hinges on the rights and responsibilities of people to participate in the decisions that affect their lives and those of future generations. It also demands the equitable sharing, North and South, of the costs of adjustment to a sustainable society.

To enable their people to exercise the right of participation, governments must guarantee civil and political rights including freedom of association, an independent judiciary and freedom of information. Participation can then lead to real empowerment through the provision of appropriate education, awareness raising and skills training to overcome the inequities perpetuated by the exclusion of the majority from the shaping of their own development.

Progress towards these goals presupposes the existence of or scope for democratic processes from the village to the global level. But these processes will be diverse; they cannot and must not be expected to conform to a particular model. International agencies and Northern governments need to exercise caution in attaching political conditions to aid programmes. There are severe limits on the extent to which a market-led economy can propel democracy in poor countries with few resources to manage the transition. Emphasis must be placed on the substance rather than the form of progress towards a pluralist society.

To manage change, it is suggested, requires in any country an interlocking network of institutions capable of acting as a power grid to harness and distribute a nation's energy. Much of the recent attention given to institutional development has focused on organizational efficiency. But institutions are not a neutral factor in development; often they are exploitative of the poor. More fundamental than their efficiency, some of the questions needing to be addressed concern the scale, orientation, relevance and values of institutions in relation to economic or social needs. At each level of organization (micro, meso and macro), enabling measures are required to help institutions fulfil their role. As a particular example, support for sustainable development calls for more coherent efforts – especially but not exclusively in the South – to strengthen the quality, representativeness and resources of local government.

Finally, as is now increasingly recognized, the pre-condition for any sustainable future lies in the mobilization of human resources to plan and manage it. A country's priorities for human resource development need to be assessed (or reassessed) not only according to the requirements of a given sector or institution but in light of the wider issues of sustainability.

Given the chance, we may conclude, people can make direct democracy work powerfully in favour of sustainable development. The more intractable problem is that of scaling up. Above the small-group or community level, systems of representative democracy have to reconcile many complex and conflicting pressures. They can only be expected to contribute to the goal of sustainability where social divisions are manageable and where there is a broad consensus on the ecological, economic and ethical criteria for a secure future. These three criteria – the ecological, the economic and the ethical – must be the measure of any organization for change in the twenty-first century.

REFERENCES AND BIBLIOGRAPHY

ACORD, 1990. *Democracy and Empowerment in Africa: The Challenge for NGOs,* ACORD, London.

Banuri, Tariq, 1991. 'Democratic decentralization', mimeo, IUCN, Islamabad.

Bebbington, Anthony, 1991. *Farmer Organizations in Ecuador: Contributions to Farmer First Research and Development,* Sustainable Agriculture Programme Gatekeeper Series no. 26, IIED, London.

CWS (Church World Service) and LWR (Lutheran World Relief), 1991. 'Democratization and development: what are we talking about?', discussion paper for an NGO workshop, Washington, DC, May.

Dag Hammarskjold Foundation, 1975. *What Now? Another Development,* Hammarskjold Foundation, Uppsala, Sweden.

Daly, Herman, 1991. 'Sustainable development is possible only if we forgo growth', *Development Forum,* 19, 5, September–October.

Damiba, Pierre-Claver, 1991. 'Governance and economic development', *Africa Forum,* 1.

Ecoforum, 1991. 15, 2, July.

Environment and Urbanization, 1990. 'Mexico's urban popular movements', 2, 1, April.

Freire, Paulo, 1970. *Pedagogy of the Oppressed,* Seaview Press, New York.

Freire, Paulo, 1973. *Education for Critical Consciousness,* Seaview Press, New York.

Gran, Guy, 1983. *Development by People: Citizen Construction of a Just World,* Praeger, New York.

Hardoy, Jorge E., Cairncross, Sandy and Satterthwaite, David (eds), 1990. *The Poor Die Young: Housing and Health in Third World Cities,* Earthscan, London.

Hasan, Mubashir, 1991. 'Empowerment, democracy, participation and development in Southeast Asia', *Development,* (journal of Society for International Development), 1.

Hofmeier, Rolf, 1991. 'Political conditions attached to development aid for Africa', paper for a conference sponsored by Queen Elizabeth House, Oxford, and the World Bank, Oxford, May.

Huxley, Aldous, 1927. *Proper Studies,* Chatto & Windus, London.

Illich, Ivan, 1970. *Deschooling Society,* Harper & Row, New York.

Israel, Arturo, 1987. *Institutional Development: Incentives to Performance,* World Bank, Washington DC.

McCracken, Jennifer A., Pretty, Jules N. and Conway, Gordon R., 1988. *An Introduction to Rapid Rural Appraisal for Agricultural Development,* Sustainable Agriculture Programme, IIED, London.

Peattie, Lisa, 1990. 'Participation: a case study of how invaders organize, negotiate and interact with government in Lima, Peru', *Environment and Urbanization,* 2, 1, April.

Pretty, Jules N. and Sandbrook, Richard, 1991. 'Operationalizing sustainable development at the community level: primary environmental care', paper for the Development Assistance Committee, OECD, Paris, October.

Stockholm Initiative on Global Security and Governance, 1991. *Common Responsibility in the 1990s,* Prime Minister's Office, Stockholm, April.

UNDP, 1991. *Human Development Report 1991,* Oxford University Press, Oxford.

World Bank, 1989. *Sub-Saharan Africa: From Crisis to Sustainable Growth. A Long-Term Perspective Study,* World Bank, Washington, DC.

World Bank, 1991. 'Community involvement and the role of non-governmental organizations in environmental review', *Environmental Assessment Sourcebook,* vol. 1, World Bank, Washington, DC.

3 Economic Policy and Sustainable Natural Resource Management

Edward Barbier, Joshua Bishop, Bruce Aylward and Joanne Burgess

INTRODUCTION

In the 1980s environmental degradation in the South received increasing recognition by governments, aid agencies and the general public as a key economic development issue. This rather recent 'discovery' that excessive resource mismanagement, depletion and degradation do indeed impose high costs on developing economies has been slow in coming. Perhaps one reason has been that the costs of environmental degradation are often difficult to assess. The impacts of environmental degradation often occur *externally* to any market system and involve complex processes of ecological–economic interaction. Both the economic *causes* and *effects* of environmental degradation are difficult to discern and analyse in developing countries.

Third World economies, especially those of the lower-income countries, are highly dependent on primary production as the foundation of long-term, sustainable economic development. Maintaining or increasing primary production – in agriculture, fishing, forestry and mining – depends in turn on efficient and sustainable management of the resource base which supports these activities. Moreover, as developing countries industrialize and as their populations increase and concentrate in urban settlements, the role of the environment in assimilating waste products will become increasingly important. Protection and conservation of key natural systems will be essential, not just for the potential value of genetic resources, recreation and tourism but also because these systems provide important ecological functions which support economic activity and human welfare.

The following section of this chapter looks in detail at the market failures and government policies that are at the centre of many environmental degradation problems facing developing countries. We then discuss the challenges facing environmental economists in redirecting policies for sustainable development. This section argues that an understanding of the economic functions performed by the environment is a necessary component of strategies aimed at ensuring the sustainable and efficient management of natural resources in developing economies. The subsequent section describes four important techniques – environmental cost-benefit analysis, resource accounting, economy–environment linkages and applied sustainability research – for integrating sound natural resource management principles into all levels of economic policy-making in developing countries. The final section draws together the conclusions of the chapter.

THE ROLE OF MARKETS AND PUBLIC POLICY IN ENVIRONMENTAL DEGRADATION

Market failure exists when markets fail to reflect fully environmental values. The presence of open-access resource exploitation, public environmental goods, externalities, incomplete information and markets, and imperfect competition all contribute to market failure. Usually some form of corrective public or collective action, involving regulation, incentives or institutional measures, is required – provided that the costs of such measures do not exceed the potential welfare benefits. *Policy failure* occurs when the public policies required to correct for market failure over- or under-correct for the problem. It also occurs when government decisions or policies – in areas where there are no market failures – are themselves responsible for excessive environmental degradation. For example, environmental damage may arise from policies designed to promote economic growth or to improve income distribution, due to inadequate attention to their impact on the environment.

Market and policy failures lead to a distortion of economic incentives. That is, the private costs of activities which result in environmental degradation do not reflect the full social cost of that damage, in terms of environmental values forgone. The failure to take full account of these social costs may result in excessive levels of environmental degradation.

Market failure

Market mechanisms determine the prices of natural resources, and of products derived from them, by reconciling demand and supply. However, *markets do not automatically account for environmental values,* such as the subsistence use of natural products for food, fuel, medicines and building materials, the protective and supportive roles of ecological functions, or the use of biodiversity for agricultural and medicinal research. Nor do markets capture *option* and *existence values,* values derived from preserving certain natural environments, species and resources today as an 'option' for future use or simply because their existence is valued. As these environmental values are not channelled through existing markets they are not reflected in producer and consumer decisions; they are *external costs.* Market mechanisms also tend to understate *user cost* – that is, the cost of forgoing future direct or indirect use benefits that results from excessive resource depletion or degradation today. A number of market failures causing this divergence of social and private costs are reviewed below.

Public goods
Certain environmental benefits may be defined as public goods – that is, they are freely available to everyone, and consumption by any one individual does not significantly diminish the quality of consumption by another. Problems arise because the cost to any individual of producing (or preserving) the environmental public good always exceeds the potential benefits they can anticipate. Hence market mechanisms tend to under-supply public goods.

Existence values, such as the satisfaction derived from the knowledge that an endangered species continues to survive, are examples of public goods. Once the existence of the panda, the rhino or the blue whales is assured there is no way to exclude others from taking part in the feeling of ethical or emotional satisfaction. Nor does one person's enjoyment detract from that of another. Given that the existence benefits of saving endangered species do not pass through formal markets and are open to all who care to entertain them, there is little economic incentive for individuals to put up the costs of conservation. Instead, there is a tendency to wait and see if others will contribute first, thereby giving the opportunity to obtain the benefits without paying.

In order to overcome the inertia of this 'free-riding' behaviour, government must intervene to determine and achieve a satisfactory level of provision of such environmental public goods. Mechanisms used include restrictions on trade (for example, in endangered species), mandating minimum quality standards (such as for air and water) and reserving natural areas which contain important resources or supply important environmental services. Alternatively, taxes and subsidies may be used to establish *privileged groups,* who will perceive a net financial benefit in the production of a public good. Institutional responses include the creation of public authorities to administer these regulations and incentives.

Open access

Environmental public goods – once available in abundant quantities – often grow increasingly scarce due to the sheer scale of exploitation. Open access or unrestricted use of natural ecosystems in many developing countries, for example, can ultimately threaten the environmental public goods or common pool resources produced by these systems.

As indicated in Chapter 7, shifting cultivation *is* a sustainable method for managing forest lands. However, when human population growth, technological improvements, socio-cultural difficulties or other pressures disrupt existing management systems, the ensuing patterns of land use may degenerate into open access. Increasing scarcity of the resource base and a lack of clearly defined or enforced rights of access to land may lead to increasingly short fallow periods as more and more users rush to maximize short-run income to the detriment of future productivity. Concern about the increasing scarcity of fallow land is overcome by the fear that restraint would only benefit other users, who would not hesitate to clear land prematurely. Similar conditions and outcomes prevail in many loosely or ineffectively managed fisheries, rangelands, forests, wetlands and other natural habitats in developing countries, most of them in the public domain.

Short concessions for renewable resources with long growth cycles can also discourage prudent land husbandry. Logging concessions which are shorter than natural tree growth cycles will discourage the protection and regeneration of growing stock, and may lead timber companies to minimize harvest costs by practising destructive clear-cutting of forest lands. In Indonesia, for example, the inappropriate logging practices prevalent in the Outer Islands are attributed to a poorly formulated concessions policy (Pearce, Barbier and Markandya, 1990, ch. 5). Concessions for the use of public property should be phased to coincide with natural regenerative cycles, and permit the extension and/or sale of concession rights.

The general solution to open-access problems is to enforce property rights, which may be defined privately or collectively. Limits on the level of exploitation must be explicit, by means of licensed quotas, closed seasons, and so on. Management of common pool resources may be undertaken by government alone, or in collaboration with local user groups, which are often better placed to define regulations or to administer incentives and dispute-resolution schemes than central authorities (see Chapter 8).

Externalities

Externalities are those costs or benefits that arise through the production or consumption process but are not reflected in market prices. Externalities may be difficult to identify, since they are usually unintended and have indirect and diffuse effects. The ecological functions and non-timber products of the forest provide salient examples of the external, on- and off-site impacts of logging activities. The sedimentation of reservoirs, hydroelectric facilities or irrigation channels due to soil erosion arising from logging activities are typical examples of negative off-site externalities. Meanwhile, the economic contribution of wild foods and other natural products collected from the forest by rural producers (such as game meat, plant medicines, fuel and construction materials) are often lost when the forest is cleared or disturbed. Neither the off-site nor the on-site costs of such degradation are reflected in the market price of timber, although they represent additional real social costs of production along with the direct costs of logging operations. In the Philippines, the social gains from logging old-growth forest were found to be negative (around –US$130 to – US$1,175 per hectare), once the social costs of reforestation, user cost and off-site damages were included (Paris and Ruzicka, 1991).

The general response to externalities is to find ways to 'internalize' any costs and benefits affecting third parties, so that market prices will reflect the full social costs and benefits of production and consumption. In theory the ideal solution is to merge the economic interests of parties to an externality (for example, polluter and victim). More frequently policy appeals to the 'polluter pays' principle, which states that the polluter should bear all expenses associated with clean-up or compensation. In the case of logging activities, the concessionaire would be responsible not only for the direct costs of production but for compensation to those who must forgo both the direct uses of biodiversity and the indirect uses of the forest's ecological functions.

Imperfect information

Imperfect information on market trends and government policy in developing countries often leads the private sector to consume natural resources rapidly and deters investment in sustainable methods of production. From a social perspective, the resulting environmental degradation will be excessive.

The many risks and high uncertainty confronting private individuals translate into short planning horizons, causing individuals to prefer immediate to long-term returns from conservation investments. On the other hand, societies as a whole are risk averse and must balance immediate returns from resource exploitation against ensuing losses of future productivity and other environmental values. Where resources without viable substitutes are being irreversibly degraded, or when the future value of resources is uncertain, society will prefer less consumption of those resources and greater investment in conservation than the individual or firm.

In some developing countries the lack of markets or institutions in which producers can hedge or pool risk skews their preference for resource exploitation towards the present. Producers of non-traded goods and small-scale operators are particularly susceptible. Unlike large firms producing internationally traded commodities such as oil and copper, or cash crops like coffee, tea and rubber, such producers cannot 'insure' themselves against medium-term risk in international futures markets. In addition, their lack of access to formal credit frequently means that such producers are forced to borrow in informal markets, where higher interest rates reflect private and small-group perceptions of risk.

Uncertainty over renewal of tenure agreements, threats of expropriation and the perceived unwillingness or inability of authorities to protect private property serve to delay investments that promote sustainable production and to encourage mining of the resource base. Uncertainty about future rental arrangements and prices, contradiction between indigenous and modern property rights and other concerns about future access to land and capital may discourage farmers from investing in soil conservation. Cases of land degradation in Botswana, Java, Sudan and Nepal all highlight the role of uncertainty and risk, much of it related to the high cost of informal credit, in reducing farmers' propensity to invest in land improvements (Pearce, Barbier and Markandya, 1990).

Imperfect competition
Natural resource and environmental problems in developing countries are frequently linked to what might be considered 'excessive' levels of competition. Monopolies or oligopolies in resource markets are often considered beneficial precisely because they lead to conservative use of natural resources, in order to maximize scarcity rents. Tax and regulation can ensure that these rents accrue to society as a whole. Unfortunately, public intervention in developing countries often distorts markets and creates conditions of imperfect competition that

either dissipate resource rents or lead to excessive private profit. Both can be devastating to the environment.

The exploitation of exhaustible resources such as oil, gas and copper, and of renewable resources such as timber for logs, pulp and paper, is often characterized by large economies of scale. With high fixed costs these natural monopolies are often operated in developing countries by public enterprises or by subsidiaries of multinational companies. Dominance of the local market is assured, but producers are often restrained from extracting monopoly rents by taxes, price controls and regulation. Ideally prices should be set close to the marginal costs of production, but in practice prices are often set at well below average costs. In Venezuela, for instance, excessive local consumption of petroleum products due to the high level of effective subsidization not only reversed the typical monopolistic impact on resource use, but aggravated the public sector deficit.

Lack of competition in markets for renewable resources in developing countries often results from the creation of agricultural marketing boards, which then act as sole (monopsonist) buyers. The resulting impacts on the environment may be ambiguous, as depressed prices for agricultural products may protect marginal lands from coming under cultivation, but also reduce farm incomes and thus deter investment in conservation. In the absence of government restrictions, monopolies are unlikely to arise in markets for non-traded agricultural products, which are usually characterized by many small-scale producers. However, collusion among a small number of firms controlling access to land, capital, fertilizer and imported machinery may result in monopolistic pricing of scarce inputs. A more common scenario is the creation of public monopolies in agricultural inputs causing distortions and restrictions in supply. Poorer farmers who desperately need inputs for land improvements may be excluded, whereas more affluent farmers willing to invest in mechanized irrigation of dryland areas and conversion of forest areas and wetlands might benefit – to the detriment of the environment.

Policy failure

In addition to the distorting effects of market failure, even the direct costs of exploiting or altering natural resource systems *are often subsidized and/or distorted by public policies*. As a result, individuals do not face even the full *private costs* of their own actions, much less the social costs. Unnecessary and excessive environmental degradation often ensues.

Regulation
Regulations covering the production and consumption of a wide range of goods and services can affect environmental quality by distorting demand and supply conditions for natural resources. Quantitative restrictions on trade often have significant effects; quotas on grain imports, for example, may result in higher local grain prices and thus encourage encroachment by farmers on marginal lands or environmentally sensitive areas. Other regulations with environmental impacts include pollution controls, licensing and permit laws, concession terms and tenancy arrangements. The effect of regulation on the use of natural resources may be indirect and ambiguous, hence the need for careful scrutiny of existing and proposed measures. In Indonesia, for example, regulations governing pesticide use in rice production were modified in 1987, after increased pest outbreaks in successive seasons were linked to problems of excessive pesticide use.

Economic policy
Macro-economic, trade and sectoral adjustment policy can alter incentives governing the use of natural resources by altering aggregate demand, as well as by distorting the relative prices of natural resources and related goods and services. Because the exploitation of natural resources is a relatively large component of economic output in many developing countries, almost any economic policy or price distortion may be suspected of having environmental effects. Figure 3.1 outlines some possible linkages between economic policy and the environment.

For example, as discussed in Chapter 9, energy subsidies are pervasive in many developing countries. Oil exporters heavily subsidize all domestic oil consumption, while several importers subsidize particular petroleum products. Electricity, natural gas and coal are also heavily subsidized and as a result the prices of these fuels do not reflect the marginal costs of resource use (Kosmo, 1989). The emission of carbon dioxide from energy utilization is a major factor contributing to the greenhouse effect. Removing existing price distortions makes a significant impact on the levels of energy consumption and thus carbon dioxide emissions. For example, in India, the annual saving in carbon emissions under privately efficient electricity pricing is estimated to be approximately 13 million tonnes, which is 12.5 per cent of the country's total annual carbon emissions from carbon combustion. Similarly, in China over 30 million tonnes of carbon are saved by privately efficient electricity pricing, which is around 7.4 per cent of the country's total current emissions (Burgess, 1990).

Figure 3.1: Economic policy and potential environmental impacts

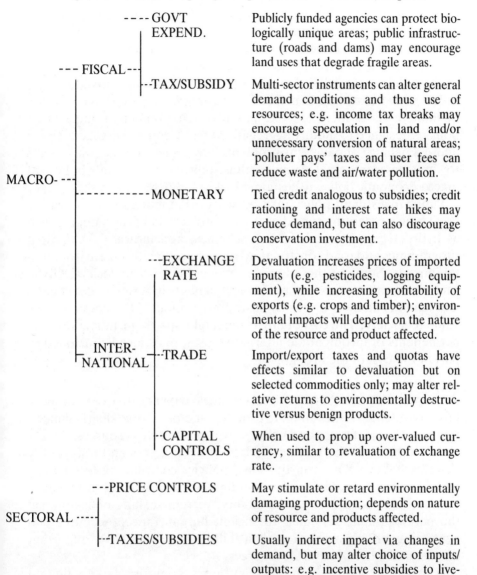

| | | Publicly funded agencies can protect biologically unique areas; public infrastructure (roads and dams) may encourage land uses that degrade fragile areas. |

GOVT EXPEND. — Publicly funded agencies can protect biologically unique areas; public infrastructure (roads and dams) may encourage land uses that degrade fragile areas.

TAX/SUBSIDY — Multi-sector instruments can alter general demand conditions and thus use of resources; e.g. income tax breaks may encourage speculation in land and/or unnecessary conversion of natural areas; 'polluter pays' taxes and user fees can reduce waste and air/water pollution.

MONETARY — Tied credit analogous to subsidies; credit rationing and interest rate hikes may reduce demand, but can also discourage conservation investment.

EXCHANGE RATE — Devaluation increases prices of imported inputs (e.g. pesticides, logging equipment), while increasing profitability of exports (e.g. crops and timber); environmental impacts will depend on the nature of the resource and product affected.

TRADE — Import/export taxes and quotas have effects similar to devaluation but on selected commodities only; may alter relative returns to environmentally destructive versus benign products.

CAPITAL CONTROLS — When used to prop up over-valued currency, similar to revaluation of exchange rate.

PRICE CONTROLS — May stimulate or retard environmentally damaging production; depends on nature of resource and products affected.

TAXES/SUBSIDIES — Usually indirect impact via changes in demand, but may alter choice of inputs/outputs: e.g. incentive subsidies to livestock production may promote deforestation; fertilizer subsidies may retard adoption of soil conservation; pesticide subsidies may increase negative health effects of agro-chemical runoff, etc.

Source: Bishop, Aylward and Barbier (1991).

Ideally, sectoral or micro-economic policy should aim to bring market prices into line with the estimated marginal social costs and benefits of natural resource use, accounting for all environmental market failures described above. In practice, however, limitations on data and research capacity usually require that initial efforts concentrate on determining the *direction* in which prices must move to better reflect social costs and benefits. On the macro-economic side, even a qualitative assessment of the potential environmental impacts of policies designed to modify aggregate demand, counter fiscal deficits or address balance of payments problems may suggest minor adjustments to limit environmental damage, thus improving the contribution of macro-economic policy to sustainable development.

Public investment policy may be analysed in much the same way as fiscal policy regarding subsidies. Large projects and programmes, such as hydroelectric dams, irrigation schemes, agricultural development programmes and road construction, often have significant environmental impacts. Some of these impacts may entail costs to society. Given such costs, the appraisal of net project benefits in terms of *direct* costs and benefits alone is a serious misrepresentation of the net economic value to society. The cost of environmental impacts, including forgone net benefits of incompatible alternative uses, must also be included as part of the cost of the investment.

Institutions

An important form of institutional weakness with negative environmental consequences is the failure to establish and/or enforce clearly defined rights of access, tenure and control over productive resources. This is clearly related to the market failures of open access and uncertainty described above. Other institutional policies contributing to environmental damage include political failings such as a lack of participatory mechanisms and public accountability, or rent-seeking behaviour on the part of public servants. Inefficient bureaucratic procedures and conflicting or mismatched responsibilities can also have important effects on the use of natural resources.

A structural failure common to developing countries, but not limited to them, is the definition of institutional authority along sectoral or geographic lines that do not correspond to the range and types of environmental problems. Many developing countries distribute responsibility for environmental affairs among a number of public agencies, creating serious problems of co-ordination. Examples may include a lack of policy co-ordination between agricultural and environmental departments over pesticides or fertilizer policy, or conflicting local government policies on the management of resources straddling administrative boundaries. In many cases all that is needed is clear delineation of areas of authority, or improved institutional linkages where there are geographical or sectoral overlaps affecting the use of natural resources.

But we should be cautious in advocating radical policy changes. As discussed below, in the case of many environmental problems in developing countries we are not even at the state of 'optimal ignorance' to begin advocating new policy directions. More difficult still is the problem of 'political will'; even when the economic evidence is clear and the policy direction self-evident, short-term political and economic interests in developing countries may predominate – especially when powerful special interest groups have a vested interest in maintaining the status quo.

THE CHALLENGE FOR ENVIRONMENTAL POLICY: 'OPTIMAL IGNORANCE'

If public policies are to be redirected to achieve efficient and sustainable management of natural resources in developing countries, then clearly major changes are required. Economic valuation of the environmental impacts arising from market and policy failures is essential for determining the appropriate policy responses. Often, however, insufficient data and information exist to allow precise estimation of the economic costs arising from market and policy failures. In most cases, cost estimates expressed as orders of magnitude and as indicators of the direction of change are sufficient for policy analysis and prescription.

However, with many natural resource problems in developing countries we are not even at this state of 'optimal ignorance' and cannot easily design appropriate policy responses. In the face of such uncertainty we should be humble in our policy prescriptions. Even the standard economic tool of 'improved pricing policy' should be invoked with caution. In most developing countries there is little empirical understanding of the mechanisms linking real price changes to short- and long-term supply and demand responses, and to natural resource impacts. Analysis is complicated by the presence of underemployment, informal and incomplete markets, labour and capital constraints and above all the problem of widespread poverty. Thus we are often ignorant of the impact of public policies on the economic incentives faced by individual producers and households for managing natural resources, particularly in the case of the poorest groups who are on the 'margin' of formal economic and social systems.

The difficulties are exemplified by problems that arise out of economic analysis of resource problems in the drylands. As indicated in Chapter 8, there is little firm evidence of the extent and costs of dryland degradation. Even further behind – and more controversial – is the analysis of the effects of economic and environmental policies on resource use in the drylands. Although degradation in the drylands is partly attributable to population growth and natural events, it is also symptomatic of an agricultural development bias that distorts agricultural pricing, investment flows, research and development, and infrastructure towards more 'favoured' agricultural land and systems (Barbier, 1989b). Where drylands 'development' is encouraged, it is often through the introduction of large-scale commercial agricultural schemes, which may conflict with indigenous farming and pastoral systems. Often, however, we lack sufficient information to anticipate the reaction of dryland producers to such investments, or to determine how resources will be affected.

Soil erosion and land degradation are not confined to the drylands; the problem is pervasive throughout all agricultural systems, degraded forest lands, public and privately owned lands, and large and small holdings in the developing world. Designing appropriate policy responses to control soil degradation is again hampered by the limitations of data, and by our poor understanding of how producers respond to resource degradation, including incentives for and against conservation.

The relationship between economic policy and resource use is often complex and difficult to substantiate. For example, there are strong indications that agricultural input pricing can influence farm-level soil erosion and conservation. Subsidies for non-labour inputs, notably inorganic fertilizers, can artificially reduce the costs to farmers of soil loss and, on more resource-poor lands, substitute for manure, mulches and nitrogen-fixing crops that might be more appropriate. On the other hand, the *inaccessibility* of inorganic fertilizers – for example, shortages caused by rationing subsidised fertilizer imports – can also lead to sub-optimal application and encourage farming practices that actually increase land degradation. Similarly, the relationship between the erodibility and profitability of different cropping systems needs to be carefully analysed, particularly in relation to changes in the *relative prices* of different crops and changes in *real producer prices and incomes* over time. More complex incentive effects arise from factors such as the availability of labour, off-farm employment, population pressure, tenure and access to frontier land, the development of post-harvesting capacity and other complementary infrastructure and the availability of credit at affordable interest rates (Southgate, 1988; Barbier, 1989a, ch. 7; Barbier, 1989b; Mortimore, 1989; Barbier and Burgess, 1990).

Gender, economics and environment

Another area of uncertainty concerns the role of women and female-headed households in economic–environment linkages. In most developing countries, women are active participants in agricultural and household production. Their *use, perception, knowledge* and *management of the land* can often be contrasted to those of men across all types of households. For example, a detailed study of the effects of agricultural commercialization among smallholders in southern Malawi emphasizes how the mix of crops grown differs between male- and female-headed households (Peters, Herrera and Randolph, 1989). Female-headed households on average cultivate maize on 90 per cent of their land, and rarely grow any cash crops, whereas male-headed households typically grow maize on 81 per cent of their land, with the remainder mostly under tobacco.

Women confront a multitude of *constraints* that are non-existent or less binding for men, and which block economic opportunities and hinder improved land management (Becker, 1990). For example, both men and women may be constrained in adopting improved crop varieties, as these typically require relatively intensive fertilizer inputs as compared to traditional crops. However, female-headed households often have extremely low income, and are unlikely to be able to raise sufficient funds from their own resources, or to obtain formal credit, in order to purchase improved seed and fertilizer (Barbier and Burgess, 1990). Large labour demands on women within the household – such as child bearing and rearing, fuel and water collection, cooking, land preparation, planting and weeding – further limit their ability to undertake improved land management, such as constructing earthworks for erosion control or planting trees. Off-farm employment opportunities for women to supplement farm income may also be constrained by gender discrimination in the labour market. Such factors help to explain the relatively low participation of women and of female-headed households generally in agricultural extension activities, credit uptake, modern input use and conservation effort (ibid.)

The causes of tropical deforestation

An equally important challenge for economic analysis in the future is to examine the impact of economic policy relative to other causes of large-scale land use changes and resource degradation. Much work has been devoted to examining the causes of tropical deforestation. For example, in the Brazilian Amazon subsidies and other policy distortions are estimated to have accounted for at least 35 per cent of all forest disturbance up to 1980, through tax incentives for capital investment (for example, industrial wood production and livestock ranching), rural credits for agricultural production (mechanized agriculture, cattle ranching and silviculture), subsidized small farmer settlement and export subsidies (Browder, 1985). In addition, government-financed investment programmes – for road building, colonial settlement and large-scale agricultural and mining activities – may *indirectly* be contributing to deforestation by 'opening up' frontier areas that were previously inaccessible to smallholders and migrants.

Studies by Capistrano (1990) and Capistrano and Kiker (1990) examine the influence of international and domestic economic factors on tropical deforestation.[1] The econometric analysis indicates the role of high agricultural export prices in inducing agricultural expansion and forest clearing, as well as the influence of macro-economic policies, such as exchange rate devaluation and increased debt servicing ratios. Similarly, in Malaysia and Indonesia, government policies to encourage the export of processed timber products rather than raw logs have led to substantial economic losses, the establishment of inefficient processing operations and accelerated deforestation (Repetto and Gillis, 1988).

There is also strong evidence that *non-economic* policy distortions contribute towards excessive land clearing (Browder, 1985; Binswanger, 1989; Southgate, Sierra and Brown, 1989; Pearce, Barbier and Markandya, 1990). As discussed in Chapter 7, formal property law as well as indigenous custom often mean that land clearing is the only way to establish a claim to tracts of forest land and thereby 'capture' potential agricultural rents. As the capacity of many developing countries' governments to manage vast tracts of publicly owned land is often minimal, encroachment into reserves and protected areas is often poorly controlled. At the same time, government agencies frequently ignore customary land tenure arrangements and the claims of indigenous inhabitants when decisions are made to allocate land.

Clearly, both micro-economic analysis of individuals' contribution and responses to environmental degradation and macro-economic analysis of the broader economic–environmental linkages will be required if coherent and effective public policies for natural resource management in developing countries are to be implemented.

PROSPECTS FOR NATURAL RESOURCE MANAGEMENT IN DEVELOPING ECONOMIES

Four important techniques that have the potential to make – and in some cases are already making – a substantial contribution to integrating sound natural resource management principles into all levels of economic policy-making in developing countries. These techniques are environmental cost-benefit analysis, resource accounting, economy–environment linkages and applied sustainability research (Barbier, 1989a).

Environmental cost-benefit analysis

As pointed out by the authors of the classic United Nations Industrial Development Organization *Guidelines,* the main rationale for conducting social cost-benefit analysis is 'to subject project choice to a consistent set of general objectives of national policy' (UNIDO, 1972). As perceptions of national policy objectives in developing countries have changed, for example emphasizing the need for scarce foreign exchange and equitable income distribution, project appraisal and planning methods have changed accordingly. The recent emphasis on the role of environmental quality and the long-term productivity of natural resource systems in sustaining economic development has led to further extensions of social cost-benefit analysis, to include environmental impacts. In contrast with traditional project evaluation, which considers only direct project benefits and costs, 'the expanded approach includes the external and environmental improvement benefits (plus the benefits from environmental protection), as well as the costs of external and/or environmental damages and of environmental control measures' (Dixon and Hufschmidt, 1986). The basic methodology comprises two steps: first, identify and measure environmental impacts in physical terms; secondly, translate these impacts into monetary terms for inclusion in the cost-benefit framework.

In recent years, considerable progress has been made in applying economic appraisal techniques to analysing the environmental impacts of investment projects and programmes in developing countries (Anderson, 1987; Gregersen *et al.*, 1987; Dixon *et al.*, 1988; Bojo, Maler and Unemo, 1990). Frequently, appraisal of the environmental impacts of major public investments has shown that the investments should be modified, and in some cases should not proceed at all. Box 3.1 summarizes an analysis of the economic benefits of the Hadejia–Jama'are floodplain in northern Nigeria, which is threatened by proposals for irrigation schemes upstream, such as the Kano River

Project. The analysis shows that the economic benefits of the existing floodplain system are considerable, and that the diversion of water to upstream developments would entail a net loss of social welfare.

Box 3.1: Comparative benefits of floodplain and upstream development in north-east Nigeria

In north-east Nigeria, an extensive natural floodplain occurs where the Hadejia and Jama'are rivers combine to form the Komadugu Yobe river, which drains into Lake Chad. The Hadejia–Jama'are floodplain provides essential income and nutrition benefits in the form of fertile soils for agriculture, grazing resources, forest products and fishing for local populations. The wetlands also serve wider regional economic needs, such as providing dry-season pasture for semi-nomadic pastoralists, agricultural surpluses for Kano and Borno states, ground-water recharge of the Chad Formation aquifer and a reserve of wild foods and other natural 'insurance' in times of drought. In addition, the wetlands are an important winter habitat for many migratory birds, and contain a number of forestry reserves. The region therefore has important tourism, educational and scientific potential.

However, in recent decades the Hadejia–Jama'are wetlands have come under increasing pressure from drought, and from upstream and downstream water developments. Upstream developments are affecting incoming water, either through dams altering the timing and size of flood flows or through diversion of surface or ground water for irrigation. Increased demand for water downstream, especially for irrigated agriculture, may lead to diversion of water past the wetlands, through construction of bypass channels. Intensified water use within the floodplain itself, notably for irrigated wheat production, is also putting pressure on the wetlands.

A recent study compared the economic benefits of fourteen agricultural crops, fuelwood and fishing in the Hadejia–Jama'are floodplain with the potential net returns to an upstream water development, the Kano River Project (Barbier, Adams and Kimmage, 1991). The economic importance of the wetlands demands that the benefits it provides must be considered an opportunity cost of any scheme that diverts water away from the floodplain system. When compared to the potential benefits of the Kano River Project, however, the economic returns to the floodplain appear much more favourable, with a net present value per hectare over five times higher. This contrast is even more apparent when relative returns are compared in terms of average water use. Traditional exploitation of the natural floodplain is a far more efficient user of scarce water resources, yielding net returns per cubic metre over a thousand times higher than the anticipated returns from the Kano River Project.

The extension of cost-benefit analysis to incorporate the environmental impacts of projects is hindered by a number of empirical problems. Physical estimation of environmental effects may be hampered by lack of necessary data. Also, most environmental resources are non-marketed common-property goods, hence the valuation of their benefits is not straightforward. Moreover, there is considerable debate concerning the validity of methods used for the evaluation of intangible environmental benefits in monetary terms and the nature of those benefits, such as the need to preserve unknown species for their intrinsic value.

As this expanded approach inevitably raises issues of intertemporal choice, the interest rate chosen to discount the future may determine the degree, if any, to which environmental degradation is 'optimal'. It is often stressed that the appropriate discount rate should emerge from the project appraisal process. In practice, imperfect capital markets, inconsistent data on the productivity of capital and large variances in domestic borrowing for investment make it difficult to establish an economic accounting rate of interest for developing countries.

Introducing environmental considerations further complicates the picture. As Markandya and Pearce (1988) observe, natural resources are more likely to be over-exploited at high discount rates than at low ones, but, at the same time, consistent use of low discount rates can lead to greater levels of investment in projects which degrade the environment. Given the additional problems posed by environmental risk and irreversible impacts, the authors conclude that it is generally preferable to adjust project costs and benefits and adopt additional sustainability criteria, rather than to adjust the discount rate.

In many cases of poverty-induced environmental degradation, the sacrifice of long-term sustainability for immediate economic returns implies a high discount rate. For example, one of the consequences of deforestation and the depletion of fuelwood supplies is that it forces poor households to use dung for fuel rather than for fertilizer. The present value of the dung as fuel is higher than its value as a soil nutrient; but 'the context is one where there is no choice anyway since there are neither fuel nor fertilizer substitutes to which households can gain access'. Therefore, this behaviour is itself 'the result of the resource degradation process which compels actions to be taken which imply high discount rates' (Pearce, 1988). In other words, the apparently high discount rates are a reflection of the constraints imposed by environmental degradation rather than the desired social choice.

Resource accounting

Another initiative in environmental economics, usually referred to as resource or environmental accounting, involves adjusting national income accounts to reflect both the direct costs inflicted by environmental degradation and the depreciation of natural capital. Although the national accounts record the income earned from harvesting resource stocks (for example, fish catch, timber or meat), the loss of future income through declining resource stocks and deteriorating environmental quality is excluded. By allowing for such depreciation in the natural capital stock, the net contribution of resource exploitation to national income is much lower but more accurately reflects the impact on economic welfare. For example, preliminary estimates of the cost of soil erosion and timber extraction in Indonesia suggest a cost of around US\$3.1 billion in 1982, or approximately 4 per cent of GDP (Repetto *et al.*, 1989).

Because resource accounting uses the existing system of national accounts it appeals to economic policy-makers. None the less, there are a number of limitations to its application. Measuring the stock of natural capital and its rate of depreciation in developing countries is in itself a complicated task. Given the difficulties in quantifying environmental 'goods', extending depreciation accounting to the stock of 'natural' capital would prove even more difficult. Some natural resources, such as forest timber, oil and fish stocks, are more readily counted as discrete units. Others, such as soils and watersheds, are not easily measurable as stocks.

There is also disagreement among some economists over the correct method of valuing the depreciation of natural capital stocks.[2] In the standard economic accounting approach, if an environmental asset is to be treated like any other capital asset, its economic depreciation should be composed of two components: the value of its physical depreciation and any change in the current price of stocks (that is, capital gains or losses). Thus an asset (such as the stock of standing Indonesian hardwoods) can suffer some degree of physical deterioration and still increase in present value, implying negative depreciation or a net capital gain. Other economists argue, however, that international commodity prices for natural resources fluctuate dramatically with little impact on projected extraction and production schedules. Including unrealized capital gains from natural resource price changes in current income could therefore lead to significant fluctuations in income between successive periods. These economists advocate that depreciation accounting should include only the value of physical changes in the resource stock (Repetto *et al.*, 1989).

Perhaps a more serious limitation is that a resource accounting approach that limits itself to a consideration of *environmental assets* – assets that produce valuable and marketed raw material – can only cover part of the economic costs of environmental degradation. Such an approach does not include all the external, off-site environmental quality effects (that is, the indirect use value of environmental assets in assimilating waste and providing ecological support for economic systems and human welfare). As mentioned earlier, the true value of the forest must include not only its productive value as a commodity – timber – but also its non-timber use value, the indirect use values of environmental functions and relevant existence values. Therefore, the figure of US$3.1 billion for the depreciation of the timber stock of Indonesia must be well below the full cost of forest degradation.

Despite such difficulties, resource accounting is a major advance over the present procedure, which essentially values natural capital at zero. Moreover, by starting to measure environmental values, resource accounting approaches ensure that better techniques for measuring such values will be developed.

Economy–environment linkages

Efforts to undertake resource accounting are part of the larger initiative to design economic policies which can balance economic efficiency with the need to correct problems of environmental degradation in developing countries. This agenda has two primary components:

- the design of investment programmes supporting environmental and natural resource objectives; and
- the promotion of economic, social and institutional policies and incentives that influence the behaviour of government agencies, major resource users and countless small-scale resource-using activities which occur throughout a nation's economy.

The appeal of such an approach is the reliance on traditional economic tools and concepts, such as marginal opportunity cost, to measure the total costs of resource degradation borne by society. Moreover, some existing economic policies in developing countries (for example, agricultural input subsidies, fiscal and financial inducements for live-stock rearing, and agricultural export taxation) may be encouraging both environmental degradation and economic inefficiency. Correcting these policies may therefore offer the opportunity to pursue both environmental and efficiency goals.

In designing appropriate incentives for sustainable development, a distinction should be made between *user-enabling incentives* focused on the resource user (such as changes in land and resource rights, increased participation in decision-making and appropriate projects); *policy-enabling incentives* focused on the policy-maker and implementing agencies (such as institutional incentives and flexibility, and political conditions); and *variable incentives* focused on price changes facing producers and consumers (such as altering input and output pricing, exchange rate modification, tax and subsidy reform, and restraining middlemen margins). User-enabling incentives are the main micro-level concerns for sustainable development, whereas appropriate policy-enabling and variable incentives are macro-level issues. Working with only one set of incentives is likely to be ineffective. At least one policy instrument is needed for each objective. The challenge for economic policy is to design the right combination of incentives for a given target group and a given environmental problem.

The design of appropriate incentives is fraught with difficulties. For example, it is often assumed that aligning agricultural producer prices with world prices will increase the incomes of farmers, which will in turn encourage resource conservation investments. The counter-argument, however, is that price increases encourage switches between crops but may have no effect on aggregate output. Farmers may not have an extra surplus to invest in resource conservation. In addition, the relationship between increased profitability of farm-level production and additional investments in land management and farming systems may not be a straightforward one. In most cases, our understanding of the linkage from producer price to agricultural supply response to natural resource effects is not sufficient to design appropriate incentives and investment strategies with confidence.

Nevertheless, macro-economic policies and incentives for natural resource management are, in the long run, essential for sustainable development. Donor agencies, led by the World Bank, are making a major effort in co-operation with the governments of some developing countries to conduct studies of how best to design an appropriate natural resource and economic policy framework for sustainable development. As these studies indicate, before any practical policy guidelines can be successfully formulated, there is a need for substantive and extensive analysis of the natural resource implications of various macro-economic, trade and sectoral policies in developing countries. At the more micro level, there is a need for more analysis of the economic costs of environmental degradation and of the natural resource allocation decisions made by rural populations. This should be co-ordinated and reviewed consistently at the national level so as to be useful for policy and investment decisions.

Applied sustainability research

If sustainable development is to be achieved, the three techniques discussed so far need to be complemented by a fourth: the applied analysis of the sustainability of farming and other production systems at the village, community and household level. For example, in agriculture, the 'farmers' needs pull' form of farming systems research and extension takes the analysis of existing farming systems as its starting-point. It then goes on to determine the needs, problems and constraints to which subsequent technological innovation is directed. The use of agroecosystem analysis and participatory rural appraisal techniques is crucial to this approach (see Chapter 4).

An even broader, and more difficult, task is the analysis of the problems of attaining sustainable and secure livelihoods. For example, rural livelihoods do not rely exclusively on farming but also rely on skills employed on the farm in the manufacture of handicrafts and in other cottage industries, on natural resources (such as timber, fuelwood, fodder, wild plants, fish and other wild animals) that may be harvested for immediate consumption or sale, on opportunities for off-farm employment or most commonly on some combination of these. Thus rural livelihoods depend on ownership of, or access to, resources, and access to product- or income-generating activities. Livelihood stability is measurable in terms of both the stock (that is, a household's reserves and assets) and the flows of food and cash. In practice, rural families decide on livelihood goals and then determine the optimal mix of activities depending on their environmental and social circumstances and the skills and resources at their disposal. Sustainable livelihood analysis must take account of this decision-making process at the household level, as well as the set of institutions, customs and systems of rights and obligations at the community level that determine much of what individuals and households can and cannot do.

Data and methodology requirements

A constraint common to these four analytical approaches is the lack of a reliable data base and widespread ignorance of the methodology needed to evaluate the impacts of environmental degradation on the resource base. Existing natural resource data bases in developing countries, where they are reliable, are often patchy, incomplete and disaggregated by administrative and political boundaries. It is often extremely difficult to obtain comparable economic and environmental data by major agro ecological and resource system zones (for example, watersheds, semi-arid lands, uplands, forests and coastal resource systems). It may be equally difficult to obtain detailed data on certain key socio-economic groups, such as agro-pastoralists, nomads, upland farmers, shifting cultivators and indigenous tribes.

In addition, although valuation techniques for measuring the environmental impacts of economic policies and projects have been developed in recent years, they have yet to be applied extensively in developing countries. Thus developing the data and methodology requirements for all levels of analysis in developing countries should be a major priority.

These four techniques – environmental cost-benefit analysis, resource accounting, economy–environment linkages and applied sustainability research – indicate the need for a multi-level approach to integrating sound natural resource management at all levels of economic policy-making and planning. Sustainable development cannot be based solely, or even largely, on the piecemeal application of resource accounting, environmental cost-benefit analysis or reform of economic policy. Each of these initiatives needs to be developed in its own right and in relation to the other approaches, and this totality of analysis used as the analytical foundation for sustainable development.

CONCLUSIONS

This chapter has argued that economics has a vital role to play in the struggle towards the sustainable use of natural resources, economic development and poverty alleviation. Improved analysis of both the impacts and the causes underlying environmental degradation will become crucial in the years ahead. Substantial policy distortions and market failures affecting natural resource management in developing countries do exist, and it is necessary to reorient public policies to correct for these distortions as best as possible. None the less, it must be accepted that in many cases our less than optimal 'ignorance' about the relationships involved means that the first step in promoting sustainable development is to correct major economy-wide problems (such as over-valued exchange rates, budgetary excesses, debt overhang and high rates of inflation). Once such distortions are corrected – and, indeed, in the early 1990s the evidence was that many developing countries were taking these economic reforms seriously – the techniques discussed earlier may be able to focus more closely on the adjustments necessary to overcome market and policy failures causing environmental degradation.

It is equally important to recognize that an economic interpretation of environmental problems relies on the outputs of many other disciplines, from anthropology to ecology to soil science. It has been said that economists feed high up on the information food chain; the truth of this statement lies in the diversity of information and disciplines that are required to support the application of environmental economics to issues of sustainable development. Significant improvements in environmental quality and the conservation of natural resources cannot always be derived from simple adjustments of macro-economic policy and micro-economic incentives. The long-term contribution of environmental economics to the process of sustainable development requires the successful integration of economics in a multidisciplinary approach.

The agenda set forth by this chapter implies continued economic analysis of the relationship between natural resource management and economic development. There is a need for substantive and extensive analysis of the implications of various macro-economic, trade and sectoral policies for management of the natural resource base. Alternative policy options that explicitly take into account the resource constraints of the most vulnerable economic groups also need to be properly formulated and analysed. At the micro level, there is a need for more analysis of the economic costs of environmental impacts. Micro-level analysis of natural resource allocation decisions at the village or farmer level is also required, as is monitoring of the impacts of policy decisions and investment programmes at this level. Although some of the information required may be available from research stations and from independent, project and provincial studies, it needs to be co-ordinated and reviewed consistently at the national level to assist policy and investment decisions.

NOTES

1 Capistrano (1990) and Capistrano and Kiker (1990) use changes in timber production forest area as a proxy for total deforestation. Although the authors argue that there is a close correlation between average area of closed broad-leaved forest and timber production forest area, there are many tropical forest countries where industrial logging is not a significant source of overall deforestation (Barbier *et al.,* 1991; Burgess, 1991). Thus their analytical results are more relevant to the deforestation of tropical timber production forests than to overall tropical deforestation.

2 For discussion and review, see Ahmad, El Serafy and Lutz (1989) and Pearce, Markandya and Barbier (1990).

REFERENCES AND BIBLIOGRAPHY

Ahmad, Y. J., El Serafy, S. and Lutz, E. (eds), 1989. *Environmental Accounting for Sustainable Development,* Environment Department, World Bank, Washington, DC.

Anderson, D., 1987. *The Economics of Afforestation,* Johns Hopkins University Press, Baltimore, Md.

Barbier, E. B., 1989a. *Economics, Natural-Resource Scarcity and Development: Conventional and Alternative Views,* Earthscan, London.

Barbier, E. B., 1989b. 'Sustaining agriculture on marginal land: a policy framework', *Environment,* 31, 9, pp. 13–17, 36–40.

Barbier, E. B., Adams, W. M. and Kimmage, K., 1991. *Economic Valuation of Wetland Benefits: The Hadejia–Jama'are Floodplain, Nigeria,* Discussion Paper 91-02, London Environmental Economics Centre, London.

Barbier, E. B. and Burgess, J. C., 1990. *Malawi – Land Degradation in Agriculture,* report to the World Bank Economic Mission of Environmental Policy, Malawi Country Operations Division, World Bank, Washington, DC.

Barbier, E. B., Aylward, B. A., Burgess, J. C. and Bishop, J. T., 1991. 'Environmental effects of trade in the forestry sector', paper for the Joint Session of Trade and Environment Experts, Environment Directorate, OECD, Paris.

Becker, H., 1990. 'Labour input decisions of subsistence farm households in southern Malawi', *Journal of Agricultural Economics,* 41, 2, pp. 162–71.

Binswanger, H., 1989. *Brazilian Policies That Encourage Deforestation in the Amazon,* Environment Department Working Paper no. 16, World Bank, Washington, DC.

Bishop, J. T., Aylward, B. A. and Barbier E. B., 1991. *Guidelines for Applying Environmental Economics in Developing Countries,* Gatekeeper Series Paper no. 91-02, London Environmental Economics Centre, London.

Bojo, J., Maler, K. G. and Unemo, L., 1990. *Environment and Development: An Economic Approach,* Kluwer Academic, Dordrecht.

Browder, J. O., 1985. *Subsidies, Deforestation, and the Forest Sector in the Brazilian Amazon,* World Resources Institute, Washington, DC.

Burgess, J. C., 1990. 'The contribution of efficient energy pricing to reducing carbon dioxide emissions', *Energy Policy,* June, pp. 449–55.

Burgess, J. C., 1991. 'Economic analysis of frontier agricultural expansion and tropical deforestation', M.Sc. thesis, Economics Department, University College London.

Capistrano, A. D., 1990. 'Macroeconomic influences on tropical forest depletion: a cross-country analysis', Ph.D. Dissertation, Food and Resource Economics Department, University of Florida, Miami.

Capistrano, A. D. and Kiker, C. F., 1990. 'Global economic influences on tropical closed broadleaved forest depletion, 1967–85', mimeo, Food and Resource Economics Department, University of Florida, Miami.

Dixon, J. A. ·and Hufschmidt, M. M. (eds), 1986. *Economic Valuation Techniques for the Environment,* Johns Hopkins University Press, Baltimore, Md.

Dixon, J. A., Carpenter, R. A., Fallon, L. A., Sherman, P. B. and Manipomoke, S., 1988. *Economic Analysis of the Environmental Impacts of Development Projects,* Earthscan, London.

Gregersen, H. M., Brooks, K. N., Dixon, J. A. and Hamilton, L. S., 1987. *Guidelines for Economic Appraisal of Watershed Management Projects,* FAO, Rome.

Kosmo, M., 1989. 'Commercial energy subsidies in developing countries: opportunity for reform', *Energy Policy,* June, pp. 244–53.

Markandya, A. and Pearce, D. W., 1988. *Environmental Considerations and the Choice of the Discount Rate,* Environment Department Working Paper no. 3, World Bank, Washington, DC.

Mortimore, M., 1989. *The Causes, Nature and Rate of Soil Degradation in the Northernmost States of Nigeria and an Assessment of the Role of Fertilizer in Counteracting the Processes of Degradation,* Environment Department Working Paper no. 17, World Bank, Washington, DC.

Palo, M., Mery, G. and Salmi, J., 1987. 'Deforestation in the tropics: pilot scenarios based on quantitative analysis', in M. Palo and J. Salmi (eds), *Deforestation or Development in the Third World,* Division of Social Economics of Forestry, Finnish Forestry Research, Helsinki.

Paris, R. and Ruzicka, I., 1991. *Barking up the Wrong Tree: The Role of Rent Appropriation in Tropical Forest Management,* Environment Office Discussion Paper, Asian Development Bank, Manila, Philippines.

Pearce, D. W., 1988. 'The economics of natural resource degradation in developing countries', in R. K. Turner (ed.), *Sustainable Environmental Management: Principles and Practices,* Westview Press, Boulder, Colo.

Pearce, D. W., Barbier, E. B. and Markandya, A., 1990. *Sustainable Development: Economics and Environment in the Third World,* Edward Elgar, London.

Peters, P. E., Herrera, M. G. and Randolph, T. F., 1989. *Cash Cropping, Food Security and Nutrition: The Effects of Agricultural Commercialization among Smallholders in Malawi,* report to the US Agency for International Development, Harvard Institute for International Development, Cambridge, Mass.

Repetto, R. and Gillis, M. (eds), 1988. *Public Policies and the Misuse of Forest Resources,* Cambridge University Press, Cambridge.

Repetto, R., Magrath, W., Wells, M., Beer, C. and Rossini, F., 1989. *Wasting Assets: Natural Resources in the National Income Accounts,* World Resources Institute, Washington, DC.

Southgate, D., 1988. *The Economics of Land Degradation in the Third World*, Environment Department Working Paper no. 2, World Bank, Washington, DC.

Southgate, D., 1991. *Tropical Deforestation and Agriculture Development in Latin America*, Discussion Paper 91-01, London Environmental Economics Centre, London.

Southgate, D., Sierra, R. and Brown, L., 1989. *The Causes of Tropical Deforestation in Ecuador: A Statistical Analysis*, Discussion Paper 89-09, London Environmental Economics Centre, London.

UNIDO, 1972. *Guidelines for Project Evaluation*, United Nations, New York.

4 Regenerating Agriculture: The Agroecology of Low-External Input and Community-Based Development

Jules Pretty, Irene Guijt, Ian Scoones and John Thompson

INTRODUCTION

Despite an agricultural revolution in the South over the course of a single generation that has produced enormous benefits for farmers, consumers and economies, many of the poorest rural people are yet to benefit. They live in regions with poor-quality soils and unpredictable rainfall. Either they are remote from agricultural services that promote the package of inputs necessary to add value, or they cannot afford to take a risk by adopting the whole package. More importantly, many simply find the package unsuitable for their needs and tastes. In addition, inappropriate use of inputs imposes costs in terms of both economic efficiency and the external costs imposed on others from agricultural pollution and environmental degradation.

If the projected world population of 8 to 13 billion people is to be fed, new efforts based on maximizing the use of renewable resources internal to the farm, rather than on a high-external input approach, will be required. These will be centred on agroecological technologies capable of achieving permanent improvements to agricultural production that do not damage the environment.

This chapter argues that low-external input technologies improve pest management, conserve soil, water and nutrients, recycle wastes and utilize local sources of water efficiently. The selection of elements appropriate to local livelihoods will best be made by rural people, who know most about local conditions. This participation in planning, implementation and maintenance has been shown to produce highly effective, efficient and sustainable solutions, but generally only on a small scale. The final element of the challenge for fostering this new revolution lies in the support by national governments in the form of appropriate institutional and legal frameworks and economic incentives to make these islands of success more widespread.

AN AGRICULTURAL REVOLUTION

Overview

During the last twenty-five years, farmers in the Third World have risen to an enormous global challenge. Although the global population has grown from 3.3 to 5.3 billion, food production per person has risen even more steeply. Farmers have both intensified their use of resources to produce more from the same amount of land and expanded into uncultivated lands. As a result, each one of us has now on average some 7 per cent more food than the prior generation had at the same age. This has been agriculture's Green Revolution.

The success of the Green Revolution lay in simplicity. Agricultural scientists bred new varieties of staple cereals that (1) matured quickly, so permitting two or three crops to be grown each year, (2) were day-length insensitive, so could be extended to farmers at a wide range of latitudes, and (3) were producers of more grain at the expense of straw. These modern varieties (MVs) were distributed to farmers together with high-cost inputs, including inorganic fertilizers, pesticides, machinery, credit and water regulation. These technical innovations were then implemented in the best-favoured agroclimatic regions and for those classes of farmers with the best expectations of and means for realizing the potential yield increases (Conway and Barbier, 1990). As a result, average cereal yields have roughly doubled in twenty-five years. The remaining production growth has been met through a 20 per cent expansion of the agricultural area.

Yet in many ways the most difficult challenges are just beginning. The world population is not thought likely to stabilize until there are between 8 and 13 billion people. Even at the lowest estimates, and given current inequitable access and rights to resources, there will be a need for agricultural production to increase substantially if current levels of nutrition are to be maintained. Without very considerable growth the prospects for many people in poor countries and regions of the world are bleak. Given the extraordinary success of the Green Revolution, many believe that this model of development continues to provide the most effective and efficient prospect for all people of the South.

However, not only have many people missed out on the benefits of this revolution but there have been hitherto hidden costs that, once taken into account, make the previous measures of efficiency less attractive.

Characteristics of high- and low-external input systems

By focusing on the import to farms of new seeds or animal breeds, the Green Revolution has encouraged the development of two distinctly different types of agriculture in countries of the South. The first type has been able to respond to the technological packages, producing high-external input (HEI) systems of agriculture. These tend to be endowed with good soils and adequate supply of water, through either stable rainfall or irrigation systems, and access to marketing infrastructure, modern farm inputs, machinery, transport, agroprocessing facilities and credit.

HEI systems are found in the large irrigated plains and deltas of South, South-east and East Asia, and parts of Latin America and North Africa, but also in patches in other regions. They tend to be focused upon monocrops and mono-animal enterprises, and geared for sale. So they include lowland irrigated rice, wheat and cotton; plantations of bananas, pineapples, oil palm and sugar cane; market gardening near to urban centres; and intensive livestock rearing and ranching.

The second type comprises all the remaining agricultural and livelihood systems which, in terms of area, are in the great majority. These are the low-external input (LEI) systems and are located in drylands, wetlands, uplands, near-deserts, mountains and hills. Farming systems in these areas are complex and diverse, and rural livelihoods are dependent on wild resources as well as agricultural produce. Agricultural yields are low, and the poorest countries tend to have higher proportions of these agricultural systems. Diversity means that what is appropriate for one farmer may not be for a neighbour; they are remote from markets and infrastructure; they are located on fragile or problem soils; they have very low productivity; they are less likely to be visited by agricultural scientists and extension workers; and they are much less likely to be studied in research institutions.

The number of people directly supported by LEI systems is enormous, probably some 1.4 billion, yet 'most agricultural development assistance . . . has emphasized external resources' (OTA, 1988). They can neither afford to sustain the use of external resources, nor produce them in their own economies; the alternative lies in LEI systems, as for most poor countries no viable alternative exists (Wolf, 1986; OTA, 1988; Chambers, Pacey and Thrupp, 1989; Horwith *et al.*, 1989).

The proportion of major crops currently planted to MVs varies widely across continents. In Asia, 45 per cent of rice is planted to MVs, but in Africa the proportion is only 5 per cent. Where HEI systems occur, in almost every case external inputs have been substituted for the internal resources, rendering them less powerful (Table 4.1). HEI systems produce up to five times more food per unit area. The result is rice yields of 4 tonnes/ha in Indonesia, where 83 per cent of the rice land is planted to MVs and 63 per cent irrigated compared with only 1.1 t/ha in Cambodia, where the use of MVs is 71 per cent but only 11 per cent of the land is irrigated (Lipton with Longhurst, 1989).

The direct economic benefits of HEI systems are clear: more food per hectare and per farm worker. Yet despite these returns, and considerable investment in research and extension, why have more farmers and countries not adopted HEI systems for agriculture?

Farmers' views of modern varieties (MVs)

Using the conventional criterion of productivity, agricultural development judges HEI systems as successes. Yet farming households do not always see the modern varieties and associated package of external inputs in the same way as researchers and extension workers. Their criteria for evaluating and making choices are frequently so different that the best products of research services are sometimes rejected, while others judged inappropriate are chosen by farmers as favourable.

In Colombia, a high-yielding variety of bush beans was rejected by farmers because the variable colour made marketing difficult; another variety rejected by researchers for its small bean size was acceptable because, as one farmer put it, 'it is good for consumption purposes because it swells to a good size when cooked – it yields in the pot' (Ashby, Quiros and Rivera, 1987). In the Philippines, sweet potato varieties bred for high yield and sweet taste were rejected by upland farmers who preferred rapidly vining varieties that prevented weed growth and rain-induced soil erosion. They also selected varieties tolerant to weevil damage during the underground storage phase, as this meant the potatoes could be harvested only as required (Acaba *et al.*, 1987).

Taste is one of the factors in the failure of maize MVs to be adopted widely in Malawi, formerly one of Africa's Green Revolution successes (Kydd, 1989; Barbier and Burgess, 1990). From the 1960s, agricultural research in Malawi has focused on 'dent' varieties that have soft starch which is easier for modern rollers to handle to produce flour. But rural people prefer 'flint' varieties for their taste and high starch content, and

Table 4.1: Internal and external resources for agroecosystems

Internal resources	*External resources*
Sun – source of energy for plant photosynthesis	*Artificial lights* – used in greenhouse food production
Water – rain and/or small-scale local irrigation schemes	*Water* – large dams, centralized distribution, deep wells
Nitrogen – fixed from air, recycled in soil organic matter	*Nitrogen* – primarily from applied synthetic fertilizer
Other nutrients – from soil reserves recycled in cropping system	*Other nutrients* – mined, processed and imported
Weed and pest control – biological, cultural, mechanical and locally available chemicals	*Weed and pest control* – synthetic chemical herbicides and insecticides
Seed – varieties produced on farm	*Seed* – hybrids or certified varieties purchased annually
Machinery – built and maintained on farm or in community	*Machinery* – purchased and replaced frequently
Labour – most work done by the family living on the farm	*Labour* – most work done by hired labour
Capital – source is family and community, reinvested locally	*Capital* – external indebtedness, benefits leave community
Management decisions – information from farmers and local community	*Management decisions* – from input suppliers and crop consultants
Varieties of plants – thrive with lower moisture and fertility	*Varieties of plants* – need high inputs to thrive

Sources: Rodale (1985) and Francis (1989).

because they are less subject to insect damage during storage. Researchers accepted these drawbacks, but suggested that further new technologies would solve the problems. This would comprise the promotion of insecticides to control storage pests, and mechanical mills to overcome the difficulties of hand-milling dents. But the package was too costly and risky to farmers. By the beginning of the 1990s, only 5 per cent of the maize area was being planted to modern dent varieties.

Adopting the whole package

The Green Revolution begins on the research station, where scientists have access to all the necessary inputs of fertilizers, pesticides and labour at all the appropriate times. But when the package is extended to farmers, even the best-performing farms display the now well recognized yield gap. For example, rice yields on the International Rice Research Institute (IRRI) station are usually 1 t/ha better than the best-performing farmers, who in turn yield at 1–1.5 t/ha more than the average adopting farmers (Barker and Herdt, 1983). Differences in soil fertility, water control, insects, weeds, cultural practices, access to inputs, labour risk averseness and credit availability experienced by farming households explain the differences in yields.

If one element of the package is missing, the seed delivery system fails or the fertilizer arrives late, or there is insufficient irrigation water, then yields may not be much better than those for traditional varieties. Farmers with access to plentiful irrigation achieve steadily increasing yields of rice for each additional increase in applied nitrogen fertilizer, yet those applying nitrogen with a poor or variable supply of water produce steadily falling yields (Barker and Herdt, 1983). For high productivity per hectare, farmers need access to the whole package: MV seeds, water, labour, capital or credit, fertilizers and pesticides. This is not always possible.

Farmers prefer biodiversity

The introduction of MVs often displaces traditional methods and varieties. During the past twenty-five years genetic stock has been greatly narrowed, and fields monocropped to single varieties are common. This is in marked contrast to the patchy mixtures that small farmers traditionally promote in the interest of minimizing the risk of crop failure, a central element of most small farmer strategies. The diversity on fields and farms can be extraordinary. In one field in the Andes in Peru, some thirty-six potato varieties were recorded growing in thirteen rows (Rhoades, 1984). Altogether some 10,000 traditional varieties are still grown by Andean farmers.

Contrary to the strategies of researchers, who have simplified and standardized agriculture, farmers of LEI agricultural systems still select for a diversity of crops and varieties. Very few fields and farms are monocropped, and for good reason – mixed cropping systems can be less risky and more productive. Farmers of LEI systems utilize intercropping and multiple cropping widely. In Africa more than 80 per cent of all cereals are intercropped, producing in some cases highly complex patterns on the ground, with up to twenty species grown in close proximity (OTA, 1988). In Latin America, about 60 per cent of maize is intercropped, and 80 to 90 per cent of beans are grown with maize or potatoes (Francis, 1986).

The hidden costs of HEI systems

The agricultural production increases brought about by HEI packages have brought great benefits. Without them many people would be worse off than they are now; many others might have died of starvation. But in order to assess the true net benefits of HEI packages, it is important also to investigate some of the hidden costs.

Intensification of agriculture means greater use of inputs and a tendency to specialize operations. The inputs of nutrients and pesticides, though, are never used entirely efficiently by the receiving crops or livestock and, as a result, some are lost to the environment (Conway and Pretty, 1991). Some 30 to 80 per cent of nitrogen and up to 2 per cent of pesticides are lost to the environment to contaminate water, food and fodder and the atmosphere. These costs to national economies and environments are growing, particularly in industrialized countries but also in developing countries.

In Tanzania, for example, US$75 million of Canadian aid has been spent over twenty years to develop 40,000 hectares of monocropped wheat farms on the dryland Hanang Plains. Yields are comparable with those on the Canadian plains, and the farms supply nearly half of the national wheat demand. Yet the scheme has displaced local Barabaig pastoralists from their prime grazing lands, disrupted their complex rotation patterns, destroyed cultural sites and induced ecological damage in the form of soil erosion and siltation of lakes (Lane and Pretty, 1990). From the viewpoint of the farms, they are financially profitable. But if these wider impacts are accounted for, then the picture changes. The financial resources spent developing an HEI system in an LEI region would have been more efficiently used by buying wheat in the world market.

Continuing the dependency on external inputs

HEI agricultural systems will continue to be immensely important for Third World farmers and economies. However, the potential for marginal improvements in growth in HEI systems is not clear. All countries where the Green Revolution has had a significant impact saw average annual output growth rates in the agricultural sector fall during the 1980s compared with the post-revolution period of 1965–80 (World Bank, 1991). For example, annual growth rates fell in the Philippines from 4.6 to 1.8 per cent, in Mexico from 3.2 to 1.2 per cent, in Indonesia from 4.3 to 3.2 per cent and in Syria from 4.8 to 0.5 per cent. There is also evidence that returns to MVs grown on the same land are now declining, despite technological advances. On IRRI farms, rice yields are now falling, and more inputs will be required to maintain current levels of productivity (Flinn and De Datta, 1984). This evidence, together with that indicating natural resource damage from pollution and depletion from over-use, indicates that many HEI systems are at or above sustainable levels of production. It will be difficult to achieve further benefits that are not outweighed by the marginal costs.

Opportunities may come with new biotechnology and genetic manipulation techniques. This may produce crops and animals that are more efficient converters of nutrients and more resistant to pests and diseases; it may succeed in incorporating nitrogen-fixing nodules to the roots of cereals; and it may produce better slow-release fertilizers containing nitrification inhibitors. All of these techniques will still be part of a package that must be supplied to farmers and paid for, however. Although offering great potential, they are likely simply to foster even greater dependency on external resources and systems. Those low-income countries that are poorly endowed with natural resources and infrastructure and where population growth is high are not likely to benefit (Hobbelink, Vellve and Abraham, 1990).

Regenerating agriculture through low external inputs

There is enormous potential in LEI systems. Productivity is certainly far below potential levels, unlike in the Green Revolution areas. The key question is now: how best can this potential be partly or fully unlocked? An alternative and regenerative agricultural strategy is quite different to that of the HEI approach exemplified by the Green Revolution (NRC, 1989; Conway and Pretty, 1991). Such a sustainable LEI agriculture pursues the following goals:

- more thorough incorporation of natural processes such as nutrient cycles, nitrogen fixation and pest–predator relationships;

- reduction in the use of external, off-farm inputs with the greatest potential to harm the environment or the health of farmers and consumers;
- greater productive use of the biological and genetic potential of plant and animal species;
- improvement of the match between cropping patterns and the productive potential and physical limitations of agricultural lands to ensure long-term sustainability of current production levels.

Evidence is now growing that the result of such a regenerative strategy will be the creation of more productive and sustainable systems that emphasize the use of available resources, do not damage the environment and avoid the dependency on external and locally uncontrollable resources and systems. Despite the diversity of LEI systems, and the range of research and extension efforts developed for them, there are certain common elements critical for their successful development. These are:

- building on local knowledge of pest management, soil and nutrient conservation, water conservation and harvesting, waste recycling and irrigation;
- building on local social organization and management systems;
- using process-oriented approaches for projects to permit sequential and adaptive planning and development.

BUILDING ON LOCAL KNOWLEDGE AND AGROECOLOGICAL PROCESSES

In rural areas the livelihoods of poor households are diverse, commonly relying on a mix of agricultural produce, wild plants and animals, remittances and trading. Over generations, people have developed a wealth of detailed knowledge about the quality and quantity of natural resources, and the means to manage and exploit them. This knowledge is a resource commonly neglected by agricultural projects, yet is critical to the success and improvement of LEI systems. The first component of success requires taking the detailed local knowledge as a starting-point and building upon it. Where agricultural development has done this, the economic benefits are remarkable. When development planning ignores this rule not only may goals not be met, but greater environmental and social damage may arise.

Provided groups or communities are involved in identification of technology needs, the design of testing and experimentation, the adaptation to their own conditions and finally the extension to others, then sustainable and cheaper solutions can be found. Development focusing on appropriate agroecological pest, nutrient and water management practices can lead to at least a 50 per cent increase in the yields of crops, livestock and trees.

Pest management strategies

Agricultural pests and pathogens are thought to destroy some 10 to 40 per cent of the world's gross agricultural production. It is this potential for damage that has driven the search for synthetic pesticides and resulted in their widespread use. Pesticides, though, are not a perfect answer to controlling pests and pathogens. They can be dangerous to human health and damage natural resources and the environment. But more importantly to the farmer, pesticides are often inefficient at controlling pests (Conway and Pretty, 1991). They can cause pest resurgences by also killing off the natural enemies of the target pests. They can also produce new pests, by killing off the natural enemies of species which hitherto were not pests. Pests can become resistant to pesticides, so encouraging further applications; there are some 470 pest species known to be resistant to at least one product (NRC, 1984). Finally, pesticides provide no lasting control, and so, at best, have to be repeatedly applied.

LEI systems make use of the agroecological processes of predation, competition and parasitism in six broad strategies of pest control:

- emphasizing natural enemies of pests and pathogens;
- breeding crop plants or livestock for resistance to pests or pathogens;
- using locally available insecticidal compounds to reduce pests;
- increasing agroecosystem diversity to reduce pest or pathogen numbers;
- disrupting pest reproduction;
- the selective use of pesticides, with low toxicity and little environmental hazard.

Integrated pest management (IPM) is the integrated use of some or all these pest control strategies in a way that not only reduces pest populations to economically acceptable levels but is sustainable and non-polluting. It is by no means a new approach. LEI farmers have long used combinations of these technologies to provide a degree of pest control. All IPM successes begin by understanding local practices and agroecological processes and building upon these. One traditional technique on citrus trees has been to encourage populations of predatory ants that feed on various insect pests. In China, bamboo bridges have for some 1,700 years been placed between branches to encourage movement of citrus ants from tree to tree, and whole orchards are colonized by securing a nest on one tree and then connecting this to others with the bamboo strips (Huang and Pei Yang, 1987).

Although IPM is a more complex process than, say, scheduled spraying of pesticides, the large-scale IPM for rice programmes in the Philippines, Indonesia and Thailand shows that ordinary farmers are capable of rapidly acquiring the principles and approaches (Kenmore *et al.*, 1987; Craig and Pisone, 1988; Kenmore, 1989). This is producing a 50 per cent reduction in insecticide use, a 10 per cent increase in profits and a reduced variance of profits. The 50 per cent reduction in pesticide use represents savings of US$5 to 10 million each to Thailand and the Philippines, and US$50 to 100 million to Indonesia.

Nutrient conservation strategies

It is virtually impossible to maintain crop production without adding nutrients. When crops are harvested, nutrients are invariably removed and so have to be replaced. There are a variety of sources: the mobilization of existing nutrients in the soil and parent rocks; the fixing of nitrogen from the atmosphere; or the supply of organic or inorganic fertilizer. The options for nutrient conservation include improving the efficiency of fertilizers, using alternative sources of nutrients and environmental manipulation.

The application of fertilizer, ideally, should closely match the needs of crops; but often farmers, for reasons of cost, will apply fertilizer only once. Fertilizer is often applied in excess of need, so some nutrients are lost from the farm as nitrates to surface or ground water, or as ammonia or nitrous oxide to the atmosphere. Efficiency of uptake is influenced by the crops themselves, the soil type and the timing and appropriate placement of fertilizers.

Farmers who can neither afford nor rely on a regular supply of inorganic fertilizers must find alternative organic sources of nutrients. Livestock manures have been the traditional key to maintaining agricultural productivity in LEI systems, replenishing nutrients and improving soil structure. Composting is a technique of similar long standing that combines the use of animal manures, green material and household wastes. The impact of legumes grown together with or before a cereal crop can further reduce and sometimes eliminate the need for nitrogen fertilizers. Symbiotic bacteria present in specialized nodules that develop on the roots of the legumes can fix a considerable amount of nitrogen from the atmosphere. In a well-nodulated and managed stand of legumes, fixation can be about 50 to 100 kg N/ha/year (NRC, 1989; Young, 1989; Sarrantonio, 1991). The cultivation of cereals and legume crops together can improve both total yields and stability of production. Bushes and trees with nitrogen-fixing capacity also have beneficial effects on plants growing with or after them.

Nutrients are supplied when vegetation is incorporated in the soil as a green manure. This technique has been practised for a long time; the Romans grew lupins and ploughed them in before sowing cereals more than 2,000 years ago. Quick-growing legumes are popular green manures for LEI systems. In Honduras, the introduction of the velvet bean as a green manure on poor soils has raised yields of maize from 850 to 2,500 kg/ha (Bunch, 1990). And in Rwanda, *Tephrosia* has increased cereal yields fivefold (Kotschi *et al.*, 1989).

Blue-green algae are another important source of nitrogen, the most widely exploited being the alga *Anabaena azollae*. This fixes atmospheric nitrogen while living in cavities in the leaves of a small fern, *Azolla*, that grows on the water of rice fields. In one year, *Azolla* can fix more than 400 kg N/ha, a rate in excess of most tropical and subtropical legumes. In the Philippines, *Azolla* increased rice yields by 12 to 25 per cent; and in India, wheat crops following rice with *Azolla* have also been shown to produce improved yields (Watanabe *et al.*, 1977; Kolhe and Mitra, 1987).

Interventions that help to conserve soil and water are powerful techniques for nutrient conservation. Soil nutrients can be conserved by a wide range of physical structures of varying scale. Most of these are designed to check the surface flow of water, and thus perform the dual role of soil conservation and water harvesting and retention. If successful they can minimize the need for fertilizer application. The simplest approach is to construct earth bunds across the slope that act as a barrier to runoff. They are suitable on shallow slopes and are often used on tropical smallholdings together with contour planting. Some-times the earth bunds are reinforced with vegetation such as crop stalks or trees. Such vegetative bunds are partly permeable, so crops planted in front of the bund also benefit from water runoff. More elaborate are various forms of retention and bench terraces, which raise crop yields by some 30 to 50 per cent over those on non-terraced slopes. A lower-input alternative is to plant crops along contours. Water flow is slowed as it meets rows of plants growing perpendicular to the flow, thus improving infiltration. In strip cropping the main row crop is grown along the contour in wide strips alternating with strips of protective crop, such as grass or a legume. Contour bunding and contour ploughing in Gujarat, India, more than doubles millet yields by improving moisture and nutrient retention (Shah, Bharadwaj and Ambastha, 1991).

Soil, water and nutrient conservation is also furthered by the uses of mulches or cover crops. Organic or inorganic material is spread on the soil surface to provide a protective physical cover, the mulch, for the topsoil. Erosion, desiccation and excessive heating are reduced, thus promoting optimal conditions for the decomposition and mineralization of organic matter. The cheapest and easiest method is to use plant residues from previous crops, from nearby perennials or from wild areas, such as reeds from swamps (Kotschi *et al.*, 1989).

These low-external input options for farmers comprise a wide range of interventions that will reduce the losses of nitrogen to the environment and act as alternatives to inorganic fertilizers. They are usually integrated on farms to give a finely tuned strategy specific to the biophysical and socio-economic conditions of individual farmers. As with IPM, integrated nutrient conservation successes have all begun with building on technologies that farmers are already using and with which they are already familiar.

In all parts of the world, where farmers' knowledge about local complexities is built upon by outside projects and programmes, the impacts on agricultural production alone can be very significant (Craig, 1987; Fujisaka, 1989; Bunch, 1990; Kerkhof, 1990; Poffenberger, 1990; Pretty, 1990; Shah, Bharadwaj and Ambastha, 1991). In all cases, yield increases of 50 to 100 per cent, and sometimes more, were achieved without the addition of inorganic fertilizers. However, access to inorganic fertilizers, even in very small quantities, will improve yields even further.

Water conservation and harvesting

Where rainfall is unreliable, inadequate and distributed erratically, water shortages often severely limit crop production. Water conservation and harvesting can carry crops over an otherwise disastrous dry period, can stabilize and increase production and can even make agricultural production possible for the first time. Water harvesting systems are used in arid and semi-arid regions where runoff is intermittent, and with water storage an essential component; they include a runoff-producing and a runoff-using area; water is not usually transported over long distances; and harvesting is carried out on a relatively small scale, in terms of area, volume and capital investment (Reij, Muller and Begemann, 1988; Reij, 1991). Water harvesting systems can be found in all parts of the world, including the Middle East, south Asia, China, North America, and sub-Saharan Africa.

Water harvesting systems from short slopes are simple and cheap. One very old system of microcatchment use is *meskat* in Tunisia, where fruit trees are fed by runoff from upper slopes in a 200 to 400 mm rainfall area. The *zay* system in Burkina Faso is another example, involving the digging of small pits, local application of manure and construction of stone bunds to catch runoff. The concentration of both water and nutrients has made *zay* a method to rehabilitate degraded land. Yields from these areas can be 1,000 kg/ha or more, in areas where average yields are only 400 to 500 kg/ha. For water harvesting from long slopes semi-permeable stone contour lines and bunds are used. Water runoff is slowed down, rather than concentrated, and so has more time to infiltrate below the stones. Half-moon-shaped bunds are used to concentrate water, almost always for forest or fodder trees.

Floodwater harvesting in the streambed, whether a valley bottom or floodplain, blocks the water which flows intermittently and often in flash floods. In North Africa and the Middle East *wadi* floors are blocked and fill with water from the adjacent slopes and the main watercourse. Many local variations of this basic principle have been documented, from Mexico, India, Pakistan, Burkina Faso and elsewhere. On the central plateau of Burkina Faso, low semi-permeable dams of loose rock are constructed in the gullies to slow the water flow and push the water out of the gullies on to the floodplain. Soil is also conserved in the process, with rapid formation of terraces between the dams. Sorghum yields are 200 to 300 per cent higher on fields connected to the dams than on unimproved fields (Reij, Muller and Begemann, 1988; Critchley, 1991; Scoones, 1991).

BUILDING ON LOCAL SOCIAL ORGANIZATION AND MANAGEMENT SYSTEMS

Individuals and co-operatives

A common element of successful implementation of agroecological technologies has been the attention paid to local social organization. Success measured in the form of change sustained over long periods has been achieved through either building on existing patterns of organization, formal or informal, or the development of new institutions.

Yet this has not always been so in agricultural development. There have been two quite different approaches, both with the same goal of widespread adoption of changes. The first ignores existing local formal and informal institutions by dealing with individual farmers or house-holds. These are chosen partly for their likelihood to adopt new technologies and are expected to induce further adoption in their community through a demonstration effect. At the other extreme is the approach of building community-wide co-operatives or collectives, whose action is governed by members and whose impact is expected to be positive on all members.

There is growing evidence to suggest that both approaches are flawed. At best only a few people benefit, and the gap between the poorest and the relatively wealthy grows. At worst the technologies are only adopted under the close supervision of external officials, the departure of whom often signifies the end of the effective use of the technology.

In the individual approach, the contact farmers are usually selected on the basis of literacy, wealth, readiness to change and progressive-ness. This often sets them apart from the rest of the community. This approach is exemplified by the training and visit (T & V) system of extension widely adopted in the South over the past ten to fifteen years (Howell, 1988; Moris, 1990). Extension agents receive regular training to enhance their technical skills, which they then pass on to farmers through regular contact with the selected contact farmers. This technical advice and knowledge are then supposed to diffuse from the contact farmers to all other farmers. The secondary transfer of the messages, though, has been much less successful than predicted, and adoption rates are commonly very low among non-contact farmers (Chapman, 1988; Mullen, 1989).

Despite the intention of involving the whole community directly, the community or collective approach to extending technologies to rural people has also resulted in inequitable development, with benefits being captured by the relatively well-off. Large co-operatives, in which the needs of different members vary enormously and which are too large for widespread participation, have to be managed by small groups, usually comprising the most wealthy, to whom decision-making has been delegated. They are thus inevitably less effective in meeting the needs of the poor (Ramaprasad and Ramachandran, 1989).

Small entrepreneurial groups

The alternative lies in the middle ground with small groups of households with a common interest in resource management and control. Sometimes these are existing formal or informal groups, such as traditional leadership structures, water users' groups, neighbour-hood groups, youth groups, housing societies, grazing management groups, and so on. On other occasions they are groups formed with outside facilitation to take charge of and manage a new resource, such as water users' associations for irrigation, credit groups for loans access or water-point committees to manage pumps. These groups promote incentives and enforce rules and penalties aimed at eliciting behaviour conducive to rational and effective use of resources (Kottak, 1985; Cernea, 1987 and 1991; *Environment and Urbanization*, 1990; Jodha, 1990; Murphy, 1990; Uphoff, 1990; Shah, Bharadwaj and Ambastha, 1991).

It is widely believed that taking social considerations into account results in greater costs. The concrete economic evidence, however, suggests quite the opposite. One study of twenty-five multilateral projects, conducted five to ten years after project completion, found the flow of benefits to have risen or remained constant where institutional development had been important (Kottak, 1985; Cernea, 1987). Where it had been ignored, economic rates of return declined markedly, and in some cases had become negative.

The benefits can have a wider social and environmental significance. Groups commonly pass through several phases. First the group establishes agreed rules for management and decision-making. These are then used by members as a vehicle to channel information or loans to individual members. As confidence grows with success, and resource bases expand, group activity evolves to an entrepreneurial stage where common action projects and programmes are initiated (Rahman, 1984; Ramaprasad and Ramachandran, 1989; D'Souza and Palghadmal, 1990; Shah, Bharadwaj and Ambastha, 1991). An example is provided in Box 4.1.

Box 4.1: Myrada small credit groups in southern India

The work of the NGO Myrada of Bangalore has shown that small-group formation or strengthening mobilizes resource flows. Seven years of concentration upon credit supply via nationalized banks and local co-operative societies had rarely produced permanent solutions. These large co-operatives were heterogeneous, too large for effective shared deci-sion-making and bound by rigid rules. One large society, built up with a great deal of external effort, broke into fourteen small groups. Myrada's first thought of reintegration was resisted by the groups. Myrada agreed to lend money, with positive results: 'Not only was the money managed more carefully, there was a far greater commitment and responsibility from the group towards repaying the amount of money, something that had not unduly bothered them when they were part of the co-operative.'

It was realised that members of small groups participated more, had common concerns and needs and, after developing their own rules and

---

decision-making, expanded their resource base and took up common action programmes. Myrada has now helped establish 1,700 groups containing 48,000 families in southern India, to whom Rs16 million have been loaned in 100,000 separate loans.

No two groups are completely alike, though all groups encourage members to save; all hold money in a common fund; all advance loans for consumption as well as production purposes; all can engage in income earning to expand their resource bases; all can engage in providing or running community services; all evolve their own set of rules and regulations; and all agree that leadership responsibility must be shared. Each group decides its own interest rates to members as well as the types of loan it will permit. What is particularly significant is that the majority of loans are taken out for consumption purposes, and many of these for less than Rs100. Rather than borrowing money from a money-lender to meet consumption or contingency needs, such as for a funeral, marriage or pre-harvest food shortage, now rural households are able easily to borrow small amounts of money. Without such groups, the rural poor inevitably get caught up in the cycle of indebtedness.

Success of credit groups programme of Myrada in two parts of Tamil Nadu, India

	Talavadi	Thally
Number of groups	72	58
Number of members	1,754	1,569
Fund size (Rs)	470,000	904,000
Total advanced (Rs)	1.5 million	1.2 million
Number of loans advanced	9,871	6,515
Total overdue (Rs)	21,000	n.d.
Proportion of money advanced overdue	1.4%	n.d.
Proportion of loans for consumption purposes (mostly food)	77%	82%
Proportion of loans for less than Rs500	98.5%	n.d.
Proportion of loans for less than Rs100	38%	n.d.
Proportion of food loans for less than Rs100	n.d.	94%

n.d. = no data

The success of this programme rests on three points: the groups have the flexibility to make their own decisions and so know the priorities of members much better than a bank; the poor are not a single group; and when confidence grows with skills and knowledge, groups turn towards community-wide development.

Source: Ramaprasad and Ramachandran (1989).

The next phase comprises inter-group co-operation as several groups might come together to federate and pool resources and knowledge. This opens up economies of scale that bring greater economic and ecological benefits. Lastly, the emergence of groups and federated groups makes it easier for government and non-governmental organizations (NGOs) to develop direct links with the poor (Bebbington, 1991). This results in greater empowerment of poor households, as they draw down on public services. It also permits more efficient passing of socially important messages relating to family planning, adult education, sanitation, and so on (Rahman, 1984).

Groups sometimes fail

Not all groups are successful. In general, external institutions find social change much less easy to promote than technical and economic change. In the Hill Resource Management Programme of Haryana, India, users' groups for natural resource management were established to fill the gap left by the decline and near disappearance of indigenous management systems. After early successes, the State Forestry Department took over implementation. But only in 30 per cent of these communities have they successfully established management societies. Technology has outpaced attention to social factors and in the long run the whole effort may be jeopardized as local people become less and less involved in planning and management (Chopra, Kadekodi and Murthy, 1990; Poffenberger, 1990).

Groups are often more effective in their early years. As they grow in confidence and become empowered, so the action taken can bring them into new conflicts (Murphy, 1990). The ZOTO people's organization in Manila began with a successful first four to five years. It was much less successful, however, as a growth in demand for concrete results caused members to neglect the formation of a secondary leadership, and local people paid to become organizers tended to dominate. Ideology came to dominate, too, and the leadership failed to see that the government was making concessions. The members observed this and left to take the compromises offered (Honculada, in Murphy, 1990).

Growth in size can also threaten effectiveness. As interest and enthusiasm spreads, so more people become interested in joining. Group sizes in the Kenya Woodfuel Development Project grew from twelve to forty, making it hard for extension workers to maintain a personal approach, and allowing social hierarchies to dominate (Chavangi and Ngugi, 1987; Huby, 1990).

INNOVATIVE APPROACHES ADOPTED BY PROJECTS AND INSTITUTIONS

Incorporating local knowledge

As has been repeatedly shown, farmers and rural households in complex, diverse environments are fully capable of contributing to development research, planning, implementation and monitoring. Agricultural development emphasizing both HEI and LEI strategies is littered with spectacular failures where local perceptions and needs have not been understood. Where these local factors are not involved, projects are less effective as fewer people adopt the new technologies, and these are often not sustained. This can mean expensive development efforts wasted for want of critical information. In Nigeria, for example, research scientists at the International Institute for Tropical Agriculture spent several years trying to break the seed dormancy of yams. Between one-quarter and one-half of the edible portion of the crop has to be set aside for replanting, yet if yams could be grown from seed then food yields would dramatically improve. The research failed when the first generation tubers were always found to be small. Yet farmers knew this already; some had been conducting their own experiments on this in the 1930s (Richards, 1985).

There are many more examples of farmers' knowledge informing the agricultural research and development process. In many cases this local knowledge has been discovered by individuals or institutions working in a participatory mode with rural people. This does not mean farmers participating in doing what outsiders want them to do or think is best for them. Participation means that outsiders learn with rural people and are willing to change their activities and direction in the light of locally articulated needs and knowledge. As Yves Cabannes, co-ordinator of the Habitat Section of the Groupe de Recherche et d'Echanges Technologiques, Paris, has said: 'Given the chance, poor communities hold the key to the solution of their own problems' (Cabannes, 1988).

Participatory methods

In recent years participatory methods have spread at a remarkable pace through NGOs and government organizations around the world. A large number of approaches for collaborative research, planning, implementation and monitoring have been developed, including rapid rural appraisal, participatory rural appraisal and other similar techniques (Farrington and Martin, 1988; McCracken, Conway and Pretty, 1988; *RRA Notes*, 1988–91; Gueye and Schoonmaker Freudenberger,

1991; Mascarenhas *et al.*, 1991). Once exposed to the culture of learning from and with rural people, more organisations are trying out various methods, inventing their own and developing variations. Already this has produced a wealth of practical field experience. Where the attitudes of outsiders are appropriate and rapport and accountability are good, it has repeatedly been shown that villagers know a great deal, and this knowledge itself helps to drive innovations.

With the devolution of planning and monitoring to villagers, people in rural communities are no longer seen simply as informants, but as teachers, extensionists, activists and monitors of change. These specialists include village para-professionals, village extensionists, experts, village game wardens, women veterinarians, and so on (Huby, 1990; Cernea, 1991; Shah, Bharadwaj and Ambastha, 1991). An emphasis on village specialists integrates marginalized groups more readily, so allowing their skills and knowledge to influence development priorities. In this way local people are able to monitor changes and articulate local demands for support.

Box 4.2: Small-scale irrigation in the Philippines

The Institute of Philippine Culture compared two types of NIA-assisted communal projects: those which NIA developed through its participatory intervention methods, and those assisted through its traditional approach. Pilot participatory projects were first established in 1976, and by 1981 the approach had been expanded to twenty-five projects countrywide. The participatory approach gives attention to the development of the irrigators' association months before project construction starts. The key mechanism used to develop these associations is farmers' involvement in the planning and construction of the irrigation system. Full-time organizers reside in the project area and prepare the association to work with the engineers.

The incorporation of local knowledge into design made a large difference. Farmers provided information on the behaviour of the proposed water source and on the location of more stable river banks; they pointed out alternative canal routes to avoid low-lying or sandy areas; they indicated routes that would include distant fields of farmers who had shown great interest in the project; they indicated where a canal would consume too much of a small farmers' land; and they suggested structures across streams that would serve their needs. As De los Reyes and Jopillo (1986) noted: 'NIA's judicious use of the farmers' knowledge of their environment resulted in more functional systems.'

The NIA participatory approach was successful in producing larger irrigated areas, greater productivity, stronger associations, improved

---

water distribution, better compliance with government policy and an improved relationship between farmers and government. NIA achieved this because it had a policy framework supportive of local involvement, the presence of a supportive bureaucracy and a new and appropriate attitude in programme implementers.

Comparison of participatory and non-participatory irrigation systems developed with the support of the NIA, Philippines (1983–5)

Indicators	Participatory	Non-participatory
(1) Sizes of irrigation systems (ha):		
Design area	205	246
Irrigated Area: wet season	104	149
dry season	76	123
(2) Cost per hectare of actual irrigated land (pesos)	15,150	15,599
(3) Proportion of NIA-built structures assessed by farmers as defective	13%	20%
(4) Proportion of NIA-built canals abandoned or rerouted by farmers	9%	18%
(5) Proportion of systems in which farmers' suggestions were incorporated in system layout and design	83%	27%
(6) Rice yields wet season: before NIA	2.84	2.59
after NIA	3.05	2.65
(7) Rice yields dry season: before NIA	2.56	2.57
after NIA	3.11	2.54
(8) Farmers' per hectare contribution to costs (pesos)	357	54
(9) Remittance of amortization payments due to NIA (by 1984–5)	82%	50%
(10) Number of group works held per association	32	14
(11) Person-hours contributed by each system user	67	28
(12) Measure of financial management capacity of irrigators' associations	5.11	2.45

Sources: De los Reyes and Jopillo (1986); Bagadion and Korten (1991).

Participatory methods have now been used by sufficient numbers of institutions that it is possible to evaluate their impact in comparison with situations where no such methods have been used. One significant case study is the irrigation development conducted by the National Irrigation Authority (NIA) in the Philippines (Box 4.2).

Project flexibility

The most successful institutions are those that start their projects small and cheaply. They promote uncomplicated design and do not try everything at once. Technologies promoted tend to be low risk to farmers, easy to teach and demonstrate and tested under local conditions, and tend to offer the prospect of clear, large, on-site benefits in the coming season or year. Paternalism in the form of financial or food incentives to encourage short-term adoption is avoided as it creates dependency and so threatens the long-term commitment of local people (Bunch, 1990; Lobo, 1990; Reij, 1991). After initiation, projects may stay small (Goethert and Hamdi, 1988; Uphoff, 1990) or be combined into larger programmes once the participatory procedures and processes have been fully elaborated (Cernea, 1983 and 1987).

It is impossible to predict the results of participatory planning and development without sustained contact with potential beneficiaries. A common feature of successful projects has been an early period of experimentation and continuous dialogue that allows outsiders to learn, return to the drawing board and replan. Investing in appropriate human resource development is also vital, which includes improving the skills of outsiders in facilitating development, and fostering multidisciplinary and multisectoral working. Many successful projects have changed priorities and adapted practices following the incorporation of people's needs and priorities. After a survey, the Kenya Woodfuel Development Project, planning to teach tree planting and raising as a major activity, discovered that 30 per cent of farms already had agroforestry micro-nurseries, and project managers were able to make a drastic change in the project design (Chavangi and Ngugi, 1987; Huby, 1990). Elsewhere in Kenya, a project in Turkana used theodolites and other complicated equipment to design water harvesting technologies for sorghum gardens for pastoralists, but social factors were overlooked as food for work was used to persuade the pastoralists to participate (Critchley, 1991). When the project realized the reasons for the ensuing lack of success, design was turned over to the Turkana people, who designed modified and simple water harvesting that has produced reliable crop yields.

The length of time for which external agencies are willing to commit funds is also critical to success. For real social and natural resource change, development projects must be of realistic lengths. Projects of less than five years' duration have a much greater chance of failure than those of five to ten or more years (Hudson, 1989; Uphoff, 1990). This need to give sustained support is increasingly being recognized. Just as local communities take a long-term and sequential view of resource use and management, so must projects and governments.

Farmer-to-farmer extension

Where there has been successful extension of LEI agroecological technologies to new communities, farmers have always been involved in the transfer of their expertise. This farmer-to-farmer extension takes many forms. Most common are farmer exchange visits, in which farmers are brought to the site of successful use of the technologies, where they are able to observe benefits and costs and discuss them with adopting farmers. Project staff can play the role of bringing interested groups together and facilitating the process of information exchange. For farmers 'seeing is believing', and the best educators of farmers are other farmers. Such farmer-to-farmer extension has resulted in the spread of *Leucaena* contour hedgerows in the Philippines (Fujisaka, 1989); management innovations for irrigation systems in Nepal (Pradan and Yoder, 1989); velvet beans for green manuring in Honduras (Bunch, 1990); and a range of watershed protection technologies in India (Mascarenhas *et al.*, 1991; Shah, Bharadwaj and Ambastha, 1991). These all have shown that farmer-to-farmer extension is a low-cost method of motivating farmer groups to change habits and practices. It also provides crucial leadership experience for villagers and provides role models that they can reasonably aspire to emulate.

POLICY FRAMEWORKS TO SUPPORT LOW-EXTERNAL INPUT SUSTAINABLE AGRICULTURE INTO THE 1990s

Current policy shortcomings

The current policy frameworks of national governments all over the world strongly favour the HEI approach to agricultural development. Many countries are under multiple stresses from rising debt servicing requirements, the long-term decline in world commodity prices, increasing populations and growing demand for food. These force debtor nations to take the short-term view, and thus emphasize the expansion of export earnings and staple production, and the curbing of public, including development, expenditure. Yet increasing supply forces down world prices even further, a situation worsened by agricultural protectionism in some industrialized country trading blocs.

To overcome these pressing problems, policy-makers tend to favour approaches for stimulating agricultural production that promise immediate returns, even if the long-term prospects are threatened. This means supporting large-scale enterprises, such as ranching operations, plantations and large farms, through the subsidy of inputs, generous tax laws, selective extension of low-interest credit and favourable product pricing (Barbier, 1989). These incentives have helped boost production on more favourable lands, so spreading the adoption of Green Revolution technologies. But the long-term benefits of this strategy are not so clear. The costs incurred include resource degradation and increased inequity if agriculture expands into common property resources, if fertilizers and pesticides are used inefficiently because of their low price, if food imports are favoured at the expense of appropriate local foods and if particular commodities are supported at the expense of diverse and mixed farming.

LEI agriculture will not flourish beyond the small-scale successes documented above unless concerted action is taken both by national governments and by multilateral and bilateral development assistance agencies to adjust institutional, economic and legal frameworks to shift the balance of support towards LEI agricultural systems.

Institutional frameworks

The appropriate institutional framework to support LEI farming will be multisectoral and co-ordinated over natural resource boundaries rather than administrative ones. It will be oriented so that local priorities and needs are articulated and influence the process of planning and financial resource allocation. This will require a high degree of institutional flexibility and adaptability.

Institutional flexibility is a difficult criterion to meet. It is not simply the greater devolving of power. It involves the development of partnerships between sectoral ministries and between government and NGOs; the reform of agricultural research and extension services; and the provision of infrastructure complementary to the support of LEI agriculture. The mixed livelihood systems that form the basis of productive and sustainable agriculture centred on internal resources are not well served by government sectoral institutions. Often crop production is the responsibility of one department in a ministry, while livestock may be in another department or ministry altogether; tree crops fall into the responsibility of a specialized department, and soil and water conservation probably into another. Such division hinders co-ordination of efforts to support complex LEI agricultural systems. It is therefore necessary for government institutions to take a more holistic view of farmers' livelihoods and to develop multidisciplinary teams capable of addressing their problems in a flexible and timely manner.

Reform must also occur in agricultural research and extension institutions. Extension services work best when they are less concerned with transferring a technology from a research station to a farmer, and more involved in creating a constructive dialogue with farmers (Moris, 1990; Thompson, 1991). Agroecological technologies must fit each farmer's livelihood system, and farming households are inevitably the best judge of new practices. A partnership, in both problem-finding and problem-solving, is essential if long-term solutions are to be found. In the British agricultural revolution of the eighteenth and nineteenth centuries, there was no national agricultural ministry – all knowledge and advice on new rotation systems, new crops and new livestock breeds was transferred by farmers extending their advice to others through tours, open days, publications and on-farm demonstration (Pretty, 1991). Extension advisers must increasingly seek rural people's knowledge to ensure better partnerships and greater success.

There is also a need to reallocate financial resources away from research on HEI agroecosystems. In Thailand and Indonesia, the overwhelming investment emphasis is on research and extension for rice in the irrigated lowlands; upland, rainfed areas, such as north-east Thailand and upland Java, receive little or no benefits (Conway and Barbier, 1990). Reform of agricultural research should focus on creating professional incentives for conducting on-farm research and working closely with resource-poor farmers, and on rigorous evaluations of the successes of conventional research and new approaches.

Attention to complementary infrastructure will also have important impacts. Increased yields in LEI agricultural systems located in 'marginal' or remote areas should have a multiplier effect on the local economy, generating income and employment opportunities, such as in food processing industries, storage, transportation, sorting, grading and packing. These changes will require complementary support through investment in physical infrastructure, such as roads, schools and markets.

Economic frameworks

Governments apply various micro-economic instruments such as subsidies and fiscal measures to their agricultural, forestry and fishery sectors. To date, these have not been used with a view to directing agricultural practices towards greater sustainability. Indeed, sometimes they have had the opposite effect. The overwhelming message about micro-economic policies is that their impact on the environment and on sustainable resource use has frequently been misconceived. Mostly this is because policies are pursuing some other objective – for example, an increase in exports, income support for low-income groups or benefits to powerful sections of society. The result is often overgrazing, deforestation, salinization, over-use of inputs, and so on. The balance between HEI and LEI systems is currently severely distorted in favour of HEI through the inappropriate application of economic instruments.

Both industrialized and developing countries adopt measures such as supporting farm prices or providing deficiency payments to farmers; subsidizing agricultural inputs such as fertilizers or pesticides; not charging for water used for irrigation; imposing tariffs or quotas on imports that would otherwise compete with home-grown produce; and giving direct income support to farmers (Barbier, 1989; OECD, 1989). There are implicit subsidies in the form of tax concessions for forest clearance, for example as has been the case in Brazil, that encourage unsustainable HEI agriculture.

These are powerful incentives that discriminate against LEI agroecological technologies. Farmers switching from HEI to LEI, or making changes to LEI systems to improve productivity, rarely can do so without incurring extra initial costs. Reducing distorting subsidies would have at least two benefits, namely a reduction in the environmental damage and an increase in government resource mobilization. With appropriate support, farmers would be encouraged to adopt LEI agroecological technologies. Examples include assistance to farmers who plant trees, construct contour bunds and leave headlands and crop boundaries unsprayed. While support of this kind is often being provided through foreign aid, there is scope for more active use of fiscal instruments towards the same end, for example through tax concessions to farmers adopting practices that protect the environment, such as planting trees or constructing soil and water conserving structures.

A key economic policy issue is the extent to which agricultural prices can provide appropriate incentives to promote LEI agriculture and farmer investment in sustainable land management. The balance between aggregate crop prices and input costs affects a range of short- and long-term decisions farmers make. Given an appropriate balance, farmers can be encouraged to intensify using local resources, invest in conservation measures and replace degrading cropping systems with environmentally benign ones. A combination of selective support for the introduction of LEI agroecological technologies together with attention to stable economic returns to crops will provide an incentive framework conducive to LEI agriculture. Higher returns to crop production will mean that farmers may be able to afford to maintain terraces and other conservation measures.

Legal frameworks

Even taken together, institutional and economic measures are rarely sufficient to control pollution or resource degradation. In theory, economic policies appear attractive and seem simple and elegant. However, if high levels of efficiency and justice are to be combined they have to be reinforced or replaced by a legal apparatus, including judiciary institutions such as police and courts that by comparison are complex and cumbersome. In many countries this apparatus is often inefficient, as well as highly discriminatory against the poor. It is useful to distinguish between private law, which individuals threatened by, for example, eviction or pollution can use to take offenders to court, and public law, which provides various mechanisms for control and support of public agencies (Conway and Pretty, 1991).

Private law is concerned with the rights of individuals and how they can obtain redress for damages they have suffered. In theory, it is a powerful deterrent, but in practice its usefulness is limited in the rural context in a developing country. The major drawback to private law solutions is the considerable cost of litigation that often arises, particularly when cases involve small farmers or poor plaintiffs (Macrory, 1990). For all practical purposes small farmers in most developing countries cannot seek redress for grievances, however well justified, in courts of law, breeding a sense of apathy and alienation and contributing to a general distrust of public authorities. Improvements in the local judiciary will often be an important prerequisite for sustainable development, including LEI agricultural practices, in rural areas (Banuri, 1991).

The primary role for public law lies in redressing the balance between HEI and LEI agriculture by making the former less favourable through anti-pollution laws and the setting of standards, and the latter more favourable through the granting of rights and access to natural resources. This implies, for example, action to grant tenurial rights to small farmers so that they feel sufficiently confident to take a long-term view. Public law provides the legal framework within which farmers, if and when the judiciary provides them with the practical possibilities to do so, can seek an end to discrimination by those better endowed.

117

CONCLUSIONS

The experiences documented in this chapter suggest that agricultural production in LEI systems can be improved by 50 per cent or more. Yield improvements through sustainable intensification would be accompanied by further indirect economic benefits. There would be no need for extensification into uncultivated areas, so ensuring that non-agricultural plant and animal species with value to local livelihoods would be sustained. Non-use benefits would also be preserved, such as locally valued cultural sites and globally valued biodiversity and ecosystems, both of which are threatened when cultivation expands. There would be reduced contamination and pollution of the environment, so reducing costs incurred by farming households, consumers of food and national economies as a whole. Migration patterns could also be reversed as economic growth based upon agricultural regeneration occurs. In the long run the benefits will extend to reduced population growth rates as rural people become better off and less in need of large supportive families.

When people's ideas and interests, not just their labour, are sought and incorporated fully in development projects and programmes, then conventional indicators of development success are all met. Effectiveness is improved as people feel an ownership of the developmental change and are willing to contribute to maintenance; and efficiency is better as cost recovery improves. Where the appropriate incentives are applied by national governments in the form of enabling institutional, economic and legal frameworks, then the potential for widespread sustainable agricultural development can be fulfilled.

REFERENCES AND BIBLIOGRAPHY

Acaba, M., Apura, D., Cabiling, J., De Pedro, R. and Lightfoot, C., 1987. *A Study of Farmers' Evaluation of Camote Varieties*, Farming Systems Development Project, Eastern Visayas, Visayas State College of Agriculture, Leyte, Philippines.

Ashby, J. A., Quiros, C. A. and Rivera, Y. M., 1987. *Farmer Participation in On-Farm Trials*, ODI, London.

Bagadion, B. U. and Korten, F. F., 1991. 'Developing irrigators' organizations: a learning process approach', in: M. M. Cernea (ed.), *Putting People First*, 2nd edn, Oxford University Press, Oxford.

Banuri, T., 1991. 'Democratic decentralization', mimeo, IUCN, Islamabad.

Barbier, E. B., 1989. 'Sustaining agriculture on marginal land: a policy framework', *Environment*, 31, 9, pp. 13–17, 36–40.

Barbier, E. B. and Burgess, J., 1990. *Malawi – Land Degradation in Agriculture*, report to the World Bank Economic Mission of Environmental Policy, IIED, London.

Barker, R. and Herdt, R., 1983. *The Rice Economy of Asia*, Resources for the Future, Washington, DC.

Bebbington, A., 1991. *Farmer Organizations in Ecuador: Contributions to Farmer First Research and Development*, Sustainable Agriculture Programme Gatekeeper Series no. 26, IIED, London.

Bunch, R., 1990. *Low Input Soil Restoration in Honduras: The Cantarranas Farmer-to-Farmer Extension Programme*, Sustainable Agriculture Programme Gatekeeper Series no. 23, IIED, London.

Cabannes, Y., 1988. 'Human settlements', in C. Conroy and M. Litvinoff (eds), *The Greening of Aid*, Earthscan, London.

Cernea, M. M., 1983. *A Social Methodology for Community Participation in Local Investments*, Staff Working Paper no. 598, World Bank, Washington, DC.

Cernea, M. M., 1987. 'Farmer organizations and institution building for sustainable development', *Regional Development Dialogue*, 8, pp. 1–24.

Cernea, M. M., 1991. 'Social actors of participatory afforestation strategies', in M. M., Cernea (ed.), *Putting People First*, 2nd edn, Oxford University Press, Oxford.

Chambers, R., Pacey, A. and Thrupp, L. A., 1989. *Farmer First: Farmer Innovation and Agricultural Research*, Intermediate Technology Publications, London.

Chapman, N., 1988. 'The impact of T & V extension in Somalia', in J. Howell (ed.), *Training and Visit Extension in Practice*, ODI, London.

Chavangi, N. A. and Ngugi, A. W., 1987. 'Innovatory participation in programme design: tree planting for increased fuelwood supply for rural households in Kenya', paper for Workshop on Farmers and Agricultural Research, Institute of Development Studies, University of Sussex.

Chopra, K., Kadekodi, G. K. and Murthy, M. V., 1990. *Participatory Development: People and Common Property Resources*, Sage Publications, New Delhi.

Conway, G. R. and Barbier, E. B., 1990. *After the Green Revolution*, Earthscan, London.

Conway, G. R. and Pretty, J. N., 1991. *Unwelcome Harvest: Agriculture and Pollution*, Earthscan, London.

Craig, I. A., 1987. 'Pre-rice crop green manuring: a technology for soil improvement under rainfed conditions in NE Thailand', NERAD Project, Tha Phra, Khon Kaen, Thailand.

Craig, I. A. and Pisone, U., 1988. *A Survey of NERAD Promising Processes: Methodologies and Technologies for Rainfed Agriculture in NE Thailand*, NERAD Project, Tha Phra, Khon Kaen, Thailand.

Critchley, W., 1991. *Looking After Our Land: New Approaches to Soil and Water Conservation in Dryland Africa*, Oxfam, Oxford, and IIED, London.

De los Reyes, R. and Jopillo, S. G., 1986. *An Evaluation of the Philippines Participatory Communal Irrigation Program*, Institute of Philippine Culture, Quezon City.

D'Souza, E. R. and Palghadmal, T. J., 1990. *Sustainable Water-Use System: A Case Study of Sase-Gandhalewadi Lift Irrigation Project*, Social Centre, Ahmednagar, India.

Environment and Urbanization, 1990. 'Community based organizations: how they develop, what they seek and what they achieve', 2, 1, IIED, London.

Farrington, J. and Martin, A., 1988. *Farmer Participatory Research: A Review of Concepts and Practices*, Agricultural Research and Extension Network Paper no. 19, ODI, London.

Flinn, J. C. and De Datta, S. K., 1984. 'Trends in irrigated rice yields under intensive cropping at Philippine research stations', *Field Crops Research*, 9, pp. 1–15.

Francis, C. A., 1986. *Multiple Cropping Systems*, Macmillan, New York.

Francis, C. A., 1989. *Internal Resources for Sustainable Agriculture*, Sustainable Agriculture Programme Gatekeeper Series no. 8, IIED, London.

Fujisaka, S., 1989. *Participation by Farmers, Researchers and Extension Workers in Soil Conservation*, Sustainable Agriculture Programme Gatekeeper Series no. 16, IIED, London.

Goethert, R. and Hamdi, N., 1988. *Making Microplans: A Community-Based Process in Programming and Development*, Intermediate Technology Publications, London.

Gueye, B. and Schoonmaker Freudenberger, K., 1991. *Introduction à la Méthode Accélérée de Recherche Participative: Quelques Notes Pour Appuyer une Formation Pratique*, IIED, London.

Hobbelink, H., Vellve, R. and Abraham, M., 1990. *Inside the Bio-Revolution*, IOCU, Penang, and GRAIN, Barcelona.

Horwith, B. J., Windle, P. N., MacDonald, E. F., Parker, J. K., Ruby, A. M. and Elfring, C., 1989. 'The role of technology in enhancing low resource agriculture in Africa', *Agriculture and Human Values*.

Howell, J. (ed.), 1988. *Training and Visit Extension in Practice*, ODI, London.

Huang, H. T. and Pei Yang, 1987. 'Ancient culture of citrus ant as a biological agent', *BioScience*, 37, pp. 665–71.

Huby, M., 1990. *Where You Can't See the Wood for the Trees*, Kenya Woodfuel Development Programme Series, Beijer Institute, Stockholm.

Hudson, N., 1989. *A Study of the Reasons for Success or Failure of Soil Conservation Projects*, FAO Soils Bulletin 64, Rome.

Jodha, N. S., 1990. *Rural Common Property Resources: A Growing Crisis*, Sustainable Agriculture Programme Gatekeeper Series no. 24, IIED, London.

Kenmore, P., 1989. 'IPM means the best mix', *MAPPS Newsletter*, 11, p. 38.

Kenmore, P., Litsinger, J. A., Bandong, J. P., Santiago, A. C. and Salac, M. M., 1987. 'Philippine rice farmers and insecticides: thirty years of growing dependency and new options for change', in E. J. Tait and B. Napometh (eds), *Management of Pests and Pesticides: Farmers' Perceptions and Practices*, Westview Press, London.

Kerkhof, P., 1990. *Agroforestry in Africa: A Survey of Project Experience*, Panos Institute, London.

Kolhe, S. S. and Mitra, B. N., 1987. 'Effects of *Azolla* as an organic source of nitrogen in rice–wheat cropping system', *Journal of Agronomy and Crop Science*, 159, pp. 212–15.

Kotschi, J., Waters-Bayer, A., Adelhelm, R. and Hoesle, U., 1989. *Ecofarming in Agricultural Development*, GTZ, Eschborn.

Kottak, C. P., 1985. 'When people don't come first: some sociological lessons from completed projects', in M. M. Cernea (ed.), *Putting People First*, Oxford University Press, Oxford.

Kydd, J., 1989. 'Maize research in Malawi: lessons from failure', *Journal of International Development*, 1, pp. 112–44.

Lane, C. and Pretty, J. N., 1990. *Displaced Pastoralists and Transferred Wheat Technology in Tanzania*, Sustainable Agriculture Programme Gatekeeper Series no. 20, IIED, London.

Lipton, M. with Longhurst, R., 1989. *New Seeds and Poor People*, Unwin Hyman, London.

Lobo, C., 1990. *Watershed Development: A Participatory Development Approach to Resource Mobilization*, Social Centre, Ahmednagar, India.

McCracken, J., Conway, G. R. and Pretty, J. N., 1988. *An Introduction to Rapid Rural Appraisal for Agricultural Development*, Sustainable Agriculture Programme, IIED, London.

Macrory, R., 1990. 'The legal control of pollution', in R. Harrison (ed.), *Pollution Cause, Effects and Controls*, 2nd edn, Royal Society of Chemistry, Nottingham.

Mascarenhas, J., Shah, P., Joseph, S., Jayakaran, R., Devavaram, J., Ramachandran, V., Fernandez, A., Chambers, R. and Pretty, J. N., (eds), 1991. *Participatory Rural Appraisal: RRA Notes 13*, Sustainable Agriculture Programme, IIED, London.

Moris, J., 1990. *Extension Alternatives in Tropical Africa*, ODI, London.

Mullen, J., 1989. 'Training and visit system in Somalia: contradictions and anomalies', *Journal of International Development*, 1, pp. 145–67.

Murphy, D., 1990. 'Community organization in Asia', *Environment and Urbanization*, 2, pp. 51–60.

NRC (National Research Council), 1984. *Pesticide Resistance Strategies and Tactics for Management*, National Academy Press, Washington, DC.

NRC, 1989. *Alternative Agriculture*, National Academy Press, Washington, DC.

OECD, 1989. *Agricultural and Environmental Policies*, OECD, Paris.

OTA (Office of Technology Assessment), 1988. *Enhancing Agriculture in Africa: A Role for US Development Assistance*, US Government Printing Office, Washington, DC.

Poffenberger, M., 1990. *Joint Management of Forest Lands: Experiences from South Asia*, Ford Foundation, New Delhi.

Pradan, N. C. and Yoder, R., 1989. *Improving Irrigation Management through Farmer-to-Farmer Training: Examples from Nepal*, Working Paper no. 12, International Irrigation Management Institute, Kathmandu.

Pretty, J. N., 1990. *Rapid Catchment Analysis for Extension Agents: Notes on the Kericho Training Workshop for the Ministry of Agriculture, Kenya*, IIED, London.

Pretty, J. N., 1991. 'Farmers' extension practice and technology adaptation: agricultural revolution in 17th–19th century Britain', *Agriculture and Human Values*, 8, 1–2.

Rahman, M. A. (ed.), 1984. *Grass-Roots Participation and Self-Reliance*, Oxford University Press, Oxford, and IBH Publication Co, New Delhi.

Ramaprasad, V. and Ramachandran, V., 1989. *Celebrating Awareness*, Myrada, Bangalore, and Foster Parents Plan International, New Delhi.

Reij, C., 1991. *Indigenous Soil and Water Conservation in Africa*, Sustainable Agriculture Programme Gatekeeper Series no. 27, IIED, London.

Reij, C., Muller, P. and Begemann, L., 1988. *Water Harvesting for Plant Production*, Technical Paper no. 91, World Bank, Washington, DC.

Rhoades, R. E., 1984. *Breaking New Ground: Agricultural Anthropology*, International Potato Center, Lima, Peru.

Richards, P., 1985. *Indigenous Agricultural Revolution*, Hutchinson, London.

Rodale, R., 1985. 'Internal resources and external inputs – the two sources of all production needs', Rodale Institute Research Center, Kutztown, Pa.

RRA Notes, 1988–91. Issues 1–14, Sustainable Agriculture Programme, IIED, London.

Sarrantonio, M., 1991. *Soil-Improving Legumes: Methodologies for Screening*, Rodale Institute Research Center, Kutztown, Pa.

Scoones, I. (ed.), 1991. *Wetlands in Drylands: The Agroecology of Savanna Systems in Africa*, Drylands Programme, IIED, London.

Shah, P., Bharadwaj, G. and Ambastha, R., 1991. 'Participatory impact monitoring of a soil and water conservation programme by farmers, extension volunteers, and AKRSP', in J. Mascarenhas *et al.* (eds), *Participatory Rural Appraisal: RRA Notes 13*, Sustainable Agriculture Programme, IIED, London.

Thompson, J., 1991. *Combining Local Knowledge with Expert Assistance in Natural Resources Management: Small-Scale Irrigation in Kenya*, Case Study no. 2, 'From the Ground Up' research programme, World Resources Institute, Washington, DC.

Uphoff, N., 1990. 'Paraprojects as new modes of international development assistance', *World Development*, 18, pp. 1401–11.

Watanbe, I., Espinas, C. R., Berja, N. S. and Alimango, B. V., 1977. *Utilization of the Azolla-Anabaena Complex as a Nitrogen Fertilizer for Rice*, Research Paper Series no. 11, IRRI, Los Baños, Philippines.

Wolf, E. C., 1986. *Beyond the Green Revolution: New Approaches for Third World Agriculture*, Worldwatch Paper no. 73, Worldwatch Institute, Washington, DC.

World Bank, 1991. *World Development Report 1991*, Oxford University Press, Oxford.

Young, A., 1989. *Agroforestry for Soil Conservation*, CAB International, Wallingford.

5 The Future City

Jorge Hardoy, Diana Mitlin and David Satterthwaite

INTRODUCTION: SUSTAINABLE RESOURCE USE OR SUSTAINABLE DEVELOPMENT?

If the main concern of sustainable development is the sustainable use of resources and of the global commons[1], urban centres in the Third World perform much better than urban centres in the North. This can be seen in the much lower levels of resource use and waste generation per person and in the much smaller contributions per person to global environmental degradation (including greenhouse gas emissions).

Lower levels of resource use are evident in different sectors. For instance, most housing construction in urban centres in Africa, Asia and Latin America makes considerable use of recycled or reclaimed materials and little use of cement, glass, aluminium, steel or other materials with a high energy input. In addition, low-income households – generally the majority within urban centres in the Third World – have too few capital goods to represent much of a draw on the world's finite non-renewable resource base. Low-income households also generate low volumes of household waste, and much of the metal, glass, paper and other items in their wastes is reused or recycled. Most people in urban centres of the Third World rely on public transport (or walk or bicycle), which ensures low average oil consumption per person.[2] City averages for water and electricity consumption per person are often low – perhaps not surprisingly when a considerable proportion of the population do not have homes connected to electricity supplies or piped water systems.

While more sustainable in terms of resource use and waste generation, most urban centres in the Third World do not sustain the health or livelihoods of the majority of their citizens. As such, they do not meet the other aspect central to the concept of sustainable development set out by *Our Common Future* (WCED, 1987): the meeting of human needs. Low averages for levels of resource use and waste generation per

124

person are largely the result of the very low incomes for such a high proportion of the population. A city with a low average for water consumption per person can hardly be held up as a model of water conservation (or sustainable development) if this is the result of much of the population lacking sufficient water for drinking, cooking and personal hygiene. Similarly, an illegal shelter where five or more persons live in a single room with inadequate protection from the elements and under constant threat of eviction can hardly be considered a model of sustainable development, however much the shelter itself makes widespread use of cardboard, plastic and wood reclaimed from industrial, commercial and domestic garbage. High levels of efficiency in recycling or reclaiming metals, glass, paper, rags and other items from city wastes are often at the cost of very poor health and disablement among the thousands of people who make their living from sorting through garbage by hand.

Despite great diversity between nations in the scale and nature of urban change, certain problems have been shown to be common to most urban centres. These include:

- a high proportion of people with incomes too low to allow them to meet their basic needs (for food, fuel, water, clothing, shelter and health care);
- an estimated 600 million people living in 'life- and health-threatening' environments in very poor-quality housing with little or no provision for infrastructure and services essential for health (Cairncross, Hardoy and Satterthwaite, 1990; WHO, 1992);
- little or no protection for workers from unsafe workplaces (where exposure to toxic chemicals is common) and over-long working hours;
- high levels of air and water pollution and inadequate controls over industrial wastes, including the collection and disposal of toxic and hazardous wastes;
- a haphazard, unplanned pattern of urban expansion in which poorer groups are often denied access to safe, legal housing or sites on which such housing can be built (and as a result, large concentrations of low-income groups construct shelters on floodplains, hillsides prone to landslides or other unsuitable sites);
- a high proportion of infants and children in the population (usually close to half the total population) but with enormous inadequacies in the services essential for child health and development such as primary health care (including a strong focus on immunization and

125

preventive measures), emergency services, schools, nurseries, crèches and safe and easily accessible play facilities;
- a physical decay in infrastructure such as roads and drainage systems, public buildings and services such as public transport, schools, hospitals and health centres.

A key question is why such problems are common to so many urban centres, despite the diversity of nations (and urban centres) within Africa, Asia and Latin America. The question has relevance for more than urban populations, since the political future of most Third World societies will be much influenced by the extent to which their urban policies incorporate the needs and priorities of their urban populations into their economic, social and political life.

It is possible to consider the differences between an urban future with no changes in government policies and an urban future which could result from new attitudes and approaches. This chapter outlines the social, economic and political context which will shape the urban future. It also describes the main actors who will be responsible for building and financing this urban future, and it contrasts an urban future where no changes are made in government policies with an urban future where urban populations' development concerns are addressed. The resource implications of meeting these development needs are also discussed, since meeting these needs might imply unsustainable levels of resource use.

THE CONTEXT FOR THE URBAN FUTURE

In recent decades, most Third World nations have experienced a very rapid growth in their urban populations. The scale of this demographic change remains poorly appreciated. Between 1950 and 1990, the South's total population grew from 1.7 billion to close to 4 billion, while its urban population grew from under 300 million to 1.5 billion (United Nations, 1991); the South's urban population is now larger than the total population of Europe, North America and Japan combined. There are many cities whose populations have grown more than tenfold in these same forty years – including Abidjan, Amman, Brasilia, Dar es Salaam, Khartoum, Kinshasa, Lagos, Nairobi, Nouakchott and Seoul. There are over twenty urban agglomerations in the South with more than 5 million inhabitants; in 1940, none had reached this size. There are dozens of cities with between 500,000 and 5 million inhabitants; many were only small urban centres forty years ago. There are hundreds of urban centres with between 100,000 and 500,000 inhabitants which did not exist forty years ago or were small towns with only a few thousand inhabitants. Finally, there are tens of thousands of urban centres with under 100,000 inhabitants.

This rapid expansion in the urban population has occurred without the needed expansion in the capacity of public authorities to manage such expansion[3] – for instance, to control pollution and to ensure the provision of services and facilities essential to a decent urban environment. Public authorities have also failed to manage land uses to ensure that sufficient land is available for housing and that natural resources (and the ecosystems on which they depend) in the areas around cities are protected. The result is that in virtually every urban centre – from the large cities and metropolitan areas to regional centres and small market towns – a large proportion of the population lives in houses and neighbourhoods with little or no provision of piped water, sanitation and storm drainage, all-weather roads and pavements, services to collect and dispose of garbage, schools and health centres. For instance, households with five or more persons often live in one or two rooms in cramped, overcrowded dwellings such as tenements, cheap boarding houses or shelters built on illegally occupied or subdivided land. In addition, in the larger urban centres (or centres with high concentrations of heavy industry), liquid, solid and, on occasion, gaseous wastes from city-based enterprises and households are damaging surrounding farmlands, forests and aquatic ecosystems.

However, it is difficult to be precise about the scale of recent changes in urban populations, since census data after 1980–2 are not available for most nations. We know very little about the scale of urban change during the 1980s. The urban population statistics given for 1985, 1990 and beyond in statistical compendia are simply projections based on older census data. Once sufficient census data become available to show urban trends for the 1980s, these are likely to reveal a considerable slow-down in the rate at which urbanization levels have increased in most Third World nations and slower growth rates for most national urban populations and for most large cities. This will reflect slower economic growth or economic stagnation during the 1980s, which in most instances implies a slower transfer of population from rural to urban areas. In the nations where rapid economic growth has been sustained, rapid urbanization is likely to have continued, although rates of increase in the level of urbanization will also tend to slow as a society becomes predominantly urban. In many nations, slower population growth rates for the largest cities and for national urban populations will also reflect lower rates of population growth within the nation.

Unless there are major changes in prevailing trends, most of the people who will live in 'the future city' will live in relatively small cities, not in large metropolitan areas or so-called 'mega-cities'. Although so much of the literature is on the mega-cities, only a small proportion of the Third World's population lives in such cities. Estimates for 1990 suggest that less than 3 per cent of the population in Africa, Asia (excluding Japan) and Latin America live in cities of 10 or more million inhabitants (Table 5.1). Most of the Third World's urban inhabitants are likely to continue living in urban centres with less than 250,000 inhabitants, and the economic and political changes needed to produce

Table 5.1: The relative importance of 'mega-cities' within the Third World's urban population

City/metropolitan area	Population (millions)	Date and source
São Paulo metropolitan area	17.4	1990 (estimate)
Mexico City metropolitan area	15.5	1990 (census; preliminary)
Calcutta	11.8	1990 (estimate)
Bombay	11.2	1990 (estimate)
Seoul	11.0	1990 (estimate)
Buenos Aires metropolitan area	10.8	1991 (census; preliminary)
Rio de Janeiro	10.7	1990 (estimate)
Beijing	10.7	1990 (estimate)
Total population in metropolitan areas with over 10 million inhabitants	99.1	
Total Third World population	4,086.0	1990 (estimate)
Percentage of Third World population in metropolitan areas of over 10 million inhabitants	2.4%	

Note
Other cities or metropolitan areas such as Cairo and Shanghai have been attributed populations exceeding 10 million inhabitants in 1990 estimates or projections. But these are for areas much larger than the metropolitan area; for instance, for Shanghai, the population only exceeds 10 million if using an area of over 6,000 square kilometres which includes large areas of highly productive land and many villages and agricultural workers (Hawkins, 1982). See Garza (1991) for discussion of figure for Mexico City.

hundreds of 'mega-cities' are very unlikely to occur. Mega-cities can only develop in countries with large non-agricultural economies and large national populations, but most nations in the South have too small a population and too weak an economy to support mega-cities. A city of 10 million can only exist if there is an economy which can provide incomes for a population concentration of that size. In addition, many of the Third World's mega-cities have been experiencing substantial falls in their population growth rates for several successive inter-census periods, while an examination of recent censuses in many nations shows that certain mid-sized cities or smaller metropolitan centres have sustained rapid population growth rates during recent decades.

The fact that the Third World is likely to be less urbanized and less dominated by mega-cities than predicted by United Nations projections for the year 2000 and beyond does not mean that urban problems are not very serious. This does not mean an end to the long-term trend towards increasingly urban societies. The economic, social and political factors which drive urbanization are unlikely to stop before a majority of people live in urban areas; but uncertainty as to the scale and nature of these factors within each nation make accurate predictions impossible. For many of the poorer nations with few possibilities (under current conditions) of developing stronger and more stable economies, increases in the level of urbanization will undoubtedly slow and may in a few instances stop.

The central characteristic of the urban problem is not the rate of population growth but the gap between the scale of population concentration in urban centres and the capacity of the public authorities to ensure this population has access to basic needs. The urban problem owes more to the fact that national societies are ill prepared and usually ill equipped to make the necessary institutional changes to address the problems which accompany rapid urban change. This includes city and municipal governments that lack the power, resources and knowledge as to how to cope. Put another way, the rate of economic, social and demographic change exceeds society's capacity to develop the institutions needed to cope with such change. The hundreds of urban centres in the Third World which have grown in recent decades from a few thousand to over 100,000 inhabitants today mostly have local governments whose form, mode of operation and resource base have changed little to reflect the enormous change in the scale and nature of the entity they are meant to manage.

THE ECONOMIC AND POLITICAL CONTEXT FOR THE FUTURE CITY

One reason why it is so difficult to generalize about urban change in different nations is the unique nature of the factors which determine the scale and spatial distribution of such change – demographic, social, economic and political change and their interaction. Each nation's urban system has been shaped by its performance within the world market. Political history has also influenced national urban systems. Many Third World cities (including virtually all the larger cities) were founded by colonial powers. Their locations were determined by the commercial and administrative needs prevailing at that time and are now often ill suited to contemporary economic factors. In certain nations, urban change can be tied quite precisely to political change – as in China since 1949 (Kwok, 1982; Kirkby, 1985) or Cuba since 1959 (Hardoy, 1979; Gugler, 1980).

The history of urbanization reveals the rise and fall of thousands of cities in response to economic and political change. While the last 150 years have brought an unprecedented increase in urbanization, this does not imply that all urban centres will grow rapidly in the future. Indeed, analyses of changes in population in urban centres in recent inter-census periods for a range of Third World nations reveal thousands of urban centres with very slow population growth or population decline.[4] Many commentators assume that all nations will become increasingly urban, until virtually all of their population lives in urban areas, without a consideration as to what will be needed to cause this change.[5] All major cities in the Third World are presumed to continue increasing in population. For instance, United Nations projections for the populations of cities such as Beirut and Baghdad assume that the population of these cities continued to grow throughout the 1980s and will continue to grow, taking no account of the civil war taking place in Beirut for the last decade or of Iraq's war first with Iran and then with the Western alliance.

In seeking some guide to the urban future, certain generalizations can be made in regard to the factors which will influence the scale and nature of urban change. For instance, the extent to which a nation will urbanize is strongly linked to the scale of economic growth. Rapid economic growth will be accompanied by rapid urbanization until a high proportion of the population already live in urban centres – although advanced transport and communications systems and changes in the nature and organization of production in the richest nations are likely to increase the scale of economic activities outside major cities, as they have done in Europe and North America. The spatial form that urbanization takes, including the extent to which one city will dominate the urban system, will be much influenced by the structure of the economic growth. For instance, economic growth based on expanding production of relatively high-value agricultural commodities and related goods (such as coffee, tea, fruit and vegetables and products based on these) will in most circumstances stimulate urbanization in the producing areas. Among the factors which can encourage a more decentralized pattern of urban development are economic growth accompanied by a sustained commitment to stronger, more effective local government, a more equitable income distribution nationally and good inter-regional transport and communications systems.

By contrast, economic stagnation is unlikely to promote rapid urban growth and increasing levels of urbanization, unless also accompanied by political and/or economic instability which can force large numbers of rural people (or refugees from neighbouring nations) to cities for security or because of more certainty of obtaining food. For instance, the very rapid growth in the population of Khartoum in the Sudan and Maputo in Mozambique in recent years cannot be explained by a growth in these cities' economy; it owes more to the movement of people there fleeing drought and civil strife. The many nations which had stagnant economies, falling public expenditures and large debt burdens during the 1980s are likely to have had much slower urban growth than that experienced during the 1960s or 1970s.

It is often forgotten that, in the vast majority of nations, the cities which grow most rapidly are the cities where most enterprises choose to locate, because that city represents the location which best serves their purposes and profits. Government attempts to stop new investments in a city (to slow its 'explosive' growth) risk damaging the city (and the national) economy; the high costs and limited impacts of government measures to slow urban growth have been documented in considerable detail (see e.g. Renaud, 1981; Hamer, 1984; World Bank, 1991). The real issue is to ensure that cities (and the urban systems of which they are part) support new productive investment while also preventing enterprises located there from deriving their profits from passing on costs to other people. This can be through dumping their externalities on the wider population (for instance, through their contribution to air and water pollution) and on their workforce (in terms of inadequate income and inadequate attention to occupational safety). It can also be through avoiding the payment of taxes and of realistic costs for the municipal infrastructure and services they use.

Five characteristics can be highlighted as important influences on the future city in most Third World nations: a minor role for government and the conventional (legal) private sector in the construction of housing and new residential areas; a minor role for international aid agencies; an inappropriate legal framework which, if unchanged, criminalizes much of the city's production, workforce and population; a considerable proportion of the population with incomes too low to afford even the most basic level of food intake, health care and housing; and population growth in larger cities concentrated in the urban districts where local authorities are least equipped to manage such growth and meet the growing population's needs.

Construction of housing

First, in most urban centres, neither the government nor the conventional (legal) private sector has a major role in the construction of housing. It is common for 30 to 60 per cent of the population of cities to live in houses and neighbourhoods which have been developed illegally; and in most urban centres, 70 to 95 per cent of all new housing is built illegally. Neither government nor the conventional private sector has contributed much to the construction of housing, to the installation of basic residential infrastructure (roads, water supply, sewers, drains, pathways) or to the provision of basic services like health care, garbage collection and street cleaning. A minor current and future role for conventional private sector enterprise is easily understood; most of the population cannot afford to buy or rent even the cheapest house or apartment which meets legal requirements in its design, use of materials and construction standards. The minor role for government is partly the result of national governments' refusal to allow city and municipal governments the powers, resources and representative character necessary to be an effective supplier of infrastructure and services.

In most Third World nations, economic circumstances are unlikely to change for the better in terms of increasing the poor's capacity to pay for housing and health services. It is unrealistic to expect governments to increase the scale of funding for housing, basic infrastructure and services to a point where it begins to match the scale of need. Even under the most optimistic scenarios for economic recovery and for institutional changes to make urban governments more democratic and effective, most public authorities will continue to lack the economic and institutional capacity to provide the majority of urban dwellers with water piped to their homes, sewers, drains, paved roads and pathways, health care and emergency services.

International aid agencies

A second characteristic of past and current urban development in the Third World which is unlikely to change is the minor role taken by international agencies in providing the funding for addressing urban poverty. The current level of funding from aid and development assistance agencies for the provision of urban infrastructure and services essential for health and well-being, and for the improvement of poorer groups' housing and living conditions, is so small in relation to need that even if current levels were multiplied severalfold it would still make little impact. At present, most multilateral and bilateral development assistance agencies allocate less than 6 per cent of their funds to primary health care (including improved water supply and sanitation, immunization, health education and community-level health services) and less than 3 per cent to other kinds of project aimed at improving housing, living conditions and basic service provision (Hardoy and Satterthwaite, 1991; UNCHS, 1991). While there is some evidence of certain development assistance agencies increasing their interest in urban problems, sectoral priorities within large agencies rarely change rapidly. In addition, the institutional structure of most development assistance agencies constrains a greater priority to basic needs projects, especially small-scale, community-based projects.

Legal framework

A third characteristic which will continue to shape most Third World cities is legal and institutional barriers which inhibit poorer groups earning an income, acquiring or building a house and acquiring a loan to permit this, and obtaining basic infrastructure and services. The fact that most neighbourhoods in major cities have been built illegally on illegally occupied or subdivided land deters governments from providing infrastructure and services to their inhabitants, since such provision would imply some legal recognition of their right to be there. The inertia and conservative bias built into laws regarding private property, as they are presently constituted, have the effect of pricing poorer groups out of the legal land and housing market.

Low incomes

A fourth characteristic will be a large group of people unable to earn sufficient income to allow them to meet their basic needs adequately. Many will have regular employment; their problem is simply that their income is insufficient. Others will have sources of income which fluctuate and they need additional work at certain times. Others will have little possibility of work. Two consequences are worth highlighting. The first is the health burden suffered by such people who cannot afford adequate health care or housing with the piped water and provision for sanitation and personal hygiene which prevents so much ill health. The second is the implications for households and their children. In such circumstances, it is common for all adult members of a household and many children to undertake some form of income earning – however poor the return in terms of income per hour worked. The continual struggle for survival places very large strains on all those concerned, and on interpersonal relationships. This is a major factor in creating the problem of street children – both in the sense of children working on the street to earn income to contribute to their household and children who have left (or been expelled from) their home and live and work on the street.

Concentration of population growth and poverty

A fifth characteristic present in cities whose populations continue to grow rapidly will be a concentration of poorer groups on the city periphery – as has generally been the case in recent decades. Where the government of the urban area is divided into separate boroughs or municipalities (as is the case with most major cities), the highest rates of population growth and the highest concentrations of poor people will be found in the peripheral boroughs or municipalities which are also generally the weakest economically, politically and technically. If there is no mechanism for redistributing revenues from richer to poorer municipalities, or greater support for poorer municipalities from higher levels of government, problems within larger urban centres will be concentrated in the peripheral areas.

WHO WILL BUILD AND FINANCE THE FUTURE CITY?

To a large extent, the future city will be planned, financed, built and shaped by people with low incomes: garbage collectors or scavengers, shoemakers, pedlars, those making clothes, foods and crafts in their homes, maids, low-paid government clerks, office messengers and drivers, low-paid factory workers, shoeshiners, market sellers, and so on. These people provide the cheap labour and cheap goods and services on which much of the city's economy depends. The city's expansion will be influenced by where such people can obtain land on which to organize the construction of their houses – either through illegal occupation or through negotiation with landowners, developers or those who traditionally allocate rights to occupy land. At present, most of these people are excluded from legal land and housing markets, legal health services and, very often, legal markets for water.

Much of this future city will be financed by residents' savings, informal loans and self-help efforts in building, maintaining or expanding their dwellings. Employment patterns, houses and settlements will reveal the inventiveness, resilience and ingenuity of the hundreds of millions of poor people whose main skills are their capacity to survive under very difficult circumstances.

Unless severely constrained by government repression, community organizations formed by low-income groups will continue to be among the most important and active groups shaping the city, especially in settlements where a high proportion of inhabitants feel they can benefit from working with and through such organizations. These organizations will take many different forms, reflecting the particular priorities of different groups. For instance, tenant organizations seeking improved security or better terms from landlords will have different priorities from squatter organizations seeking basic services or negotiating for legal tenure. The scale and nature of their role will be much influenced by official attitudes; and where official bodies support their work, they can take a central role in organizing the design and implementation of improvements to infrastructure and services and the quality of the living environment. In democratic societies, they often take on overtly political roles – mobilizing support for particular parties or candidates.

Women from all social groups are likely to acquire more explicit political and professional roles, and their economic roles will become more visible. This trend has been evident for some time, although taking very different forms in different nations and cultures. Part of this is due to the strategies for survival of poorer groups in urban areas which have forced women to take on additional income-earning responsibilities, while also retaining their more traditional roles of household management and child rearing. It is also common to find a high proportion of women-headed households in low-income settlements with their households dependent on the woman's income-earning capacity (Moser and Peake, 1987). Part of the change is also due to women challenging their exclusion from jobs and roles traditionally dominated by men. There are many examples of women becoming increasingly active politically within poor urban communities, even if men remain the 'official' representatives (see e.g. Moser, 1987).

Apart from some downtown areas in the more prosperous cities, urban centres will grow horizontally, not vertically, with most buildings being one or at most two storeys. Homes and neighbourhoods built informally or illegally by an incremental building process with ambig- uous tenure and limited capital do not provide the basis for multi-storey buildings. Some of the housing in older or better-established low- income settlements can be developed to two or three storeys, and the incentives to do so will be greater in areas which are relatively well located within the city.

Local governments will inevitably be a significant influence on the future city – for what they do (or do not do) and for what they encourage or repress. At worst, they can be a negative influence, as in the many instances of municipal governments that have repressed community organizations, evicted those living in illegal settlements, refused resources to programmes which meet poorer groups' needs and concentrated available resources on major road programmes and other investments to benefit a small élite. It is more common for them to be a less active influence because their powers and resources are so limited.

THE FUTURE CITY WITHOUT CHANGED POLICIES

It is possible to predict some characteristics of the future city assuming no changes in the attitudes and policies of governments, simply by extrapolating current trends into the future. This allows a consideration of what the future city may imply for the urban citizens and for urban sustainability. Without changes in the attitudes and policies of govern- ments, the urban future for tens of millions of people will be one of constant insecurity. In cities with rapidly growing economies, increasing numbers of poor people will face forced eviction from their dwellings. Many poorer groups who developed their homes on illegally occupied or subdivided land on what was the urban periphery when they moved there now find that, with rapid city expansion, their land has become more valuable and is in demand for commercial or industrial develop- ment or public works. In many cities, relatively central districts which developed as locations for cheap tenements or boarding houses are now being redeveloped and the poorer groups living there are being expelled or under threat of expulsion.

The nature of the political system will have a major influence on whether poorer groups living as tenants, squatters or owners of illegal subdivisions can retain their homes in the face of such pressures or influence a compromise so they obtain a level of compensation which allows them to find alternative accommodation. Over the last twenty to thirty years, it has generally been non-democratic governments which have implemented the largest eviction programmes with the least concern for the welfare of those evicted. The example of Seoul is an illustration of what can happen within a system of government which gives little consideration to the needs and rights of poorer groups; some 5 million people were forcibly evicted over the last three decades to accommodate the redevelopments which were part of South Korea's remarkable economic transformation (Asian Coalition for Housing Rights, 1989).

As a consequence of evictions and high land prices, increasing numbers of city dwellers will live on sites ill suited to housing. Cities will increasingly be made up of settlements built on dangerous sites, continuing the long-established trends noted already whereby poorer groups illegally occupy or purchase land and develop housing on steep hillsides, around solid waste dumps, beside open drains or in industrial areas subject to high levels of pollution.

There will be an increase in the number of people suffering from diseases relating to poor, overcrowded and contaminated living environments. Combined with inadequate incomes (and inadequate nutritional intakes), this means an increase in the number suffering from the malnutrition-infection complex with its high levels of disease, disablement and premature death. The increase will largely be the result of the growing number of people living in settlements without adequate water supply, sanitation, drainage, health care and emergency life-saving services. It will be exacerbated by growth in overcrowded tenements or boarding houses as a result of increased competition among poorer groups for cheap rental accommodation within easy reach of jobs or income sources.

In many urban centres, current levels of service provision are likely to deteriorate, especially where economies are stagnant. Most agencies involved in running or maintaining infrastructure and services lack the resources to maintain them. Constrained national budgets imply a postponement of new investments in city infrastructure and no expansion in the provision of basic services. They usually imply little or no investment in maintenance – and this is reflected in the deterioration of bus and train services, in roads and public buildings.

People's health will suffer not only from inadequate and unsafe water but also from inadequate or lack of provision for sanitation, drainage, garbage collection, curative and preventive health care and measures to control disease vectors. Table 5.2 outlines the many diseases associated with water and gives estimates of the morbidity and mortality for which they are responsible. Diseases arising from the ingestion of pathogens in contaminated food and water represent the communicable diseases

Table 5.2: Examples of the main water-related infections with estimates of morbidity, mortality and population at risk

Disease		Morbidity	Mortality	Population
Common name	*Scientific name*		*(no of deaths/year)*	*at risk*
(1) *Waterborne* (and water-washed; also food-borne where indicated by *)				
Cholera	Cholera	More than 300,000	More than 3,000	
Diarrhoeal diseases	This group includes salmonellosis*, shigellosis*, Campylobacter, *E. coli*, rota-virus, amoebiasis* and giardiasis*	700 million or more infected each year	More than 5 million	More than 2,000 million
Enteric fevers	Paratyphoid Typhoid	500,000 cases; 1 million infections (1977–8)	25,000	
Infective jaundice Pinworm	Hepatitis 'A'* Enterobiasis			
Polio	Poliomyelitis	204,000 (1990)	25,000	
Roundworm	Ascariasis	800–1,000 million cases; 1 million cases of disease	20,000	
Leptospirosis Whipworm	Trichuriasis			
(2) *Water-washed*				
Skin and eye infections				
Scabies	Scabies			
School sores	Impetigo			
Trachoma	Trachoma	6–9 million people blind		500 million
Leishmaniasis	Leishmaniasis	12 million infected; 400,000 new infections/year		350 million
Others				
Relapsing fever	Relapsing fever			
Typhus	Rickettsial diseases			
(3) *Water-Based*				
Penetrating skin				
Bilharzia	Schistosomiasis	200 million	Over 200,000	500-600 million
Ingested				
Guinea worm	Dracunculiasis	Over 10 million		Over 100 million
(4) *Water-Related Insect Vector*				
Biting near water				
Sleeping sickness	African trypanosomiasis	20,000 new cases annually (thought to be an underestimate)		50 million
Breeding in water				
Filaria	Filariasis (lymphatic)	90 million		900 million
Malaria	Malaria	267 million (107 million clinical cases)	1–2 million (three-quarters of children under 5)	2,100 million
River blindness	Onchocerciasis	18 million (over 300,000 blind)		85–90 million
Yellow fever	Yellow fever	10–25,000		
Dengue; breakbone fever	Dengue fever	30–60 million infected every year		

Note
Gaps in table due to insufficient data.
Source: Based on WHO (1992); derived from Cairncross and Feachem (1983) and White, Bradley and White (1972). Figures for morbidity, mortality and population at risk from WHO (1990).

with the largest health impact worldwide (WHO, 1992). More than 5 million people die each year from diarrhoeal diseases in Africa, Asia and Latin America. The cholera epidemic which began in Peru in January 1991 and which has now spread to several other Latin American nations with over 300,000 reported cases and over 3,000 deaths is a reminder of the speed with which certain water-borne or water-washed infections can spread – although it is also forgotten that cholera remains a significant cause of death in many African and several Asian nations (ibid.).

Malaria remains one of the most significant causes of death in many urban districts, especially where there is poor drainage and pools of water provide breeding grounds for the anopheline mosquito. There are also hundreds of millions of people in urban area of the Third World who suffer from diseases associated with contaminated water or inadequate sanitation which rarely kill – for instance, intestinal worms, trachoma, scabies, filariasis and dengue fever. Certain diseases traditionally associated with rural areas, such as the debilitating parasitic disease American trypanosomiasis (Chagas' disease) and schistosomiasis are becoming increasingly common in urban areas, as infected rural people move there (Gomes Pereira, 1981; WHO, 1992).

To the diseases associated with contaminated food and water must be added those associated with overcrowding, high levels of air and water pollution and exposure in work places to toxic chemicals and other health hazards. Some 5 million people die annually from acute bacterial and viral respiratory infections and tuberculosis (WHO, 1992); tuberculosis accounts for some 3 million of these deaths (virtually all of them in the Third World), and overcrowding and malnutrition (both underpinned by inadequate incomes) are major contributors. One important (and often overlooked) problem of urban air pollution arises from the use of biomass fuels or coal on open fires or in inadequately vented stoves. The indoor air pollution they cause contributes to serious respiratory problems for tens of millions of urban households; in certain cities, they are also a major cause of outdoor air pollution (CSE, 1982; Smil, 1984). Overcrowding is associated with many diseases and physical hazards, including household accidents and airborne infections whose transmission is increased by people's close proximity to each other – not only tuberculosis but also influenza, meningitis and many respiratory infections. There are also the chemical pathogens introduced into the environment by human activities. We know very little about the long-term health consequences of the concentration and mix of air pollutants which is now common in many Third World cities, and the next twenty to thirty years may show that the health impact has been greatly underestimated. Few urban governments in the Third World have adequate provision to control the dumping of toxic or hazardous wastes (Leonard and Morell, 1981; WHO, 1992).

Most Third World cities of the 1990s will be cities of young people, as children, adolescents and young adults will make up most of the population. Many children will leave school early to work; most will not have completed primary school. The contribution that even small children working for very low returns (and often under highly exploitative conditions) can make to household income is often of great importance for survival. Western commentators sometimes forget that this was also common practice in the richest nations little more than a century ago (see e.g. Hibbert, 1980). Without major changes in government policies towards support for low-income households, many children will abandon their homes and live on their own in the city streets, threatened by the many forms of violence and exploitation.

Cities will become increasingly segregated: the poor on the worst-quality, worst-served and often worst-located sites, with richer groups in the best-located, best-quality, best-serviced locations. Cities' physical growth will be defined by where poorer groups can invade or illegally negotiate for land. This will produce a pattern of urban development which makes the provision of basic services increasingly costly. One of the great advantages of a planned urban expansion is the large cost savings in the provision of infrastructure and services. New housing developments or commercial sites located to take advantage of existing roads, drains, water mains and sewers result in major cost savings in the provision of these services. The uncontrolled process of urban expansion creates the opposite of this: large areas of land left undeveloped because the owners benefit from rising values (partly created by public investments) and a patchwork of illegal settlements wherever poorer groups have found it possible to settle.

There will be an ever-increasing expansion of the urban landscape, visually monotonous because it is characterized by ever-expanding numbers of illegal dwellings. Very little land will be allocated to public space, for secure and easily supervised places where children can play, for recreation or for culture. A failure today to ensure that each neighbourhood has open space for recreation and leisure and safe places for children to play, away from dangerous streets, means a legacy for the future of many children disabled by accidents and a greater number whose potential has been diminished by the lack of stimulus during their early development (Hughes, 1990). Once an area is built up, it is very difficult to remedy such shortages. Natural landscapes and historic districts and buildings, once destroyed, cannot be recreated.

URBAN SUSTAINABILITY

In terms of sustainability, without changes in direction, larger cities in the Third World will have increasingly serious environmental impacts on their wider region and develop with levels of resource use and waste generation which will prove increasingly unsustainable. A failure of the market to respond to increasing levels of waste and of governments to adopt or implement pollution controls and to install and operate adequate systems for sanitation and solid waste collection will mean ever-increasing pollution loads in local water bodies. A failure by public authorities to encourage water conservation and to instigate a realistic pricing structure will put increasing strains on water authorities' capacity to meet rising demands and to extend piped water to those inadequately served. Many large cities are already facing serious constraints on increasing supplies and have long drawn on aquifers beyond their rate of natural recharge.

Among the richer cities, a failure to restrict the use of private automobiles (including inadequate provision for alternatives to their use) implies serious environmental impacts at different levels: from increasing air pollution loads and traffic congestion to increased oil import bills for the national economy and increased greenhouse gas emissions. City authorities with responsibilities for solid waste collection and management will face increasingly severe cost problems, especially if they serve the poorer neighbourhoods scattered around the urban periphery. The larger the city, the more difficult it is to find a site for dumping solid wastes; and the more distant the site from the city, the greater the cost.

A final characteristic worth highlighting in the urban future without changed government policies is social instability. In cities where the above trends continue, and which are ruled from above with the poor majority segregated in unserviced illegal settlements or deteriorating and overcrowded rented accommodation, the society is likely to become increasingly violent and unstable. A failure today to develop competent representative local government which can work with community organizations has damaging long-term consequences. If the habits of democracy and participation become lost, they must be relearned, and this takes time. In many of the Third World nations which over the last decade returned to democratic forms of government, citizen expectations exceed government capacities to deliver improvements. In many nations, this is in turn linked to debt burdens and to the constraints on increasing export earnings imposed by the trade barriers around the world's richest consumer markets. These are structural constraints for Third World economies which have serious implications for the social and political stability of the future city.

AN ALTERNATIVE URBAN FUTURE

For over forty years, certain observers of urban developments have pointed to the dynamism shown by people who organize the occupation of land illegally, who build their housing there, who organize its defence against attempts to evict them, who mobilize to negotiate for secure tenure and for some public provision of infrastructure and services.[6] It is within an informal and largely illegal market for real estate, building materials and builders that most new urban neighbourhoods have developed and a high proportion of new employment has been created by their inhabitants. In recent years, more governments have shown greater tolerance of these activities and, in some instances, have provided some support. But what is lacking in virtually all these instances is a realistic public framework.

It is possible to conceive of an alternative urban future where the central role for government is to support individual and community initiatives within all urban centres and to ensure that all urban dwellers have access to essential infrastructure and services. There are dozens of case studies of successful community-based projects which show how houses can be built or improved and infrastructure and services provided at low cost – often with good cost recovery.[7] What is needed above all is government support for a vast multiplication of such successful projects. The lessons coming from the leaders of successful community-based projects is that such projects cannot simply be 'scaled up'. It is not the aim of these community leaders to replicate them elsewhere. They are also aware that the success has largely been due to making best use of existing resources and working with existing institutions within a particular context. This makes it difficult to repeat them in different cities or districts where circumstances differ.

What we learn from successful projects is that there are certain preconditions which allowed them to take place. These include the possibility for low-income groups to organize; they usually include technical help from outside agencies and collaboration between community organizations and local governments (or other agencies) in the installation of infrastructure and services. The lessons which must be sought from projects judged by their beneficiaries to be a success are the pre-conditions which would allow hundreds of other small-scale local 'success stories' to develop – each rooted in its own particular context, addressing the priorities of the local populations and making best use of local resources.

It is obvious that hundreds of local 'success stories' will require that poorer groups can obtain access to land, finance and materials. One key role for public authorities is to ensure a great increase in supply and a reduction in cost for all the components of an adequate house, including cheap and well-located sites, cheap building materials and advice available to low-income groups on how to build healthy and safe houses at minimum cost. Increasing the supply and reducing the cost of land sites for low-income groups' housing is a high priority – although politically often the most difficult.

There is a critical need to ensure that there are *local* institutions from which community organizations can obtain loans and technical advice for this kind of programme. Here, the role of local non-government organizations is often important. NGOs can serve as technical advisers to community organizations, as has been documented in many case studies.[8] They could also act as supervisors of loans or credits. Many Third World NGOs have demonstrated new ways of working with low-income groups and their community organizations.[9] These are helping to develop new breeds of professionals; within the alternative urban future, there is less of a role for traditional planners and technocrats, but a great demand for social agents who work with community organizations and their leaders and for new types of project managers, architects, medical personnel, environmentalists, lawyers and sanitary engineers. They will be skilled at managing programmes and projects which make best possible use of local knowledge, skills and enthusiasm and rely little or not at all on imported knowledge, machinery and skilled personnel.

Another important aspect of the alternative urban future is public authorities with the power and the motivation to control private market abuses which have serious negative consequences for the environment and the health of the population. This includes enforcing pollution control and also includes providing broad physical guidelines for urban expansion to avoid many of the problems associated with uncontrolled urban expansion noted earlier. It also includes considerable flexibility in any system of incentives and making available resources to individuals and community organizations in the building of homes and neighbourhoods.

For instance, different households will have differing preferences as to the extent to which they have the time, resources and skills to build their own dwellings (and reduce costs by doing so). There is often an assumption that poorer households have the time to build their own houses, yet many adults work such long hours that this is not the case. This is especially the case for women-headed households, since the women have responsibility for income, child rearing and household management and thus have obvious difficulties finding time to contribute to house construction (Falu and Curutchet, 1991). Different households will also have differing preferences as to the size of the dwelling and its design; poorer households with several children are often allocated 'low-cost' houses or serviced sites which are too small and ill designed in regard to the size and composition of the family (ibid.). The extent to which low-income housing programmes misunderstand the particular needs of women have been well documented (ibid.; Moser and Peake, 1987).

An alternative urban future which seeks to meet development needs must include a strong commitment to health. Three components of this commitment are worth stressing. *First*, a 'safety net' which guarantees all urban dwellers sufficient nutritional intake and health care – with special provision for particularly vulnerable groups (for instance, pregnant and lactating women, infants and young children). The means by which this safety net is put in place will vary according to local circumstances; but it is now clear that the costs of a combination of specific health and nutritional interventions aimed at vulnerable groups, and public works programmes which provide a minimum income to those unable to find income elsewhere, need not be expensive.

Second, a strong focus on prevention. The safeguards to human health arising from safe and sufficient water, provision for sanitation, drainage and garbage collection, paved roads, safe settlement sites and the prevention aspects of primary health care are far more important for health than a good curative system. Such safeguards supported by adequately funded primary health care services can radically improve health (World Bank, 1990). Table 5.3 provides some examples of the potential reduction in morbidity from different diseases as a result of improvements in the quantity and quality of water and sanitation.

Third, a strong participatory element in shelter programmes and service provision so that low-income groups and their community organizations can influence the scale and nature of health interventions. Health centres cannot be effective if they are not used, and there are many examples of such centres with inappropriate working hours (for instance, not open before or after working hours), inappropriate locations and professional attitudes which discourage poorer groups from using them. In addition, many health centres give insufficient attention to community outreach including the involvement of the

Table 5.3 Potential reductions in morbidity for different diseases as a result of improvements in water and sanitation

Diseases	Projected reduction in morbidity (%)
Cholera, typhoid, leptospirosis, scabies, guinea worm infection	80–100
Trachoma, conjunctivitis, yaws, schistosomiasis	60–70
Tularaemia, paratyphoid, bacillary dysentery, amoebic dysentery, gastroenteritis, louse-borne diseases, diarrhoeal diseases, ascariasis, skin infections	40–50

Source: WHO (1986).

inhabitants in health service management and in community liaison, working with schools in immunization programmes and health education and home visits.

This raises the question of the political structure needed to implement an alternative urban future. Government support for a participatory 'bottom-up' approach at local level can hardly be implemented by a non-representative 'top-down' city or national government. The achievement of an alternative urban future depends on the extent to which poorer groups are able (or allowed) to organize not only within their district but also to become a greater political force within the city and the nation. Unless the needs of the poor majority acquire much greater influence within local and national government, public sector investments financed by governments, banks and international development institutions will continue to have little relevance to their needs. Governments (and aid agencies) will continue to give priority to a few major projects and concentrate scarce resources on major highways, industrial estates, 'prestige' buildings, airports and metro systems; their list of priorities bears little resemblance to those of most citizens. Poorer citizens' right to vote and so to influence new developments in their own city (and neighbourhood) is perhaps the only effective check against the exclusion of their needs in government decisions. But the possibilities open to more democratic local governments will be limited unless there are substantial increases in their power and the resources available to them.

Box 5.1 illustrates three different ways of spending US$20 million to improve poorer groups' housing and living conditions. Option 1 was the most common approach during the 1960s and part of the 1970s; its high cost and narrow impact are evident. Option 2 represents one of the most common 'new' approaches of the last twenty years; its limitations are also all too evident. Option 3 represents a far more effective model and illustrates this alternative urban policy; its effectiveness has been proven by hundreds of small projects implemented by community organizations with the help of NGOs or church groups over the last thirty years. What makes Option 3 unusual is the support it receives from local government in ways which catalyse and support hundreds of small-scale locally based actions.

Box 5.1: Different options for government spending US$20 million on improving housing and living environments

Option 1: US$20 million is spent on the construction of two-bedroom 'low-cost' housing units for 'low-income groups'. The cost of each unit is some US$10,000, once the land has been purchased, the site prepared, the contractor paid for building the units and the infrastructure and the units allocated. Thus, 2,000 households or 12,000 people receive a good-quality house – if we assume that on average there are six persons per household. Cost recovery would be difficult if these were from among the poorer households.

Option 2: US$20 million is spent on a serviced site project, so that more households can be reached than in public housing projects. Knowing that poorer households need to live close to the main centres of employment, a relatively central site was purchased for US$12 million with the other US$8 million spent on site preparation and installing infrastructure and services. At a cost of US$2,000 per plot, 10,000 households (or 60,000 people) could benefit. It would be easier to recover some costs than in the public housing project, but for the poorer households US$2,000 for a site on top of the cost of having to construct their own house would be too much.

Option 3: Local government makes available to any residents' organization formed by the majority of the inhabitants of an area the sum of US$100,000 for site improvements. These residents' organizations have considerable flexibility as to how they choose to spend these funds and who they turn to for technical advice. For instance, they can use local NGOs for technical advice, as long as certain basic standards are met. Although what can be achieved with such a sum will vary greatly depending on site characteristics, local costs and the extent to which residents contribute their skills and labour free, within an area with 500

---

households it should be possible to 'reblock' the site to allow better access roads and to pave them and also to greatly improve site drainage, water supply and sanitation. Support could be given to local artisans to fabricate the materials, fixtures and fittings which are most cheaply and effectively made on site – for instance, a carpenters' co-operative to make doors and windows, or cheap building block fabrication. Of the US$100,000, an average of US$150 is spent per household on improved infrastructure and services, with US$10,000 spent on technical advice and US$15,000 on support for local businesses. The 'reblocking' of the site also frees sufficient land to allow 50 more housing plots to be developed within the existing site or on adjacent land as yet undeveloped, and the cost of providing these with infrastructure and services and of building a community health centre is paid for by selling them.

With US$100,000 provided to 150 community organizations with an average of 500 households (3,000 people) the total cost was US$15 million and the whole programme reached 150 × 3,000 people, that is, 450,000 people. Since an average of 50 new housing plots were produced in each reblocking, not only did 450,000 people benefit from improved housing, infrastructure and services but 7,500 new plots with services were developed and new health centres constructed in each site. The possibility of cost recovery was much better than for Options 1 and 2 since most households could afford to pay US$200 – or take out a loan which allowed repayment over a few years. Spending US$15 million in this way still left US$5 million from the original US$20 million which could be used to improve some city-wide service – for instance, training community health workers to run health clinics and health campaigns in each settlement.

Source: Hardoy and Satterthwaite (1989).

Consider these options in the context of a city of one million inhabitants, growing at 5 per cent a year. Each would take several years to implement. Options 1 and 2 would do nothing to improve conditions in existing settlements. Option 1 would not produce sufficient new housing for one year's growth in population, and Option 2's 10,000 units would only just do so. Option 3 would reach nearly half the city's population with improved infrastructure and services and contribute much more than the other options to employment creation. It would support the development of local NGOs as centres of advice and support for low-income organizations and would create almost as many new units as Option 2. Furthermore, US$5 million would be left for investment in improving some city-wide service, and prospects for cost recovery would be much better than for the other two options.

Approaches like those outlined in Option 3 in part save money because local residents contribute labour free. But many poor people have little or no 'free time' to contribute because of very long working hours. Governments and international agencies may describe them as unemployed or underemployed because they have no registered employment; but in reality, most work long hours, six or seven days a week. But approaches like those outlined in Option 3 also mean major savings in the time of architects, planners, surveyors and other expensive professionals who would otherwise be involved in community-level consultations to resolve such issues as moving certain houses out of the way of access roads and collecting funds from households to pay for the improvements. There are also major savings as specialized equipment and materials can be used to install not only piped water but also sanitation, drainage and all-weather roads and paths. The match between what is provided and capacity to pay is much improved when local community organizations are fully involved in such decisions.

New approaches will also demand changes among professionals and researchers in international organizations. Outside professionals often misunderstand community needs and priorities. Many also advocate urban policies to slow urban growth or change the spatial distribution of urban development, with little understanding of the particular social, economic and political factors which drive urbanization within any nation or region, or the extreme cost to poor people if such policies were actually implemented. Many repressive, regressive policies have been advocated (and sometimes implemented) under the heading of 'managing urban development'. Virtually all are based on inaccurate stereotypes of the poor being passive and ignorant.

RESOURCE IMPLICATIONS OF THE ALTERNATIVE URBAN FUTURE

The alternative future outlined above should better meet the needs of urban inhabitants – but is it likely to prove more sustainable in terms of resource use and waste generation? At first sight, it might seem contradictory. For instance, guaranteeing all urban citizens adequate supplies of piped water might increase the demand for fresh water beyond the sustainable yield from exploiting water sources nearby.

However, this alternative future capitalizes on the frugal and efficient resource use evident among poorer groups. While ensuring that their needs are met, it does not increase the use of resources and the generation of wastes to unsustainable levels. Indeed, there are many examples of community-based initiatives to improve water supply, sanitation, housing or garbage collection which contribute much towards sustainability.

Improving the housing and living environment of poor groups can also bring major benefits in terms of lessening environmental degradation. Cities with comprehensive provision for sewers and storm drains concentrate the waste waters so these can be treated, prior to disposal into rivers, lakes or the sea. This greatly lowers water pollution since in cities without sewers and drains much of the human excreta finds its way into the water bodies either through open drains or through runoff. Cities with garbage collection services covering all households and businesses have much reduced levels of non-point source water pollution[10] than those where such services are lacking – and of course have higher-quality living and working environments in the city itself. Effective controls on air and water pollution for road vehicles, power stations and industries can also mean improved health and environment within the city and reduced environmental degradation in the wider region.

Planning, guiding and regulating the built environment – building materials production, building construction, building design and performance, site and settlement planning, and so on – has a considerable role in helping to limit fossil fuel combustion and thus the scale of carbon dioxide input into the atmosphere, quite apart from the other health and environmental benefits of reduced fossil fuel use. Most fossil fuel combustion (the major contributor to global warming) is to heat or cool buildings and to move people and goods within and between settlements. The potential contribution to reduced fuel use of better building design and construction, transport planning and settlement planning is obvious.

Cities' water supplies can usually be increased very considerably by encouraging conservation in water-intensive industries, by ensuring water consumers pay realistic prices for water and by better maintenance and leakage prevention in existing water distribution systems. Water losses within urban distribution systems continue to be very high, especially in Third World cities. A survey in 1986 of fifteen large Latin American cities found that unaccounted-for water ranged from 39 to 67 per cent (Hueb, 1986), around half of which was due to water loss. In Geneva, unaccounted-for water was estimated at only 13 per cent in 1989. In the city of São Paulo, an intensive programme to reduce water losses in water distribution systems reduced the unaccounted-for water from 36 per cent in 1977 to 27 per cent in 1982; the savings allowed for an increase of about 46 per cent in the number of house connections without the need to increase water production (Yassuda, Kochen and Borba, 1981).

In addition, in regions where water resources are short, a water management plan at the regional level can often free water resources for priority uses within a city. Water supply for domestic and municipal use is usually only a small proportion of total freshwater withdrawals. Most freshwater withdrawal is for agriculture, especially irrigated agriculture.

Garbage collection is another service which brings important benefits to poorer households and major reductions in land and water pollution. This is a service whose importance for health rises as population density rises, and as household incomes grow (with a corresponding increase in the volume of waste material). While the typical Northern-type garbage collection and disposal service is relatively expensive, there are examples of alternative approaches servicing relatively poor households at per capita costs they can afford (see e.g Cuentro and Gadji, 1990).

In recent years, there have been four important changes in the attitude among many professionals to the collection and processing of garbage (Cointreau, 1982). The *first* is the recognition of the need to develop local solutions which match local needs and possibilities. Conditions vary greatly from city to city in the scale and type of refuse generation, the amount residents can afford to pay for refuse collection, local possibilities for recycling part of the refuse, the availability of land sites for city dumps, the resources at the disposal of local authorities for the management of garbage disposal and other factors. This usually implies solutions very different from those taught to engineers whose training is overwhelmingly based on Western models and precedents (Flintoff, 1976). A *second* change, linked to this, is the need to reconcile a much more effective system to remove garbage (especially in poorer communities) with very limited budgets. The poorer, more distant, more inaccessible settlements whose inhabitants have the least capacity to pay are usually those in most need of better services. A *third* change is the recognition that district- or neighbourhood-level garbage collection schemes, devised and managed with the residents, are often the cheapest and most effective solution. This is especially the case when there is also reclamation of materials and recycling of part of the waste (for instance, use of organic wastes for making compost). This leads not only to additional employment but also to cost savings, since a reduction in the volume of waste needing to be collected and transported to a waste dump means a reduction in one of the major costs in a garbage collection service (Cuentro and Gadji, 1990). A *fourth* change is the recognition that scavengers, rag pickers and recycling businesses can be made an important component within garbage management systems but they need a supportive framework – perhaps most especially in the provision of services to address their health problems (Furedy, 1989 and 1990).

Another change in attitude needed among professionals is the recognition of the complementarities between garbage collection and other improvements in infrastructure and services. For instance, paving roads to and within peripheral settlements can cheapen garbage collection costs, while improved garbage collection ensures that drainage systems work better and lessens water pollution.

The economic constraints on the improvement of water supplies, sanitation and the collection and disposal of garbage for those inadequately served or not served at all are certainly overstated. Local solutions worked out in partnership between local authorities and local communities which are rooted in the residents' priorities and make optimum use of local resources can often improve housing and living conditions at much lower costs than conventional systems. In many instances, most or all the costs can be recovered from user charges (see e.g. Cairncross, 1990, on water supply, and Sinnatamby, 1990, on sanitation). The major constraint on their implementation is far more to do with the limited capacity of local government. One returns to the fact that most municipal governments lack the trained personnel and the financial base and autonomy to provide the needed investments. This weakness of local governments also makes other needed changes difficult to implement – from the enforcement of environmental legislation to the management of solid waste sites and improvement of traffic management.

A priority to meeting the transport needs of poorer groups can also promote more sustainable resource use. Poor groups suffer from the congestion, accidents and air pollution which result from widespread use of private automobiles; these costs are rarely recouped through taxes and fees paid by private automobile users. Private automobiles are one of the major sources of air pollution within cities. Higher charges on private road vehicles and on gasoline can both reduce air pollution and fossil fuel use and also help to fund improvements to public transport. Incentives can also be used to reduce and in the long term phase out the use of lead additives in petrol; there are increasing worries about the impact of lead pollution on children's mental development (see e.g. USAID, 1990, on the possible impact of lead on child health and development in Bangkok). Efficient public transport, combined with controls on the use of private automobiles in city centres (especially during peak periods), can encourage substantial shifts in consumer preferences towards public transport. Improved public transport also brings substantial benefits to poorer groups who have to rely on public transport. A variety of measures can both enhance city environments and encourage more people to walk or bicycle.

CONCLUSIONS

The most important resource for the future city is the knowledge, ingenuity and organizational capacity of citizens themselves. Much could be achieved in terms of the direct improvement of living conditions and of services if governments no longer deemed illegal and repressed but instead supported the vast range of individual, household and community-based actions which are the most dynamic force within most cities. This great range of activities could be helped and co-ordinated by government actions to guarantee the availability of essential resources: land sites, technical advice, infrastructure networks and basic services. Such an approach also demands a legal system to protect the human environment from contamination by industries and to protect individuals from exploitation by employers, landlords and landowners. This approach cannot solve more fundamental problems which are rooted in unequal distribution of wealth and power both within nations and internationally. But it can support the efforts of the true builders of their cities. With government support adapted to each culture and society, it would help promote more effective responses to contemporary problems in Third World cities.

NOTES

Special thanks to Jo Burgess and to Johan Holmberg for their comments on an earlier draft.

1 Most of the literature on sustainable development concentrates on 'sustainability', not sustainability and development; see Mitlin (1992).
2 A small proportion of the urban centres in the Third World do have high levels of automobiles relative to populations; some have higher ratios of automobiles to population than many cities in the North. But an average figure for per capita fuel consumption taken across all urban centres would produce a much lower figure than that for urban centres in the North. However, governments in the North have taken actions to limit certain air pollutants which can arise from automobile exhausts (e.g. through the use of catalytic converters and the promotion of petrol without lead additives) and some have also encouraged the use of more fuel-efficient cars.

3 See e.g. Cochrane (1983), Stren and White (1989), Clichevsky *et al.* (1990), Bubba and Lamba (1991) and the special issue of *Environment and Urbanization* on local government, vol. 3, no. 1, 1991.

4 This was a particularly striking finding from an analysis of inter-census growth rates for all urban centres with over 10,000 inhabitants in the last census for all of Latin America for all available censuses since 1850 undertaken by IIED-America Latina and IIED. Similar analyses undertaken for a selected group of African and Asian nations also supported this.

5 This assumption underlies the trends and projections in the United Nations Population Division's regular statistical, compendia on world urban statistics, and most publications about urban change in the Third World do not question this.

6 See e.g. Matos Mar (1962), Abrams (1964), Turner (1966 and 1976) and Mangin (1967).

7 See Turner (1976), SINA (1988), Turner (1988) and Hardoy and Satterthwaite (1989).

8 See UNCHS (1987), SINA (1988), Turner (1988) and Conroy and Litvinoff (1988).

9 See e.g. Harth Deneke and Silva (1982), Stein (1989), SPARC (1990) and Hardoy, Hardoy and Schusterman (1991).

10 Water pollution from wastes not released at specific identifiable (point) sources; in this instance, mainly from garbage washed into water bodies by storm and surface runoff.

REFERENCES AND BIBLIOGRAPHY

Abrams, Charles, 1964. *Man's Struggle for Shelter in an Urbanizing World*, MIT Press Cambridge, Mass.

Asian Coalition for Housing Rights, 1989. 'Evictions in Seoul, South Korea', *Environment and Urbanization*, 1, 1, April, pp. 89–94.

Bubba, Ndinda and Lamba, Davinder, 1991. 'Local government in Kenya' *Environment and Urbanization*, 3, 1, April, pp. 37–59.

Cairncross, Sandy, 1990. 'Water supply and the urban poor', in Jorge E. Hardoy, Sandy Cairncross and David Satterthwaite (eds), *The Poor Die Young: Housing and Health in Third World Cities*, Earthscan, London.

Caincross, Sandy and Feachem, Richard G., 1983. *Environmental Health Engineering in the Tropics – an Introductory Text,* Wiley, Chichester.

Cairncross, Sandy, Hardoy, Jorge E. and Satterthwaite, David, 1990. 'The urban context', in Jorge E. Hardoy, Sandy Cairncross and David Satterthwaite (eds), *The Poor Die Young: Housing and Health in Third World Cities,* Earthscan, London.

Clichevsy, Nora, Herzer, Hilda, Pirez, Pedro, Satterthwaite, David *et al.*, 1990. *Construcción y administracion de la ciudad Latinoamericana*, Grupo Editor Latinoamericano, Buenos Aires.

Cochrane, Glynn, 1983. *Policies for Strengthening Local Government in Developing Countries,* Staff Working Paper no. 582, World Bank, Washington, DC.

Cointreau, Sandra, 1982. *Environmental Management of Urban Solid Waste in Developing Countries,* Urban Development Technical Paper no. 5, World Bank, Washington, DC.

Conroy, Czech and Litvinoff, Miles (eds), 1988. *The Greening of Aid,* Earthscan, London.

CSE (Centre for Science and Environment), 1982. *The State of India's Environment – a Citizen's Report,* CSE, Delhi.

Cuentro, Stenio de Coura and Gadji, Dji Malla, 1990. 'The collection and management of household garbage' in Jorge E. Hardoy, Sandy Cairncross and David Satterthwaite (eds), *The Poor Die Young: Housing and Health in Third World Cities,* Earthscan, London.

Davila, Julio D., 1990. 'Mexico's urban popular movements: a conversation with Pedro Moctezuma', *Environment and Urbanization,* 2, 1, April, pp. 35–50.

Environment and Urbanization, 1991. Special issue on local government, 3, 1.

Falu, Ana and Curutchet, Mirina, 1991. 'Rehousing the urban poor: looking at women first', *Environment and Urbanization,* 3, 2, October, pp. 23–38.

Flintoff, F., 1976. *Management of Solid Wastes in Developing Countries,* WHO (SEARO), New Delhi.

Furedy, Christine, 1989. 'Social considerations in solid waste management in Asian cities', *Regional Development Dialogue,* 10, 3, Autumn.

Furedy, Christine, 1990. 'Social aspects of solid waste recovery in Asian cities', *Environmental Sanitation Reviews,* (ENSIC: Asian Institute of Technology, Bangkok), 30, December pp. 2–52.

Garza, Gustavo, 1991. 'The metropolitan character of urbanization in Mexico, 1900–1988' mimeo, April.

Gomes Pereira, Mauricio, 1981. 'Characteristics of urban mortality from Chagas' disease in Brazil's Federal District", *Bulletin of the Pan American Health Organization,* 18, 1.

Gugler, J., 1980. 'A minimum of urbanism and a maximum of ruralism: the Cuban experience', *International Journal of Urban and Regional Research,* 4, pp. 516–35.

Hamer, Andrew, 1984. 'Decentralized urban development and industrial location behaviour in São Paulo, Brazil', discussion paper, Water Supply and Urban Development Department, World Bank, Washington, DC.

Hardoy, Ana, Hardoy, Jorge E. and Schusterman, Ricardo, 1991. Building community organization: the history of a squatter settlement and its own organizations in Buenos Aires', *Environment and Urbanization,* 3, 2, October, pp. 104–20.

Hardoy, Jorge E., 1979. *Urban and Agrarian Reform in Cuba,* IDRC/SIAP Ediciones SIAP, Buenos Aires.

Hardoy, Jorge E. and Satterthwaite, David, 1986. *Small and Intermediate Urban Centres,* Hodder & Stoughton, London.

Hardoy, Jorge E. and Satterthwaite, David, 1989. *Squatter Citizen: Life in the Urban Third World,* Earthscan, London.

Hardoy, Jorge E. and Satterthwaite, David (1991. 'Environmental problems in Third World cities: a global issue ignored?', *Public Administration and Development,* 11, pp 341–61.

Harth Deneke, A. and Silva, M., 1982. 'Mutual help and progressive housing development: for what purpose? Notes on the Salvadorean experience', in Peter Ward (ed.), *Self-Help Housing: A Critique,* Mansell, London.

Hawkins, J. N., 1982. 'Shanghai: an exploratory report on food for a city', *GeoJournal,* supplementary issue.

Hibbert, Christopher, 1980. *London: A Biography of a City,* Penguin Books, London.

Hueb, J. A., 1986. *El programa de control de perdidas como estrategia para el desarrollo de institución es de agua potable e saneamiento,* Hojas de Divulgación Tecnica no. 34, CEPIS, Lima.

Hughes, Bob, 1990. 'Children's play – a forgotten right', *Environment and Urbanization,* 2, 2, October, pp. 58–64.

Kirkby, Richard, 1985. *Urbanization in China: Town and Country in a Developing Economy 1949–2000 AD,* Croom Helm, London.

Kwok, R. Yin-Wang, 1982. 'The role of small cities in Chinese urban development', *International Journal of Urban and Regional Research,* 6, 4, pp. 549–65.

Leonard, Jeffrey H. and Morell, David, 1981. 'Emergence of environmental concern in developing countries: a political perspective', *Stanford Journal of International Law,* 17, 2, pp. 281–313.

Mangin, William, 1967. 'Latin American squatter settlements; a problem and a solution', *Latin American Research Review,* 2, 3, Summer.

Matos Mar, José, 1962. 'Migración y urbanización – las barriadas Limenas: un case de integración a la vida urbana' in Philip Hauser (ed.), *La urbanizacion en America Latina,* UNESCO, Paris.

Mitlin, Diana, 1992. 'Sustainable development – guide to the literature', *Environment and Urbanization,* 4, 1, April.

Moser, Caroline O. N., 1987. 'Mobilization is women's work: struggles for infrastructure in Guayaquil, Ecuador', in Caroline O. N. Moser and Linda Peake (eds), *Women, Housing and Human Settlements,* Tavistock Publications, London and New York.

Moser, Caroline O. N. and Peake, Linda, (eds), 1987. *Women, Human Settlements and Housing,* Tavistock Publications, London and New York.

Peattie, Lisa, 1990. 'Participation: a case study of how invaders organize, negotiate and interact with government in Lima, Peru', *Environment and Urbanization,* 2, 1, April, pp. 19–30.

Renaud, Bertrand, 1981. *National Urbanization Policy in Developing Countries,* Oxford University Press for the World Bank, Oxford and New York.

SINA, 1988. *NGOs and Shelter,* Mazingira Institute, Nairobi.

Sinnatamby, Gehan, 1990. 'Low cost sanitation', in Jorge E. Hardoy, Sandy Cairncross and David Satterthwaite (eds), *The Poor Die Young: Housing and Health in Third World Cities,* Earthscan, London.

Smil, Vaclav, 1984. *The Bad Earth: Environmental Degradation in China,* M. E. Sharpe, New York.

SPARC, 1990. 'NGO profile: SPARC – developing new NGO lines', *Environment and Urbanization,* 2, 1, April, pp. 91–104.

Stein, Alfredo, 1989. 'The Tugurios of San Salvador: a place to live, work and struggle', *Environment and Urbanization,* 1, 2, October, pp. 6–15.

Stren, Richard E. and White, Rodney R. (eds), 1989. *African Cities in Crisis: Managing Rapid Urban Growth,* Westview Press, Boulder, Colo.

Turner, Bertha (ed.), 1988. *Building Community – a Third World Case Book,* Habitat International Coalition, London.

Turner, John F. C., 1966. *Uncontrolled Urban Settlements: Problems and Policies,* report for the United Nations Seminar on Urbanization, Pittsburgh, Pa.

Turner, John F. C., 1976. *Housing by People – Towards Autonomy in Building Environments,* Ideas in Progress, Marion Boyars, London.

UNCHS, 1987. *Shelter for the Homeless: The Role of Non-Governmental Organizations,* United Nations Centre for Human Settlements, Nairobi.

UNCHS, 1991. *Financial and Other Assistance Provided to and among Developing Countries for Human Settlements – Report of the Executive Director,* biennial report for the UN Commission on Human Settlements meeting in Harare, April.

United Nations, 1991. *World Urbanization Prospects 1990: Estimates and Projections of Urban and Rural Populations and of Urban Agglomerations,* ST/ESA/SER.a/121, United Nations, New York.

USAID, 1990. *Ranking Environmental Health Risks in Bangkok,* Office of Housing and Urban Programs, Washington, DC.

WCED, 1987. *Our Common Future,* (Brundtland Report) Oxford University Press, Oxford.

White, G. F., Bradley, D. J. and White, A. U., 1972. *Drawers of Water: Domestic Water Use in East Africa,* University of Chicago Press, Chicago.

WHO, 1986. *Intersectoral Action for Health,* WHO, Geneva.

WHO, 1990. *Global Estimates for Health Situation Assessment and Projections 1990,* WHO, Geneva.

WHO, 1992. *Our Planet, Our Health – Report of the WHO Commission on Health and the Environment,* WHO, Geneva.

World Bank, 1990. *World Development Report 1990,* Oxford University Press, Oxford.

World Bank, 1991. *Urban Policy and Economic Development: An Agenda for the 1990s,* World Bank, Washington, DC.

Yassuda, E. R., Kochen, J. V. and Borba, E. F., 1981. *Reduction of Losses and Costs in Water Distribution Systems through Appropriate Technology,* SABESP, São Paulo.

6 Restructuring Industry for Sustainable Development

Nick Robins and Alex Trisoglio

INTRODUCTION: THE NEED FOR AN ECO-INDUSTRIAL REVOLUTION

In the debate on how to achieve sustainable development, industry plays a paradoxical role. One the one hand, it is one of the major productive and wealth-creating sectors of society, contributing on average one-third of measured national income. However, industry is also a major polluter, both directly through its production processes and indirectly through the products it sells. The challenge for companies, governments and the public at large is, how can industry both produce products to meet needs and generate wealth in ways that do not degrade the environment or exacerbate growing global inequality? As the World Commission on Environment and Development stated in 1987: 'Industry has the power to enhance or degrade the environment; it invariably does both' (WCED, 1987).

Industry is also an elusive and ever-changing sector of the economy. Currently, the traditional division between manufacturing and services is becoming blurred as products and processes become redefined in the light of the shift to a global, information-based economy. Environmental impacts are also changing in intensity and location as some regions de-industrialize and others go through rapid industrialization. But the basic expansionary drive that has led to a sevenfold increase in manufacturing output since 1950 remains. Indeed, WCED projected a further five- to tenfold expansion of production by the time that world population stabilizes some time in the next century.

But WCED, like countless other government or business analyses of the problems related to industry and sustainability, declined to assess whether an expansion at the rate predicted was either desirable or feasible, given the accelerating depletion of natural 'capital stocks'.

Furthermore, there has been no serious attempt to pursue to its logical extent the Brundtland Report's objective of 'meeting needs' of current and future generations in the industrial context. In a world of increasing poverty and inequality, this would mean questioning the continuing concentration of industrial process and product development funding in the saturated markets of the North, which the 'green consumer' movements of Europe and North America have scarcely begun to challenge.

Since sustainable development is essentially a global concept, as far as industry is concerned it means the ability of production and consumption patterns to be universalized so that needs are met and environmental integrity guaranteed for the future. However, the dominant industrial model of the North is far from sustainable. In the USA, for example, hazardous waste generation is growing at an annual rate of 7.5 per cent, considerably more than the rate of economic growth. Energy and materials consumption levels remain excessive, although some progress towards greater efficiency was made during the 1970s, particularly in Japan. And despite considerable improvements in environmental awareness and, in some cases, performance, industry remains resistant to the restructuring that will be required, for instance, to reduce fossil fuel consumption and phase out toxic substances.

The eco-industrial revolution

Maurice Strong, the Secretary General of UNCED, has spoken of the need for an 'eco-industrial revolution'. Its purpose would be to redefine the goals of industrialization and the tools and technologies used to achieve them. This process of industrial restructuring for sustainable development would have two main priorities:

- The first priority would be to redirect corporate energies to satisfy the broader human aspects of development. This would mean refocusing product and process development to ensure that basic human needs are met on a global basis, establishing formal commitments to transparency and community access to decision-making, and collaborating in the creation of sustainable livelihoods for the growing labour force of developing countries.
- The second priority would be to maximize long-run efficiency in the use of environmental resources in the production and consumption of useful goods and services. This would involve a move to industrial ecosystems that are increasingly 'closed' in environmental terms, with increasing bias in favour of renewable or recyclable resources.

Unlike previous industrial revolutions, the restructuring needed to achieve sustainable development will require conscious and deliberate changes in corporate goals, business practice and regulatory frameworks. Sustainable development cannot be left to the market, since markets fail to internalize social and environmental costs and to reflect the full range of human choices. But neither can it be planned or driven solely by governments. Instead, both industry and governments need to become more open and accountable, and develop effective partnerships with stakeholders, whether citizens, employees or consumers. In the particular case of governments, without the active support of both industry and society, state action to promote sustainable industry will be futile. Governments need to provide an empowering framework, and within this stimulate, cajole and sometimes force a long-term shift in industrial behaviour. This will involve the application of a range of policy tools at different levels from the global to the local.

The concept of an 'eco-industrial revolution' has only just emerged, and the possible scope, timescale and contours of the required changes remain unclear. This chapter seeks to fill some of these gaps. It begins by examining structural changes in industry that have occurred since the UN Conference on the Human Environment in Stockholm in 1972, and then looks at some of the ways that industry has moved to improve its environmental performance. The key obstacles to further improvement are then discussed, leading to an outline of some of the main priorities for an eco-industrial policy.

STOCKHOLM TO RIO: STRUCTURAL CHANGE IN INDUSTRY 1970–90

Industry has historically been a significant consumer of energy and raw materials, as well as a major generator of pollution and wastes. But industry is also a dynamic and constantly changing sector of the economy. As Ruprecht Vondran, president of the German Steel Federation, said at the Second World Industry Conference on Environmental Management in April 1991: 'The history of industrialization is the history of constant structural change, without which economic growth would not have been possible' (WICEM, 1991). Often change comes in waves, characterized by new technologies, energy sources, transport systems and social arrangements.

Since the late 1960s, there has been a 'volatile and turbulent transitional period' towards a new pattern of industrial development (Grubler and Nowotny, 1990). This has changed the balance of industry around the world and brought a shift towards relative 'dematerializa-tion' of production in the North, in which the volume of raw materials and energy needed to generate added value is reduced. There has also been rapid industrialization in some parts of the South. However, this period of structural change has not reduced the total burden of industry on the environment, and there is growing concern about the environ-mental implications of high-consumption lifestyles.

The changing balance of industry

In the OECD, industry's share of gross domestic product has fallen from an average of about 40 per cent to about 30 per cent. During this process of restructuring one-third of the '*Fortune* 500' list of leading industrial companies has disappeared through merger or closure. In the developing world, the trend has been the reverse; in China, for example, industry now accounts for almost 50 per cent of GDP, compared with less than 40 per cent in 1965. The changes are particularly marked in Nigeria, where industry grew from 13 per cent to 44 per cent of GDP over the same period. Thus as the economies of the OECD become increasingly dominated by the service sectors, many developing countries are developing proportionately larger industrial sectors.

'Dematerialization' in the North

The Brundtland Commission and others have noted a number of environmental benefits flowing from this shift to a 'post-industrial, information-based era' in the developed world (WCED, 1987). One of the most notable aspects of these changes has been the relative 'dematerialization' of production in the OECD region. Following the two oil crises of the 1970s, a drive for efficiency improvements ensured that while the output of the chemicals industry has more than doubled since 1970, its energy consumption per unit of output has fallen by 57 per cent (OECD, 1991a). A recent study by the International Monetary Fund has shown that improved resource productivity is a long-term trend: 'raw material requirements for a given unit of output have fallen by an average of 1.25 per cent a year since the start of the century' (ibid.). Companies have found that they can deliver the same or a better service with fewer materials; for example, the average weight of a car has declined by nearly 400 kg since 1975, through improved design and the partial substitution of plastics for steel.

Despite the often considerable 'environmental gratis' effects of increasing production efficiencies, these improvements have to be placed in context (see Simonis, 1990). Although average energy intensity – the amount of energy used to generate one unit of GDP – in the OECD has fallen, total energy consumption has increased by over 30 per cent in the last twenty years. Despite all the regulatory efforts to date, no country has yet managed to fill the gulf between the social and environmental costs externalized by industry and other sections of society, or to delink economic growth from the production of waste. For example, in Germany total spending on environmental protection reached 1.5 per cent of GDP in the mid-1980s. However, the costs of pollution have been estimated to be in the region of 10 per cent of GDP (Weizsäcker, 1991). Similarly, in France, every 1 per cent of growth generates 2 per cent extra waste. Continued growth has meant that add-on technical solutions to pollution problems, such as catalytic converters for auto emissions, have been overwhelmed. In addition, from the middle of the 1980s falling oil prices have removed the stimulus for conservation. As a result, the positive trend decoupling economic growth from energy growth has actually been reversed. Finally, while relative dematerialization has occurred in the OECD in certain sectors, to a significant degree this has been brought about by the net transfer of energy- and resource-intensive industries to the developing world, in effect displacing rather than solving the environmental problems of production.

Industrialization in the South

Developing countries' proportion of global industrial production has increased from 9.3 per cent to 13.2 per cent, although most of this increase occurred during the 1970s. In particular, there has been a marked redeployment of traditional industries such as textiles, leather, iron and steel, industrial chemicals and petrochemicals from North to South. Unfortunately, most of these industries are heavily polluting; and, in the absence of adequate financial resources and management practices, 'such structural change could lead to increased environmental pressures in the South unless clean and efficient technologies are adopted on a large scale' (UNIDO, 1990). Among the newly industrializing countries (NICs) of East Asia, such as Taiwan, Thailand and South Korea, the output of waste is beginning to reach levels in the OECD (Hirschhorn and Oldenberg, 1991) (see Table 6.1).

In Thailand, 'the share of hazardous waste generating factories has increased from 29 per cent in 1979 to 58 per cent in 1989. The trend towards more hazardous waste producing industries is expected to continue during the next 15 to 20 years' (Phantumvanit and Panayotou,

Table 6.1: Hazardous waste generation

Country	Tons per capita	GNP per capita (US$)
Japan (1983)	0.01	16,000
West Germany (1988)	0.1	15,000
UK (1988)	0.1	8,000
Taiwan (1986)	0.2	3,000
South Korea (1985)	0.01	2,000
China (1987)	0.0004	250

Source: Hirschhorn and Oldenberg (1991)

1990); only one area in Thailand has adequate treatment facilities (ibid.). But as happened earlier in the OECD region, industrial accidents are generating a mounting wave of public outrage at corporate environmental performance. For example, in South Korea, the environment minister was dismissed in February 1991 following national protests after an affiliate of the giant Doosan group had dumped 30 tons of phenol in the Naktong River.

The trend to dematerialization in the OECD has also had important economic impacts. The increasing use of synthetic substances (such as artificial sweeteners for sugar) or new materials (such as fibre optics for copper) is undermining the competitive basis of resource-based developing economies, often resulting in increased exploitation of natural resources to compensate for reduced market prices. And although the consumption of raw materials and energy has continued to increase in the OECD, the relative decline in importance of resource inputs has been reflected in declining real prices for commodities. Between 1980 and 1988 the real prices of non-fuel commodities from developing countries declined by 40 per cent; fuel prices declined by 50 per cent in the same period (UNCED, 1991b). The full-scale entry of the resource-rich former Soviet Union into world markets will increase the supply of commodities, depressing prices even further. These trends have reinforced the urgent need for developing countries to industrialize.

However, developing countries' efforts to diversify their economies have been severely hampered by increasing trade and technological protectionism within the OECD, a lack of industrial know-how and a shortage of financial resources to purchase or develop the necessary technology, exacerbated by the debt crisis. Furthermore, according to the United Nations Economic Commission for Latin America and the Caribbean, there has been an 'erosion of traditional competitive advantages', with information technology and flexible automation undermining the attraction of cheap labour and natural resources for multinational corporations (ECLAC, 1991). In some cases, this has meant that industry has begun to return to the developed world. For example, Fairchild Semiconductors, one of the pioneers of offshore manufacturing, has returned its assembly operations back to the USA after automating the welding of semiconductor chips and the inventory tracking system (Bello, 1990).

Although 'human capital' is now held to be the key to economic progress in the 1990s, this is not labour as traditionally conceived, but the highly sophisticated application of relatively few skilled workers together with costly hardware. Management, organization and information management skills are rapidly becoming the basis of competitiveness. This contrasts with the growing numbers of low-skilled and unskilled workers in the developing world, where under-employment and unemployment now affect half a billion people out of a total working population of 1.8 billion, as many as the entire workforce of the industrialized world (UNCED, 1991c). Many developing countries are in any case afflicted by a 'brain drain' of their more skilled workers and scientists to the developed world.

The trends in foreign investment during the 1980s reflect this changing balance of competitive advantage. Although total foreign investment increased faster than the growth in world trade, four-fifths of this was between North America, Western Europe and Japan. Developing countries' share of global investment declined from 25 per cent in the first half of the 1980s to 18 per cent in the second half. Furthermore, about 75 per cent of foreign investment in developing countries was accounted for by only ten countries, with close links to the markets of the OECD, whereas during the second half of the decade, the least developed countries received only 0.7 per cent (UNCTC, 1991a). These trends highlight the difficulty of achieving what the United Nations Centre on Transnational Corporations has identified as one of the key criteria for sustainable industrial development, 'the diversification of appropriate productive activities around the planet'.

Developing countries appear to be faced with a no-win situation. Without industrial development, they will continue to be plagued with poverty-induced environmental degradation and plummeting competitive advantage in the world market. But industrialization, when it does occur in developing countries, is often repeating all the environmental mistakes of the developed world.

Consumerism and the environment

In this context, the environmental performance of the 'post-industrial' economies offers only a limited guide. Indeed, Maurice Strong, has commented that 'the livelihoods of the rich are the real security risk and greatest threat to our common future'. In the North, new environmental problems are emerging, linked to high-consumption lifestyles, and the focus of concern is shifting from industry's production processes to the environmental impact of its products. An analysis of the total life cycle of a car, for instance, shows that 90 per cent of energy consumption and pollution occurs during use, and only 10 per cent during production. Managing the consumption habits of millions of individual consumers, however, poses new problems for governments. The problem has been accentuated by the shift from mass production to mass customization, where advanced manufacturing techniques are able to produce products tailored individually to consumer demands. This has greatly increased the number and variety of products: 'if present trends continue, 50 per cent of the products which will be used in 15 years' time do not yet exist' (OECD, 1991a).

The profitability of industry relies on constantly growing consumption, relentlessly promoted through the marketing and advertising of unsustainable lifestyles. By contrast, sustainable development requires 'a concerted approach at remoulding the consumer's sovereignty, and steering wants in the direction of environmentally benign activities' (Goodland *et al.*, 1991). Furthermore, a number of consumption patterns are also 'inherently dissipative' in their use of dangerous substances, such as mercury in disposable batteries (Ayres, 1991). One of the clearest symbols of environmentally dissipative lifestyles has been the rise in packaging; in the last forty years, the amount of packaging in Paris's municipal waste stream has increased from 13.5 per cent to 61.8 per cent (McCarthy, 1991). But packaging has also been at the forefront of government and consumer efforts to establish effective recycling schemes and reduce the unnecessary consumption of scarce resources. In the Netherlands, for example, the government decided in the mid-1980s that plastic containers for soft drinks could only be used provided that efficient recycling was adopted. Countries have found that the only effective way to deal with dissipative uses of toxic substances is to develop 'sunset' policies to phase out their use (for example, lead in petrol). But because of industry resistance, the elimination of toxic substances remains the exception rather than the rule. Unfortunately, too, new substances that are toxic in even small amounts continue to be developed at a rate that exceeds the possibilities of testing and regulation (UNCED, 1991a).

THE PARTIAL GREENING OF BUSINESS

Across the world, company responses to environmental issues have mostly been driven by legislative demands, with 'probably no more than 100–200 companies worldwide having made environmental performance one of their top concerns' (Cairncross, 1990). By the late 1980s, a number of multinationals in environmentally intensive industries, such as chemicals, had begun to develop a kind of 'corporate environmentalism'. As well as individual company efforts, industry associations have introduced numerous codes of conduct to exert peer pressure and improve public image. This has coincided with the emergence of new market-driven pressures on companies from the 'green consumer' movement. For developing countries, however, a prime concern has been how to ensure that multinational corporations do not abuse their weak regulatory regimes by operating according to double standards.

If companies have been largely reactive, this mirrors the behaviour of society at large, which has often only been galvanized into action following major accidents, such as the release of dioxin at Hoffmann La Roche's Seveso plant in Italy in 1976 and the disaster at Union Carbide's plant at Bhopal in India in 1984. But behind these incidents have been two noticeable waves of environmental concern, the first of which peaked in the early 1970s, when some major multinationals such as Philips and IBM introduced corporate environmental policies. The second 'green' wave, which grew in strength through the 1980s, was marked by a significant broadening of the industrial base affected by tightening regulation and public scrutiny. But the diffusion of new ideas and clean technologies has been highly erratic, with the developing countries suffering from a weak 'trickle down' of best practice from the developed world.

Company actions on the environment have been shaped predominantly by regulatory requirements. Industrial unwillingness to consider fundamental changes in processes or products, and government desires for a quick fix to pollution problems, has resulted in unsystematic and 'end-of-pipe' solutions. Wastes have been disposed of through dilution, dispersion and dumping. Emissions to different environmental media have generally been treated separately, leading to the transfer of pollution from one medium to another (such as from water to land). Nevertheless, government regulation focusing on pollution control has

165

spawned a rapidly expanding pollution control and waste management industry which, rather than being 'green', relies on the continued growth in pollution for its profitability.

It was not until the late 1980s that the common-sense concepts of resource conservation, risk reduction and pollution prevention (or waste minimization), which had been pioneered almost two decades before with initiatives such as the 'Pollution Prevention Pays' programme at 3M, became more widely accepted by both government and industry. In the USA, for example, Congress passed a Pollution Prevention Act, requiring companies to detail their efforts to reduce pollution. These concepts have now been integrated under the single heading of 'cleaner production' by the United Nations Environment Programme's Industry Office (UNEP, 1991). Rather than focusing simply on 'clean technology', UNEP stresses the importance of effective management and organization, and the need for constant improvement in performance (thus cleaner rather than clean).

Nevertheless, as the 3M and other cases show, good environmental practice is good for business, and the payback of investments is often short. Furthermore, companies have barely begun to take advantage of the low- or no-cost prevention options. In the USA, the Office of Technology Assessment estimated in 1986 that 50 per cent of all industrial waste could be prevented using current technologies (quoted in Hirschhorn and Oldenberg, 1991), while the Dutch Prisma Project concluded that 'a substantial part (an estimated 30–60 per cent) of pollution caused by industry can be reduced by the prevention of waste and emission, keeping within business economic conditions, by using existing management techniques, and by employing today's technology' (Prisma, 1991) (see Table 6.2).

The same potential for cleaner production exists in developing countries. Fritz Balkau of UNEP's Industry and Environment Office believes that 'a general industrial rule of thumb for old plant is that 50 per cent of pollution abatement can be achieved by better operation and minor plant modifications' (Balkau, 1990). In the Hong Kong textile industry, for example, the amount of waste water has been substantially reduced by relatively simple 'good housekeeping' practices, such as the 'shutting off of water supply to equipment not in use, installing automatic shut-off valves in hoses and supplying only the optimum amount of water to the machine'. But companies can quickly reach a plateau of such 'good housekeeping' improvements. Further measures require investments in time, training, technology and know-how, which many companies do not have.

Table 6.2: Good environmental practice – good business practice

Industry	Method	Reduction of wastes	Payback
Pharmaceutical production	Water-based solvent replaced organic solvent	100%	< 1 year
Equipment manufacture	Ultrafiltration	100% (solvent/oil) 98% (paint)	2 years
Automotive manufacture	Pneumatic process replaced caustic process	100% (sludge)	2 years
Organic chemical production	Adsorption, scrap condenser, conservation vent, floating roof	95% of cumene	1 month
Photographic film processing	Electrolytic recovery ion exchange	85% (developer) 95% (fixer, silver and solvent)	< 1 year

Source: Huisingh (1987).

By necessity, environmental efforts have been greatest in environment-intensive industries, such as petrochemicals, where most of the large US, European and Japanese multinationals have now established specialized environmental departments, introduced regular internal monitoring and auditing procedures and inaugurated company-wide programmes to reduce environmental impacts. Successful corporate programmes have relied on strong support from senior management and significant reforms in organization and management structures to allocate responsibility and provide effective incentives for reducing environmental impacts.

This more positive approach to environmental management in leading companies is reflected in a survey carried out by the management consultancy McKinsey of 290 senior executives during 1991, 12 per cent of whom were from the Third World. The survey found 'a positive, growing awareness'; 80 per cent of those surveyed belonged to companies that had published an environmental policy statement, and 25 per cent carried out evaluations of their suppliers' environmental performance to minimize the waste they received (McKinsey & Co., 1991). The survey found that on average companies spent 3 per cent of sales on environmental protection; this was expected to increase to 5 per cent by 2000. A survey of 12,000 managers by the *Harvard Business Review* found that companies now accept that solving environmental problems is the responsibility of those that create them (Kanter, 1991).

A few companies have declared their intention to go beyond current requirements and anticipate future regulations, thereby hoping to exercise greater control over their environmental destiny. This more active stance has not come from altruism, but from a recognition that the scale of government and public expectations has turned the environment into an issue. For example, the UK chemical company ICI has stated that 'unless we treat environmental matters seriously, we are not going to survive as a company' (Robins, 1990). ICI subsequently announced that it will reduce waste by 50 per cent by 1995, and require all new plants to be built to standards that anticipate future regulations 'in the most environmentally demanding country' in which it operates that process. The change towards an anticipatory approach is shown by reference to ICI's operations in Taiwan. Local opposition to the marine dumping of wastes forced the closure of a plant producing acrylic intermediates in 1989. The same year, ICI announced the opening of a new plant to produce terephthalic acid, which will produce little or no waste.

Corporate environmentalism?

In the USA, the shock produced by the Bhopal disaster and the passage of the Superfund Amendment and Reauthorization Act (SARA) stimulated a similar response. A number of chemical companies such as Dow, Du Pont and Monsanto introduced company-wide programmes to minimize waste and reduce risks. Enhanced liability laws and rapidly rising waste disposal costs made waste minimization programmes increasingly attractive, and also necessary. The new mood was exemplified by Edgar Woolard, chief executive of Du Pont, who coined the phrase 'corporate environmentalism' in a speech in London in May 1989. By this he meant 'an attitude and a performance commitment that place corporate environmental stewardship fully in line with public desires and expectations'. Du Pont believes that an environmental management paradigm shift is under way, so that, rather than regarding environmental quality as an added burden for business, it is now considered a vital part of a company's competitive advantage. Instead of the traditional reactive response to pollution problems, seeking to comply with regulations and no more, the aim is now to prevent pollution at source and aim for 'environmental excellence'.

Collaborative efforts

From the beginning of the first wave of environmental concern, individual company initiatives to improve environmental performance have been supplemented by collective efforts at the sectoral, national and international levels. Industry has come to realize that it is judged by the performance of its worst member. Codes of conduct and statements of principle can help to exert pressure on these companies, and can provide the framework for technology and know-how transfer to pull up standards. A good example of this is the chemical industry's 'Responsible Care' initiative, started by the Canadian Chemical Producers' Association in the late 1970s, and since adopted by industry associations in Australia, Europe and the USA.

Responsible Care requires companies to make a formal commitment to continuous improvement in performance as a condition of membership. This commitment is detailed in a series of binding codes of conduct, such as on process safety, community awareness, emergency response and pollution prevention. In the USA, each company has to complete an annual self-evaluation form for each code, from which public reports on progress will be released. Furthermore, in a number of countries, an advisory panel has been established to act as a formal conduit for public concerns about the chemical industry. The mandatory nature of the programme marks a new stage in voluntary agreements by industry, and provides a vital mechanism for providing peer pressure and assistance to chemical companies that are performing below acceptable standards. Although Responsible Care is operated by nationally based industry associations, the aim is to spread the programme throughout the global chemicals industry. In the developing world, industry associations in India, Mexico and Taiwan have programmes under preparation.

As with individual company programmes, collective efforts need to be more than statements of good intent to be effective; they need to be followed up with detailed commitments and plans of action. However, in most cases industry codes have stopped at the formulation of principles. This is the case with the Business Charter for Sustainable Development, issued by the International Chamber of Commerce (ICC) at the Second World Industry Conference on Environment and Development in April 1991. The charter details sixteen principles for environmental management, ranging from giving the environment 'corporate priority' to adopting the precautionary principle regarding environmental risks. The charter has been supported by over 500 companies and business associations; but unlike the Responsible Care programme (or the rival Valdez Principles – launched by US environmental investment group CERES in 1989), the ICC has chosen not to require companies to report on the integration of the principles into daily practice. This lack of rigour in the implementation of the charter has raised a number of doubts about its effectiveness.

The green consumer pull

In addition to the regulatory 'push' and voluntary initiatives, companies now face a market 'pull' for cleaner products and processes. The advent of the 'green consumer' movement in Europe and North America in the late 1980s was in some sense a reflection of growing popular dissatisfaction with the slow pace of environmental improvement according to the traditional regulatory model. It built on a number of environmentalist product boycott campaigns, most notably against CFC-powered aerosols and natural fur coats. Initially, many of the company responses to this new environmental challenge were inept, leading to the establishment of the 'Green Con' award by the UK branch of Friends of the Earth in 1990. However, companies have become increasingly sophisticated at analysing the environmental implications of their product portfolios and redesigning them to reduce impacts. In some sectors, the result has been dramatic. For example, consumer pressure rather than government regulation has led to considerable reductions in the use of phosphate-based detergents in Europe. Many supermarket chains have introduced own-brand ranges of 'green' products to satisfy niche market demand.

The green consumer movement has the potential to go far deeper into the corporate psyche than regulatory compulsion, for the basic reason that it affects the primary aim of companies in a consumer economy, to provide products to meet demand. For this to happen, however, consumers will need greater access to objective information about the relative environmental impacts of difference products. False claims by companies have led to considerable scepticism. But current 'eco-label' schemes, such as Germany's 'Blue Angel' and Canada's 'Environmental Choice', only scratch the surface of the immensely complex interactions between a product and the environment. A handful of companies have begun to apply life cycle analysis to explore the relative environmental merits of different product options (such as between plastics and steel for cars, or between cloth and paper for diapers). For these to be credible, the public must be given access to the data upon which materials and technology choices are made. Furthermore, standardized methodologies need to be developed so that different eco-balances can be compared.

170

Avoiding double standards

For developing countries, a prominent issue is to ensure that multinational companies do not operate according to double standards, abusing the often weak regulatory and enforcement regimes in these countries. Multinational companies often have a better environmental record than local companies, largely because of their visibility and exposure to pressure and because of their superior access to finance, know-how and clean technologies. As one observer has commented: 'even if multinational corporations do use a double standard, their performance looks good by comparison' (Gruber, 1991). None of the ninety-eight US multinationals surveyed by Tufts University's Center for Environmental Management in 1991 set standards that met or exceeded the requirements in place in all countries of operation (Rappaport and Flaherty, 1991). In fact, 40 per cent of the respondents agreed that one of the reasons US corporations locate abroad is because of weak regulatory systems.

Research undertaken by the Thailand Development Research Institute shows that between 1987 and 1989 the proportion of foreign investment projects which would produce significant amounts of hazardous waste, and which attracted incentives from Thailand's Board of Investment, rose from 25 per cent to 55 per cent (Phantumvanit and Charnpratheep, 1991). The consequences for the local environment can be profound, as shown by the impacts of Mexico's border industrialization programme, which has encouraged major multinationals and local operators to establish 'maquiladora' (assembly) plants for the US market. The US$3 billion in foreign exchange earnings produced by the 'maquiladoras' is second only to Mexico's oil and gas exports. But this is produced at a cost of 20 million tons of hazardous waste, with inadequate treatment facilities and no incentive for waste minimization (Ladou, 1991). The approach of legislation to establish a free trade area between the USA and Mexico has, however, led to efforts to clean up the border zone. Many companies now recognize that the establishment of a tough code of conduct for multinationals could provide a basis for minimizing the damage done by 'free riders', exploiting the differences between the developed and the developing world (McKinsey & Co., 1991).

OBSTACLES TO SUSTAINABLE INDUSTRIAL DEVELOPMENT

While the quality and the scope of environmental management have improved considerably since 1970, there is little evidence that the full integration of environmental considerations into industrial practices called for by the Brundtland Report has occurred in a concerted fashion. After twenty years of environmental policy, all that the Dutch government could point to in its 1989 National Environmental Policy Plan (NEPP) was 'bending' and not elimination of negative environmental trends. Environmental management remains on the periphery of corporate concern, despite increasing awareness in recent years. A recent survey found that while companies' 'overall environmental intentions are good, they are often let down by the lack of systematic planning and implementation' (DRT International, 1991). Furthermore, the enormous potential for cleaner production has not been realized. Even in the OECD region, 'scarcely more than 20 per cent of pollution control investments' are made in so-called 'clean technologies', which reduce the use of raw materials and the production of pollution at source (OECD, 1985).

A reputation for resistance

Industry has gained a reputation for resisting public pressure and legislative efforts. Rather than preventing pollution, one analyst has described industry's attitude as 'to prevent, delay and water down' legislation (Mayr, 1991). In some instances, this opposition to legislation could possibly be justified; traditional 'command and control' legislation is increasingly viewed as an inefficient way of achieving environmental quality improvements. In particular, companies are not given a continuous stimulus to improve their performance. One recent survey of US corporate waste specialists concluded that 'command and control laws often impede prevention efforts'.

But industry frequently overestimates the costs of change. For example, during the debate on the phase-out of ozone-depleting chemicals, manufacturers which produced CFCs 'mobilized research and public relations efforts to stress the scientific uncertainties, the necessity of CFCs for modern lifestyles, the infeasibility of substitutes, and the alleged high costs and economic dislocations associated with controls on these chemicals' (Benedick, 1991). Even when companies admitted that alternatives were possible, they held back; for example, Du Pont announced in 1986 that it could develop CFC substitutes within about five years but that 'neither the marketplace nor regulatory policy . . . has provided the needed incentives to justify the required investment' (Du Pont, 1986). As soon as the Montreal Protocol was signed in 1987, companies began to move in directions that two years earlier had been considered impossible, making it clear that industry's claims regarding the costs and difficulties of adapting to new regulations had been 'greatly overstated' (Benedick, 1991). One estimate has now put the cost of CFC/halon production phase-out at half that estimated by industry in 1987 (Lovins and Lovins, 1990).

A number of barriers stand in the way of industrial sustainability, and there is increasing consensus that these 'obstacles to sustainability are not mainly technical; they are social, institutional and political' (MacNeill, Winsemius and Yakushiji, 1991). The most basic is industry's ability to extract resources and emit pollution as if the environment were a 'free good'. Furthermore, the capital markets and shareholders who ultimately judge industry's achievements are setting increasingly short-term financial performance goals, which make it difficult to make the necessary environmental investments. Scale can also be an obstacle. Although most environmental initiatives have taken place among large multinational corporations, most of industry is small-scale, often lacking the necessary managerial, technological or financial resources to take action. Industry in developing countries has often been hamstrung by misdirected government policies. But perhaps the greatest obstacle is a lack of will to change and innovate, and an absence of appreciation of the scale of the changes needed to shift industry towards sustainability. This is linked to a tradition of secretive and closed decision-making.

Competitive pressures

Without countervailing legislative or community constraints, the pursuit of individual advantage by industry will lead inexorably to the 'tragedy of the commons'. The competitive pressures of the market economy act as a constant stimulus to companies to externalize their social and environmental costs as much as possible. This means that the negative consequences of industrial activities, such as accidents, pollution or the disruption of community life, are borne by the environment or society (including future generations). Unfortunately, companies risk becoming uncompetitive if they 'seek profits only in a manner that leaves the Earth healthy and safe', as the US environmental investment group CERES declared in its 1989 Valdez Principles. The pressures for companies to externalize their costs are mounting steadily as competition becomes increasingly aggressive and global.

Despite almost two decades of commitment to the 'polluter pays' principle, no industrial sector yet pays the full cost of the pollution it generates or the resources it depletes. The situation is particularly stark in many developing countries where the process of internalizing these costs into corporate decision-making has barely begun. In Thailand, for example, 'in the absence of some form of government intervention, free disposal of uncontrolled and untreated waste, the use of low-cost, high-polluting fuels and haphazard development are the most "economical" and therefore the preferred choice of private industry' (Phantumvanit and Panayotou, 1990). For multinational corporations, cost considerations are an important factor determining the standards they set for their subsidiaries in developing countries. As one of the US respondents commented in a Tufts survey concerning one of its subsidiaries: 'we're not screwing things up, but if the economics change, we might do more' (Rappaport and Flaherty, 1991).

Even if companies have resources available for investing in new, cleaner processes, these investments must compete against other project proposals, which could have higher returns. The issue is exemplified by the remarks of an executive from a UK water company who explained inadequate investment in environmental protection by the fact that other investments were 'better for shareholders' (*Sunday Times,* 1991). In addition, pollution costs may be small relative to turnover, and therefore represent a low priority for managers. Companies can also be constrained from changing their basic technology by the large costs sunk in existing capital equipment which would need to be written off. In many cases, fully integrated solutions can only be inserted during the capital renewal phase.

Financial short-termism

A concern for the welfare of future generations is one of the aspects that distinguish sustainable development from traditional environmental protection. Beyond the moral imperative, there are a number of practical reasons why a long-term, precautionary approach is required. Toxic materials can accumulate in the environment, with few noticeable effects for many years, producing chemical 'time bombs' for the future. Often there is a lag between the moment that measures are taken and when they take effect. Industry also argues that it needs time to adjust to new regulations, making early action vital. Since capital markets strongly influence corporate behaviour, Juan Rada, the former Director-General of the IMD business school, believes that 'a sustainable economy requires capital markets, tax structures and regulations that privilege investments and savings over consumption, the long over the short term and the stakeholders over a narrow definition of shareholders' (WICEM, 1991). However, this requirement appears to be in direct contradiction to the increasingly short-term time horizons operating in the world's financial markets, where speculation is favoured over strategic investments.

Nevertheless, in North America and Europe in the late 1980s there was a rapid growth of 'ethical' and 'green' investment funds. According to the US Social Investment Forum, an estimated $650 billion is now invested in the USA according to a range of social, environmental and ethical criteria. It was a group of these environmentally concerned shareholders that launched the Valdez Principles, named after the 1989 *Exxon Valdez* oil spill in Alaska. The principles are intended to act as 'broad standards for evaluating activities by corporations that directly or indirectly impact the Earth's biosphere' (CERES, 1990). Without accurate information and reporting, investors are unable to make fully informed decisions. Signatory companies agree to abide by ten principles, including to 'conduct and make public an annual self-evaluation of our progress' (ibid.). However, by late 1991 only twenty-nine smaller 'green' companies had signed up, although CERES expected to have some '*Fortune* 500' companies sign during 1991.

As concern for liability for pollution problems spreads, banks are beginning to scrutinize the environmental impacts of loan projects. Increasing numbers of merger and acquisition proposals are being called off because of concerns about contaminated property. But investor pressure is still low overall, and only 10 per cent of European executives in the 1991 DRT International survey acknowledged that they had been influenced by shareholders or insurers to alter their processes or products for environmental reasons (DRT, 1991).

Problems of scale

The weak environmental capacity of the small business sector is one of the many paradoxes of sustainable industrial development. In both the developed and the developing world, policy-makers are beginning to appreciate the job-creation potential of small businesses, within both the formal and the informal sector. Indeed, in developing countries, 'many planners see the informal sector as probably the greatest source of new urban jobs in the next few decades' (World Resources Institute, 1990). Already more than 60 per cent of employment in sub-Saharan Africa is in the informal sector, according to the International Labour Organization. Small companies in developing countries also tend to rely more on local resources to produce basic consumer and producer goods, often avoiding complex pollution problems caused by larger-scale industry. Nevertheless, small firms in developing countries suffer from a lack of resources simply to keep in touch with potential improvements in environmental technologies or management practice. Even in advanced industrial countries, like Germany, a survey in the town of Nuremberg found that 33 per cent of small and medium sized companies were not complying with state regulations; in addition, 71 per cent failed to obtain regular information on environmentally sound production processes (Winter, 1990).

As the divide between the public and private sectors ceases to be the major division in industry, due to the wave of liberalization and privatization sweeping the world, a new fault line appears to be emerging between a few hundred multinationals which dominate technology, investment and trade flows and a mass of small and micro-industrial enterprises, often without the capacity for either economic or environmental improvement.

Institutional inadequacies and attitudinal barriers

There is growing consensus that excessive state intervention, poorly functioning markets and legal systems are also at fault. Moreover, public resources are often misallocated, undervaluing the importance of building human capital through education and research, and resulting in insufficient numbers of skilled workers. Where countries have invested in basic education and training, and maintained a competitive economy, the results have been good. The World Bank argues that Japan's rapid industrialization since the Meiji Restoration was founded upon 'its aggressive accumulation of technical skills, which in turn was based on a high level of literacy and a strong commitment to training' (World Bank, 1991). A failure to appreciate the importance of the human factor in technological development (including management practices and methodologies) partly explains the twenty-year stand-off between North and South over 'technology transfer'. Technological hardware can only be used effectively within a framework which contains trained staff who can absorb and adapt the technology that is transferred and then begin their own innovation. Without this capacity to develop technology, obsolescence quickly sets in.

Ultimately, however, the most powerful obstacle to the restructuring of industry for sustainable development is habit and human conservatism. Pollution prevention consultants have found that it is often management attitudes rather than technology or cost which is the barrier to change: 'the "Not Invented Here" syndrome is a very strong impediment to the transference of cleaner production' (Huisingh, 1990). Even where companies have introduced environmental protection measures, the possibilities for further improvement might be missed: 'the fact that "someone else handles it" is a barrier to understanding of waste management problems and opportunities' (Dickens, 1991). The root of this problem often lies in ignorance; most companies still have no idea of the amounts of pollution and waste they are producing, and thus are unable to undertake elementary assessments to minimize waste and conserve raw materials.

The same psychological block to innovation and new value systems was encountered when companies tried to introduce total quality systems in the early 1980s to cut down on production and product waste and enhance customers' satisfaction. Many executives believed there was an inevitable trade-off between quality and cost. However, experience has shown that improved quality can yield financial benefits through improved efficiency and productivity. In the case of environmental 'quality', success will only be achieved if there is a fundamental overhaul of corporate priorities, adopting a 'total systems approach' in place of the traditional 'blinkered approach' (Davis, 1991).

Linear industrial ecosystems

The need for industry to shift from a 'linear' to a 'circular' approach to environmental management demonstrates the urgent need for this total systems approach (see Jackson, 1991). The way that industrial operations interact with the environment can be likened to an ecosystem. In an ideal world, the flow of materials from extraction through manufacturing to use and disposal would ensure that the waste products could be reinserted into the system as raw materials for the same or another process. Currently, however, the design of the industrial ecosystem is flawed; rather than acting according to the circular principles of natural ecosystems, the flow of goods and services is essentially linear. Products are produced, purchased, used and dumped, essentially without regard for environmental efficiency or impact.

Numerous opportunities for reducing resource consumption and pollution are missed because of the lack of a systematic approach to materials use. Considerable benefits can be gained from materials recycling, apart from resource conservation, in particular by avoiding the energy- and pollution-intensive materials extraction and processing stages. In the case of steel, approximately 1.5 barrels of oil is saved every time one ton of steel is produced from scrap instead of from iron ore. Steel produced from scrap also 'reduces air pollution by 85 per cent, cuts water pollution by 76 per cent and eliminates mining wastes altogether' (Brown *et al.*, 1990). Currently, on average only 25 per cent of steel is recycled. The gains are even greater with aluminium, where a

95 per cent saving in energy is possible through the reuse of recycled scrap. Closing resource loops in this way will 'reduce the amount of materials that enter and exit the economy, thus avoiding the environmental costs of extracting and processing virgin materials and of waste disposal' (Brown *et al.*, 1991).

Closed decision-making processes

The maintenance of closed and secretive decision-making processes within both government and industry is a major obstacle to making them more responsive to consumer and citizen demands for improved environmental quality. Citizen and employee action has often been a vital spur to industrial change, and formal rights of access need to be established to stimulate further progress. The provision of information on environmental performance is merely a first step in improving community access to corporate decision-making.

Not only do companies have a broad duty to disclose their environmental impacts to all their stakeholders, in the same way as financial auditing displays their economic activities, but experience has demonstrated that public disclosure has a powerful catalytic effect on corporate behaviour. The clearest example of this is the US Toxics Release Inventory (TRI), introduced as part of the 1984 SARA legislation. This requires all firms to report their emissions of just over 300 relatively common industrial chemicals. The information from over 20,000 companies is compiled on a publicly accessible data base. This has meant that US companies have started to operate 'within glass walls' (Kleiner, 1991). Local and national league tables of polluters are publicized by the press and environmentalists, prompting companies to introduce waste minimization programmes independent of any new regulatory requirements. The Environmental Protection Agency recently introduced the '33–50' initiative, which builds on the experience of corporate voluntary waste minimization programmes to ask companies to pledge publicly to cut wastes by 33 per cent by 1993 and by 50 per cent by 1995; over 100 large corporations have responded to the challenge. Rather than spurring further conflicts as industry fears, increased environmental transparency could form the foundation for partnership between industry and its external stakeholders.

BUILDING AN ECO-INDUSTRIAL POLICY

In the face of such deep-seated obstacles, only a fundamental reorientation of the underlying logic, corporate goals, sectoral balance and geographical spread of industrial development will be sufficient to ensure sustainability in the coming decades. As John Davis has written recently: 'Sustainable development challenges the entire industrial and commercial system to restructure itself, based on a completely new set of assumptions and beliefs about the ways we must conduct our economic affairs. We should be making a profound mistake if we perceived the change in terms any less fundamental than that' (Davis, 1991). But the evidence is unclear as to whether an 'eco-industrial revolution' is likely to occur on current trends. In the OECD region, increased awareness and improved environmental performance among industry have led some commentators to suggest that 'a radical transformation of the industrial paradigm' is under way towards an 'economy of reconsumption' (Vandermerwe and Oliff, 1991). From a global perspective, however, the 1990 UNIDO report declared that 'if the current patterns of structural change in world industry should continue unchecked, environmental problems in developing countries will be likely to reach crisis proportions in the near future' (UNIDO, 1990).

Recent developments suggest that there could be considerable opportunities for large-scale, discontinuous changes, which could dramatically tip the scales in favour of an eco-industrial revolution. For example, although the original Montreal Protocol reduction targets were not at a level to eliminate CFCs, 'the negotiators effectively signalled the market that research into solutions would now be profitable. Competitive forces then took over, and the later phase-out decisions became technically easier' (Benedick, 1991). Again, with the rise of 'green consumerism' in North America and Western Europe in the late 1980s, an atmosphere of generalized environmental concern was transformed into a movement through a few very small campaigns by environmental groups (for instance, to ban CFCs in aerosols). Similar discontinuous shifts could await us in the future if the supporters of sustainability target their efforts effectively.

Environmental policies alone will not be sufficient to achieve this turn-around. As the Brundtland Report recognized, sustainable development requires the integration of equity and environmental considerations into all other policy areas. Governments will need to develop a new type of eco-industrial policy to guide and encourage companies to develop cleaner products and processes. The overall goals of this new eco-industrial policy should be to balance the needs for sustainability with those of equity and market competitiveness. This need not be as difficult as first thought. Harvard business professor Michael Porter, for example, argues that 'tough [environmental] standards trigger innovation and upgrading' and concludes that 'the Environmental Protection Agency must see its mandate as stimulating investment and innovation, not just setting limits' (Porter, 1991). Governments now need to take the next step and design policies which directly contribute to sustainable industrial development.

However, the rebirth of an active industrial policy, intervening in the direction of corporate development, is likely to be controversial. Industrial policy has been linked in popular imagination with the subsidizing of loss-making 'lame duck' companies and the failure of government bureaucrats to pick 'winners'. Furthermore, industrial policy, especially when linked to generous financial support, can lead to 'cronyism and corruption rather than to policy and development' in the absence of competent and scrupulous administration (Drucker, 1989). Nevertheless, it has proved possible in some countries for government and industry to collaborate successfully for mutual social and commercial benefit. For example, after the Second World War, Japan's comparative advantage was in labour-intensive industries and low-cost products. But the Japanese Ministry of International Trade and Industry encouraged industry to move away from existing businesses and into technology-based businesses such as steel, oil refining, petrochemicals and automobiles (OECD, 1986).

The challenge for eco-industrial policy is to ensure that it does not remove one structural constraint to sustainable development at the cost of creating one far larger. In the past, large-scale government intervention in the economy has sometimes had both negative and unintended effects. Government should concentrate on what it does best: providing strategic direction, overcoming sectional interests, preventing market failures, assisting those without resources and universalizing best practice. Rather than acting on their behalf, governments should aim to stimulate those who are responsible for environmental problems, whether producers or consumers, to take action themselves.

The following priorities are intended to give an indication of the scope of an eco-industrial policy that needs to be adopted by 2000 by governments committed to restructuring industry for sustainable development. Clearly, they will have to be adapted to local priorities and resource availability.

1. Establishing a strategic vision

Governments have a vital role to play as catalysts for the development of shared principles and for long-term industrial targets. A new generation of environmental planning, which seeks to design transition paths out of unsustainability, and develop ways of anticipating and avoiding possible problems in the future, has already begun, notably in Japan and the Netherlands. The Japanese 'New Earth 21' action plan sets a 100-year time frame 'for the recovery of this planet from 200 years of the accumulation of carbon dioxide and other greenhouse gases' (MITI, 1991). The transition to sustainable development cannot, however, be planned in the traditional way. Increasingly sophisticated and borderless markets often make government intervention a very blunt and ineffective instrument. The key to the success of the recent wave of national planning exercises, such as the Dutch NEPP, the Canadian 'Green Plan' and the Japanese 'New Earth 21' programme, was the definition of key targets and principles for long-term development.

In the Netherlands, the government has realized that sustainable development requires a range of 'target groups' in society, from industry sectors such as chemicals and retail to consumers and environmental activists, to accept their responsibilities for change. As part of the NEPP process, the government has established a dialogue with these groups to identify the most effective way to meet their targets. In the process, a habit of co-operation has been established which should help in overcoming some of the deep attitudinal and institutional barriers to structural change. However, governments need to ensure that co-operation does not degenerate into a situation where 'interest groups are given the opportunity to successfully delay structural measures' (Wams, 1991).

2. Managing structural change

In the transition to sustainable industrial development, a number of sectors could be faced with the prospect of ecologically induced obsolescence. As one executive of a heavy metals industry association has commented: 'For some sectors clean production will mean no production.' For other sectors, while the services they provide are highly valued, the long-term future of their current production processes and products is in doubt. Perhaps the largest restructuring will have to come in the energy industries, moving away from oil and coal towards renewable sources. In the automobile industry, some companies like Volvo are seeking to reposition themselves as transport companies, building significant stakes in public transport to compensate for possible contraction of the auto market. The future of the chemicals industry is also likely to be increasingly moulded by environmental pressures. The environmental pressure group Greenpeace has launched a major campaign against the chlor-alkali process, central to the chemicals industry ('Chlorine Free by '93'). One trade magazine has concluded that 'the chlor-alkali sector is in serious danger of becoming the first major casualty of globally increasing sensitivity towards environmental issues' (*European Chemical News,* 1990).

The rise and fall of industrial sectors has, however, been the hallmark of industrial development. The question for business, governments and the rest of society is whether they can overcome past reluctance to make positive choices for structural change to improve environmental performance and combine this with investments in human capital and technology development for the new 'sunrise' sectors. Governments can help to build new sectors through technology-forcing regulation. Studies made in the OECD suggest that the stimulus to new investment brought about by environmentally induced change has had a positive impact. For example, in the early 1970s at a time of recession, Sweden introduced strict pollution control measures, combined with 75 per cent cash grants towards the purchase of new technology: 'The result was a massive stimulation to the construction, equipment and chemical industries, which helped pull the country out of recession' (Royston, 1991).

3. Shifting to circular industrial ecosystems

Governments can do a great deal to facilitate the shift to more circular industrial ecosystems by progressively closing off pollution options, thereby stimulating competition within industry towards higher standards.

Companies are beginning to think in quite different ways about their responsibilities for the environmental impact of their products, as governments increasingly close off easy or cheap waste disposal options. Companies now need to minimize environmental impacts throughout the entire product life cycle, from the extraction of the raw materials through the manufacturing stage to use by the consumer and final disposal. In Germany, for example, the threat of government action to tackle the problem of the waste produced by cars at the end of their useful life has spurred car manufacturers to establish recycling systems and redesign their products for easy disassembly. A race began within the industry to develop the best recycling system, with BMW, Opel and Volkswagen all announcing at the 1991 Frankfurt Motor Show a variety of pledges to take back and recycle their cars.

Governments should continue to force the pace of change by making life-cycle responsibility the rule rather than the exception as it is today.

This means requiring companies to produce only those products that can be used and disposed of within a comprehensive environmental management system which minimizes environmental impacts and maximizes environmental efficiency. In the USA, the state of Rhode Island has decided that the term 'recyclable' can be used on product packaging only if there is a state-wide recycling rate of at least 50 per cent for that product category. The shift to a circular system of industrial development should also be regarded as a positive opportunity to develop a more comprehensive materials use strategy, and is likely to result in the creation of a completely new industrial sector focusing on recycling. Environmental management to date has largely been focused on reducing and eliminating the negative (that is, pollution or wasteful resource use). As well as involving the phase-out of 'sunset' materials (such as CFCs, lead and asbestos), sustainable industrial development should also involve the introduction of 'sunrise' materials 'that intentionally provide lower risks' (Geiser, 1991).

4. Designing products for needs

While an increasing number of companies have begun to respond to the 'green consumer' demand for 'life-styles within the planet's ecological means' (WCED, 1987), few companies have yet appreciated the need to redirect their product development strategies towards the unmet needs of the poor in both North and South. Some observers have stated that in a sustainable economy, world needs rather than existing product portfolios will determine which markets businesses enter and leave. In Japan, the high social and environmental costs of the post-war period of rapid growth have stimulated both government and industry to start thinking through the implications of a switch away from mass production and consumption. For example, a recent report from the leading Japanese business organization, the Keidanren, states that 'Japanese corporations . . . have to change traditional business activities by establishing new concepts of management focusing more on humanity than profit-seeking' (Keidanren, 1991).

A strong ethical commitment to more appropriate products and processes will facilitate this transition, but this will need to be bolstered by government and public action. In particular, governments could encourage the establishment of a new type of firm, whose constitution commits it to sustainable development, in the same way as co-operatives are committed to common ownership. It is no accident that some of the leading 'green' companies either are co-operatives (such as Migros, the largest supermarket chain in Switzerland) or have been founded with environmental goals in mind (such as the UK Body Shop). In addition, governments could help to promote product design to meet the needs of developing countries, through targeted research and development funding and award schemes, such as the UK's Better Environment Award for Appropriate Technology.

5. Building human capacity

Awareness raising and skill formation are critical to changing management and worker attitudes in favour of sustainable development. Governments should ensure that the environment becomes a core component of all education and training programmes for managers and professionals such as engineers and accountants.

Governments can also help with targeted assistance programmes to overcome managerial and organizational bottlenecks to improved environmental performance. Particularly in the case of smaller companies, it is highly unlikely that they will be able to develop the necessary managerial competencies without outside assistance, whether from governments, industry associations or committed companies willing to share their experience.

However, it is not only managers and employees who need training and awareness raising. The potential for 'green consumers' truly to shift patterns of demand is frequently held back by both a lack of accurate information and an inability to assess the impacts of different products. While eco-label schemes can offer a baseline for consumers, these need to be supplemented by locally based education schemes. In France, the Institut Eco-conseil, established in 1989, trains 'eco-counsellors', who are then appointed by municipal authorities to act as catalysts for changed household consumption patterns in the area.

6. Ensuring corporate accountability

Citizen and employee rights to information and participation are often impotent without the force of law. As a result, governments should introduce mandatory requirements for companies to assess and disclose to the public the environmental impacts of their processes and products, as well as their plans for new plant and product development. The need to publish details will also force companies to establish monitoring capabilities, the basis for effective pollution prevention. Without the regulatory push, many firms, particularly small companies, will not take the initiative. Furthermore, the most effective way of anticipating and preventing environmental problems is to open industrial activity to public scrutiny. Around the world, governments are considering how to encourage the diffusion of environmental auditing, and they are at the same time coming under pressure to require greater transparency of corporate operations. However, rather than focusing on the environmental audit, which has developed as an internal management tool, governments, in collaboration with standards institutes, the accounting profession, industry and the community, must begin as a matter of urgency to draw up 'generally accepted environment accounting principles', which could form the basis for externally verified statements of a company's past, present and expected environmental impacts and resource use.

But not only do citizens and employees have a right to know about industrial performance, they also have a right to participate in corporate decision-making. In particular, many environmental problems start in the workplace, and employees are often the first to be affected by poor environmental performance. In addition, employees frequently fear that environmental measures could lead to job losses, while company managers often invoke 'jobs blackmail' to prevent environmental action. New fora are needed to give managers and employees the opportunity to discuss and resolve these and other issues (including rights to environmental training). In the UK, the Trades Union Congress is encouraging member unions to sign broad environmental agreements with corporate management, establishing 'principles for participation, partnership and active co-operation' for joint environmental policies (TUC, 1991).

7. Using market mechanisms for industrial transformation

The current structure of market prices, government subsidies and taxes is heavily weighted against sustainable development. Governments should use the range of emerging economic instruments – charges, taxes and return deposits – set at sufficiently high levels to promote the transformation of industry. In recent years there has been an acceleration in the use of such mechanisms, particularly in Scandinavia, where Finland and Sweden have led the way in levying 'carbon taxes' to restrain global warming. This could be combined with a restructuring of the taxation system away from desirable activities such as financial saving, employment and productive activity, and on to pollution and resource use. The aim of such change would not be to give some abstract price to the environment, but to send signals through the price mechanism to consumers and producers to cease unsustainable activities.

There are an increasing number of sectoral models of the role that economic instruments can play in industrial restructuring. For example,

Professor Ernst von Weizsäcker of the Wuppertal Institute has developed some indicative scenarios to examine the impact on the transport sector of a steady 5 per cent annual increase in the price of petrol. He concluded that it would take only a few years for substitute fuels to enter the market and high-fuel-efficiency cars to become dominant. After fifteen years, solar and hydrogen fuel cars become competitive, and after twenty years infrastructure changes will provide realistic alternatives to daily private car use. After forty-two years, petrol and diesel will have increased eightfold in price, and will have virtually disappeared from the market (Weizsäcker, 1991). In the USA, the 'feebate' has emerged as another innovative idea for transforming the transportation system. First proposed in California in 1990, the 'feebate' would act as a revenue-neutral system whereby buyers of dirty, inefficient cars would pay two fees, and buyers of cleaner, more efficient cars would get two rebates (Lovins and Lovins, 1990). The system could also be fine-tuned to encourage accelerated scrapping of old, inefficient cars, one of the priorities for improving the overall efficiency of the car fleet.

8. Guiding technological development

Although much can be achieved with existing technologies, new technological development is urgently required. The key task for governments is to set in place the appropriate mix of policies which will accelerate the dissemination of best practice, while prompting research into alternative technologies (such as solar power). Japan's 'New Earth 21' action plan foresees the first fifty years of the next century being devoted to the 'application and development of available and new technology', including clean energy sources and measures to enhance the capacity of natural sinks to absorb carbon dioxide emissions (MITI, 1991). There is great potential for governments to use public procurement programmes to pump-prime the market for new technologies. As the definition of security is increasingly modified to incorporate environmental factors, so government R & D support should be refocused towards supporting new technologies to guarantee sustainable development. There are clear parallels with past technological innovations: 'the first generation of computers arose from far-reaching military support for a revolutionary technology' (Heaton, Repetto and Sobin, 1991).

For developing countries, the issue is how to avoid sinking capital into today's ecologically obsolete production machinery. 'That pollution prevention is cheaper than clean-up and repair is the great lesson learned by every nation that has been through development' (Gruber, 1991). Although there has been little evidence of such 'leapfrogging' in the past, some are hopeful that the environmental imperative will now provide a new opportunity: 'While the low industrial state of Africa has largely been seen as a problem, it also constitutes an opportunity to "leap-frog" into the use of environmentally sound technologies' (ACTS, 1991). For this to happen, technology assistance programmes will need to be re-examined to discover whether they risk locking developing countries into unsustainable systems.

9. Fostering sustainable livelihoods

The current pattern of industrial development places great emphasis on both capital and environmental resources. Government intervention is needed to support the development of labour-intensive projects with the aim of providing employment for the growing labour forces of the developing world. An eco-industrial policy would also aim to foster employment and income opportunities in rural areas to stem and perhaps reverse the unsustainable flow of people to urban areas. But subsidizing employment in large-scale public and private enterprises has not proven effective or efficient. Resources should therefore be redirected to small business development and building human capital through focused training programmes. Fortunately, many environmental measures are also labour intensive, which can make them particularly attractive for developing countries. One African study has concluded that 'promoting environmental conservation can be a major source of industrial activity and employment generation' (Juma, Karani and Ng'weno, 1990).

Industry has a major role to play in generating employment opportunities. However, current mentalities and market incentives make labour a cost to be minimized and replaced with capital. Just as companies are beginning to adopt corporate environmental policies committing them to improved environmental performance, so they should start to consider introducing corporate livelihood policies, which aim to promote satisfying employment for the greatest number of workers. There are already models which can be built upon, particularly in Japan. As Hiroyuky Itami has observed: 'In the United States, management focuses on maximizing profits. By contrast, in Japan, a corporation is responsible for the creation and maintenance of employment' (Itami, 1985).

10. Building global partnerships

Efforts in the developing world to provide attractive investment opportunities for multinational corporations should continue and they should be supplemented on the side of industry by a commitment to diversify production activities wherever possible to developing countries. But it would be fruitless if this much needed relocation of industry to the developing world simply resulted in the application of today's 'dirty' technologies and the production of polluting products. The environmental quality of investments in the developing world must therefore be far higher than today, and steps need to be taken to build innovative global partnerships to share the necessary skills and technologies. Unfortunately, the current debate over 'technology transfer' has become a dialogue of the deaf between free-market ideologues in industry who resist any form of public intervention to provide subsidized access to know-how and developing countries' governments demanding greatly increased financial flows.

The concentration on financial transfers has diverted attention from the central issue of investing in 'human capital', which has become the basis of competitive advantage. Unless developing countries can create competitive niches around the skills of their populations, aid flows alone will not provide a basis for development. Since foreign direct investment by business and industry is becoming the most important source of technology, know-how and management skills for many developing countries, it is vital that industrial policy forms a key part of international co-operation. The governments of the North need to foster the flows of technologies and techniques in a context of genuine long-term partnerships between private sector enterprises, governments and citizen groups. Business or governments alone are incapable of achieving the necessary exchange of skills and ideas. One step towards such partnerships would be for industry, through its various representative organizations, to agree a code of conduct for technology transfer that discourages unsustainable investment projects. Osama El-Kholy, adviser to UNEP, has stressed that 'the current market is distinguished by an exceptionally asymmetric relation between buyer and seller', which could be overcome through new rules of the game, drawn up by the various stakeholders in the technology transfer process (WICEM, 1991).

CONCLUSIONS

The eco-industrial revolution needed as part of a broader strategy for sustainable development will involve structural change on a number of levels: geographical, sectoral, managerial, technological and societal.

This has led most observers to emphasize the complexities and difficulties of making the necessary changes; industry in particular has stressed the need for a very gradual shift. However, because of the continuing lack of appreciation in environmental policy circles of the dynamic nature of industrial development, these difficulties have been overstated. Industrial development is a process of constant restructuring, as seen in the far-ranging changes in industry composition and location since the 1970s and in the rapid diffusion of personal computers during the 1980s. The issue is now how to harness this dynamic potential for sustainable development.

Invocations of the need for time sit uneasily with industry's manifest ability to adapt to new circumstances and the pressing urgency of the human and environmental situation. Policymakers, industrialists and environmentalists have largely failed either to explore or act upon the multiple benefits that could flow from the pursuit of a vigorous eco-industrial policy. The continuing resistance to such a 'fast track' to sustainable industrial development is thus evidence not only of a lack of imagination and courage, but also a clear statement that most political and business leaders still do not take the sustainability imperative seriously.

NOTES

The authors would like to thank the following for their comments: John Adams, Jacqueline Aloisi de Larderel, Vijay Bhardwaj, Tom Burke, David Fleming, Paul Hackett, Tahar Hadj-Sadok, Nay Htun, Kerry ten Kate, Larry Kohler, Juan Rada, Francisco Szekely, Beverley Thorpe, Teo Wams and Mark Wilson.

REFERENCES AND BIBLIOGRAPHY

ACTS (African Centre for Technology Studies), 1991. *Sustainable Industrial Development in Africa: Agenda for the 1990s*, workshop report, ACTS, Nairobi, March.

Ayres, Robert U., 1991. *Eco-Restructuring: Managing the Transition to an Ecologically Sustainable Economy*, IIASA, Vienna.

Balkau, Fritz, 1990. 'Tanning and the environment in the 1990s', *Journal of the Society of Leather Technologists and Chemists*, 74.

Bello, Walden, 1990. *Brave New Third World*, Earthscan, London.

Benedick, Richard E., 1991. 'Protecting the ozone layer: new directions in diplomacy', in J.T. Mathews (ed.), *Preserving the Global Environment: The Challenge of Shared Leadership,* Norton, New York.

Brown, Lester R. *et al.*, 1990. *State of the World 1990* (Worldwatch Institute), Norton, New York.

Brown, Lester R. *et al.*, 1991. *State of the World 1991* (Worldwatch Institute), Earthscan, London.

Cairncross, Frances, 1990. 'Cleaning up: the *Economist* survey of industry and the environment', *The Economist*, 9 September 1990.

CERES, 1990. *The 1990 Guide to the Valdez Principles*, CERES, New York.

Commoner, Barry, 1990. *Making Peace with the Planet*, Gollancz, London.

Conroy, Czech and Litvinoff, Miles (eds), 1988. *The Greening of Aid*, Earthscan, London.

Davis, John, 1991. *Greening Business*, Blackwell, Oxford.

Dickens, Paul S., 1991. 'Waste elimination – challenge for the 1990s', paper for the Global Pollution Prevention Conference, Washington, DC, June.

DRT International, 1991. *The DRT International 1991 Survey of Managers' Attitudes to the Environment*, Touche Ross & Co., London.

Drucker, Peter, 1989. *The New Realities*, Heinemann, London.

Du Pont, 1986. 'Du Pont position statement on the chlorofluorocarbon–ozone–greenhouse issues', *Environmental Conservation*, 13, 4, Winter, p. 363

ECLAC (Economic Commission for Latin America and the Caribbean), 1991. *Sustainable Development: Changing Production Patterns, Social Equity and the Environment*, ECLAC, Santiago.

Ehrenfeld, John R., 1990. 'Technology and the environment', paper for the World Resources Institute Symposium, 'Toward 2000', June.

European Chemical News, 1990. 'Chlor-alkali to work for industrial eco-system', 8 October.

Frosch, Robert A. and Gallapoulos, Nicholas E., 1989. 'Strategies for manufacturing', *Scientific American*, September.

Geiser, Ken, 1991. 'From hazardous waste reduction to national materials policy', paper for the Global Pollution Prevention Conference, Washington, DC, June.

Geus, A. P. de, 1988. 'Planning as learning', *Harvard Business Review*, March–April, pp. 70–4.

Goodland, Robert, Daly, Herman, El Serafy, Salah and Drost, Bernd von (eds), 1991. *Environmentally Sustainable Economic Development: Building on Brundtland*, UNESCO, Paris.

Gruber, Michael A., 1991. *Sustainable Development in the Pacific Rim*, National Wildlife Federation, Washington, DC.

Grubler, A. and Nowotny, H., 1990. 'Towards a fifth Kondratiev upswing', *International Journal of Technology Management*, 5, 4.

Haavelmo, Trygve and Hansen, Stein, 1991. 'On the strategy of trying to reduce economic inequality by expanding the scale of human activity' in R. Goodland *et al.*, *Environmentally Sustainable Economic Development: Building on Brundtland*, UNESCO, Paris.

Heaton, George, Repetto, Robert and Sobin, Rodney, 1991. *Transforming Technology*, World Resources Institute, Washington, DC.

Hirschhorn, Joel S. and Oldenberg, Kirsten U., 1991. *Prosperity without Pollution*, Van Nostrand Reinhold, New York.

Huisingh, Don, 1987. *Good Environmental Practices, Good Business Practices*, WZB, Berlin.

Huisingh, Don, 1990. What role can universities play in helping to effect the societal transition to cleaner production?', paper for the UNEP–IEO Cleaner Production Conference, Canterbury, September.

ILO, 1990. *Environment and the World of Work*, ILO, Geneva.

Itami, Hiroyuky, 1985. 'The firm and the market in Japan', in Lester C. Thurow (ed.), *The Management Challenge,* MIT Press, Cambridge, Mass.

Jackson, Tim, 1991. 'The principles of clean production', discussion document, Stockholm Environment Institute, Stockholm.

JEA (Japanese Environment Agency), 1991. *Pollution in Japan: Our Tragic Experiences*, Study Group for Global Environment and Economics, JEA, Tokyo.

Juma, Calestous, Karani, Patrick and Ng'weno, Bettina, 1990. *Industrialization, Environment and Employment*, ACTS, Nairobi.

Kanter, Rosabeth Moss, 1991. 'Transcending business boundaries: 12,000 world managers view change', *Harvard Business Review*, May–June, pp. 151–64.

Keidanren, 1991. 'Outlook for the Japanese economy in the 1990s and its challenges: towards a harmonious market economy, *Keidanren Review*, 128, April.

Kleiner, A., 1991. 'What does it mean to be Green?', *Harvard Business Review*, July–August, pp. 38–47.

Kornai, Janos, 1990. *The Road to a Free Economy*, Norton, New York.

Ladou, Joseph, 1991. 'Deadly migration', *Technology Review* (MIT), July.

Leontiades, M., 1991. 'The Japanese art of managing diversity', *Journal of Business Strategy*, March–April.

Lovins, Amory and Lovins, L. Hunter, 1990. *Least-Cost Climate Stabilization*, Rocky Mountain Institute, Colo.

McCarthy, James E., 1991. 'Environmental regulation of packaging in OECD countries', in *Packaging and the Environment*, Lund University, Lund, Sweden.

McKinsey & Co., 1991. *The Corporate Response to the Environmental Challenge*, McKinsey & Co., Amsterdam.

MacNeill, Jim, Winsemius, Pieter and Yakushiji, Taijo, 1991. *Beyond Interdependence*, Oxford University Press, Oxford.

Mathews, Jessica Tuchman (ed.), 1991. *Preserving the Global Environment: The Challenge of Shared Leadership*, Norton, New York.

Mayr, Johann, 1991. 'Packaging and environment in Austria', in *Packaging and the Environment*, Lund University, Lund, Sweden.

MITI (Ministry for International Trade and Industry), 1990. *International Trade and Industrial Policy in the 1990s: Towards Creating Human Values in the Global Age*, MITI, Tokyo.

MITI, 1991. *The New Earth 21 – Action Program for the Twenty-First Century*, MITI, Tokyo.

Modak, Prasad, 1991. *Environmental Aspects of the Textile Industry*, UNEP–IEO, Paris.

OECD, 1985. *Environmental Policy and Technical Change,* OECD, Paris.

OECD, 1986. 'The industrial policy of Japan', in T. K. McGraw (ed.), *America versus Japan*, Harvard University Press, Boston, Mass.

OECD, 1987. *The Promotion and Diffusion of Clean Technologies in Industry*, OECD, Paris.

OECD, 1989. *OECD Environmental Data 1989*, OECD, Paris.

OECD, 1991a. *Technology in a Changing World*, OECD, Paris.

OECD, 1991b. *The State of the Environment*, OECD, Paris.

Ohmae, Kenichi, 1990. 'Managing in a global environment', *McKinsey Quarterly*, 3.

Phantumvanit, Dhira and Charnpratheep, Krerkpon, 1991. *The Greening of Thai Industry: Producing More with Less*, Thailand Development Research Institute, Bangkok.

Phantumvanit, Dhira and Panayotou, Theodore, 1990. *Industrialization and Environmental Quality: Paying the Price*, Thailand Development Research Institute, Bangkok.

Porter, Michael E., 1991. 'America's green strategy', *Scientific American*, April.

Prisma, 1991. *Prevention is the Winning Option!*, Prisma Project, The Hague.

Rada, Juan, 1990. 'New demands on decision-makers in governments and industry', in International Chamber of Commerce, *The Greening of Enterprise*, ICC, Paris.

Rappaport, Ann and Flaherty, Margaret, 1991. 'Multinational corporations and the environment: context and challenges', *International Environment Reporter*, 8 May.

Robins, Nick, 1990. *Managing the Environment: The Greening of European Business*, Business International, London.

Royston, Michael, 1991. 'Responsibility of industry towards the environment', *Productivity* (India), 31, 4, January–March.

Senge, Peter M., 1990. 'The leader's new work: building learning organizations', *Sloan Management Review*, Fall, pp. 7–23.

Simonis, Udo E., 1990. *Beyond Growth*, Edition Sigma, Berlin.

South Commission, 1990. *The Challenge to the South*, Oxford University Press, Oxford.

Stata, Ray, 1989. 'Organizational learning: the key to management innovation', *Sloan Management Review*, Spring, pp. 63–74.

Sunday Times, 1991. 'Rivers get dirtier as water firms divert their profits', 16 June.

TUC (Trades Union Congress), 1991. *Greening the Workplace*, TUC, London.

UNCED, 1991a. *The Relationship between Demographic Trends, Economic Growth, Unsustainable Consumption Patterns and Environmental Degradation*, A/CONF.151/PC/46, UNCED, Geneva, August.

UNCED, 1991b. *The International Economy and Environment and Development*, A/CONF.151/PC/47, UNCED, Geneva, August.

UNCED, 1991c. *Poverty and Environmental Degradation*, A/CONF.151/PC/45, UNCED, Geneva, August.

UNCTC, 1991a. *The Triad in Foreign Direct Investment*, UNCTC, New York.

UNCTC, 1991b. *Criteria for Sustainable Development Management*, UNCTC, New York.

UNDP, 1991. *Human Development Report 1991*, Oxford University Press, Oxford.

UNEP, 1991. *Cleaner Production*, Canterbury conference report, UNEP–IEO, Paris.

UNIDO, 1990. *Industry and Development: Global Report 1990–91*, UNIDO, Vienna.

Vandermerwe, Sandra and Oliff, Michael, 1991. 'Corporate challenges for an age of reconsumption', *Columbia Journal of World Business,* Fall 1991, pp. 6–25.

Wams, Teo, 1991. *The Deceptive Appearance of the Dutch Environmental Plan*, Milieu Defensie, Amsterdam.

WCED, 1987. *Our Common Future* (Brundtland Report), Oxford University Press, Oxford.

Weizsäcker, Ernst Ulrich von, 1991. 'Sustainability is a task for the North', *Journal of International Affairs,* Winter.

White, Allen L., 1991. 'Total cost assessment', working paper for the National Academy of Engineering Workshop, 'Engineering our Way Out of the Dump', July.

WICEM, 1991. *WICEM II: Conference Report and Background Papers*, ICC, Paris.

Wilkinson, Paul R., 1991. 'Measuring and tracking waste', paper for the Du Pont Safety and Environment Seminars, Global Pollution Prevention Conference, Washington, DC.

Winter, Georg, 1990. 'The challenge of environmental management', in International Chamber of Commerce, *The Greening of Enterprise,* ICC, Paris.

World Bank, 1991. *World Development Report 1991,* Oxford University Press, Oxford.

World Resources Institute, 1990. *World Resources 1990–91*, Oxford University Press, Oxford.

Wykle, Lucinda, Morehouse, Ward and Dembo, David, 1991. *Worker Empowerment in a Changing Economy*, Apex Press, New York.

Yawson, Gregory E., 1990. 'Towards the promotion and implementation of pollution prevention in developing countries: the case of Ghana', paper for the EPA–IACT International Conference on Pollution Prevention, June.

7 The Future Shape of Forests

Caroline Sargent and Stephen Bass

INTRODUCTION

People have feared, worshipped, culled, cleared and planted forests. Although people's perceptions of forests and their actions are complex and changing, the invariable result has been a simplification of the forest.

Forests are dynamic. 'Primary forest' is a term which has been used loosely to describe undisturbed, old-growth forest. 'Secondary forest' describes forest which has regenerated following disturbances. When any dying or diseased tree falls in primary forest, a gap is created, in which the forest becomes, at least for a time, secondary. The gap creates conditions which are different from the rest of the forest – there is more light and the soil is drier – and 'pioneer' species invade it[1]. Pioneers are able to grow independently of other trees, in a physical environment which is harsher than within the old-growth forest. In its natural state, therefore, a forest is a sea of primary forest with secondary islands.

When people harvest and clear forests, other disturbances are added to the naturally occurring changes. Anthropogenic (human-induced) disturbances at their most benign – for example, in traditional shifting cultivation and forest gardening systems at low population densities – are close analogues of natural disturbances. The forest's ecological processes – of nutrient recycling, water regulation, fertilization and seed dispersal – are maintained by such systems, even if certain species become absent for a while. As human impacts on the forest become more intrusive, the landscape becomes a 'sea of secondary forest with primary islands' (Ashton, 1991). However, extreme human disturbances can cause a catastrophic breakdown of the forest's ecological processes, and the forest cannot regenerate. The usual first indicator of such breakdown is a sharp drop in soil nutrients. The trend towards simplifying forest diversity and the increasing physical independence between trees thereby approaches its extreme – no forest at all.

195

Through the ages, people have observed the effects of forest disturbance – in particular the flux of pioneer species within a forest. They have noted the ability of pioneers to grow in isolation or under relatively harsh environmental conditions. Where such species have material value, or can be used to restore or protect the environment, they have been taken into cultivation, and have been selected and often bred for particular characteristics. With greater circumspection, the species of the primary forest have also been taken into cultivation. For these (generally slower-growing) species, it has been noted that the best growing environment approximates that of the natural forest. Thus, in the process of domesticating the forest, people have also domesticated certain of its component species; they have taken some of these species out of the forest to create landscapes of planted trees.

The replacement of natural vegetation with landscapes of planted trees is invariably a simplification. Unfortunately, simplification usually brings with it increased instability. In a forest of many species, each with genetically complex populations, there is a stronger basis for surviving change than in a simplified system. The loss of species diversity, and of genetic variability within species, can lead to a loss of resilience to change. And resilience is a most desirable characteristic wherever environmental and anthropogenic change is rapid. Current expectations are that unprecedented and rapid change will occur: in environmental conditions (associated with increasing instability of global and regional climates) and in societal demands upon forests (associated with growing numbers of people and their demands upon forests).

Today's forests are increasingly less resilient than undisturbed natural forests, or than those subject to the benign anthropogenic disturbances of small populations of forest-inhabiting people. Large areas of diverse natural forests have given way to landscapes of simpler residual forests and planted trees, which have fewer biological interdependences than in the natural forest. Biological independence permits spatial independence, but brings new dependences – on human management, on fertilizers and on pesticides. Michon (1985) provides an apt description of the trend as 'from the man of the forests to the peasant of the trees'.

With such a trend, there is a danger of forest systems losing resilience. To retain resilience, it is important to conserve both the diversity of biological information – forest species and their genetic make-up – and the diversity of human information – knowledge of the processes, use and management of forests and associated cultural traditions. But it is just as important to avoid or mitigate gross changes which provoke instability. Sawyer (1990) describes these as:

- the 'centrifugal' forces which force people into the forest (social and economic problems outside the forest);
- the 'centripetal' forces which attract people to the forest (infrastructure, subsidies and tenure policies);
- and the destabilizing forces which encourage predatory behaviour within the forest (policies and economic signals which undervalue forest resources, encourage speculation and render investments precarious).

At the same time, there must be a pragmatic realization that societies, like forests, are dynamic. Remaining forests will not therefore stay intact. Efforts to solve forest problems cannot progress if they remain confined to the simple trade-off of 'deforestation' versus 'saving the forest', an inappropriate focus on a conflict which does not acknowledge the fact that forests can and should perform a variety of economic, social and environmental functions. Forests must be used, not merely either preserved or liquidated; and the critical issue is sustainable use versus abuse (Box 7.1). The pertinent decisions are: Which forests are to be used? For what mix of functions? By whom? How? And when? These decisions will shape the forests and wooded landscapes of the twenty-first century.

RE-EXAMINING DEFINITIONS OF FORESTS

We are barely at the beginning of knowing what mix of forest functions to strive for in specific circumstances. We have only very basic data concerning forest area, its decline or increase, the current use of forests and forest ecosystem characteristics. We know little of the forest's biological diversity, productivity and response to disturbances.

Part of the difficulty lies with the myriad definitions of what a forest is. For example:

- 'land where trees cover a high proportion of the ground and where grass does not form a continuous layer' (FAO, 1988);
- 'ecological systems with a minimum of 10 per cent crown cover of trees and/or bamboos generally associated with wild flora, fauna and natural soil conditions, and not subject to agricultural practices' (FAO Forest Resources Assessment Project);
- 'not just the stand of trees which represent only a synusia [link between species in one ecosystem] of the forest, but the whole complex of woody and herbaceous life-forms, with trees dominant, together with accompanying animals and microorganisms' (Longman and Jenik, 1974);

197

- 'the forest is not a bunch of wild trees, but is a place in which our history and future is written . . . to remember the dead, or to provide some day for our sons and daughters. It is our world' (Ailton Krenak, 1989).

Box 7.1: Sustainable forestry practice

For all types of forestry, whether plantations or natural forest management for timber or other products, sustainability can be achieved through:

- *maintaining the harvest of all products at sustainable levels* – by careful control of harvesting levels, timing and frequency, and by minimizing harvesting damage to residual stock; monitoring and feedback into silvicultural management;
- *maintaining essential ecosystem processes* – by retaining continuous vegetation cover; returning nutrients to the soil through e.g. in-forest debarking and conversion; minimizing soil compaction by the careful use of light machinery and animals; maintaining watercourse patterns; careful control of chemical use;
- *maintaining biological diversity at ecosystem, species and gene levels* – by adopting multi-species/variety/clone systems wherever feasible; incorporating secondary succession as far as possible, rather than treating it as a weed problem; integrated pest management;
- *satisfying the needs of people living in and around the forest* – by involving local people at all stages in forest boundary definition, planning, management, harvesting and monitoring of the forest, and forest product processing; employing local people; compensating for rights and privileges forgone; providing access and usufruct rights; providing recreation facilities; ensuring landscape and cultural compatibility;
- *ensuring economic sustainability* – (1) on the part of the *forest user*, through investing in processes that minimize external inputs of materials and energy, that recycle and that reduce waste and especially turn 'waste' into products; and through investment in forestry research, species/provenance selection and breeding; and
  (2) on the part of *governments*, creating conditions that will ensure that forest users stay in business but do not reap an excessive proportion of forest rent.

Source: based on Poore and Sayer (1987).

Forest lands, on the other hand, have been eloquently defined as those lands in which the training of foresters is useful!

In this chapter, forests are taken generically to mean a predominantly woody association of species, of variable complexity in component species and their interdependences, which is able to reproduce and dominate a landscape both in space and over time. This is a loose ecological description; what is more interesting, however, is a functional decription.

There is a great need for standardization and definition of terminology. If people hold very different perceptions of forests, their understanding of the roles and importance of forests will differ. For this reason, a helpful way to describe a forest is by the use we make of it, as a functional forest rather than as an ecological or territorial unit (Romm, 1991). In this way, forests are highlighted as attributes of dynamic landscapes that people shape through their diverse motivations, rather than as the static forest property jurisdictions that typically dominate policy discussion, or as abstract ecological entities. Trees and forests which are used for direct production can be distinguished from those used for protection and nurture of other production systems, 'nurture and fallow', or from those which are set aside for environmental conservation. This spectrum of uses can occur either in a natural forest or wooded landscape, or as a consequence of planting. These categories are reviewed below:

Direct production

In addition to timber, natural forests are used and managed for the production of food, drugs and other products. The diverse range of products is critical in many subsistence economies (see e.g. Hladik, Bahuchet and de Garine, 1990). Its translation and development into present-day market and export-led economies, while common, have not always been sustainable; prevalent economic and policy signals tend to favour certain commodities above others, resulting in predatory production systems that cause ecological and social imbalances (see e.g. Denslow and Padoch, 1988).

Palmer (1989) writes that the 'currently popular view of the tropical forest as a . . . vast storehouse of directly usable plants is somewhat mistaken'. Where mass markets are concerned, the diversity and variability of forest products, and the difficulties associated with harvesting continuously on a large scale, are generally surmountable only by a process of taking them into cultivation. Often, in the case of drugs and chemicals, the active principles can eventually be synthesized artificially, which will further remove the process from the forest. Furthermore, royalties on drugs are not returned to the forest. In the case of high-value tropical hardwood timbers of the natural forest, however, it has so far proven impossible or very expensive to cultivate most of the desirable species outside the forest. In a nutshell, natural forest management for timber will continue to be viable in many areas.

Nurture and fallow

Natural forests and trees may be managed for a nurturing, rather than a direct, function in production; forest ecosystem processes (soil and water conservation, shelter and shade, and so on) form part of the productive 'infrastructure' for other activities. Such forests are said by economists to have indirect use values. Such indirect use values are distinct from the direct use values obtained by harvesting forest plants and animals. Thus the primary function of a rotational forest fallow is to regenerate the soil for agricultural cultivation – restoring chemical fertility and physical structure, and reducing weed infestation. Grazing forests are used to nurture domestic animals. Domestic bees may be kept. Introduced fruit trees may be grown as a crop within the protection of a natural forest.

Environmental conservation

Natural forests and indigenous trees provide vital environmental functions. Of particular importance are the functions of gene conservation, local and global climate amelioration and the maintenance of hydrological cycles (again, these are indirect use values). In practice, one of the most important roles of forests in most parts of the world is to regulate water supplies – without which extremes of water flow, droughts and floods, would be far more common. Plantations can help in climatic and hydrological regulation, but natural forests are uniquely able to conserve high levels of biological diversity.

Plantation

Trees are planted or introduced into a landscape as woodlots, gardens, orchards or timber or commodity plantations, within an agroforestry complex or as roadside plantings. This occurs wherever people define a need for trees – aesthetic, productive or protective – and possess the ability and resources to fulfil it. The earliest plantation efforts, such as for spices, were made to produce a desirable commodity which was rare, because the natural forests in which it was found were diminishing, or distant, or because the species was present only at low densities. Large-scale plantations have arisen from the need to produce comparatively large and uniform quantities of industrial wood, to supply increasingly automated processing industries, with minimum harvesting costs, mainly in this century.

There is considerable overlap between any of the above forest use categories. For example, wood is harvested from a forest fallow; and plantation silviculture includes practices which promote the natural regeneration of secondary species within the matrix of planted species. Each type can play a legitimate role in a stable landscape of different forest types performing a wide range of forest functions.

REASONS FOR FOREST INSTABILITY

There are two fundamental reasons which explain why worldwide – but especially at present in the tropics – it is rare to find a stable forest landscape:

- 'frontier' development models and policies; and
- numbers of people, their demands and their relative powers.

'Frontier' development policies

The prevalent mode of development in forests this century has been characterized by predation – a 'frontier' approach to forest resources. This has deep historical roots in European expansionism, and it has since become a global phenomenon. In Ghana, for example, regions with a predominance of natural forest are termed 'frontier regions'. This mode of development has become widely discredited, but it is still embedded in policies, institutions and the attitudes of many individuals today.

Medieval European agriculture depended upon intensive techniques of resource husbandry, because of the increasingly confined European land base. The 'New World' of the colonies, however, afforded rich possibilities for agricultural expansion. In ensuing centuries, predatory expansive agriculture came to characterize imperial European civilization, leading some emergent settler cultures (perhaps most notably that of the USA) to cultivate a mythology of 'expanding frontiers'. The profits from imperial agriculture helped to finance urban-based industries; and the dynamic of industrial growth served in turn to sustain the mythology of unlimited frontiers, and further transformed formative frontier myths into a belief in perpetual economic growth, as a phenomenon which was both good and natural: 'Having expanded on the things of nature, the West came to believe that expansion was in the nature of things' (Weiskel, 1990).

Forests are the classic historical case of a resource 'frontier', and are still treated as such by prevailing development policies – as a costless source of income, rather than part of a nation's capital stock, the sustainable income from which can be used for development (Repetto, 1988). Forests have been undervalued. Their full range of benefits are not taken into account in policies and economic decisions. Timber values have dominated such decisions; but even so, the price of trees has not reflected the cost of their replacement – merely the cost of cutting and transporting them. Nor do timber values reflect the wider environmental values provided by forests. Capital and labour have been attracted into the forest by policies which encouraged predatory behaviour – rapid removal of forest stock and speculative control of land – rather than productive investment (Mahar, 1988). Degraded forest has been laid to waste, and the predatory enterprises have expanded into fresh forest areas. Many factors have exacerbated the problem, notably precarious political regimes and unfavourable economic climates. The trend has been particularly evident in tropical countries in the last two decades, with West Africa and the Amazon providing stark examples of abuse.

Consequently, forest quantity and quality have diminished rapidly in the tropics (but also in the Pacific north-west of America). Little of lasting value has replaced the cleared forests, principal exceptions including some perennial crop plantation agriculture in South-east Asia. Very few people have benefited from this degradation and destruction, but many groups of forest-dependent people have suffered greatly. The biological and human information that confers resilience on forests has diminished. Many forests have been eliminated. The forest resources remaining today are quantified in Box 7.2.

Too many people?

Much of the world, however, has not subscribed, consciously or subconsciously, to the notion of forests as a frontier. Indeed, many cultures, such as those of India and the Amazon, treat the forest as a finite, life-sustaining universe demanding respect (Bandyopadhyay and Shiva, 1990). Yet many of their forests are also diminishing, and for reasons which cannot always be ascribed to perverse development policy. For these areas, there is a popular conviction that population increase is the root cause of forest clearance and degradation.

Malthusians continue to predict resource depletion and extinction as an inevitable consequence of population growth (Coleman, 1985). In contrast, a significant body of opinion considers that an increasing

---

Box 7.2: Forest resources and forest loss
Current area of closed canopy forest

Total area	28.4 million km²

of which:

Tropical forest	42 per cent
Boreal (subarctic) forest	32 per cent
Temperate forest	26 per cent

Source: World Resources Institute (1990).

Change in forest/woodland area, 1850–1980 (million hectares)

Region	1850	1900	1950	1980	% change 1850–1980
N. Africa/Middle East	34	30	18	14	− 59%
Tropical Africa	1,336	1,306	1,188	1,074	− 20%
Latin America	1,420	1,394	1,273	1,151	− 19%
S. and SE Asia	569	548	493	415	− 27%
China	96	84	69	58	− 40%
Total 'developing'	3,455	3,362	3,041	2,712	− 21%
Europe	160	156	154	167	+ 4%
North America	971	954	939	942	− 3%
USSR	1,067	1,014	952	941	− 12%
Pacific developed	267	263	258	246	− 8%
Total 'developed'	2,465	2,387	2,303	2,296	− 7%

Source: based on World Resources Institute (1987).

---

population is essential for stimulating the development of new technology and institutions – and hence for introducing ways of reducing forest loss. Extremes of vision such as these obscure the complexities and may have drawn attention away from essential policy measures and investment to accommodate population increases.

It is useful to remember that 'population' is only an aggregate measure of diverse individuals. The population impacts on the forest are the aggregates of the actions of millions of individuals; and the context for their individual actions is always unique (Romm, 1991). Population impacts on the forest are therefore not a function of numbers alone, but also of the political, economic and social signals that cause individuals to move into and within forests. The most critical impact is the migration of people to clear new agricultural land along the forest margin.

Cruz (1991; after Thiesenhusen, 1989) considers that there are three general scenarios which lead to migration and forest conversion. These happen when population growth rates are 'rapid such that the labor absorbing mechanisms of intensive farming are insufficient in accommodating surplus labor', or 'less-rapid and agriculture is more labor-absorptive, but the capacity for absorbing labor will only work in the short run', or 'not as rapid, but because land ownership is highly inequitable, labor is prematurely expelled to the frontier and environmental damage ensues'. One might also add low labour absorption in urban areas as leading to migration to the forests, as experience in the Amazon demonstrates (see e.g. Browder, 1989).

The 'population' problem is hence also one of the power structures within and between social groups – of who owns the agricultural hinterland and the forest, of employment, of relative poverty and hence the levels of investment that can be made, and of the conditions that make that investment precarious. It will not, therefore, be possible within the forestry sector alone to find effective ways to protect and develop forests in isolation from other land use sectors, or from social and macro-economic policies.

CHANGING PRESSURES ON FORESTS

Economists accord the various forest functions with direct use value, indirect use value, option value and existence value. Table 7.1 lists a taxonomy of forest values for tropical forests. The challenge is to establish forest landscapes which provide the mix of values which best meet demands; but which also ensure that the forest is resilient to change. In this section we shall consider briefly the trends in demand.

The demand for *land for agriculture* will continue to increase. FAO predicts that, given current technology and rates of agricultural inputs, 10 million hectares of land must be cleared and brought into production each year for the immediately foreseeable future. A large part of this new land will undoubtedly be provided by converting forests. The important tasks are to ensure that forests are converted only if suitable land of lower total value is unavailable; to determine which forests should be converted; and to encourage farm systems – such as agroforestry – that retain as many forest benefits as possible. The conversion of forest land to agriculture does not merely represent 'forest loss', however, but also an opportunity to create a wooded agricultural landscape, and to form complementary relationships between agriculture and forestry.

Table 7.1: Economic values of tropical forests

Total economic value			
Use values			**Non-use values**
Direct uses	*Indirect uses*	*Option values*	*Existence values*
Timber	Nutrient cycling	Premium/discount on direct and indirect uses	Endangered species
Non-timber products	Watershed protection		Charismatic species
Recreation	Air pollution reduction		Threatened habitats
Ecotourism	Microclimatic function		Cherished landscapes
Genetic resources	Carbon store		
Medicine			
Education			
Human habitat			

Source: WCMC (forthcoming).

The demand for *forest products*, which already constitute the third major primary product in international trade, will increase. Wood is fundamental to development in all its 'stages', especially in developing countries, where alternatives are few. The types of product demanded change with national development, however. With industrialization, there is a general trend towards reconstituted wood (particle board and fibre board) and wood fibre products; these are dimensionally stable and easily machined, and are thus more favourable to automation. Such products can also take more advantage of recycling and waste reduction technologies, and technologies which allow a wider range of species and sizes to be used. Industrialization also brings about a trend away from solid wood (Arnold, 1991).

The underlying trend has been a gradual 1 per cent per year increase in the global demand for *industrial wood* over the last two decades, with some of the highest rates of increase in developing countries, principally for construction. Yet 90 per cent of the production and consumption of industrial wood remains concentrated in the temperate zone (Montalembert, 1991).

There are considerable uncertainties regarding future global demands (various projections range from from a 33 to a 75 per cent increase between 1985 and 2030/2040). Yet overall, there are unlikely to be fundamental changes in the place of the main wood products in the economy. None is likely to be displaced from its principal end uses by other materials (Arnold, 1991).

The market system has by and large extended to all wood products and has ensured that demands for industrial wood are met. In many countries, wood is grown by farmers in effective competition with agricultural crops; and large corporations are investing in plantations. Improvements have also been made in processing efficiency – and more products are being made of wood particles. This is a global view, however, and there will be local variations. In the tropics in particular, as long as natural forests are undervalued, investment in plantations will be inadequate, and logging may continue to degrade forests.

With the slow pace of electrification, *fuelwood* demands will continue to constitute the principal economic pressure on open forests around villages, towns and cities in developing countries. Fuelwood and charcoal already account for 80 per cent of total wood consumption in developing countries, for over 2 billion people use biomass as their primary source of energy. Consumption is expected to rise at 1.7 per cent a year (Montalembert, 1991).

There will be increasing commoditization of *non-timber forest products* (NTFPs). In India, the harvest of tendu leaves from *Diospyros melanoxylon*, used for cigarette paper, is already worth US$100 million a year, income which mostly accrues to the peasantry. The Indonesian rattan harvest is valued at over US$200 million. And Chinese gum resin (from *Pinus massoniana*), used for naval stores, is valued at over US$100 million a year. In many tropical areas, however, subsistence NTFPs which are not traded through the market can be critical to local welfare. Commercial harvest of NTFPs has been mooted as a way to sustain forest structure and at the same time to provide for local people's needs. Yet, historically, commercial NTFP extraction has marginalized local people. Therefore, for 'extractive reserves' truly to benefit local communities, improved local participation in forest management, processing and marketing will be required.

Forest services, such as the conservation of biological diversity and watersheds, have rarely been accorded high value in making decisions about forest use. Yet general economic trends are moving towards an increasing proportion of services in national economies. This could be beneficial for forests as more people become prepared to pay for fundamental forest services. In coming years, payment by individuals (for services such as water supplies, recreation and nature conservation) and by governments and corporations (for services such as carbon storage and sequestration, land reclamation and nature conservation) may be expected as part of increasing bargains involving natural resource use.

Even taking into account the higher use of fuelwood in developing countries, the consumption per person of all major forest products in industrialized countries is three and a half times that of someone in a developing country. The pressure that people in industrialized countries put on forest services (particularly the forest's absorption of carbon dioxide from transport and industry) is also far higher.

Recent years have witnessed marked social trends: towards greater democracy, decentralization of power and global communications that penetrate even into the remotest areas. With respect to forests, these trends have converged on the one hand in many strong voices calling for control of forests by local people, such as the Chipko movement. On the other hand, they have led to more global forestry initiatives (the Tropical Forest Action Programme, the International Tropical Timber Organization and in the future possibly an international forests convention). In between the global and local extremes, the appropriateness of current government roles has widely been called into question. Many governments have been ineffective managers of the large areas of production forest for which they have formal responsibility; and they have kept out of forests people who might otherwise have been able to manage the forests sustainably for subsistence and income (Douglas, 1983). These tensions in social control of forests will become more acute in the coming years; and clearly, changes in roles and responsibilities can be expected at all levels.

CHANGING CIRCUMSTANCES AND THE IMPERATIVE OF RESILIENCE

How can changing demands on forest products and services be met, and how can forests retain the ability to adapt in light of the unpredictability of these changes? Special attention must be paid to the ecological functions of forests. With cumulative human pressures, there will inevitably be a continued appropriation of natural habitat, a phenomenon which could result in some irreversible losses. Natural forests kept in an undisturbed state provide services that cannot be obtained from managed forests or from plantations. Principal among these is the conservation of biological diversity. Certain natural forest areas must, therefore, be set aside and conserved.

Most existing forests have evolved in response to both natural and anthropogenic disturbances. These disturbances can be both gradual, such as climate change, and rapid, such as hurricanes, fire and epidemics. Natural forests recover from infestations of pests and diseases; they can regenerate after typhoons, after inundations, after felling and in fallows in rotation with agriculture. The resulting forest may have an altered genetic composition and physiognomy, but it has maintained its capacity to function, to reproduce and to dominate the landscape. Managed forests are more susceptible to these disturbances, however. Anthropogenic environmental change (such as acid rain and increasing carbon dioxide levels) has been more intense in recent years. The levels and rates of disturbance may be greater still in the future, as demands on forests rise and as the climate changes. If forests are to adapt, they must have the property of resilience.

Resilience is conferred by the information content of the forest – both the biological information (principally the genetic diversity) and the human information (forest management and local knowledge systems) that provide the ability to adapt to change. The property of resilience is present in the natural forest, ultimately by virtue of its biological diversity. But it must be consciously included in managed forests, because human activity tends to simplify natural systems. Techniques for building up resilience will include:

- conservation of biological diversity and ecological processes;
- conservation of local knowledge systems;
- development of scientific knowledge and technology;
- forest management regimes that mimic natural forest disturbances in size, duration and frequency;
- and spatial arrangements of trees in the agricultural and urban landscapes that confer resilience, such as forest corridors enabling plant and animal migration.

Many traditional forest landscapes incorporate high degrees of biological and spatial resilience. In the following sections, traditional rotational fallowing and indigenous agroforestry systems are described. These are resilient because they incorporate large numbers of species from neighbouring and residual forests, and they are characterized by a high degree of management responsiveness.

SUSTAINABLE FOREST CONVERSION

Much discussion has centred on whether the conversion of natural forests to forms of utilized forest or to agriculture is planned or unplanned, but this is not the paramount question. What is critical is whether the resulting use is sustainable, that is:

- whether ecological processes which confer renewability and resilience remain intact; and

- whether the land is put to a mix of economic, social and ecological functions which is preferred by affected local people and, where appropriate, also provides for regional and global needs.

Ninety per cent of all forest clearance is thought to be for agriculture. Nearly all of this occurs in the tropics. Myers (1990) suggests that this is of the order of 11 million hectares per year. Rao (1991) defines three broad categories of agro-conversion: planned agriculture, unorganized agriculture and shifting agriculture.

Planned agriculture

Planned agricultural settlement frequently involves the clearing of large areas of natural forests. In South-east Asia, it is associated with government socio-economic reforms (Tho, 1991). A prominent example is the transmigration programme in Indonesia, which is aimed at relocating families from the densely populated islands of Java and Bali to less densely populated, forested islands; or the Vietnamese policy to resettle people from the rice-growing Red River and Mekong deltas into relatively underpopulated upland areas. Both of these policies have led to a certain degree of social and environmental disintegration.

A. A. Anderson (1990) observes that similar settlement schemes in the Amazon have rarely proceeded according to plan – for they did not take account of the many policy and economic signals to which people would react, in addition to the settlement policy. The Transamazon schemes attracted too little settlement. The Rondônia schemes attracted too much settlement (a growth rate of 28 per cent per year) because the extreme landlessness elsewhere was underestimated.

Unorganized agriculture

Unorganized agricultural settlement has also led to much forest clearance. In Thailand, for example, there are 8 million landless people, a proportion of whom are attempting to establish usufructuary rights (rights to use the forest short of degradation or waste) within the government forest estate. The people have few resources for investment, and consequently the planting of sago is widespread, for it requires low capital. Yet, without adequate inputs, sago exhausts soils within four to five years, and the people are forced to move further into the forest, leaving unproductive grassland behind. The resulting land use is not sustainable, and further investment is urgently needed for agricultural improvements and to legalize small landholding.

In contrast, in Bolivia, approximately 200,000 hectares of lowland forest are cleared annually by upland farmers attempting to establish permanent holdings, with cocoa as a principal crop (Reyes, 1991). These farmers are driven into the forest by poverty, which derives from inequitable land distribution and a traditional non-intensive agricultural technology. Where cocoa becomes successfully established, landholdings may become secure and land use sustainable. Unorganized forest settlement and the introduction of a tree crop are not, therefore, necessarily unsustainable.

A substantial proportion of the forest clearance which is attributed to improper forest management for timber production is, in fact, due to the advantage taken of logged or partially logged areas by agricultural immigrants, or by local inhabitants who do not receive adequate benefits from forest management. In Papua New Guinea, lowland farmers use logged forest to grow cocoa, or to plant permanent farm gardens, wherever the soil is sufficiently fertile. Where forest is left after logging or even after clear felling, it will generally regenerate, except under certain specific (and rather unusual) ecological conditions. *Terminalia brassii*, for example, forms more or less pure stands of timber in coastal swampy areas in Papua New Guinea. If this is felled when there are no trees in seed, regeneration does not occur, and the site will become densely overrun with creepers. Such unplanned conversion activities are quite distinct from (although very generally confused with) shifting agriculture.

Shifting agriculture

Shifting agriculture is a spectrum of technologies enabling relatively infertile forest land to be cultivated on a rotational or fallowing basis. In 1980, FAO found that 45 per cent of forest clearing could be attributed to shifting agriculture (70 per cent in Africa; 50 per cent in Asia). It is not certain what definition of shifting agriculture was used, particularly as no data are given for the area of land which will return to closed-canopy forest under the rotation; nor is it clear that the entire area of land reported had been cleared for the first time. In Vietnam, for example, all data are treated as new clearance, and no records are kept of forest which has regenerated (Sargent, 1991).

Richards (1973) writes that much of the forest of West Africa has been farmed previously through shifting agriculture. He attributes the relatively low numbers of species (compared with, say, the Amazon basin or Indonesian forests) to such use. It has been suggested that in West Africa the relative frequency of trees which are of domestic importance, for example *Dacryoides edulis*, *Irvingia gabonensis*, *Sphondias mon*, is also indicative of extensive cultivation in the forest.

Davies and Richards (1991) write of the Mende people in Sierra Leone that their

> orientation towards the boundary between forest and farm, as distinct from a concern for the forest itself . . . has a most important consequence for forest conservation. The priority area for a conservation strategy sensitive to local interests and concerns should be the bush fallow system, and not, in the first instance, the forest itself. [However,] whereas the change from forest to farm bush is, from a subsistence perspective, probably on balance positive, the shift from farm bush to grassland is widely perceived to have a major negative impact because the secondary succession contains so many useful species. Annual fires in grassland suppress the regrowth of many useful species and lengthen the period of fallow recovery, to the major detriment of gathering activities and population–land ratios.

Worldwide, forest fallowing or shifting agriculture is practised by several hundred million people. It has an important role in conserving many wild relatives of cultivated plants, in domesticating new plants and in providing a niche for many forest species in the fallow – and yet it is popularly considered to have a deleterious impact on the forest. This received wisdom has generated extensive, and frequently misguided, attempts to 'stabilize' rotational fallow systems. 'Stable' agroforestry and plantation systems have been widely advocated in the environmental interest. However, these have not always been successful with farmers, who find that fallowing can return high yields with low capital and labour inputs (see e.g. Rambo, 1983).

Rotational fallowing of forest land may be an entirely appropriate and effective way of managing land for conserving biodiversity, soils and ecological processes, and providing goods for the local community. In West Africa, a large proportion of minor forest products is obtained from the bush fallow; in Papua New Guinea, certain species are actively encouraged during this phase; in Vietnam, fruit trees are grown as a supplement within the rotation.

Why have foresters paid so little attention to the importance of protective natural forest fallows? Perhaps because they have valued intact forests principally for their trees. In contrast, for traditional forest users, 'the forest is not just trees, but rather it is the natural regenerative processes, the successional stages, the forest animals . . . and the other useful plants' (Alcorn, 1990). The instances where forest fallows have failed, where land has become degraded or turned to a coarse, infertile grassland, have been conspicuous. The unfortunate consequence is that foresters have decried all forms of shifting agriculture. Yet failure has usually been due to external pressures beyond the control of the traditional forest user.

There are concrete advantages to counteracting these prejudices. For shifting agriculture can be a process that allows for substantial and varied products with minimal input, while protecting biodiversity and conserving soil and water processes. More importantly, the pressures that destabilize shifting agriculture, and cause it to become destructive, should be curtailed or mitigated.

Logging

While agriculture has been responsible for the conversion of most forests, logging is also significant. One hundred years ago, both the West African and the South-east Asian rainforests contributed a much greater diversity of produce to the world market than at present. Today, the production of timber, and only a few species at that, is by far the most significant forest extraction industry. Much of this activity is not sustainable, for it commonly damages the trees remaining in the forest, and occasionally results in complete forest removal – 80 per cent of moist forests have been removed in West Africa since 1850 (Gerstin, 1990). Much attention is, and should continue to be, paid to methods of making timber production more sustainable; that is, ensuring a continuing supply of the product while maintaining intact environmental processes.

In timber production, there are a number of approaches which can promote a balance between economic, social and ecological functions. These include:

- Reducing the volume of timber extracted. Queensland foresters, who have kept generally good records, found minimal environmental deterioration at a rate of extraction of half a cubic metre per hectare per annum. This is considerably less than the generally accepted rate of two to three cubic metres per hectare (Poore, 1989).
- Restricting extraction to high-value timbers, as a corollary to reducing the volume extracted and maintaining the economic value of the forest. The considerable research and development efforts currently being made towards bringing lesser-known species, with variable properties, on to the market may not be appropriate in the conservation interest (Alfred Leslie, personal communication, 1991).
- Improving harvesting techniques to reduce damage to soil, ground vegetation and residual trees. Use of elephants or other draught animals is generally more appropriate than heavy machinery. Introduction of helicopters may be locally feasible. Detailed planning of all harvesting is essential (Jonsson and Lindgren, 1990).

SUSTAINABLE TREE ESTABLISHMENT

The creation of a domesticated forest landscape has been achieved as much by planting trees as by manipulating natural forests. Relative to logging, tree plantations require a high economic investment and continuing social commitment, and returns are not immediate. Tree planting is not, therefore, common until tree products or services become scarce, and until local economies are sufficiently stable and diverse to be able to establish and protect long-term forestry investments.

Romm (1991; after Romm and Washburn, 1985) hypothesizes that 'the proportion of land in forest cover has a U-shaped relation with population density and a direct relation with income level'. Thus, natural forests are most abundant where populations and incomes are very low – when both the needs and the technology to alter the forest are inconsequential. Where populations increase, the natural forest is liquidated to generate income. But at higher population densities still, the needs for trees become important; and when incomes rise, those needs can be met. Hence the numbers of trees increase, but a higher proportion of these trees will be planted (see Figure 7.1).

Figure 7.1: Changing proportions of land under tree cover

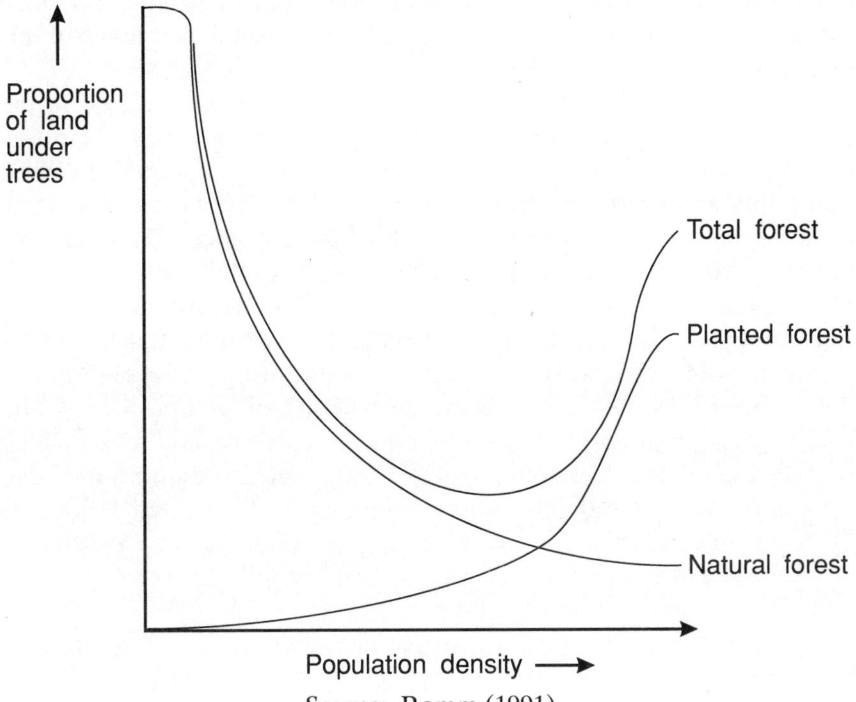

Population density ⟶

Source: Romm (1991).

Recent studies in Nepal (Carter and Gilmour, 1989; Campbell, Shrestha and Euphrat, n.d.) show that the numbers of trees within the agricultural landscape are increasing. In two hill districts in Nepal, results indicated a two- to threefold increase in tree cover (up to 30 million new trees) in the 24-year period ending 1988 (Carter and Gilmour, 1989). In Kenya (Dewees, 1991), numbers of trees on large, wealthy farms tend to be high. They are also high on small, poor farms, with insufficient labour.

Tree cover in Europe is also increasing, for afforestation has exceeded deforestation since 1950. Many European cities already have a highly complex 'cover' of trees, established for a host of reasons. The reclamation of degraded land and mining wastes has been an established practice for some time. Recently in Britain, large urban 'community forests' schemes have been set up, ostensibly for recreation and aesthetic reasons. This pattern of 'social forest' spreading out from urban centres is also reported by Romm (1991) for India, Thailand and California. In California, the mature stage of the U-curve is observed with dense populations of high economic well-being; when land requirements for food production are low, the retreat of the natural forest stops and social forest extends to meet it. Some 500,000 hectares of British agricultural land have been taken out of production since 1981, and it is thought that trees have been established over much of this area.

At the end of 1980, there were over 90 million hectares of forest plantations throughout the world (Hyde and Sedjo, 1991), including approximately 11.7 million in the tropics (Allan and Lanly, 1991). Plantation areas are favoured because of their potential for scale economies and the specific input needs of the growing pulp and paper industry. Although large-scale investments may enable greater attention to environmental care (D. Anderson, 1990), the widely held belief that large plantations are beneficial from both environmental and socio-economic points of view is not always justified. Frequently, plantations have been established through the destruction of natural forests and have resulted in people being removed from common land upon which they depended for subsistence. In contrast, smaller plantations have been better integrated into a tight landscape of different land uses (Bass, 1991). They have also retained higher genetic diversity, because farmers have tended to plant trees from locally gathered seeds or cuttings (see e.g. Carter and Gilmour, 1989).

At present, genetic uniformity is the inevitable consequence of commercially oriented plantation management. In order to supply large markets and automated forest industries, forest practices emphasize uniform outputs, with plantation trees that are necessarily similar or identical genetically. However, the structural and genetic uniformity of these plantations is less resilient to environmental or anthropogenic stress. Consequently, the plantations need a relatively high degree of external input, including management.

Palmer (1989) has called the genetic uniformity of a plantation 'intentional instability'. Forest investors weigh the risks associated with genetic uniformity against its likely higher productivity, against the greater control over – and predictability of – output and against the greater ease of protecting the boundaries of plantations (compared to natural forests) from social pressures. In economic terms, forest investors must be clear where the marginal benefits of putting land under monoculture plantations exceed the marginal costs of the lack of resilience, and the reduced range of products and services provided. Clearly, the benefits are likely to be higher where plantations replace highly degraded land than where they replace pristine natural forests. But in between these clear extremes, it is currently difficult to make rational decisions, for information on the many values of natural forests is scanty. Isolated examples of the valuation of natural forests have been made (e.g. Peters, Gentry and Mendelsohn, 1989) which suggest that the values can be very high. While the direct use components are often valued for particular forests, it is rare for comprehensive assessments to be made of direct, indirect, option and existence values (Table 7.1), particularly in developing countries.

In preparing assessments of world forest cover, FAO aggregates natural forest with timber plantations but, interestingly, not with plantations of rubber (which are now also used for timber), oil palm or other tree crops. Many people would not consider such plantations to be forests. Nevertheless, plantations may move towards a 'forest state', as Dawkins (1988) suggested when he defined success in tropical silviculture to be 'when a fine stand of timber trees has been brought to maturity, and is producing natural regeneration on a site where it has matured before'. For example, many forests that people would perceive to be natural today, such as some of the Chilterns beechwoods in the UK, are in fact the result of earlier planting. Such plantations can thus be said to have resulted in forest types that are sustainable, at least in ecological terms.

What precedents are there for ensuring sustainability in social and economic terms too? In the same way that we can learn from traditional shifting agriculture as a form of forest conversion that can provide economic, social and ecological benefits, we can learn from traditional agroforestry as a sustainable form of afforestation. Both can provide insights into sustaining forests with low external inputs within an increasingly agricultural and urban landscape, where large blocks of forest property are of decreasing significance. Alcorn (1990) identifies attributes of traditional agroforestry that account for its sustainability:

- incorporating native species, through planting or natural regeneration;
- incorporating numerous species for resilience;
- relying on ecological succession – to produce resources, protect and improve soils, and reduce pests – rather than treating it solely as a weed problem;
- varying the agroforestry system to use local natural variations in the landscape;
- adopting flexible strategies through constant experimentation – creating systems that can be modified to meet changing socio-economic needs in future years;
- relating the agroforestry systems to surrounding wild forest – for supplying seeds and famine/reserve products;
- complementing surrounding intensively managed fields – the agroforestry providing low-energy, low-labour sources of subsistence in times of illness, and providing opportunities for off-farm labour.

Traditional agroforestry systems thus not only help in achieving local food security – a fundamental aim of sustainable development – but they also retain the forest, its species and its regenerative processes. At any given time, secondary successional species are reproducing somewhere in the mosaic; and, in this way, the elements necessary to regenerate the forest are retained in the system. The systems are effective within the constraints faced by peasant farmers the world over: limited labour, limited land, low capital, low availability of inputs, unpredictable markets and family needs.

CONCLUSION: TOWARDS SUSTAINABLE FOREST STRATEGIES

Despite the 1972 UN Conference on the Human Environment, despite increasing adherence to various concepts of sustainable development and despite the work of some institutions to resolve environment and development conflicts, there remains a polarization of thought. When it comes to forests, the polarization is between those who wish to cash in forest capital and those who wish to preserve all remaining forests for ecological and social values. However, as we have explored above, the financial, social and ecological values of forests are not necessarily incompatible – rather, complementary relationships between them must be constructed actively.

Many insights can be gained from traditional forest conversion and afforestation processes in seeking complementarities between forest values. Traditional processes have resulted in forest types that retain resilience through conserving biological diversity and ecological processes.

Traditional forest conversion and afforestation processes can also be socially sustainable. Boundaries are created between forest and non-forest, and between different types of forest, that delineate genuine social spaces. The boundaries are the result of careful negotiation between neighbouring land users, more or less on an equitable basis, and they are drawn partly according to the forest's ecological capabilities. In the English countryside, the result has been a system of relatively permanent, but highly complex, boundaries: hedgerow planting aligned to allow for rights of way; wooded copses retained in specific places for hunting interests; or tree plantations sited to shield a view considered unattractive by the public (Hoskins, 1955). In a tropical bush fallow system, the result is an equally complex landscape but with impermanent boundaries that shift continually within limits.

In contrast to traditional processes, in many places and particularly at present in the tropics, the natural forests are continually being cut back in favour of non-forest uses that soon prove to be unsustainable. The boundary between forest and non-forest is an unstable 'frontier'.

The optimum mix of forest values, and a capacity of resilience, cannot be achieved through the unstable 'frontier' approach to forests. Rather, it must be achieved through the establishment of a stable forest continuum which can accommodate changing circumstances. This would comprise a system of interlinked forest types, subject to various degrees of human intervention, and with reasonably stable boundaries:

- protected forest in its natural state;
- managed natural forests;
- shifting cultivation;
- agroforestry;
- plantations.

Throughout the world, the combined effect of continuous forest conversion and afforestation has been the progressive fragmentation of the forest, with an increasing boundary–area ratio (Dembner, 1991).

The forest boundary, stable or unstable, will therefore become an increasingly significant element of the forest resource in future.

What strategies can be taken to move from the unstable frontier to the stable forest continuum? We must look both outside and within the forest. Inside the forest, it is widely agreed that the preservation of intact natural forest is fundamental to the conservation of biological diversity, as well as to the production of commodities that cannot be produced outside natural forests. Yet there are great uncertainties, in the level of biological diversity present, in the extent to which it can be put to social/economic use and in the extent to which it is being degraded. These uncertainties make it wise to adopt the precautionary principle – which dictates that we should take action to maintain values, and to stave off problems which potentially are very costly, without waiting for scientific proof of their cause and extent. Hence there is a social imperative to protect those forests which are of the highest ecological value. Once these are defined, their boundaries should be set more or less permanently.

The boundaries within the different *managed* forest types, however, may be set by the market and/or social processes. Wherever these can signal the multiple values of forests, the boundaries may be more sustainable. Good information about forest values is therefore important.

Outside the forest, it is clear that many prevailing economic and policy signals marginalize people, forcing them into the forest. These signals must be understood and altered where necessary. Particularly important will be a review of land use and landownership policies and practices in the agricultural hinterland. It is equally important to look at the signals which attract farmers and loggers into the forest, to ensure that the signals encourage them to make forest land more productive on a sustainable basis.

At the national level, the most critical element in a strategy for sustainable forestry development is to establish the right policy framework (Box 7.3). Current forestry policies have been formulated with economic and strategic needs paramount. Many are several decades old. And it is inadequately realized that, today, forested landscapes are just as significant as the formal forest estate, and that they are impacted upon by many policies, apart from the official forestry policy. Hence there is a need to ensure that all policies that affect forests – and not just forestry policy – foster conservation and sustainable development of forest landscapes.

Box 7.3: Policy framework for conservation and sustainable development of forests

In every country, the *policy framework* should:

- *Halt inappropriate incentives*: the subsidies, logging concession terms, tenurial policies, pricing policies, and so on, which attract people to the forest to treat it in a predatory, short-term manner.
- *Relieve problems outside the forest*: the problems of health, population, agriculture, employment, and so on, that impoverish and deprive people, and thereby force them into the forest.
- *Consolidate existing settlement in the forest and on its fringe*, to create a stable forest continuum. This will entail providing appropriate incentives to encourage a long-term approach to forests: the infrastructure, tenurial and financial security, technology, knowledge and resources.
- *Integrate forestry into rural development*: recognizing that forestry is no longer restricted to large blocks of 'pure' forest producing industrial materials, but is carried out in the wider landscape for many purposes. Policy attention should be paid to land and tree tenure, sustaining and developing traditional forestry knowledge, integrating forestry and agriculture and encouraging participation in multipurpose forestry/ agroforestry.
- *Set up a clear forest ownership structure, a stable forest authority and a stable framework of regulations and incentives*. Generally, government should own forests with important watersheds and areas of the highest biological diversity. However, it may be more appropriate for the private sector and communities to own and manage production forests. Private/community ownership affords more possibilities to integrate forestry with surrounding agricultural and urban land uses. Institutional and legal frameworks must ensure equitable access to forest resources and ensure balances in control between top-down and bottom-up interests. The policy framework for forestry must be stable over the long term.
- *Co-ordinate the authorities responsible for forest functions* – notably forestry, water and agriculture – to achieve convergent approaches to the management of forests.
- *Make clear distinctions between policies for forest production and policies for conserving forest ecosystems*. The precautionary principle should be applied in setting forest conservation policy.
- *Evaluate, and keep account of, the economic, social and ecological functions of forests*. New systems of forest resource accounting need to be developed: to measure the values of different forest functions and forest types, and their value relative to other assets. These need to be reviewed regularly.

- *Ensure participation of local people* in all policy and planning that affects forests, and in forest management and use. This will entail making provision for access to forests and to inputs necessary for sustainable management. Special recognition must be given to poor and landless groups who depend upon the forest but who have no codified tenure.
- *Diversify forest research*. Research should diversify from its commodity focus (which concentrates on the economic function of forests) to a focus on the forest ecosystem (to explore the ecological function) and a focus on forest people's livelihoods (to explore the social function). In practice, this will mean greater attention to multiple use/user systems, to the forest boundary and to forest services.
- *Improve international co-operation* in forestry matters: to assist technology transfer and the sharing of skills and information; to ensure that trade in forest products is sustainable and equitably rewarded; to co-ordinate forest monitoring and accounting; and to compensate countries that protect forest assets for global benefits, on the basis of services supplied.

While international co-operation should define and work towards common goals and standards, global regulation and enforcement are not appropriate. Rather, recognizing the very different circumstances of each country, countries would devise their own approaches to encourage different social groups to meet those goals and standards. Further, countries should not be penalized for gross rates of deforestation. Instead, on the basis of a full forest valuation, countries might identify those forests which should be protected in perpetuity, and also a minimum percentage of land under tree cover of all types; it is these areas which might legitimately be held up for international scrutiny.

The policy framework needs to be better informed by ecological and social realities. Policies must establish the primacy of maintaining forest ecological processes and biological diversity. Further, policies should be formulated with much greater public participation than at present. Specific groups of people determine what happens in the forest, and policies will only be effective if they are built on knowledge of the diverse behaviour and aspirations of these people.

NOTES

1 A pioneer species is a colonizer of open land. It is characterized by vigorous growth, dependency on and tolerance of full sunlight, and abundant readily

dispersed seed, which may remain dormant for a long time. Pioneer trees may be unable to compete successfully in a close-canopy forest and be relatively short lived.

REFERENCES AND BIBLIOGRAPHY

Ailton Krenak, 1989. Quoted in S. Hecht and A. Cockburn, *The Fate of the Forest*, Verso, London.

Alcorn, J. B., 1990. 'Indigenous agroforestry strategies meeting farmers' needs', in A. A. Anderson (ed.), *Alternatives to Deforestation: Steps towards Sustainable Use of the Amazon Rain Forest,* Columbia University Press, New York.

Allan, T. and Lanly, J. P., 1991. 'Global overview of status and trends of world's forests', in D. Howlett and C. Sargent (eds), *Proceedings of the Technical Workshop to Explore Options for Global Forest Management*, IIED, London.

Anderson, A. A., 1990. 'Introduction', in A. A. Anderson (ed.), *Alternatives to Deforestation: Steps towards Sustainable Use of the Amazon Rain Forest*, Columbia University Press, New York.

Anderson, D., 1990. *Economic Growth and the Environment*, selected papers, Shell International Petroleum Co., London.

Arnold, J. E. M., 1991. *Long-Term Trends in Global Demand for and Supply of Industrial Wood*, Oxford Forestry Institute, Oxford.

Ashton, P., 1991. Paper for World Resources Institute Colloquium on Sustainability in Natural Tropical Forest Management, Washington, DC.

Bandyopadhyay, J. and Shiva, V., 1990. 'Asia's forest cultures', in S. Head and R. Heinzman (eds), *Lessons of the Rainforest*, Sierra Club Books, San Francisco.

Bass, S. M. J., 1991. *The Social and Cultural Implications of Tree Plantations in Local Economies*, Shell Tree Plantation Review Paper no. 5, Shell International Petroleum Co., London.

Browder, J. O., 1989. 'Lumber production and economic development in the Brazilian Amazon: regional trends and a case study', *Journal of World Forest Resource Management*, 4.

Bruenig, E. F. and Schneider, T. W., 1991. 'Forests and microclimate: old neglects and new challenges', paper for the World Forestry Congress, Paris.

Campbell, J. G., Shrestha, R. P. and Euphrat, F., n.d. 'Socio-economic factors in traditional forest use and management', *Banko Janakari*, 1, 4, pp. 45–54.

Carter, A. S., and Gilmour, D. A., 1989. 'Increase in tree cover on private land in central Nepal', *Mountain Research and Development*, 9, 4, pp. 381–91.

Coleman, D., 1985. 'Population regulations: a long-range view', in D. Coleman and R. Schofield (eds), *The State of Population Theory: Funeral for Malthus*, Blackwell, New York.

Cruz, M. C. J., 1991. *Population Pressure in Tropical Developing Countries*, Population Reference Bureau, Washington, DC.

Davies, A. G. and Richards, P., 1991. *Rain Forest in Mende Life*, report to ESCOR, ODA, London.

Dawkins, H. C., 1988. 'The first century of tropical silviculture: successes forgotten and failures misunderstood', in *Oxford Rainforest Conference Proceedings*, Oxford Forestry Institute, Oxford.

Dembner, S., 1991. 'Provisional data from the Forest Resources Assessment 1990 project', *Unasylva*, 164, 42.

Denslow, J. S. and Padoch, C., 1988. *People of the Tropical Rainforest*, University of California Press, Berkeley, Calif.

Dewees, P. A., 1991. 'Woodlots, labour use and farming systems in Kenya', paper for the Institute of Rural Management, Anand, India: Socio-Economic Aspects of Tree-Growing by Farmers.

Douglas, J. D., 1983. *A Reappraisal of Forestry Development in Developing Countries*, Martinus Nijhoff and Dr W. Junk Publishers, The Hague.

Falconer, J., 1991. *The Significance of Forest Resources in Rural Economies of Southern Ghana*, report to the Government of Ghana, ODA, London.

FAO, 1988. *An Interim Report on the State of Forest Resources in the Developing Countries*, FO:MISC/88/7, FAO, Rome.

Gerstin, J., 1990. 'No condition permanent: the rainforests of Africa', in S. Head and R. O. Heinzman (eds). *Lessons of the Rainforest*, Sierra Club Books, San Francisco.

Hladik, C. M., Bahuchet, S. and de Garine, I. 1990. *Food and Nutrition in the African Rain Forest*, UNESCO Man and Biosphere programme, Paris.

Hoskins, W. G., 1955. *The Making of the English Landscape*, Hodder & Stoughton, London.

Hyde, W. S. and Sedjo, R. A., 1991. 'Managing tropical forests: reflections on the rent distribution discussion', appendix 10 in W. S. Hyde and D. H. Newman, *Forest Economics in Brief – with Summary Observations for Policy Analysis*, draft report, Agricultural and Rural Development, World Bank, Washington, DC.

Jonsson, T. and Lindgren, P., 1990. *Logging Technology: For or Against?*, Forest Operations Institute 'Skogsarbeten', Kista, Sweden.

Longman, K. A. and Jenik, J., 1974. *Tropical Forestry Ecology*, Cambridge University Press, Cambridge.

Mahar, D. J., 1988. *Government Politics and Deforestation in Brazil's Amazon Region*, World Bank, Washington, DC.

Michon, G., 1985. 'De l'homme de la forêt au paysan de l'arbre: agroforesteries indonesiennes', unpublished thesis, l'Université des Sciences et Techniques du Languedoc.

Montalembert, M. R., 1991. 'Key forestry policy issues in the early 1990s', *Unasylva*, 166, 14.

Myers, N., 1990. 'The world's forests and human populations: the environmental interconnections', *Population and Development Review*, 16, pp. 1–14.

Oxford Forestry Institute, 1991. *Incentives in Producer and Consumer Countries to Promote Sustainable Development of Tropical Forests*, pre-project report to International Tropical Timber Organization, PCM.PCF.PCI(V)/1/Rev.3, OFI, Oxford.

Palmer, J., 1989. 'Management of natural forest for sustainable timber production: a commentary', in D. Poore (ed.), *No Timber without Trees*, Earthscan, London.

Peters, C. M., Gentry, A. H. and Mendelsohn, R. O., 1989. 'Valuation of the Amazon rainforest', *Nature*, 339.

Poore, D. (ed.), 1989. *No Timber without Trees*, Earthscan, London.

Poore, D. and Sayer, J., 1987. *The Management of Tropical Moist Forest Lands: Ecological Guidelines*, IUCN, Gland, Switzerland.

Rambo, A. T., 1983. *Why Shifting Cultivators Keep Shifting: Understanding Farmer Decision Making in Traditional Agroforestry Systems*, East–West Environment and Policy Institute, Hawaii.

Rao, Y. S., 1991. 'State of forestry in the Asia-Pacific region', in D. Howlett and C. Sargent (eds), *Proceedings of the Technical Workshop to Explore Options for Global Forest Management*, IIED, London.

Repetto, R., 1988. *The Forest for the Trees? Government Policies and the Misuse of Forest Resources*, World Resources Institute, Washington, DC.

Reyes, J. M., 1991. 'Deforestation and reforestation in Bolivia', in D. Howlett and C. Sargent (eds), *Proceedings of the Technical Workshop to Explore Options for Global Forest Management*, IIED, London.

Richards, P. W., 1973. 'Africa – "odd man out"', in B. J. Meggers, E. Ayensu and W. D. Duckworth (eds), *Tropical Forest Ecosystems in Africa and South America: A Comparative Review*, Smithsonian Institute Press, Washington, DC.

Romm, J., 1991. 'Exploring institutional options for global forest management', in D. Howlett and C. Sargent (eds), *Proceedings of the Technical Workshop to Explore Options for Global Forest Management*, IIED, London.

Romm, J. and Washburn, C., 1985. *State Policy and County Control: Their Effects on the Formation of California's Timberland Production Zone*, University of California Press, Berkeley, Calif.

Sargent, C., 1990. *Defining the Issues*, IIED, London.

Sargent, C., 1991. *Land Use Issues in the Forestry Sector in Vietnam*, TFAP report to the Government of Vietnam, FAO, Rome.

Sawyer, D., 1990. 'The future of deforestation in Amazonia: a socioeconomic and political analysis', in A. A. Anderson (ed.), *Alternatives to Deforestation: Steps towards Sustainable Use of the Amazon Rain Forest*, Columbia University Press, New York.

Thiesenhusen, W. C. (ed.), 1989. *Searching for Agricultural Reform in Latin America*, Unwin Hyman, Boston, Mass.

Tho, Y. P., 1991. 'Tropical moist forests – facts and issues', in D. Howlett and C. Sargent (eds), *Proceedings of the Technical Workshop to Explore Options for Global Forest Management*, IIED, London.

Weiskel, T. C., 1983. 'Rubbish and racism: problems of boundary in an ecosystem', *Yale Review*, 72, 2.

Weiskel, T. C., 1990. *The Anthropology of Environmental Decline: Historical Aspects of Anthropogenic Ecological Degradation*, Reference Services Bureau, USA.

WCMC (World Conservation Monitoring Centre), forthcoming. *Global Biodiversity 1992*, WCMC, Cambridge.

World Resources Institute, 1987. *World Resources 1987–88*, Basic Books, New York.

World Resources Institute, 1990. *World Resources 1990–91*, Oxford University Press, Oxford.

8 The Future of Africa's Drylands: Is Local Resource Management the Answer?

Camilla Toulmin, Ian Scoones and Joshua Bishop

INTRODUCTION

The dryland regions of sub-Saharan Africa stretch across the continent, from Senegal in the west to Sudan, Somalia and Ethiopia in the east, descending through parts of Kenya and Tanzania to southern Africa (Figure 8.1). Excluding the hyper-arid deserts, dryland areas cover an estimated 43 per cent of the surface area of the continent, and are home to 66 per cent of Africa's human population. Subject to low and uncertain rainfall within a short rainy season, dryland peoples have always had to cope with drought. However, the past few decades have witnessed growing problems of environmental degradation, food shortages, impoverishment and conflict through much of the drylands. In their acute form, rainfall failure and crop failure, combined with political conflict, have produced refugees in their millions and a heavy cost in human lives. Less clearly in evidence but of increasing importance has been the rising pressure of demand on all resources within the dryland region and the increasing conflicts between different users for control over farmland, water, forests and pastures.

While much of the experience of recent decades provides little comfort for the future of Africa's drylands, there are also more promising examples of development activity from which some hope can be sought. In general, these more successful instances comprise small-scale programmes, based on simple technologies, developed with the full participation of local people and providing fairly immediate benefits to them. The product of work by both governmental and non-governmental organizations, these programmes tend to place special

Figure 8.1: Africa's dryland regions

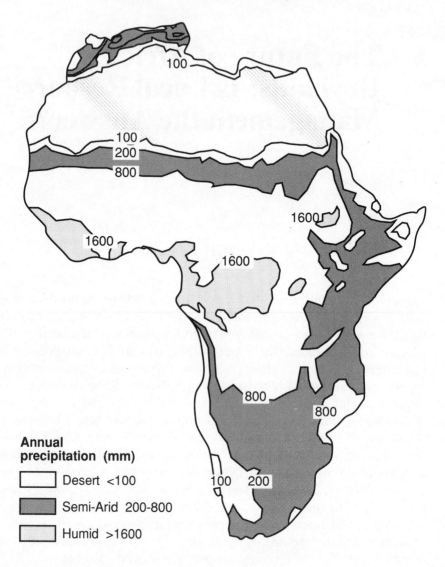

Source: Glantz (1987).

emphasis on training and support for the development of local institutions.

This chapter aims to examine several examples of more successful development activity, and to assess whether these can provide a model for broader drylands development. It will argue that the transfer of rights and responsibilities to manage natural resources to local user groups is a necessary condition for more sustainable development in these regions. It will outline some of the other necessary conditions required in different fields and at different levels (from grass roots to global) for such local-level solutions to bear the fruit so greatly hoped of them.

CONSTRAINTS ON SUSTAINABLE LIVELIHOODS IN DRYLAND AFRICA

The vulnerability of dryland Africa to food shortage and famine is usually attributed to poor rainfall. Yet, while low and unreliable rainfall certainly plays its part, there are also other very important contributory factors. These include institutional issues such as land tenure, economic policy such as food prices, questions related to international trade and debt, the low priority given to marginal regions by national governments and the increasing incidence of military conflict. Together, these factors help explain why tens of millions of people in Africa are at risk of serious food shortage while many millions more are chronically malnourished.

How much environmental degradation?

Much has been written about environmental degradation and 'desertification' in Africa and a variety of statistics have been used to estimate their importance across the continent. Certain difficulties arise in assessing the rate and incidence of degradation, because we lack clear and unambiguous data over a period of some years from which trends could be discerned. It is also hard to unravel the relative importance of different factors in causing a particular trend in resource degradation. For example, where rainfall is highly variable and itself subject to a long downward trend, it is very difficult to judge whether a fall in crop productivity is due to falling rainfall or to soil erosion, or to some other factor such as labour shortages at harvest time.

Box 8.1 distinguishes between 'desert advance' and desertification and highlights the priority which needs to be given to coping with problems of land degradation in more densely settled regions. Box 8.2 presents the findings of several studies on land degradation undertaken in the Sudan over recent years and the conflicting evidence which they provide.

Box 8.1: Of deserts and desertification

It is widely believed that much of dryland Africa is suffering from the spread of deserts. For example, figures are quoted that claim the desert is advancing at the rate of 5 to 10 km a year. At the same time, the term 'desertification' has crept into common parlance and has become associated with the idea of spreading deserts.

There are two reasons behind the thinking that deserts are expanding. First, in prehistoric times, the area which is now the Sahara Desert was formerly well watered and harboured lakes, woodland, pastures and wild game, as archaeological research and the rock paintings in the Hoggar mountains eloquently testify. Clearly, the Sahara Desert has 'spread' over past millennia and could do so again, although the exact causes of this drying up are not well known. Second, during the severe drought years of 1968–73, 'normal' rainfall patterns shifted substantially, in many places by up to 150 km. If the 'desert border' is defined strictly in rainfall terms in a given year, then those years saw a massive advance in the desert border. Conversely, the desert has 'shrunk' in years such as 1988, when heavy rainfall has brought grasses to germinate and flourish in areas which have not seen them for many years.

In the mid-1970s, several surveys were carried out to assess the rate of 'desert advance' (Lamprey, 1975; Ibrahim, 1984). The report written following Lamprey's three-week trek across Kordofan in the Sudan in 1975 has been particularly influential in promoting the idea of the desert creeping forward, and helped gain currency for the figure of 5 to 10 km a year as the speed of this advance. However, severe reservations about the methods used and the choice of sites and years taken for comparison have largely discredited the substance of this and other work.

Recent surveys have followed more careful methods and, as a result, have produced a more complex interpretation of what is happening. This can be summarized as follows:

Rainfall isohyets[1] have shifted substantially along much of the southern edge of the Sahara Desert over the past twenty to twenty-five years. This has meant that areas that formerly could support crops with some confidence of a harvest are now no longer able to do so. Similarly, the bush and tree populations which flourished in the wetter years of the 1950s and 1960s now find themselves in an ever more hostile environment, with water-tables falling too far for their roots to reach. Trees are thus dying in huge numbers. Grasslands have not escaped the consequences of rainfall decline, and have experienced the disappearance of many valued perennial grasses within the Sahelian zone.

Scientists are still unsure why this shift in climatic patterns has occurred. After the first major drought in the early 1970s, it was widely believed that grazing and farming practices within the Sahelian region were baring the soils and thus largely to blame for persistent drought.

Now the view has turned towards the likely role of global climatic influences on African rainfall, given our growing understanding of the interconnections between regional weather systems. Whatever the causes, this area of sub-Saharan Africa seems to be experiencing an extended dry period of weather, of unknown duration. It is this fall in rainfall that is creating problems rather than a physical movement of the desert itself.

Problems of *desertification* first attracted widespread attention following the United Nations Conference on Desertification (UNCOD) held in Nairobi in 1977. Considerable confusion surrounds the meaning of the term; it has, in the public mind, frequently been taken as meaning the movement of the desert. Criticism of the muddled and inconsistent way in which the term has been used (Nelson, 1988; Warren and Agnew, 1988) has led UNEP to revise its definition to cover the *degradation of soil and vegetation within the arid, semi-arid and sub-humid zones caused largely by harmful human activities*. This redefinition of desertification has been helpful in removing from consideration changes in resource productivity that are due to rainfall variability alone. It has also helped shift attention to the areas where problems of resource degradation are most important. Desertification, or dryland degradation, does not pose its greatest challenge on the desert edge, where few people live and there is little productive activity. Rather attention is needed in higher-rainfall zones where dense human and livestock populations put considerable pressure on the available resources, and where inappropriate land use can bring about serious problems of soil erosion.

Rainfall data for dryland Africa present a mixed picture. In West Africa, there is an increasingly clear shift in rainfall patterns leading to lower and more erratic levels (IUCN, 1989), as can be seen in Figure 8.2. It is reckoned that since the mid-1960s, rainfall isohyets have shifted southwards by more than 100 km (Shaikh *et al.*, 1988). This means that places where the average rainfall used to be 600 mm are now getting 400 mm, while places where rainfall was formerly 400 mm (the limit needed for crop growth) are now receiving as little as 200 mm. In the eastern Sahel, there have also been some years of exceptional drought, such as 1973, 1984 and 1988, as shown in Figure 8.3. However, the longer-term trend is less clear than for the western Sahel (Hulme, 1991). Southern Africa has not suffered a clear downward trend in rainfall, but seems to experience regular cycles of years of better and then years of less than normal rainfall (Tyson, 1991).

Box 8.2: Is the environment degrading, and why?

A series of studies carried out in the Sudan by researchers from Lund University, Sweden represent an important attempt to establish the nature of 'degradation' processes in a dryland area. The results of these studies conflict with the conventional wisdom that the dry areas of Sudan are suffering from a process of human-induced 'desertification' and challenge the conclusions derived from more general geographical studies (e.g. Ibrahim, 1984).

The Lund studies (Hellden, 1984; Olsson, 1985; Ahlcrona, 1988) used a variety of methods: meteorological statistics, agricultural statistics, remote sensing data, ground surveys and farmer interviews. Long time-series data were required to test whether there had been irreversible changes in productivity and if these were due to human-related impact.

Ahlcrona correlated rainfall data with agricultural production for various parts of dry Sudan over a period of more than twenty years. She found that rainfall was highly correlated with millet and sorghum yields (correlation: $r^2 = 0.75$), suggesting that rainfall decline was the major factor in falling crop yields, rather than a long-term decline in soil fertility. This would suggest that were rainfall levels to improve, so also should crop yields.

Detailed examination of aerial photographs over the period 1961–83 showed that there had been no systematic expansion of barren areas around villages; nor was there any evidence of moving sand dunes in these areas over the same period (Ahlcrona, 1988). These findings contrast with the popular conception of the 'advancing desert' and 'desertified village zones', generated by earlier surveys.

Clearly changes in the study areas had occurred, such as a shift in the composition of tree and pasture species, towards less valuable forms of vegetation. These changes have been aggravated in certain sites by heavy pressures from human and livestock populations. However, most changes appear to be largely related to rainfall decline, rather than to a broader process of degradation or 'desert advance'. Appropriate responses to land degradation in dryland areas require a localized analysis that pinpoints key problems in particular places. Assessments of land degradation or desertification on a broad scale provide poor-quality data which are difficult to evaluate and impossible to use for the design of appropriate resource management interventions.

The Intergovernmental Panel on Climate Change makes few detailed predictions about future rainfall in dryland Africa and confirms the current poor understanding of global climate systems. Nevertheless, it suggests that rain is likely to come in fiercer storms, bringing increased problems of runoff and erosion of soils (IPCC, 1990). If these

Figure 8.2: Annual rainfall departure index for the Sahel, 1898–1991

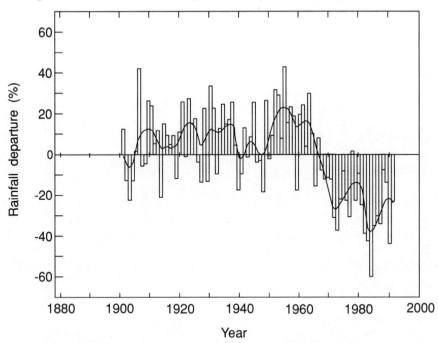

Source: Mike Hulme, Climate Research Unit, University of East Anglia, June 1991. © Mike Hulme 1991.

predictions are accurate, then careful management of soils and vegetation becomes an even greater priority.

In the past, people have coped with variability in rainfall from year to year and from place to place by developing a number of strategies, such as diversifying the crops grown and animal species herded. In addition, people have usually maintained reciprocal relations of support between different areas, so that villages suffering drought in one year can send people to harvest and glean the fields of more favoured villages elsewhere. Rainfall in future is likely to be at least as unreliable and patchy as in the past, which means that resource management systems must maintain considerable flexibility to allow for the movement of people, livestock and food between areas of deficit and surplus.

The impact of development.

Research and development activity in Africa's drylands has generated few quick and readily replicable results. Work in the 1960s and 1970s focused on the generation and spread of new technologies in the farming sector, such as the introduction of mechanization, high-yield

Figure 8.3: Rainfall trends, Ethiopia, 1898–1990

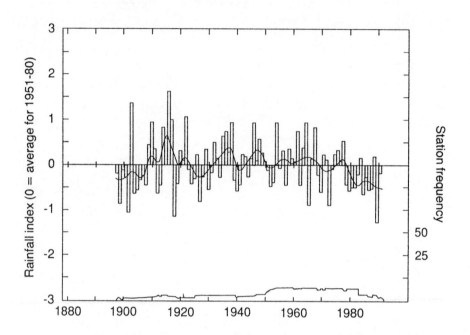

Source: Mike Hulme, Climate Research Unit, University of East Anglia, June 1991. © Mike Hulme 1991.

seed varieties and chemical fertilizers. Hopes were raised that the Green Revolution technology that had been developed with such apparent success in South Asia might be transferred to the African context. However, the high cost of such inputs has frequently hindered the poorer farmer from making this investment, particularly where there are substantial risks of crop failure due to the rain falling at the wrong time. Large-scale irrigation schemes were also perceived as providing a means to protect harvests from the hazards of drought, but have run into serious problems of maintenance, high costs, low yields and poor incentives to farmers (GRET, 1991).

Even where there are apparent successes from the use of modern technology, closer examination reveals that such gains have often been achieved at considerable cost. For example, in the eastern Sudan, there are large mechanized farming schemes which produce much grain but at high environmental and social cost, and which absorb large amounts of foreign exchange. Similarly, the large-scale wheat farms of north-east Tanzania provide more than half the country's wheat requirements, but require large amounts of imported fuel, fertilizer and spare parts and have displaced thousands of local herders (Lane and Pretty, 1990).

One reason why standard approaches to development in Africa's drylands have brought little success is that these environments are immensely heterogeneous. Some parts of dryland landscapes represent areas of high agricultural or grazing potential; understanding the role of such key 'micro-environments' within dryland ecosystems may indicate directions for future development (Chambers, 1990). Low-lying valley bottomlands (*fadamas, dambos, mbugas, wadis*) represent one type of high-potential patch. Compared to surrounding drylands, these areas offer potential for intensification (such as through water harvesting) and diversification (such as through cash cropping of vegetables). Because of their high value, such areas are also often contested, both among agriculturalists and between cultivators and pastoralists (Scoones, 1991).

Despite the difficulties in defining, quantifying and explaining trends in resource productivity and degradation, it is clear that many parts of dryland Africa are experiencing great difficulties in feeding their populations and in controlling environmental damage, such as soil erosion, reduced tree cover, loss of wildlife and falling water-tables. Pressures on resources come from a combination of increased demands stemming from increased commercialization and growing populations and from weaknesses in institutions and economic policy which contribute to create insecurity and poor management practices. Frequently, the causal mechanisms behind resource degradation are complex and interlinked. For example, a problem with soil erosion and exhausted soil fertility in one village may be linked to the in-migration of families displaced by a development scheme elsewhere.

Meeting energy needs

Most countries in sub-Saharan Africa rely heavily on woody biomass for fuel, either directly or in the form of charcoal. Between 60 and 95 per cent of all energy needs are derived from woodfuels, with the poorer countries of the region particularly dependent (Leach and Mearns, 1988). A slightly lesser dependence is found within the SADCC region, where greater industrial growth and the development of alternative fuels, such as coal and hydropower, have shifted the burden of energy supply away from woodfuels.

Experience from Senegal shows that it is difficult to shift habits away from traditional fuels. Here, considerable progress has been made with encouraging the use of gas for cooking in the main urban areas. A survey carried out in 1989 in Senegal's capital, Dakar, showed that

80 per cent of households use a gas ring. However, only 5 per cent of households had completely abandoned charcoal as a fuel in favour of gas. As a result, there has been little reduction in the demand for charcoal, since this is the preferred fuel for certain cooking operations (Club du Sahel, 1991).

Conventional analysis usually presents the deforestation of land for provision of fuel needs as a major contributor to land degradation, by removing the tree cover and hence rendering the land more vulnerable to erosion. However, as recent research has shown, in many cases woodfuel supply is largely the by-product of land being cleared for other, usually agricultural purposes (Leach and Mearns, 1988). Hence, attempts to stem deforestation must address farming practices and means to control the clearing of new land by developing, for example, more intensive forms of cultivation. In some cases, however, urban demand for charcoal and other wood products is making very damaging demands on wood stocks, in the more accessible rural areas. Local people are often unable to assert control over the use of their trees by outsiders, so that woodcutters and charcoal burners can operate with impunity (Shepherd, 1988; Bergeret with Ribot, 1990). Even where legislation exists which is meant to protect the interests of local communities over their tree resources, these rights are frequently overturned, due to the political and economic power wielded by those involved in the wood and charcoal trade.

Growth in human numbers

One factor behind the increased pressure on resources in dry Africa concerns the demands of a growing human population. Within sub-Saharan Africa, population densities vary enormously. In the more arid pastoral areas of the northern Sahel, there are fewer than 5 people per square kilometre. Here survival is only possible through extensive grazing of animal herds, which limits the number of people the land can support. Population densities rise as rainfall increases and as crop growing becomes a more assured source of subsistence. In much of the southern Sahel, for instance, population densities of 30 to 50 people per square kilometre are common, while in areas such as Machakos, Kenya, densities can reach 80 people per square kilometre. With the development of substantial off-farm incomes, population densities can rise to much higher levels. Around major cities, such as Kano in the north of Nigeria, a mixture of intensive farming developed over past centuries combined with trade and other activities has enabled the support of more than 150 people per square kilometre (Mortimore, 1989).

The human population of sub-Saharan Africa has been growing at around 3 per cent each year, so that numbers are now double what they were twenty-five years ago. Rates of population growth within the drylands vary between countries, with the highest rates for the period 1980–7 found in Kenya (4.1 per cent), Tanzania (3.5 per cent) and the Gambia (3.3 per cent). In the poorer countries of the West African Sahel, growth rates are lower, at around 2.6 per cent per annum over the same period, due to lower levels of fertility, higher mortality and emigration to neighbouring countries with higher rainfall and greater economic potential.

The population which a region can support depends on the productivity of resources available and the technologies used to exploit them. While the overall population density in dryland Africa is fairly low, so also are levels of productivity in both agriculture and the non-farm sector. Rising population densities pose a problem for resource management where people do not adapt their methods of farming and land use accordingly, to take account of the reduced availability of land. For example, in traditional farming systems, fallowing of land was widely used to re-establish the fertility of soils following several years of farming. Now, in many regions, there is no longer enough land available for it to be left idle for long enough to recover. Where soil nutrients and organic matter are not replaced on a regular basis, the fertility of soils will continue to decline with a resultant fall in crop and pasture yields (van Keulen and Breman, 1990).

Recent evidence from a number of developing countries points to certain important factors which can help slow rates of population growth and improve levels of human welfare. These include economic and social progress, improvements in women's status, education and economic position, the availability of family planning education and services, and reduced child deaths (UNICEF, 1991). These factors tend to be interlinked so that, for example, improving educational and economic prospects for women produces lower levels of child mortality and greater economic and social welfare. The results of a survey carried out in Kenya in 1989 indicate that a slowing of its very high rate of population growth is now occurring, probably due to the educational reforms and the increased associated cost to parents of sending children through school, combined with a strong desire by parents to educate their children and the increased availability of contraception (Kelley and Nobbe, 1990).

Migrants and refugees

Human migration has long been a means by which local pressures on resources have been resolved. Movement to urban areas is an important phenomenon throughout the drylands and several countries have witnessed very high rates of urban growth. For example, in Mauritania, the proportion of the population living in urban areas has risen from 10 per cent in 1965 to 27 per cent in 1980 and to 38 per cent in 1987. Elsewhere, the trend is similar, though not perhaps so rapid. For example, in the nine Sahelian states as a whole, the urban population has grown from 13 per cent in 1965 to 19 per cent in 1980 and 23 per cent in 1987 (World Bank, 1989).

Migration by people to settle new areas has always been an important strategy to gain access to increased land. The drier parts of Kenya, for example, have seen a steady inflow of people from higher-rainfall areas in the highlands where land pressure has become acute. Similarly, in Ethiopia, for decades people have been moving off the more densely settled highlands down towards the drier plains where land is in greater supply. This movement of people into more marginal farming regions has increased the vulnerability of communities in the dry zone and is becoming increasingly difficult as little unoccupied land remains. However, there has also been a converse flow from lower- to higher-rainfall areas where, for example, tsetse control programmes and the opening up of new areas have increased the availability of land. For example, in south-west Burkina Faso, incoming families originally from the drier north of the country have been arriving in large numbers over the last ten to fifteen years, largely as a result of successful programmes to eliminate river blindness. In certain districts, these incomers now constitute nearly 50 per cent of the farming population.

The forced migration of people has also been a growing problem throughout Africa's drylands, often the combined result of military conflict, recurrent drought and famine. There are now millions of displaced people in refugee camps in border areas and on the outskirts of many towns. For example, it is estimated that the city of Khartoum, in the Sudan, contains a total population of 3.5 million people of whom 1.8 million are refugees from the south and west of the country, displaced by drought and war (Ahmad, 1989; Omer, 1990). It is not just capital cities which have experienced this growth. Many smaller towns have also seen their populations swollen greatly by people fleeing both famine and harassment. These refugees often cannot acquire rights to settle and farm in their new place of residence, and while they may hope to return home soon, many camp sites have now become permanent.

Economic structures

Most countries in dryland Africa depend heavily in terms of total output and employment on rainfed agricultural production, much of it at a subsistence level. The agricultural sector is generally characterized by low inputs and low yields, producing grains (such as millet, maize and sorghum), cash crops (such as cotton and groundnuts) and livestock (meat, milk, animal power and hides). The small industrial sector tends to be dominated by food processing, textiles and light manufacturing largely for import substitution. Most of the larger manufacturing enterprises are publicly owned and heavily subsidized, and have been plagued by poor management, overvalued exchange rates and weak infrastructure and support services. Recent pressure from donors and the implementation of structural adjustment programmes have led to the closure or privatization of many of these enterprises.

In contrast to manufacturing, commerce in the drylands is often a lively sector dominated by small private traders in agricultural products and imported consumption goods. National frontiers usually represent less of a boundary and more of an opportunity for traders to benefit from exchange rate differences and from local shortages of certain commodities.

Major exports from the drylands remain primarily agricultural, despite earlier attempts to diversify away from reliance on cash crops. For example, in 1988 the proportion of export earnings contributed by agricultural and natural resource commodities was for Ethiopia 99 per cent, Somalia 95 per cent, Chad 89 per cent and Kenya 83 per cent. Such exports were made up of commodities such as coffee, livestock, cotton and tea, with some additional earnings from mineral exports such as phosphates and uranium. Production of these commodities relies heavily on the natural resource base of the region. Maintaining and improving the productivity of farming and herding systems are therefore crucial to ensure continued foreign exchange earnings. However, world market prices continue to be highly variable and many commodities experienced a marked decline in world price levels over the late 1980s. These declines have come on top of years of deliberate underpricing by many African governments. Producer prices of most food crops were fixed at very low levels, largely for the benefit of urban consumers. Export crops were often heavily taxed, generating a large surplus for state marketing boards, but little reinvestment in the farm sector. Attempts to increase the value of exports by processing have registered little progress, partly because of domestic constraints, but also as a result of protectionist barriers erected by consuming nations of the developed world.

Aid and debt

Aid flows per capita to sub-Saharan Africa as a whole are the highest in the world. The nine Sahelian states of West Africa received the most with an estimated US$59/head in 1987 compared with US$25/head for all of sub-Saharan Africa and US$5/head for the countries of South Asia. Such aid has not brought the results hoped for, in part because of the small proportion allocated to small-scale rainfed agriculture, and in part because aid has frequently not reached its intended recipients, but instead has been used to prop up systems of power and patronage.

The combined debt owed by the countries of sub-Saharan Africa is little more than that of Brazil, and is almost all owed to governments and multilateral banks and agencies, rather than to commercial banks. However, in terms of ability to pay, these levels of debt have proved crippling to many countries. In 1989, foreign debt in sub-Saharan Africa was equivalent to 112 per cent of the region's GNP and to 352 per cent of its exports; service of this debt consumed 24 per cent of export revenue. Any solution to the current difficulties faced by national governments requires some reduction in the debt burden, by cancelling of some loans and converting others to grants. Given the small size of these debts in relation to that owed by other countries, debt relief continues to be a high priority.

New stresses: institutional and political change

Since the end of the 1980s, much of Africa has experienced great political change. In many countries, the political systems which evolved over the post-independence period have lost their legitimacy in the eyes of their people and outside funders, the central role of the state has been overturned, there is growing civil and military conflict in many areas, and there are unstoppable pressures for multi-party democracy. These changes stem from internal dissent and from external donor pressure, through programmes of structural adjustment and the new political conditionality being imposed by many donors. The collapse of the centralized states of Eastern Europe has removed them as funders and models for African state development. Financial constraints due to trends in trade and debt have forced governments to accept a disengagement of state structures from key areas of economic life and a reduction in power and resources held by centralized national administrations.

Parallel to the collapse of the state in much of Africa, at a global level a new paradigm is emerging in which decentralization of power and responsibility and the growing importance of local-level institution building are key components (Hjort, 1991). This shift in thinking towards a transfer of power and responsibilities to local-level institutions represents an important opportunity for establishing more effective resource use in much of dryland Africa. Throughout the region, land tenure systems are now under review to redefine the respective powers and duties of local people and the state.

There are strong grounds for thinking that local users are the best managers of the resources on which their own livelihoods depend. This is because, first, local people have a strong interest in ensuring the continued productivity of resources on which the lives of their children and grandchildren depend and, second, the weakness of most African administrations precludes any effective management of resource use by central governments, hence the need to rely on structures which involve local users (Bishop, 1988). However, the shift in rights and responsibilities from central state structures to local people should not imply that there is no longer any important role for the state to play. As will be argued below, there are some very important activities required of the administration if such local-level resource management is to be sustainable.

VISIONS OF THE FUTURE IN AFRICA'S DRYLANDS

Dryland Africa is facing, according to some observers, a long-term decline in its ability to support its population. The combination of highly variable rainfall, increased pressure on natural resources and a growth of conflict and insecurity in many areas has, during the 1980s, pushed millions of people into severe famine and caused migrations on a massive scale. If there are no solutions to falling agricultural yields, continued rapid population growth, rising inter-ethnic strife and the general breakdown of social and political structures, the future for much of dryland Africa looks bleak. The external circumstances for this region are hardly more encouraging, with a continuous decline in the terms of trade and its growing marginalization in the world economy and global affairs.

The picture may not, however, be as dismal as the above suggests. There are, for example, ways in which rainfed farming can be made more resistant to drought. Such adaptation is sometimes born from traditional practice, as a result of farmers experimenting with new ways to use their land. In other cases, changes in technology have been prompted by access to ideas and skills from outside. Examples of promising approaches to improved resource use are presented in Box 8.3.

Box 8.3: Promising approaches to improving rural livelihoods

Building rock dams in Burkina Faso

In the Rissiam district of northern Burkina Faso, a technique has been developed using permeable rock dams to help slow soil erosion and increase the moisture available for crop growth. Since 1977, the Association Française des Volontaires du Progrès (the French volunteer association) has been helping villages develop ways to stem the formation of gulleys on their farm land. This involves building a series of long, low dams constructed of rocks placed across the streambed. As rainwater rushes down the gulley, each dam forces the water to spread out and filter slowly through the rocks. By treating an entire gulley, a series of stepped fields are created by the deposition of the soil and organic matter borne by the rainwater. Crop-growing conditions are much improved as a result, since moisture is retained in the soil and soil nutrients remain within these fields rather than being washed away (Rochette, 1989).

Soil conservation using local self-help groups

In the Machakos district of south-east Kenya, more than 70 per cent of farmed land is now terraced, bringing better and more reliable yields of maize. The National Soil and Water Conservation Project initiated fieldwork in 1979 and on the basis of its success there has been expanded since 1986 to cover the entire country. Funded by the Swedish International Development Authority (SIDA), which has provided long-term donor support, this project demonstrates the promise of working with local groups in building upon locally known techniques for stemming soil erosion in this densely populated area. The main technique for soil conservation is an improved version of the traditional *fanya juu* terrace, constructed by communal work groups largely made up of women (Critchley, 1991).

Building on success

Certain lessons can be drawn from the range of case studies now available which document more successful projects. These lessons typically include:

- the need to work with and build upon existing groups and institutions;
- flexibility in project objectives and design, to incorporate changes to meet better the priorities and resources of the local community as the project develops;
- development of techniques based on indigenous knowledge and traditional practice;
- training and motivation for local people to acquire new skills and understanding of underlying processes related to the environment.

Many of the examples found of small-scale, locally appropriate development have been initiated by NGOs – both indigenous and international. This has drawn great interest from among the larger agencies about the role which NGOs could play more broadly, in channelling aid funds and implementing projects on a much wider scale. National governments have been less keen about NGOs, and have focused on their weaker attributes, such as their decision often to bypass formal government structures, their weak technical capacity and their limited and usually highly localized impact.

The current enthusiasm for NGOs among donors and the development community raises serious questions regarding the ability of NGOs to 'scale up' their project work from, say, working with five villages in a given area to covering 500 in a whole province. Close working relations between the NGO and the villagers concerned cannot be maintained where the organization is now responsible for a far larger number of people. The flexibility and adaptiveness of the organization often depend on its staying small. There may also be few economies of scale for NGO work. The appropriateness of any particular technical intervention depends on it being developed with a particular group of people who have a common problem. For example, many of the recent successes with small-scale soil and water conservation have been based on adapting structures and technologies to the soils, sites and materials available in a particular place. An alternative strategy would be to create the conditions in which local organizations, based on village groups and herders' associations, could call upon the expertise of governmental and non-governmental bodies willing to work with them on a less intensive basis.

The greatest challenge of the 1990s in dryland Africa will be to provide the context within which good practice can multiply from specific project sites to the larger population. As pointed out above, this process of replication cannot depend alone on a 'scaling up' of NGO work, as there are distinct constraints on their capacity to do this effectively. Many of the key elements behind NGO practice need to be adopted more widely by governments and the larger agencies if Africa is to escape the gloomier forecasts made. This will require:

- sufficient resources available to decentralized bodies able to respond to the needs of local people, raising issues of local revenue-generating capacity, accountability of such bodies, access to training, and so on;
- political will at national level to enable local people to participate more fully in decisions about their future, through the establishment

241

of a representative political structure able to mediate between the different interest groups involved;

- a more flexible approach to research, training and extension so that the people of a given community take part in the development of technical and institutional solutions adapted to locally specific conditions;
- policies at national and international levels that provide the context within which local and national decision-makers can make longer-term choices.

These broad requirements are discussed more fully in the last part of this chapter. The importance of giving local people a central role in managing the resources on which they depend is examined below.

TENURE AND INVESTMENT

Local-level resource management systems will play an important role in promoting more sustainable resource use under certain assumptions:

(1) that firm rights to resources provide users with the security they need to invest and manage resources in a way which ensures that their longer-term productivity is maintained; and

(2) that investment opportunities and technologies exist which could improve the productivity of soils and plant growth and bring greater and more stable returns to crop and livestock production and to other associated activities, at accessible cost to the resource-poor farming and herding communities of these regions.

Land tenure systems

Considerable debate surrounds the role of tenure systems in providing people with sufficient security to manage and invest in their land. Some argue that traditional systems of land tenure in much of Africa provide insufficient security, and that farmers need firmer title to their land before they will carry out more than the most rudimentary investments. Within the context of irrigated agriculture, such schemes as the Office du Niger, in Mali, have suffered from poor levels of productivity due to the weak rights held by tenant farmers on their plots (Tiffen, 1985). New rules regarding tenure and responsibility for maintenance, brought into effect from 1988 onwards, now enable farmers to retain rights over their irrigated plots. As a result of this increased security over land, devolution of responsibility to farmer groups and the rehabilitation of irrigation channels, rice yields are estimated to have risen from an average of 1.9 t/ha to over 5 t/ha (Jaujay, 1990; Wageningen, 1990).

Varying forms of common property resource management, especially in the pastoral sector, have been particularly subject to attack on the grounds that they inevitably lead to resource degradation. The 'tragedy of the commons' has been widely referred to in arguing for the privatization of common grazing lands (Hardin, 1968). Such arguments confuse common property regimes in which there is completely free and open access and those where there is some control and decision-making exercised by the community (Bromley and Cernea, 1989; Lane, 1990). Resources held under open-access regimes are no doubt subject to environmental degradation, but management by the community of certain common resources need not result in over-use. Communal management may provide the best means for controlling access to resources where the community is small but resources are sufficiently valuable for it to be worth excluding outsiders (Feder and Feeny, 1991). The small size of the community means that outsiders are easily recognized and it is relatively simple to regulate the behaviour of group members. However, as the size of the group grows and the interests of different members diverge, for example as a result of new technologies and possibilities for commercialization, communal systems of management may come under stress and break down (ibid.).

In general, the actual form of tenure is probably less important than whether farmers and herders believe their rights will be enforced in cases of conflict. A survey in Kenya, Ghana and Rwanda shows that the formal registering of individual title to land does not significantly improve levels of investment and agricultural productivity (Migot-Adholla *et al.*, 1991). Indigenous tenure systems do not seem to be a constraint on productivity. Customary land tenure probably provides sufficient incentive for farmers to engage in construction and maintenance of soil and water conservation structures, as long as farmers can be sure that their use rights will be confirmed by the administration in cases of dispute (Reij *et al.*, 1986). Whether or not this happens depends on the value of these resources to other potential users and the effectiveness of the institutions meant to enforce rights. 'Enforcement depends on a constellation of supporting arrangements and mechanisms such as courts, police, financial institutions, the legal profession, land surveys, record-keeping systems, and titling agencies, in addition to the social legitimacy of property rights in land' (Feder and Feeny, 1991). The weak capacity of systems of public administration in many poor countries means that rights are not enforced firmly and fairly. Instead, officials see their role in arbitrating land conflicts as a means of earning additional sums 'under the table'.

Investment opportunities and technologies

The argument surrounding tenure and resource management presupposes that technologies exist in which farmers and herders could invest which would lead to higher and more sustainable yields in crop and livestock production in the Sahel. The transfer of Green Revolution technology to the drier parts of Africa is now acknowledged to have brought few of the hoped-for returns. Given this apparent failure, more recent project interventions have been focusing on a range of interventions that require fewer purchased inputs and which aim to reduce risk, rather than achieve spectacular yields. These interventions include soil and water conservation, agroforestry and organic farming methods (mulches, manuring, and so on) (Shaikh *et al.*, 1988; Rochette, 1989; Kerkhof, 1990; Critchley, 1991). In many cases, projects are building upon existing practice to improve techniques, such as by better definition of contours for rock dams in Burkina Faso (Box 8.3) or by getting proper manuring pits dug rather than relying on more haphazard systems of spreading dung and household waste. By associating a range of different interventions, yields can be increased and a greater level of protection provided for harvests in years of poor rainfall (Chambers, Pacey and Thrupp, 1988).

In the pastoral sector, there are a few examples of innovative work to raise herd and pasture productivity and to reduce vulnerability to drought. These include pasture management by setting aside reserve grazing areas, programmes to train para-veterinary workers, storage of hay and water harvesting methods to provide small patches of moisture where grains or forage can be grown (Oxby, 1989; Peyre de Fabrègues and Dalibard, 1990; Grandin *et al.*, 1991).

Experience shows that there are improvements to be made to farming and herding systems which will bring higher and more stable returns. Firmer title to land and its assured enforcement will encourage more of this activity. However, it must be remembered that intensification within the agricultural system bears a cost, in terms of increased labour and other inputs; whether such intensification happens depends on the returns to the use of labour and investment in these activities, in comparison with returns elsewhere. For example, much of the soil and water conservation work in northern Burkina Faso is carried out in the dry-season months of December to March, a time when most young men will have set off on migration further south to earn money. For poorer households there will be a stark trade-off between investing in on-farm soil and water conservation and getting the cash income they need to survive until the following harvest.

244

LOCAL RESOURCE MANAGEMENT: THREE CASE STUDIES

Below are examined three examples of the progress achieved and problems encountered with managing particular resources in dryland Africa, covering pastures, trees and wildlife. In each case, while programmes are being established to shift rights and responsibilities for managing these resources to local people, this transfer of management raises certain difficulties.

Case study 1: Pastoral resource management in West Africa

Water points play a central role in the management of pastoral resources in Sahelian West Africa. While in the rainy season herds can use surface water, such as ponds, for much of the long dry season herds can only have access to pastures if there is a nearby well or borehole. By maintaining broad equivalence between the output of a water point (in terms of the number of livestock that can be watered there in a day) with the availability of grazing within an accessible zone, some kind of equilibrium can be maintained between the two (Thébaud, 1990). In practice, the management of pastoral resources has not been so easy. Boreholes have been dug throughout the Sahelian pastoral zone which have an output, in terms of water, far in excess of what the neighbouring grazing lands can support. Such boreholes, constructed by governments and aid programmes, have been considered public property by herders and thus have not been under the control of a particular group. Pastoralists using a particular zone have not been able to acquire a formal and recognized title which would enable them to control access to the grazing resources which they have traditionally used. Also variation in rainfall and pasture productivity from one year to the next means that the establishment of equivalence between water point capacity and that of neighbouring grasslands is not clearly defined.

The attribution of water points to particular pastoral groups is an essential first step towards achieving a more sustainable system of pasture management in the Sahel and elsewhere in dry Africa (Marty, 1990; Thébaud, 1990). However, certain questions arise in putting the attribution of water points into practice:

- How to define the group which is to manage the water point and neighbouring pasture lands?
- How to transfer sufficient rights to the group to encourage more careful management and investment while maintaining enough flexibility to allow people to move to other areas in times of drought?

245

- How to ensure an equitable distribution of rights between different herding groups?

Trade-offs exist between, on the one hand, the more sustainable and greater level of resource productivity which it is hoped will be attained as a result of granting firmer rights to pastoral communities and, on the other hand, the possibility that this process will disenfranchise certain of the weaker pastoral groups who will lose access to essential resources. Thus increased security for some may be at the expense of reduced security for others.

Case study 2: Investing in trees in the Sahel

Trees play a particularly important role in improving the sustainability of agricultural and pastoral systems in drier parts of Africa. Trees help slow wind speeds and reduce wind erosion; they slow rainfall runoff in fields, reducing soil loss and increasing infiltration; they provide leaf-litter to enrich soils, and leaves as fodder for livestock; they contribute to a more effective recycling of water and nutrients in the soil and provide beneficial micro-climatic conditions for crop growth. In addition, trees can provide important cash incomes from the sale of fruit, wood for building, and so on, and serve as assets that can be sold in times of need (Chambers and Leach, 1987).

Encouraging people to grow more trees will have beneficial effects on their incomes and on the ecosystem as a whole. Current forestry legislation in many parts of Africa discourages farmers from tree planting and tree care. Forestry codes often rely heavily on direct state regulation of how trees and their products can be used by local people, yet ineffective systems of administration make such regulation impossible to carry out in practice, except in an arbitrary manner. All governments now recognize the importance of promoting greater public participation in forestry activities and greater private investment in trees on farms. Yet if these policies are to succeed, communities and farmers will need stronger guarantees that they will benefit from investing in trees.

A reassessment of tree tenure is under way in much of the Sahel, with governments in Senegal, Mali, Niger and Burkina Faso considering revisions to tenure law in general. Allocating much firmer rights to manage and exploit trees at the local level should provide greater incentives for farmers to plant more trees. However, there are other necessary policies which must be put in place. It is not clear that transferring all responsibility to local people will produce the hoped-for increase in tree-planting activities. As Lawry (1989) notes: 'the social and economic bases for collective control are eroding. Policies must be based on a recognition of the limits and opportunities for local management. The role of the state can be decisive in providing a legal framework and in improving economic incentives for desirable management practices.'

Examining the role of tenure in encouraging forestry activity in the Sahel raises a number of questions, which include:

- Will the introduction of clearer rights to trees encourage much more tree planting, and has weak tenure been the main constraint?
- Are there appropriate techniques for tree planting and propagation which will ensure high rates of survival in the drier parts of the Sahel?
- What are the labour inputs required, and how do returns from tree planting compare with other uses of labour?
- How will rights to trees and their products be allocated within the local population, between and within households?

The permanent stabling of sheep and goats and careful herding of cattle can bring about much natural regeneration of trees and woodland around the village. However, there are certain costs, in terms of the labour needed to maintain a cut-and-carry system of livestock production, where fodder is brought to the tethered animals. Where livestock are numerous and play an important role in the production system, there is a trade-off between improved rates of natural regeneration and higher seedling survival, on the one hand, and the labour costs of careful herding of stock throughout the year and/or stabling of herds and fetching fodder, on the other.

Case study 3: Local control over wildlife in Zimbabwe

Most of Zimbabwe's small-scale farming population lives in the dry, marginal communal lands of the country. Many of these areas are far from urban centres, transport routes and marketing facilities. Some areas are on the edge of the major wildlife areas of the country, where elephants and other large animals regularly damage the crops during the growing season. In such areas, wildlife are usually regarded as pests by the local inhabitants. However, an approach to wildlife management, pioneered by the Zimbabwe government and various NGOs, attempts to offset the costs of wildlife by turning them into a resource for exploitation and for local revenue earning.

In marginal areas, with a high population of existing wildlife resources, the returns from wildlife use can potentially be higher than alternative options of dryland agriculture and extensive cattle rearing.

High economic returns from wildlife are attained if safari operations, particularly trophy hunting, are established. Large-scale commercial farmers in many parts of the country have also switched to wildlife enterprises over the past twenty years as returns from beef ranching have proven less attractive (Child, 1988).

The CAMPFIRE (Communal Area Management Programme for Indigenous Resource Exploitation) project was launched in 1986, but had various antecedents dating back over the previous decade. Its aims, as outlined in the original project document (DNPWM, 1986) include:

- the introduction of group ownership with defined rights of access to natural resources for the local communities;
- the provision of appropriate institutions under which resources can be managed and exploited for local benefit;
- the provision of technical and financial assistance to communities.

For local resource management schemes to be successful, it became increasingly evident that a clear legal framework for their operation needed to be established; local institutions needed to be strengthened with real power devolved to them; financial mechanisms for revenue extraction and redistribution needed to be established; and technical, managerial and administrative support for emergent local groups had to be supplied. The comparative success of the CAMPFIRE schemes in the late 1980s and early 1990s has been based on this analysis.

Nyaminyami Council, situated in the Zambezi valley, was the first of several local councils to legally establish a wildlife trust, which since late 1988 has been supported by a local NGO. Several safari operations on short contracts provided much of the income during the first year of operation, with revenue supplemented by a number of game culls. The trust has shown a significant operating profit, even after aid subsidies are accounted for. The revenues are received directly by the trust and can be redistributed by the council. The first revenues were shared among the many wards in the district for the support of community development projects (Jansen, 1990).

A number of the problems faced by early schemes have been overcome. No longer does money get diverted to the central treasury; local claims have priority. A local institution is the prime authority and the scheme is not imposed from outside. The lack of technical and managerial capacity at council level is compensated for by the support provided by NGOs and government departments.

However, challenges still remain. How sustainable and replicable is the Nyaminyami experience? A next stage must include the development of capacity within local councils either to provide services themselves or to contract in the technical support they require.

Long-term financial control and involvement by the local institution in wildlife utilization operations must be ensured if these schemes are to be sustainable. The degree of long-term investment and financial security is limited by the short-term nature of many of the agreements reached to date. However, new financial arrangements are being sought. Joint venture agreements are being worked out where local councils have a direct share in the operation, resulting in increased control and greater opportunities for long-term investment. The distribution of benefits within the community poses certain questions. In the past, wildlife revenues have been shared at the ward level by elected committees and spent on projects considered by the community to be a priority. But is this sufficient incentive to ensure the commitment of individual people?

The devolution of responsibility over wildlife requires a realistic assessment of the conflicting claims of different groups at national and local levels. For local control and proprietorship to become a reality, effective legal and institutional frameworks need to be in place, lest the acquisitive desire for resources and power of central government takes precedence over local priorities.

CONCLUSIONS

The examples given above show some of the gains achieved by setting up local systems of resource management, and some of the associated difficulties. For such examples to spread more widely and to address the problems raised, several pre-conditions must be met:

Availability of resources

Recent promising approaches to natural resource management involve close contact between the community concerned and the outside agency, over a period of several years. These projects have taken time to develop a series of appropriate activities which address the priorities of local people and which are within their grasp. This way of working ties up human and financial resources over a long period, which constrains their widespread replicability. Alternative means of spreading new ideas and techniques must be sought which build upon successful practice and permit a far wider diffusion of information to farmers than would be possible by working through existing projects. Examples of innovative means of dissemination include:

- funding farmer-to-farmer visits, allowing people to see for themselves how others have tackled problems similar to those they face;
- production of educational materials which are lively and stimulate discussion among development agents and local people, such as by using videos, songs, theatre and radio programmes;
- building up regional resource centres able to draw upon NGO, research and extension experience and to provide advice on where help on particular problems and technologies can be obtained.

The resources required for such activities are not themselves likely to be very substantial. However, the kind of funding needed is often difficult to get from major donors, as it is small in scale and costly to administer. A greater constraint is likely to be the availability of personnel with the skills and attitudes needed to provide support to local organizations by non-conventional means.

Resources will also be needed to help support more effective forms of research and extension. Often extension agents have no money to travel to the villages and camps for which they have responsibility. Similarly, researchers frequently face such tight budget constraints as to prevent them carrying out any fieldwork. However, as will be argued below, research and extension systems need not only financial support but also to make major changes in terms of the definition of their objectives. Systems of extension need to move away from providing 'experts' to tell local people what they should be doing, and towards the development of staff who can act as 'catalyst, convenor and colleague' (Chambers, Pacey and Thrupp, 1988).

Political will

An effective local-level system for managing resources requires a substantial shift in power and responsibilities from the central government and local administrations to the populations directly concerned. It also requires the setting up of an enforcement system which operates fairly and effectively. Governments are unwilling to see control over the country's resources move from their hands, as this deprives them of important sources of power and patronage. The importance of such patronage over the allocation of resources has been shown recently in Senegal, where a forest reserve of 45,000 hectares has been declassified and allocated to a religious community for peanut cultivation. Given this religious group's considerable economic and political power, the government felt unable to deny them this land (Schoonmaker, 1991).

However, there is now considerable momentum behind the new paradigm sweeping through development circles which advocates greater decentralization and the vesting of increased authority in local community institutions. Governments have been pushed by donors into talking about greater participation by local people in the management of their own affairs. The new conditionality pursued by many bilateral donors, in which aid flows will depend on moves towards multi-party democracy, is a further trend in this direction. However, governments are skilled in mastering the development discourse and in highlighting their engagement with the rhetoric in vogue among donors. In reality, governments have often made little if any progress in transferring real power away from the centre. So far, making local communities responsible for resource management seems restricted to cases where the government wants to divest itself of certain costly obligations, such as borehole maintenance or cleaning out irrigation canals. Responsibility for funding maintenance costs is unlikely to be rewarded by the transfer of real power where this runs counter to current or future interests of a government and its supporters.

A cynical view of the current situation regarding land rights and their lack of clarity sees this as a conscious strategy on the part of governments to justify continued central control, on the grounds that local populations are evidently incapable of managing their own resources. Local administrators help create chaos by arbitrary decisions regarding who has access to certain resources and thus ensure that contesting parties will try to get a decision made in their favour by providing large bribes. Clear land legislation and the vesting of authority at local level would damage the interests of these administrators by removing the power to allocate as they see fit. In the case of pastoral tenure, any devolution of power over water and grazing to these politically marginal groups is seen as very unlikely as this would strengthen their autonomy, itself perceived as a threat to central government power.

Supposing governments were to commit themselves to the real transfer of power to local community bodies to manage their lands, several other conditions would need to be met for this power to be made effective:

- the establishment of a representative and accountable body at village or camp level, capable of managing fairly and effectively the distribution of rights between competing parties;
- the transfer of legal powers to this body to allow it to carry out its functions;
- the local administration to affirm the decisions made by the local management group when these are brought into dispute;

- provision of the necessary technical support to the community body managing resources to enable it to plan how to manage and improve the resources over which it now exercises formal responsibility.

New approaches to research, training and extension

Over the past three decades, research in dryland Africa has been singularly unsuccessful in developing solutions to problems of sustained food production. There are several reasons for this. Researchers have usually had very little contact with the supposed beneficiaries of their research work. Extension systems have performed poorly in channelling information on farmer and herder priorities back to the research services. Even where extension systems have been well funded, the results of their activity have been limited by reliance on the transfer of technical packages to farmers, rather than on a broader problem-solving approach. The latter is especially necessary in the complex, diverse and risk-prone environments of dryland Africa (Toulmin and Chambers, 1990). At the same time, NGOs which have been working closely with certain grass-roots groups have themselves rarely built up links with researchers and are often poorly informed on the range of technical options available. Thus, the role that NGOs might play as intermediaries between village and research station has rarely been fulfilled.

Research and extension systems need to be reversed, so that, for example, it is farmers not researchers who decide on research priorities and evaluate new technologies, and it is for scientists to learn from farmers rather than the other way round (Chambers, Pacey and Thrupp, 1988). This new agenda has major implications for the way in which decisions are made and resources allocated. 'Normal bureaucracy tends to centralize, standardize and simplify, and agricultural research and extension are no exceptions. They fit badly with the conditions of resource-poor families with their geographic scatter, heterogeneity and complexity' (ibid.). This change in research and extension practice requires new methods for working with local people, eliciting ideas, knowledge and priorities and supporting analysis within the community of how particular problems might best be solved. A variety of new methods are now being developed under a variety of different names – rapid rural appraisal, farmer participatory research, and so on (Farrington and Martin, 1988; McCracken, Pretty and Conway, 1988).

Policy change at national and international levels

The choices and decisions faced by millions of small farmers and herders in dryland Africa must be set within the broader context provided by policies at the national and international levels. These higher levels set the conditions and constraints which limit their choices.

At national levels, producers need to be assured some certainty of being able to sell their output at a reasonable return, and thus make longer-term investments in resource management. Many governments have now lifted controls on grain prices which formerly were fixed at a low level, in order to benefit urban consumers. While price liberalization has not produced an increase in total farm output, due to constraints on labour and other factors, farmers have altered the mix of crops grown in response to relative price changes (Barbier and Burgess, 1991). Liberalization in other areas of economic policy should also improve returns to the small farm sector, such as by the devaluation of exchange rates and increased investment in transport and communications. Given the relative neglect of small-scale rainfed farming, ways need to be found of improving access to credit by, for example, giving recognition to informal systems of credit provision and support to community-based savings and credit schemes.

International trading policies need to be examined to identify where these damage the interests of producers in dryland Africa. Examples include the heavy protection imposed on processed products, and the dumping of surplus commodities. For example, the Common Agricultural Policy of the European Community has generated large surpluses of meat. Frozen meat exports from the EC have now taken over many of the traditional meat markets in coastal West Africa formerly served by Sahelian livestock keepers. As a result, Sahelian pastoralists face much weaker prices and levels of demand and thus lower returns to their labour. In this case, there is an inconsistency in trade and aid policies which needs to be addressed, so that the trading practices of developed nations do not adversely damage the development of rural producers in Africa's poorest states.

The emergence of a new global paradigm in favour of the decentralization of power provides an important opportunity to relocate the rights and responsibilities for resource management in the hands of local users. However, by itself this devolution of control over resources to local communities will not be sufficient to ensure a more sustainable development for Africa's drylands. There are also other policies at local, national and international levels which need substantial change if the promise of decentralization is to bear the fruit of more secure livelihoods for dryland peoples.

NOTES

1 Isohyets are map lines joining all points with equal rainfall.

REFERENCES AND BIBLIOGRAPHY

Ahlcrona, E., 1988. *The Impact of Climate and Man on Land Transformation in Central Sudan: Applications of Remote Sensing,* Lund University Press, Lund, Sweden.

Ahmad, A. M., 1989. 'Housing submarkets for the urban poor – the case of Greater Khartoum, the Sudan', *Environment and Urbanization,* 1, 2, pp. 50–9.

Barbier, E. and Burgess, J., 1991. 'Agricultural pricing and environmental degradation', paper for the World Bank, IIED, London.

Bergeret, A. with Ribot, J. C., 1990. *L'arbre nourricier en pays Sahéliens,* Editions de la Maison des Sciences de l'Homme, Paris.

Bishop, J., 1988. 'Indigenous social structures, formal institutions, and the management of renewable natural resources in Mali', draft paper for the Sahelian Department, Agriculture Division, World Bank, Washington, DC.

Bromley, D. and Cernea, M., 1989. *The Management of Common Property Natural Resources: Conceptual and Operational Fallacies,* Discussion Paper no. 57, World Bank, Washington, DC.

Chambers, R., 1990. *Microenvironments Unobserved,* Sustainable Agriculture Programme Gatekeeper Series no. 22, IIED, London.

Chambers, R. and Leach, M. 1987. *Trees to Meet Contingencies: Savings and Security for the Rural Poor,* Discussion Paper no. 228, Institute of Development Studies, University of Sussex, Brighton.

Chambers, R., Pacey, A. and Thrupp, L. A. 1989. *Farmer First: Farmer Innovation and Agricultural Research,* Intermediate Technology Publications, London.

Child, B., 1988. 'The role of wildlife utilization in the sustainable economic development of semi-arid rangelands in Zimbabwe', D.Phil. thesis, University of Oxford.

Club du Sahel, 1991. 'Senegal makes inroads into neighbors' forest resources', *OECD Newsletter,* 10, Paris.

Critchley, W., 1991. *Looking after our Land: New Approaches to Soil and Water Conservation in Dryland Africa,* Oxfam, Oxford, and IIED, London.

DNPWM (Department of National Parks and Wildlife Management), 1986. *Communal Areas Management Programme for Indigenous Resources (CAMPFIRE),* Branch of Terrestrial Ecology, DNPWM, Government of Zimbabwe, Harare.

Farrington, J. and Martin, A., 1988. *Farmer Participatory Research: A Review of Concepts and Practices,* Agricultural Research and Extension Network Paper no. 19, ODI, London.

Feder, G. and Feeny, D., 1991. 'Land tenure and property rights: theory and implications for development policy', *World Bank Economic Review*, 5, 1, pp. 135–53.

Grandin, B. *et al.*, 1991. *Village Animal Healthcare: A Community-Based Approach to Livestock Development in Kenya*, Intermediate Technology Publications, London.

Glantz, M. H. (ed.), 1987. *Drought and Hunger in Africa*, Cambridge University Press, Cambridge.

GRET (Groupe de Recherche et d'Echanges Technologiques), 1991. *La réhabilitation des périmètres irrigués*, GRET, Paris.

Hardin, G., 1968. 'The tragedy of the commons', *Science*, 162, pp. 1243–8.

Hellden, U., 1984. *Drought Impact Monitoring: A Remote Sensing Study of Desertification in Kordofan, Sudan*, Lund University, Lund, Sweden.

Hjort, A., 1991. 'Environment reconsidered', mimeo, paper for seminar at IIED, London, June.

Hulme, M., 1991. 'Rainfall Ethiopia 1898–1990', personal communication, Climatic Research Unit, University of East Anglia, Norwich.

Ibrahim, F. N., 1984. 'Ecological imbalances in the Republic of the Sudan, with reference to desertification in Darfur', *Bayreuther Geowissenschaftliche Arbeiten*, 6.

IPCC (Intergovernmental Panel on Climate Change), 1990. *Potential Impacts of Climate Change*, World Metereological Organization and UNEP, Geneva.

IUCN, 1989. *Sahel Studies*, IUCN, Gland, Switzerland.

Jansen, D., 1990. *Sustainable Wildlife Utilization in the Zambezi Valley of Zimbabwe: Economic, Ecological and Political Trade-Offs*, World Wide Fund for Nature, Harare.

Jaujay, J., 1990. *The Operation and Maintenance of a Pilot Rehabilitated Zone in the Office du Niger, Mali*, Irrigation Management Network Paper no. 90/1c, ODI, London.

Kelley, A. C. and Nobbe, C. E. 1990. *Kenya at the Demographic Turning Point? Hypotheses and a Proposed Research Agenda*, Discussion Paper no. 107, World Bank, Washington, DC.

Kerkhof, P., 1990. *Agroforestry in Africa: A Survey of Project Experience*, Panos Institute, London.

Lamprey, H., 1975. 'Report on the desert encroachment reconnaissance in northern Sudan, October/November 1975', mimeo, UNESCO and UNEP, Nairobi.

Lane, C., 1990. 'Alienation of Barabaig pasture land: policy implications for pastoral development in Tanzania', Ph.D. thesis, University of Sussex.

Lane, C. and Pretty, J., 1990. *Displaced Pastoralists and Transferred Wheat Technology in Tanzania*, Sustainable Agriculture Programme Gatekeeper Series no. 20, IIED, London.

Lawry, S., 1989. *Tenure Policy towards Common Property Natural Resources*, Land Tenure Center Paper no. 134, University of Wisconsin, Madison, Wis.

Leach, G. and Mearns, R., 1988. *Beyond the Woodfuel Crisis: People, Land and Trees in Africa,* Earthscan, London.

McCracken, J. A., Pretty, J. N. and Conway, G. R., 1988. *An Introduction to Rapid Rural Appraisal for Agricultural Development,* Sustainable Agriculture Programme, IIED, London.

Marty, A., 1990. 'Les organizations coopératives en milieu pastoral: héritage et enjeux', *Sociétés pastorales et développement: cahiers des sciences humaines,* 26, 1–2, pp. 121–35.

Migot-Adholla, S. *et al.,* 1991. 'Indigenous land rights systems in sub-Saharan Africa: a constraint on productivity?', *World Bank Economic Review,* 5, 1, pp. 155–75.

Mortimore, M., 1989. *Adapting to Drought: Farmers, Famines and Desertification in West Africa,* Cambridge University Press, Cambridge.

Murphree, M., 1990. *Decentralizing the Proprietorship of Wildlife Resources in Zimbabwe's Communal Lands,* Centre for Applied Social Sciences, University of Zimbabwe, Harare.

Nelson, R., 1988. *Dryland Management: The 'Desertification' Problem,* Environment Department Working Paper no. 8, World Bank, Washington, DC.

Olsson, K., 1985. 'Remote sensing for fuelwood resources and land degradation studies in Kordofan, the Sudan', Ph.D. thesis, Lund University.

Omer, M. I. A., 1990. *Child health in the spontaneous settlements around Khartoum',* Environment and Urbanization, 2, 2, pp. 65–70.

Oxby, C., 1989. *African Livestock Keepers in Recurrent Crisis: Policy Issues Arising from the NGO Response,* ACORD and Drylands Programme, IIED, London.

Peyre de Fabrègues, B. and Dalibard, Ch., 1990. 'La confection et l'utilization des meules de paille dans la gestion des ressources fourragères au Sahel', *Révue d'élevage et de médicine vétérinaire des pays tropicaux,* 43, 3, pp. 409–15.

Reij, C. *et al.,* 1986. *Soil and Water Conservation in Sub-Saharan Africa: Issues and Options,* IFAD and CDCS, Free University, Amsterdam.

Rochette, R. N., 1989. *Le Sahel en lutte contre la désertification,* Margraf, Weikersheim, Germany.

Sandford, S., 1983. *Management of Pastoral Development in the Third World,* Wiley and ODI, London.

Schoonmaker, K., 1991. *Mbegué: The Disingenuous Destruction of a Sahelian Forest,* Drylands Programme Issues Paper no. 29, IIED, London.

Scoones, I., 1991. *Wetlands in Drylands: The Agroecology of Savanna Systems in Africa. Part One: Overview – Ecological, Economic and Social Issues,* Drylands Programme, IIED, London.

Shaikh, A. *et al.,* 1988. *Opportunities for Sustained Development: Successful Natural Resources Management in the Sahel,* Energy/Development International, Washington, DC.

Shepherd, G., 1988. *The Reality of the Commons: Answering Hardin from Somalia,* Social Forestry Network Paper no. 6d, ODI, London.

Sylla, D., 1989. *The Experience of Pastoral Organization in African Countries,* Unité Pastoral, Ministère de l'Elevage, Chad, and Drylands Programme, IIED, London.

Thébaud, B., 1990. 'Politiques hydrauliques pastorales et gestion de l'espace au Sahel', *Sociétés pastorales et développement: cahiers des sciences humaines,* 26, 1–2, pp.13–31.

Tiffen, 1985. 'Land tenure issues in irrigation planning, design and management in sub-Saharan Africa', Working Paper no. 16, ODI, London.

Toulmin, C. and Chambers, R., 1990. *Farmer First: Achieving Sustainable Dryland Development in Africa,* Drylands Programme Issues Paper no. 19, IIED, London.

Touré, O., 1990. *Where Herders Don't Herd Anymore: Experience from the Ferlo, Northern Senegal,* Drylands Programme Issues Paper no. 22, IIED, London.

Tyson, P. D., 1991. 'Climatic change in southern Africa: past and present conditions and possible future scenarios', *Climatic change,* 18, pp. 241–58.

UNDP, 1991. *Human Development Report 1991,* Oxford University Press, Oxford.

UNICEF, 1991. 'Child survival and population growth', in *The State of the World's Children 1991,* UNICEF, New York.

van Keulen, H. and Breman, H., 1990. 'Agricultural development in the West African Sahelian region: a cure against land hunger?', *Agriculture, Ecosystems and Environment,* 32, pp. 177–97.

Wageningen, University of, 1990. *Design for Sustainable Farmer-Managed Irrigation Schemes in Sub-Saharan Africa,* contributions to an international workshop, 5–8 February, Wageningen, Netherlands.

Warren, A. and Agnew, C., 1988. *An Assessment of Desertification and Land Degradation in Arid and Semi-Arid Areas,* Drylands Programme, IIED, London.

Whitlow, R., 1988. *Land Degradation in Zimbabwe: A Geographical Study,* Department of Natural Resources, Harare.

World Bank, 1989. *Sub-Saharan Africa: From Crisis to Sustainable Growth. A Long-Term Perspective Study,* World Bank, Washington, DC.

Zimbabwe Trust, 1990. *People, Wildlife and Natural Resources – the CAMP-FIRE Approach to Rural Development in Zimbabwe,* Zimbabwe Trust, Harare.

9 Achieving Sustainability in Energy Use in Developing Countries

Gregory Kats

INTRODUCTION

Patterns of energy use in the developing world are wasteful – the result of poor policies and planning and the self-serving development assistance offered by the industrialized West. As a consequence, developing nations almost universally have failed to share in the large gains in energy efficiency enjoyed by industrialized countries over the past two decades. Developing nations, which can least afford it, are now stuck with the most wasteful, expensive and environmentally destructive technologies for both the production and the use of energy. Unless transfer and investment policies change, energy shortages will worsen while the environment and human health suffer. Sustainability will become an ever more remote goal.

A number of studies demonstrate that energy needs in developing countries can be met at much lower financial and environmental costs through a shift to energy efficiency and to new and renewable energy technologies (see e.g. Goldemberg *et al.*, 1987a; Levine *et al.*, 1991; OTA, 1991; Phillips, 1991). This chapter draws on these studies and examines the implications and requirements for achieving sustainable energy use in the developing world. The chapter assumes that the objective of energy policy is to provide energy services at the lowest financial, environmental and health costs rather than just to increase gross energy production.

Developing countries, with three-quarters of the world's population, consume about 30 per cent of global energy, including about 23 per cent of commercial energy and 85 per cent of biomass fuel. Per capita energy use varies widely between and within developing countries: China accounts for almost 10 per cent of the world's commercial energy use, while 50 countries of Africa consume under 3 per cent (OTA, 1991). Perhaps a billion rural poor have inadequate access to any affordable fuel, while the urban rich may consume as much energy as their counterparts in industrialized nations.

Natural resource limitations make it impossible for developing nations to consume fossil fuels and nuclear power at the same rate as industrialized nations. If the world used oil at the same rate as the USA, reserves would last for less than a decade. Similarly, if world per capita reliance on nuclear power was as great as in France, commercially recoverable reserves of U-235 would last less than two years (Hohmeyer, 1991). This indicates that the current energy consumption patterns of the industrialized countries are unsustainable and are not feasible as models for the developing world. A sustainable energy strategy will involve a sharp reduction in use of fossil fuels in industrialized nations and a global transition to efficiency and renewable energies. Some industrialized countries have begun this costly transition. Developing countries should avoid very large, wasteful investments in costly and energy-inefficient infrastructure, and instead adopt the less costly and less environmentally damaging strategy of efficiency and renewables. In this way, developing nations can turn the fact of having relatively less built infrastructure into an advantage.

Although electricity accounted for only 7 per cent of primary energy consumed in the developing world in 1985, this chapter pays particular attention to electricity because this is where the lion's share of domestic investment and external aid in energy is focused. For example, electricity accounts for over three-quarters of the US$78 billion energy-related debt (1988) in Latin America, and almost one-third of total financing from multilateral and bilateral lending to the region (Berkovski, 1991). More than 80 per cent of the World Bank's energy lending goes to electricity (OTA, 1991). And electricity is projected to account for half or more of energy investment in developing nations in the coming decades. Continued concentration of resources on expanding inefficiently used electricity will deprive other energy sectors of needed investment. On the other hand, implementing greater efficiency in the electricity sector would release substantial investment capital to develop alternative energy sources, including the improved use of biomass, natural gas and renewable energy sources such as wind and solar power.

THE MEANING OF ENERGY SUSTAINABILITY

What does energy sustainability mean for developing countries? Four basic requirements are essential:

- increasing availability of energy services to provide improved standard of living, especially for those with the greatest need;
- reducing the health burdens of current energy production and consumption patterns;
- cutting the environmental damage caused by energy use, including limiting the rate of global warming to a level that does not exceed the ability of ecosystems to adjust;
- reversing the rising financial and economic costs of current energy investment and use patterns.

Based on these criteria, energy use in developing nations is currently unsustainable. However, the technology and institutional know-how exist to provide more people with energy services required for improved quality of life at lower environmental and financial costs. Innovative programmes in some developing countries demonstrate that this is achievable. These programmes emphasize efficiency of energy production, distribution and use, greater local control of resources and a broader array of energy sources, with expanding emphasis on renewable energy.

Increasing availability of energy services

Services that require energy use are central to improving quality of life, enabling economic and industrial growth and encouraging development. These services can be achieved using either much or little energy, depending on efficiency of use. Thus, the quantity and quality of energy services depend as much on *how* energy is produced and used as on the gross amount consumed.

There is widespread recognition that inefficiency of energy usage in developing countries imposes enormous financial and environmental costs (Kats, 1989). None the less, per capita energy consumption – rather than increases in energy services (such as lighting and cooling) – continues to be viewed as the primary energy development measure, in turn promoting wasteful energy investment (Box 9.1.)

Continued emphasis on what Indian energy experts call a 'consumption-obsessed supply approach' exacerbates shortages of energy (Reddy *et al.*, 1990a). Over-investment in expanding production and consequent lack of investment in cutting waste means that a large

---

Box 9.1: The fallacy of energy statistics

Consider an ongoing Brazilian utility programme to replace inefficient 60 watt incandescent bulbs with 9 watt compact fluorescent bulbs (Phillips, 1990a). Providing efficient bulbs to clients costs far less than building new power plants to provide the electricity required to run inefficient bulbs, so the programme offers large saving to the utility, expanded lighting services to customers and lower financial and environmental costs to society. Imagine that one Brazilian household has a single inefficient lightbulb drawing 60 watts of electricity, while a second household with three efficient lightbulbs uses a total of 27 watts of electricity. According to most current measurements of development, the first household is better off because more electricity is used, and therefore must, by definition of quantity of energy used, be more developed.

Current development statistics for energy would also show that a country where every household has one inefficient lightbulb and every other household one refrigerator using 1,100 kWh (Kilowatt-hours) of electricity per year is more developed than a country where every household has three efficient light bulbs and each household has one efficient refrigerator the same size as the 1,100 kWh model but using only 300 kWh per year.

---

portion of energy is wasted. Further, over-concentration on expanding supply allows little investment in more promising alternatives, such as sustainable biomass production or wind-powered water pumping. The net effect is that the needs of a large portion of the population are not met.

One study observes that the large cost of continued expansion of energy 'lead many to believe – if rarely to state in public – that living standards cannot be substantially improved in developing countries' (Goldemberg *et al.*, 1987b). The authors demonstrate that a strategy designed to meet energy needs at the lowest cost (and emphasizing cutting waste) would provide more and improved energy services in developing countries at lower financial and environmental costs.

Reducing the health burden of energy

A recent World Health Organization (WHO) study found that 'development policies can create or exacerbate the diseases of poverty as well as the health problems of industrialization' (Cooper Weil *et al.*, 1990). Commercial energy use, such as dam construction and vehicle exhaust in cities, as well as non-commercial energy use, such as rural burning of biomass, has very large and negative impacts on health.

Household exposure to pollutants from fuel burning is the single largest energy-related health threat, with exposure levels estimated to be an average of twenty times higher in developing nations than in industrialized countries (ibid.). At least 300 to 400 million people worldwide, primarily in rural areas of developing countries, suffer from indoor air pollution resulting from burning of biomass – firewood, dung and agricultural waste products – in open hearths or inefficient stoves with poor venting. Pollutants including carbon monoxide, sulphur dioxide, nitrogen oxides, ammonia, hydrochloric acid and volatile hydrocarbons result in respiratory diseases, including chronic obstructive pulmonary disease, nasopharyngeal cancer, bronchitis and emphysema (UNEP, 1986).

Household air quality can be improved through improved design of cookstoves and construction of adequate venting. Smoke reduction features or venting must become a standard part of stove design if the health damage of biomass burning is to be reduced.

Energy use in cities results in levels of suspended particulates of lead (largely from gasoline use in cars and trucks) and other pollutants that make the air quality conditions 'unacceptable' for 70 per cent of Third World urban populations, according to WHO and UNEP (Cooper Weil *et al.*, 1990). The Worldwatch Institute has suggested that very high ambient levels of lead from gasoline use in transport may result in a generation of intellectually stunted children in Mexico City (Brown *et al.*, 1991). Up to 60 per cent of residents of Calcutta suffer from respiratory diseases related to air pollution (CSE, 1982).

Increasingly severe traffic congestion and widespread damage to health throughout the developing (and the industrialized) world results from unregulated traffic and inadequate investment in public transport. Large financial and health savings can be achieved through expanded public transport programmes.

Expanded dam construction and irrigation create vast new areas for insect breeding and disease transmission and are a primary cause of the spread of water-borne diseases. For example, prevalence of schistosomiasis in children living in the area around the Akosombo dam in Ghana jumped from 5–10 per cent before construction to 90 per cent one year after the dam filled (Hunter, Rey and Scott, 1983). Two hundred million people, overwhelmingly in developing nations, now suffer from schistosomiasis (UNEP, 1986).

Health effects from energy usage have generally been ignored or underestimated. These costs should be measured and included as part of assessments of energy options. Recognizing this cost would make dams and fossil fuels relatively less attractive compared to alternatives that cause little or no damage to health, such as energy efficiency programmes or renewables. Expanded health protection measures and education are also required and can often be achieved with far greater support for and involvement of local NGOs. In most developing countries, 70 to 95 per cent of new urban housing is illegally built (Hardoy and Satterthwaite, 1990). The only way to ensure that these buildings include energy-efficient stoves that are designed to minimize health damage is to involve the informal institutions that undertake housing construction and to supply them with technical support, training and resources.

Limiting financial and economic costs of energy use

The portion of national expenditure going to energy has grown rapidly over the past decades and has reached 30 or 40 per cent of total national public investment in many developing nations (Munasinghe, 1990). In India, for example, energy as a percentage of total government expenditure rose from 10 per cent in 1956–61 to 31 per cent in 1985–90. If past investment policies continue, energy will consume 56 per cent of total government expenditure in fifteen years' time (CMIE, 1988).

These figures do not capture the full cost of required energy investment since they exclude growing and very costly private investment in independent generation required because of unreliable electricity supply. Despite mounting expenditure, electricity shortages and grid instability increasingly constrain economic growth. In 1983–4, power shortages cost India an estimated US$2.7 billion, or 1.5 per cent of GDP in direct costs (USAID, 1988). In Pakistan, load shedding and supply interruption reduced GNP by 1.8 per cent. And in the Philippines, power shortages now cost industry over US$1 million per day and could cut economic growth by more than 20 per cent (*Far Eastern Economic Review*, 1990).

Various developing nations have estimated the average overall cost of supply outages (power failures) at between US$0.40 and US$1.10 per kWh, US$1.00 to US$7.00 per kWh for industrial users and US$1.50 to US$ 1.65 per kWh for commercial users (Foley, 1990). These estimates indicate that the cost of supply outages is roughly ten times more than the cost of supplying electricity, indicating a huge financial penalty for electricity shortages. Unreliable electricity supply also discourages investment in new technologies by existing firms and puts off potential new investors, in turn slowing technical transfer and economic development. These financial and economic costs underline the importance of implementing energy efficiency programmes to reduce electricity waste and limit demand growth.

The World Bank estimates losses in transmission and distribution (T & D) of electricity in 100 developing countries at about 17 per cent

(Escay, 1990), about twice that of industrialized countries. In some countries, these losses are rising. In India, for example, electricity losses rose from 18 per cent in 1970–1 to 21.7 per cent in 1988–9 (Felix, 1990; Pachauri and Suri, 1990). These losses can often be often be reduced cost-effectively. For example, cutting Sudan's 32 per cent T & D loss by 5 per cent would cost US$1 million and provide US$12 million in direct savings (USAID, 1988). Greater investment in maintenance and equipment would cut T & D losses in the Third World to perhaps 10 to 12 per cent, providing a relatively quick and cost-effective method to extract 5 to 20 per cent more energy services from existing electricity supplies in many developing countries.

Reducing environmental damage from energy use

It has traditionally been assumed that market prices reflect the full costs of energy. However, it is now widely recognized that fossil fuels and nuclear power impose large costs in the forms of pollution, health effects and waste disposal costs that are not reflected in the price of the fuels. Many of these costs, such as global warming from burning fossil fuels, are effectively passed on to future generations. Similarly, dam construction can result in the loss of large areas of biologically rich and diverse land and may displace indigenous peoples and damage their cultures in ways that may be devastating but difficult to quantify.

Hidden costs have been estimated roughly to double the current costs of fossil fuels and nuclear power. In contrast, the hidden costs of renewable energies such as wind and solar photovoltaics are negligible (Hohmeyer, 1988). Because important costs are not reflected in energy prices, energy investment is misallocated, with over-investment in expanding fossil fuel consumption and under-investment in efficiency and renewables. Failure to account for these costs has effectively subsidized consumption of fossil fuels and biased energy investment away from efficiency and renewables, thereby accelerating global warming, the most prominent threat to the global environment.

The Intergovernmental Panel on Climate Change and others project that, if current energy use trends continue, the future rate of global warming will be about 0.3°C per decade. This is viewed as exceeding the rate at which many flora can adapt and may lead to extinction of some species (Peters, 1988). In turn, tree and plant loss is projected to increase release of carbon dioxide, further accelerating warming. Based on current scientific understanding, 0.1°C per decade global warming, with a limit on cumulative total of 2.5°C, constitutes a maximum acceptable target for achieving environmentally sustainable energy use (IPCC, 1990; Krause, Bach and Kooney, 1990).

The Brundtland Commission and others have suggested that this target can best be achieved by a sustained reduction in emissions by industrialized nations, matched by a limit in growth of energy-related carbon dioxide emissions from developing nations that would allow expansion of energy services required for continued development. This can best be achieved through a shift from a focus on expanding consumption of fossil fuels towards efficiency and renewable energy sources.

ENERGY EFFICIENCY

It is sometimes argued that, because developing nations use relatively little energy, there is little point in trying to cut energy waste. In fact, the reverse is true: because developing countries have fewer resources, they are less able to afford waste. Further, because the Third World has not shared in the efficiency gains enjoyed by industrialized countries over the past two decades, they are more wasteful of energy and therefore have more potential to cut waste. As the Brundtland Commission noted, 'developing countries will gain much more from such reductions' (WCED, 1987).

Energy use and the wealth of nations

The process of development and the creation of wealth through expansion of economic activities and services are successfully achieved when resources are used efficiently. However, it is still sometimes argued that economic growth must be accompanied by increased energy usage. This has been shown to be false since the early 1970s. Energy intensity (energy used per unit of economic output) rose 0.6 per cent annually in OECD countries, between 1965 and 1973, but declined by 1.9 per cent per year thereafter (Hanen, 1990). No parallel improvement in the efficiency of energy occurred in developing or Soviet bloc countries. Failure to use energy efficiently helps explain the relatively weak economic performance of many of these countries over the past two decades.

In 1985, Czechoslovakia, East Germany, Poland and Romania used more energy per person than Japan, yet Japan's economic output is four or five times as high (Chandler, 1990; Kolar, 1991). Japan's high economic growth rate can be partly explained by its frugal use of energy: sustained government and industrial support for energy efficiency allows Japan to spend less on energy and more on manufacturing, education and other productive sectors.

High per capita energy consumption in Eastern Europe has resulted in part from a structural bias towards energy-intensive industries, in turn representing wasteful investment patterns (Chandler, 1990). Past rapid expansion of energy production in Eastern Europe was not a prerequisite to development but rather an alternative to development (Kats, 1991b). The severe pollution, health problems and economic uncompetitiveness of the former Soviet bloc offer a cautionary vision of the possible effect that continued practice of the 'more energy is better' ideology might have on developing nations.

In every country where energy use is wasteful, continued high levels of investment in energy production without adequate investment in improving efficiency of energy usage will slow rather than enhance development (Kats, 1989). As Amulya Reddy and Indian Institute of Science colleagues observe:

> The true indicator of development is not the magnitude of energy used, but the level of energy services provided. It has therefore become essential to extend the list of options for energy decision-making so as to include both decentralized sources of supply and energy efficiency improvements and other conservation options.

(Reddy *et al.*, 1990b).

Current patterns of energy use, including projections for expanding energy production, are clearly not sustainable.

If developing nations are to avoid worsening power shortages, continuing capital drain from non-energy sectors and declining economic performance, they must embrace energy efficiency. Efficient production and use of energy are a prerequisite to achieving sustainable development.

Support for energy efficiency

Industrialized nations save several hundred billion US dollars each year from gains in energy efficiency achieved since the early 1970s. However, the development assistance and loan institutions of these industrialized countries have done almost nothing to share their gains with the developing world. According to the International Institute for Energy Conservation, since 1980, multilateral development banks have spent a paltry 1 per cent of their energy investment supporting efficiency (Phillips, 1991). This is remarkable in view of the potential that efficiency holds for cutting energy investment requirements.

The experience of Tunisia demonstrates that large savings are potentially available to developing countries. Between 1970 and 1986, Tunisia decreased annual energy consumption growth from 11.5 to

6.5 per cent, largely by phasing out energy subsidies. A national industrial and commercial energy conservation programme, begun in 1986, cut this further, from 6.5 to 3 per cent by 1990 (Phillips, 1990b)

Development assistance has provided indirect support for efficiency. Structural loans from aid agencies and loan institutions, such as the World Bank, help developing nations lift energy prices towards market rates, in turn encouraging efficiency. Similarly, funding for new industries usually supports introduction of technologies and processes that are relatively efficient. There is also growing support for energy efficiency in aid agencies. For example, USAID recently provided US$20 million pre-investment funding to help Indian utilities shift investment strategy to include energy efficiency (Gerard, 1991). Establishment of the US$1.3 billion Global Environment Facility (GEF) by the World Bank, UNEP and UNDP is also a positive step (World Bank, 1990; *Finance and Development*, 1991). The GEF has begun to fund the transfer of institutional training and equipment to support the adoption of least-cost planning practices and efficient technologies by Jamaica's electricity utility. But, encouraging as these steps are, they remain entirely inadequate to overcome barriers to efficiency and to capture the enormous savings it offers.

The lack of transfer of OECD efficiency savings to developing nations can in large part be attributed to self-serving objectives of 'tied' aid and to the relative convenience of larger power projects rather than many smaller programmes. Two-thirds of development assistance is 'tied' aid, with loans offered on condition that they are used to acquire equipment from companies of the same nationality as the lender. Since energy expansion costs far more than energy efficiency, and generally has a much higher imported content, promoting energy efficiency sharply reduces the potential sales for domestic manufacturers. Thus, *tied aid is innately biased against energy inefficiency*.

Efficiency improvements tend to be small scale, geographically diffuse and more reliant on domestic institutions, such as utilities, and therefore harder to implement than new power plant construction. In agencies such as the World Bank, evaluation of the performance of loan officers is based in part on volume of loans made. This creates a powerful bias for large, centralized projects. Generally limited administrative budgets of aid agencies and loan institutions also favour large power plants because they are less expensive to administer than many smaller efficiency projects. Similarly, politicians in developing nations also tend to be more attracted to large projects; the prospect of being photographed in front of a new power plant is more appealing than standing by an efficient refrigerator, even though increasing the

267

efficiency of appliances is generally a far more cost-effective way of increasing energy services than building new power stations.

The potential for energy efficiency

Most energy plans in developing countries call for continued rapid expansion of energy production, with little attention to cutting energy waste. The consequence is that despite huge investments, power shortages will worsen throughout much of the developing world. Efficiency could cut the cost of this required investment sharply. A recent study of capital requirements for the electricity sector in developing countries over the period 1985–2025 found that total costs would be roughly halved under an 'efficiency scenario'. This saving is in comparison with a reference scenario that projects continuation of the current emphasis on constructing large new generating plants, with little effort to cut energy waste. Annual costs under the efficiency scenario would average US$65 billion compared to US$138 billion over the period 1985–2000 for the business-as-usual reference scenario (Levine *et al.*, 1991).

As Chapter 10 suggests, foreign aid is unlikely to grow at rates commensurate with the needs of the Third World. Lack of capital during the 1990s may increasingly constrain development, particularly in the poorest countries. The cost of continuing present patterns of investment in energy suggests that these patterns are financially as well as environmentally unsustainable. For financial reasons alone, it is necessary to shift energy investment towards an emphasis on energy efficiency. This shift is clearly feasible.

The government energy plan for the Indian state of Karnataka calls for a near quadrupling of electricity production from 2,500 MW in 1986 to 9,500 MW in 1999. Despite this massive projected investment, the plan warns that 'energy shortages will continue' (Reddy *et al.*, 1990a). An alternative strategy emphasizing energy efficiency can better meet energy service needs, but do so with a growth of energy and electricity consumption that is 60 per cent lower than the official government energy programme. Financial, environmental and health costs of the efficiency approach are commensurately lower (ibid.). Similarly, detailed studies demonstrate that Brazil can either spend US$55 billion in expanding the electricity sector over the next fifteen years or provide the same energy services by investing US$20 billion in efficient equipment and cutting energy waste, a saving of US$35 billion, or over 60 per cent (Geller, 1990). Nor does this include large additional benefits of lessened pollution and health damage and reduced global warming.

Demand-side management: doing more with less

Most energy investment in developing countries remains geared towards expanding energy supply, with little integrated planning or funding committed to delivering the mix of supply, delivery and demand adjustments that achieves the most cost-effective supply of energy services.

An essential step in escaping the trap of increasing investment in energy that is then largely wasted is an approach called demand-side management or *least-cost planning* that is being widely adopted in industrialized nations. Simply put, least-cost planning involves determining the services that are desired for development and choosing the lowest cost combination of supply and gains available through efficiency improvements in supply, distribution and use of energy.

Traditionally, utilities have been rewarded for increasing power production but are prohibited from investing in energy efficiency. This can be changed by modifying regulations to permit utility investment in conservation and to provide larger financial incentives for utilities to save energy than to import energy or build new power plants.

A conservation programme might involve a utility buying 100,000 efficient lightbulbs (at a discount because of volume) and installing them in an office building. The clients would benefit from lower electricity bills. The utility would recover the cost of the lightbulbs by keeping some of the savings from lower electricity use each month until the lightbulbs were paid off. Because efficiency is far less expensive than building new power plants, utilities increase profitability, customers pay smaller bills and pollution is reduced. This approach has been adopted by more than half of US utilities as well as a growing number of utilities in Europe, Canada and a few developing countries.

An ongoing project in Bombay, India, has involved installation of 1,000 efficient lamps for trial and monitoring purposes. This will help pave the way for domestic manufacture and larger-scale introduction of efficient lighting. Because lighting accounts for up to half of Bombay's peak electricity demand, reducing consumption of electricity by the lighting sector can eliminate periods of excess demand and consequent power failures, in turn reducing damage caused to fragile equipment, such as efficient lightbulbs, by grid instability (Gadgil, 1990). Lower demand growth allows utilities to avoid construction of expensive new plants and to concentrate instead on improving reliability and efficiency of generation and transmission.

Private domestic and foreign direct investment can play an important role in independent power generation and in improving efficiency of energy production and use. However, the energy sector in most developing countries does not offer an attractive investment opportunity (Williams, 1988). By lowering the risk and cost associated with uncertain future demand growth, efficiency standards can increase the likelihood of direct foreign and domestic investment. Reduction of risk has been found to be more important than economics or capital budget constraints in determining commercial sector participation in energy expansion programmes in the USA (Hirst and Brown, 1990). Through reducing demand uncertainty, demand-side management can both save utilities hundreds of millions of dollars in capital expense (Ford and Geinzer, 1990) and encourage domestic and international private investment in the power sector.

Achieving sustainable energy use requires cutting waste in all three phases of energy: supply, distribution and end use. Waste in electricity distribution and consumption in the Indian state of Karnataka means that 2.02 kW of electricity must be generated for every 1 kW of consumption. Thus, 1 kW of electricity savings is effectively equal to 2.02 kW of additional generation capacity (Reddy *et al.*, 1990b). The savings potential is particularly large in the end use sector, which has largely been ignored to date.

Policies for improved transport and efficient appliances

Transport
Transport is one of the sectors with the most rapid growth in energy use in the developing world. Between 1984 and 1988, private car ownership rose 26 per cent per year in Kenya and 10 per cent annually in Brazil, Pakistan and Thailand (Faiz *et al.*, 1990). Rapidly expanding fleets of cars, trucks and other vehicles increase fuel imports and exacerbate health problems. Successful strategies for improving transport while reducing the costs of traffic congestion and pollution are offered by Manila, Philippines, and Curitaba, Brazil.

In the early 1970s, the Philippines responded to worsening traffic congestion and rising oil costs with an innovative light rail system for Manila. It raised fuel prices to encourage conservation and trained drivers and vehicle maintenance workers in ways to use less gasoline and oil. As a result, traffic speed on routes served by the rail system increased by about one-third, reducing commuting time, cutting gasoline and oil use, and reducing emissions. Gasoline consumption declined by 43 per cent between 1976 and 1985, while population, income and travel all increased (Giminez, 1988). If gasoline consumption in the Philippines had increased as much as economic growth, consumption would have doubled. This programme helped save the country as much as US$500 million in oil imports annually and reduce national carbon dioxide emissions by about 20 per cent (Kats, 1991a).

Few people in Brazil's fifth largest city drive to work. Two-thirds of the people living in Curitiba take buses that run on dedicated lanes following routes radiating from the city centre. The largest housing and commercial centres are located on express lanes. Smaller developments are on lanes linked to the central lines. Since the early 1970s, city planners have been required to place services such as schools and shopping centres on the bus routes, creating a model integrated transport and land use programme.

While citizens of Curitiba have more cars per capita than inhabitants of any other Brazilian city except Brasilia, they use their automobiles little, finding it more pleasant to take the bus. They also find it cheaper to take the bus, while the city benefits from reduced pollution and fewer accidents.

Desire to reduce congestion has prompted much more modest transport reform in Singapore, Thailand and Venezuela (OTA, 1991). This is only a beginning. The spectre of widespread brain damage to the children in Mexico City from transport fumes serves as a stark warning that the unchecked growth of private transport is a terrible health threat. The Philippine light rail and the Brazilian dedicated bus system both demonstrate that there are better alternatives. These programmes have succeeded in improving transport and reducing congestion, pollution and health damage while saving money. They should be widely emulated if developing nations want to avoid mounting health and environmental damages and costs imposed by unregulated and subsidized private transport systems.

Appliances

Rapid increase in appliance use is a major contributor to rapid growth in electricity consumption in developing nations. In Beijing, the portion of households with refrigerators rose from 1.5 per cent in 1981 to 62 per cent in 1987 (Sathaye *et al.*, 1989). The refrigerator plants were purchased from Japanese firms and were outdated technology that use about three times as much electricity as conventional refrigerators. The choice of very inefficient design has required construction of additional, very costly and polluting electricity plants. This could have been avoided through a wiser choice of appliance production design.

Establishing efficiency standards will cost governments little but may increase the cost of domestic production since it involves redesign (such as adding more insulation and moving the compressor from the bottom to the top of refrigerators). However, a slight design cost increase is repaid many times over by far lower energy use during the lifetime of the appliance. These savings can best be captured by establishing performance standards.

US and European Community standards for energy efficiency of appliances exceed or will exceed performance levels of many appliances manufactured in developing countries. Appliances and other energy-using equipment that do not meet these efficiency standards will be difficult to sell into the world's two largest markets. Thus, inefficient energy design is not only extremely wasteful of resources, it may also severely limit export potential for energy-using equipment manufactured by developing nations.

Improving efficiency of non-renewable energy supply options

Future decisions on new sources of power for developing countries will be bounded by the twin constraints of limited financial resources and the need to contain environment and health-damaging emissions. This will require a transition to much greater reliance on renewables. The transition to a renewable energy-based economy would include more efficient use of current energy sources, such as cogeneration in fossil fuel plants and more efficient gas turbine technologies. These options, along with the prospect for an expanded nuclear power programme in the Third World, are evaluated below. Renewable energy options will be addressed in the following section.

Cogeneration
Cogeneration, or combined heat and power systems, involves burning fuel to generate both electricity and useful heat, for use in food processing plants, for example. This can increase efficiency of energy use by 50 per cent or more at very low costs since the heat is otherwise vented and not used. Cogeneration potential is more fully used in industrialized than in developing nations. For example, Pakistan uses less than a quarter of its total cogeneration potential (1985), while unused cogeneration potential in India exceeds 20 per cent of total grid capacity (USAID, 1988).

Gas turbines
Rising gas reserves and the availability of very efficient gas turbines will make gas an important bridging fuel from fossil fuels to renewable energy sources. Switching from coal or oil to gas is an option for some developing nations and would allow reduction in emissions of green-house gases. In the mid-1980s, 47 per cent of gas produced in developing

nations was flared, compared to only 4 per cent in OECD nations (Kosmo, 1987).

Recent models of gas turbines offer generating efficiencies of 50 per cent or better, a gain of half on existing turbines. The relatively small size of these units (fifty to several hundred MW) and relatively rapid construction times of one to two years make them ideal low-cost power units for developing countries. Advanced gas turbine technologies promise even higher levels of efficiency at a capital cost of US$400 per kW, or roughly one-third the cost of US coal plants and one-fifth the cost of US nuclear reactors (Williams, 1989).

Nuclear power
Growing concern over global warming has renewed interest in nuclear power, since it has much lower greenhouse gas emissions than fossil fuels. However, this is unlikely to prompt a real revival of nuclear power because more cost-effective options exist to slow warming. A study published in 1988 determined that a dollar invested in energy efficiency in the USA reduces carbon dioxide emissions seven times as much as a dollar spent on nuclear power (Keepin and Kats, 1988). Nuclear power is also far more costly than efficiency in developing countries. For example, nuclear electricity costs about US$0.16 per kWh in India, between five and six times as much as efficiency gains at US$0.03 per kWh (Felix, 1990; Reddy *et al.*, 1990a).

In developing nations (excluding newly industrialized countries), there are only a dozen, mostly small commercial nuclear reactors in operation. These are generally among the least reliable electricity plants, with an average operating capacity of 42 per cent in 1988 and 1989. This is roughly half the level of plants that use coal or oil as fuel. Unreliability of these nuclear plants worsens grid instability, in turn discouraging investment. Cost overruns, construction delays and poor performance of reactors in the Third World are likely to discourage large future nuclear plant construction programmes.

RENEWABLE ENERGY

Many past renewable energy programmes in the Third World have not succeeded, in part because the technology was not proven first in OECD nations. However, improved performance, declining cost and increased experience with some renewable energy sources in OECD nations pave the way for application of proven renewable energy technologies in developing nations. These technologies include wind and solar power, as well as sustainable biomass use.

Research and development funding for energy in OECD countries has been heavily biased towards nuclear power and away from renewables. For example, in 1988 renewables received only 6 per cent of European Community R & D energy funding. In contrast, nuclear power is destined to receive 81 per cent of the new energy programme for European Community R & D (McGowan, 1991). Development assistance to support renewables has been correspondingly imbalanced.

This bias against renewables has influenced the energy investment priorities of developing countries, which have spent tens of billions of US dollars on nuclear power over the past three decades, but only a small fraction of this on renewables. But lack of government funding is only one of several barriers to renewable energy in developing countries. Another such barrier involves the relationship between foreign capital and the electric utilities of developing countries. Most developing countries are served by large, nationally owned utility companies that usually operate with some autonomy. These tend to be strong institutions with personnel who are better trained than in most Third World public agencies. Commercial banks and foreign aid agencies prefer to deal with strong central authorities and, as discussed above, often have a bias in favour of large, discrete projects. The result is a continuing trend towards large, capital-intensive schemes managed by these utilities. In contrast, renewable energy sources tend to be small and decentralized, giving rise to problems of management and scale that utilities and foreign aid agencies are poorly equipped to deal with (Flavin, 1986).

Another barrier to renewables is that fossil fuels and nuclear power are often subsidized. These fuels impose large costs in the form of pollution, health effects and waste disposal that are not included in the fuel price. Many of these costs – such as the contribution of fossil fuels to global warming – are effectively passed on to future generations. It has been estimated that, if passed on to consumers, these hidden costs would roughly double the present cost of these energy sources. Because these costs are not reflected in current energy pricing structures, there is over-investment in polluting energy sources, principally fossil fuels, and under-investment in renewables. The hidden costs of renewable energies, such as wind and solar photovoltaics are negligible (Hohmeyer, 1988).

Wind power, photovoltaics and solar thermal technologies are experiencing steeply declining costs and rising efficiencies, patterns that are projected to continue (Table 9.1).

Table 9.1: Cost of selected renewable electricity sources, 1980–2030 (1988 US cents per kilowatt hour)

Technology	1980	1988	2000	2030
Wind	32	8	5	3
Photovoltaic	339	30	10	4
Solar thermal:				
Trough with gas assistance	24	8	6	—
Parabolic/central receiver	85	16	8	5
Biomass	5	5	—	—

Note
Costs are averaged over the expected life of the technology and rounded; projected costs assume return to high government R & D levels.
Source: Brown *et al.* (1991).

The pattern of declining costs for renewable energy sources differs from fossil fuels, whose prices have been volatile but with a historically upward trend. Because they emit little or no carbon dioxide and continue to experience declining costs, renewables can be expected to play a rapidly growing role in developing as well as in industrialized countries. As noted by the Bruntland Commission: 'renewable energy sources . . . should form the foundation of the global energy structure during the 21st century' (WCED, 1987).

Wind power

Wind has been criticized as an unreliable power source, yet recent experience with US and European windfarms indicates availability above 90 per cent, which is as good as or better than most current power plants. Mitsubishi even offers a ten-year performance guarantee on its wind turbines, much better than guarantees on most conventional plants. A recent review of the potential for renewables dismisses five 'myths' about wind power: that it (1) is too costly, (2) is unreliable, (3) is too variable to be of value, (4) has only very small potential and (5) is proven to have the above problems by the lack of commercial development to date (Grubb, 1990).

The cost of wind power has been cut by two-thirds over the past decade, to between 7 and 9 US cents per kWh, making it a competitive power source in the USA (Rader *et al.*, 1989). The US Department of Energy expects this to drop to 5 cents per kWh by the year 2000 (see Table 9.1). There are about 20,000 electricity-generating wind machines installed globally, representing an investment of US$2 to 3 billion (Frandsen, 1991). In Denmark, generous government subsidies were phased out in 1989 as wind became fully commercially viable. With an annual growth rate of 40 per cent in installed wind-generating capacity, Denmark is likely to meet its target of 10 per cent of electricity from windmills by the year 2000. Overall European wind potential has been reported at 2.5 times total current electricity demand (Grubb, 1990; Frandsen, 1991).

Box 9.2: Powering irrigation

Use of small windmills is often the most cost-effective solution for lifting water for irrigation in developing countries. Electric pumps are generally used by farmers only because of large subsidies (Foley, 1990). However, from the perspective of efficient allocation of scarce resources, electric water pumping is often very wasteful. The cost of building the generating plants to provide the electricity required for irrigation pumping in Pakistan has been estimated at US$600 to 800 million. Pumping already accounts for most of rural electric demand in Pakistan, and consumes a quarter of total national electricity demand in peak use periods (Levine *et al.*, 1991). In India, 5.8 million electric pumps have been installed, adding 20,000 MW of demand (Felix, 1990).

Subsidies mean there is little incentive for improving the efficiency of pumping equipment. A random sample of the 200,000 tubewells used for irrigation in Pakistan found that improved design would allow energy use to be halved with no reduction in performance (Beg and Armstrong, 1989). Similarly, it is estimated that a 50 per cent reduction in energy use in India's agricultural sector can be achieved by proper installation and sizing of irrigation systems (Phillips, 1990b).

Inefficient equipment contributes to rapid demand growth: electricity subsidies were a major reason for an annual growth rate of agricultural electricity usage in India of 25 per cent annually from 1985 to 1989 (Felix, 1990). Rapid demand growth increases electricity shortages and unre-liability of electricity supply. This leads some farmers to invest in back-up diesel pumps, which is also expensive to the many governments that subsidize diesel fuel. But because diesel motors are too large for many pumping applications and are used only intermittently, they often do not justify the cost.

The potential for wind-powered water pumps in developing nations is very large and would allow more reliable performance at much lower overall costs, while replacing imported fuel or power-generation tech-nologies with domestically manufactured equipment. Achieving this potential will require a reduction in electricity and diesel fuel subsidies, support for domestic equipment manufacture and access to credit for purchase of renewable-energy-based pumping technologies.

Developing countries are well placed to manufacture windmills and other labour-intensive renewable energy technologies. For example, lower labour costs help reduce the cost of manufacture of Argentine windmills – designed for pumping water in agricultural applications – to one-half the cost in the USA. Windmills for lifting water for agriculture are a large potential market in many developing countries (see Box 9.2). Argentina manufactures the bulk of its own windmills (60,000 are now in operation in the country) and windmills are a growing Argentine export industry (Hurst, 1990).

Solar Power

Solar power (like other renewables) is sometimes dismissed as being a second-rate or not advanced technology. However, it should be noted that Pacific Gas & Electric, the world's largest private utility, based in California – perhaps the most advanced energy market in the world – has cancelled nuclear construction and is investing in large-array solar electricity plants because they cost one-third less than nuclear and the same as fossil-fuel-fired electricity, but without the environmental costs (Flannigan, 1991). At 8 US cents per kWh, this kind of solar electricity is already cost competitive for electricity generation in developing countries.

The major manufacturers and exporters of solar hot water heaters are industrialized countries. Yet at least five developing countries, including Morocco, Tunisia, Egypt, Senegal and Zimbabwe, manufacture parts of or entire solar hot water heating systems. Imported solar hot water heaters can be cost effective in industrial applications in developing nations up to a price of about US$25 per barrel of oil (Terrado, Mendis and Fitzgerald, 1989). Domestic manufacture can be expected to reduce this cost, making them competitive at lower oil prices and in a broader range of applications.

Photovoltaic (PV) cells, which convert sunlight into electricity, have experienced a more than tenfold reduction in cost over the past decade. A recent study by the US Department of Energy concluded that US sales of PV cells are growing at 30 per cent a year and that 'PV appears to be a long-term and desirable solution to US and global concerns for energy and environment'. The study indicated that the growth of this technology may be 'explosive' when the price drops to about 8 cents per kWh, which the Department of Energy predicts could happen by the year 2000 (US DOE, 1990). A similar conclusion was reached by a German study, which found that solar PV will be commercially viable as a baseload electricity source in the year 2000. However, when hidden costs, such as pollution, are included in a cost comparison between solar PV and fossil fuels, PV-generated electricity had become equal in cost to fossil-fuel-fired electricity plants in Germany by 1987 and now is the least-cost option (Hohmeyer, 1991). In developing countries with more sunshine than Germany, solar-generated electricity already costs less than fossil fuels when hidden costs are taken into account.

A major limitation on solar electricity plants is that most designs generate electricity only during the day, requiring back-up generation at night or on overcast days. This problem is solved with the addition of one-day water storage and back-up gas heating to supplement solar. In areas of high solar radiation, such as most of Africa and much of South America, this system is expected to generate electricity at about US$0.045 per kWh, with solar contributing about 80 per cent of the heating, and with emissions equal to about 12 per cent of coal plants, or one-quarter those of combined cycle gas systems. In areas of low solar radiation, such as the UK or parts of China, the solar–gas thermal system would cost about US$0.055 per kWh, with solar and gas each providing half the heating load (Mills, 1991).

Construction time for these hybrid solar–gas plants is projected to be one year, which allows avoidance of the high interest costs associated with large plants. Commercial interest in the manufacture of these systems is growing, and the first plant is expected to be operational in under five years (Mills, 1991). If these cost figures are correct, it indicates that a solar–gas hybrid can provide electricity at prices that are very competitive with fossil fuels and with a small fraction of emissions by the middle or late 1990s. It should be noted that the Australian government has accepted these projections in calculating that the country could rely primarily on renewable energy sources by 2020 at about the same cost as a strategy based primarily on fossil fuels (Government of Australia, 1991).

Solar hydrogen

One promising renewable energy option is solar hydrogen. Hydrogen production is a process of conversion using energy to release hydrogen from hydrogen compounds, such as water. Hydrogen is currently derived primarily from fossil fuels, and almost all production is used in the petroleum refining and chemicals industries. An alternative method of producing hydrogen is to separate out hydrogen through electrolysis using electricity derived from renewable energy sources, especially photovoltaic solar cells.

A recent study on the potential of solar hydrogen observed that 'because it is based on the exploitation of renewable resources (water and sunlight) and on abundant materials (silicon from ordinary sand in the case of amorphous silicon thin-film cells), PV hydrogen is a fuel with none of the resource limitation worries of oil, natural gas and uranium' (Ogden and Williams, 1989). Hydrogen derived from renewables is an extraordinarily clean fuel that by replacing fossil fuels would cut emissions of carbon dioxide, sulphur dioxide and particulates.

Solar hydrogen holds the potential of offering developing nations an environmentally benign, renewable and widely available commercial source of energy. Continued sharp decline in the cost of electricity from solar photovoltaic cells indicates that PV-derived hydrogen may become an economically competitive new energy source around the year 2000 for a large portion of commercial energy needs, including heating and transport. Hydrogen can be transported over long distances and in large volumes at a cost that is reported to be competitive with or lower than electricity transmission (Winter *et al.*, 1990). This suggests the prospect of solar hydrogen derived from, for example, the sun-rich desert areas in North Africa and exported by pipeline to the industrial nations in Europe. This would provide a potentially large new source of export earnings for some developing countries.

Biomass

Biomass is the predominant and often only source of energy for about 2.5 billion people in developing countries, primarily in rural areas. Biomass includes both products grown for biomass (such as woodfuel or sugar alcohol plantations) and the by-products of other activities (such as tree prunings, agricultural waste and dung). In sub-Saharan Africa, these fuels account for 60 to 95 per cent of total energy use, with the highest proportions in the poorest countries and households. FAO has estimated that in 1980 just over one billion people were living in areas of fuelwood deficit, a figure that according to some estimates could almost double by the year 2000 (Leach and Mearns, 1988).

Population pressure and failure to intensify farming lead to land clearance for agriculture and are often the major reasons for deforestation. According to one estimate, land clearance from 1950 to 1983 was responsible for about 70 per cent of the permanent forest destruction in Africa. Studies from Botswana, Zimbabwe and Zambia illustrate that land clearance provides woodfuel in the short term, while permanently degrading forest cover and contributing to long-term soil erosion (ibid.).

Most rural areas will continue to rely on biomass for their energy needs. Slowing deforestation and erosion will require the participatory approaches to rural development, including community reforestation, that are described elsewhere in this book (see, for example, Chapters 4 and 8). Only through such broad-based community processes can the current accelerating cycle of forest loss and land degradation that results from poverty, population pressures and energy needs be reversed.

Burning of biomass offers great scope for expanded rural electricity generation and fuel production. However, this must be weighed against the loss of alternative uses of biomass, including for agriculture (Larson *et al.*, 1989). Burning of bagasse (fibrous residue from sugar-cane crushing) to generate electricity now provides a financial rate of return of about 30 per cent in Ethiopian power plants (Terrado, Mendis and Fitzgerald, 1989). Bagasse may be an economically competitive electricity source for up to 40 GW of generating capacity worldwide, equivalent to forty large nuclear reactors (Goldemberg *et al.*, 1987b). A recent study indicates that use of efficient bagasse gasifier/steam-injected gas turbine technologies using trees from Brazilian forest plantations as fuel would be competitive in cost with hydroelectricity (Carpentieri, 1991).

Alcohol programmes use ethanol fermented from sugar-cane juice or molasses as feedstock. The most ambitious programme to date has been in Brazil. Although programme expansion has been suspended due to lower oil prices, the programme has had substantial benefits. These include substituting for imported fuel, reducing pollution and creating about half a million jobs. One job is created for each US$12,000 to US$22,000 invested in the ethanol programme, as opposed to US$200,000 per job in the oil refining industry (Goldemberg *et al.*, 1987b; Hall and Rosillo-Calle, 1991). At least four African countries produce ethanol to meet 3 to 15 per cent of gasoline demand (Terrado, Mendis and Fitzgerald, 1989). Expansion of these programmes is limited because of the value of bagasse or other biomass fuel for other uses, alternative uses of land and the difficulty of matching a stable bagasse-based fuel supply to applications in such areas such as transportation.

CONCLUSIONS: TOWARDS A STRATEGY OF ENERGY EFFICIENCY

Energy efficiency saves OECD nations hundreds of billions of dollars per year and has become a key competitive trade advantage for the most economically successful nations, such as Japan. The UN General Assembly resolution that established UNCED called for 'favourable access to, and transfer of, environmentally sound technologies, in particular to the developing countries on concessional and preferential terms' (United Nations, 1989). During the UNCED preparatory process, developing countries repeatedly called for an 'affordable and equitable' transfer of 'environmentally benign technology', with energy technology foremost in mind.

But many of the barriers to the acquisition of appropriate energy technology are in the developing countries themselves (Markandya and Ayres, 1991). Often they do not provide adequate legal protection to foreign developers or patent holders. Developing nations also often impose tariff barriers on efficient equipment while subsidizing fossil fuels, and frequently favour construction of large energy plants rather than buying the equipment and making the institutional changes required to achieve more energy-efficient economies.

None the less, it is clear that industrialized nations are guilty of not sharing efficiency techniques and technologies with the developing world. Loans to support energy purchases by developing nations often promote technologies selected more on the basis of the lender's self-interest than a desire to promote cost-effective energy services.

Current energy production and use patterns are clearly wasteful and unsustainable. Without a fundamental shift in priorities to embrace least-cost planning, developing nations face worsening power short-ages, stalled economic growth and mounting energy-related debt, in addition to continued environmental degradation.

An efficiency strategy would involve reforming utility regulations to promote least-cost planning, investing in training and expanding staff capable of performing least-cost analysis, setting appliance standards and undertaking other steps to promote the efficient use of energy. This will require that industrialized countries share the know-how of energy departments and utilities and universities with the developing world.

An energy efficiency strategy would require political commitment and institution building rather than vast amounts of capital. It would focus on meeting energy needs at the lowest cost, including decentralizing electricity production. It would involve more efficient use of biomass and expanded use of wind power – especially for water lifting – as well as a range of solar technologies.

The specific policy options open to governments and foreign agencies supporting energy development in the Third World include:

(1) *Eliminating subsidies for energy and gradually replacing these with energy taxes.* Widespread energy subsidies in developing nations promote wasteful consumption, increased imports, growing pollution

and accompanying health problems, while discouraging the development of domestic renewable energy sources. Subsidies – particularly of fossil fuels – reduce production of domestic energy sources and renewables. These subsidies should be replaced with taxes to encourage efficiency. Revenue from such taxes can be redistributed to provide the poor with free or subsidized efficient technologies, such as stoves, pumps or appliances.

(2) *Changing unfavourable fiscal regimes*. Many developing countries subsidize fossil fuels use but impose import duties on efficient equipment and technologies. For example, in India, subsidies reduce the cost of coal to one-fifth the level of US prices, while efficient equipment is taxed at between 35 and 125 per cent. Some developing countries permit tax deductions on the cost of plant expansions but not on efficiency improvements. These tax policies should be changed to promote efficiency.

(3) *Carrying out regulatory reform*. Electricity boards regularly prohibit utilities from buying back privately generated electricity, which discourages expansion of private power generation and development of efficiency, cogeneration and renewable energy sources. Regulatory reform would allow independent producers and industries to generate electricity and sell it to utilities at fair prices. It would encourage efficiency through adoption of least-cost approaches that increase energy services at the lowest cost. Some developing countries, including the Philippines, Indonesia and Pakistan, have already taken important steps in this direction.

(4) *Introducing energy efficiency standards for government procurement and construction*. In many developing countries, the government is the single largest purchaser of goods and services, including construction. By introducing and enforcing efficiency standards for all new government buildings and equipment purchases (such as appliances and vehicles), governments would establish norms to be followed by domestic and foreign bidders that would very likely be adopted by the private sector.

(5) *Improving access to credit*. Low-interest or subsidized loans are generally available for construction or plant expansion but not for efficiency improvements nor for purchase of efficient equipment or renewable technologies. Decentralized energy systems, increasingly based on renewables, often will require improved access to credit in rural areas.

(6) *Introducing new funding mechanisms*. Third-party financing, such as performance contracting, may be introduced through instituting least-cost planning to reduce investment risk. Under this arrangement,

third-party contractors undertake work required to save energy in industrial and commercial facilities and then share in the resulting savings.

(7) *Untying development assistance.* Only about one-third of development assistance is freely available for worldwide procurement (see Chapter 10). The bulk of aid has a secondary objective of promoting exports from the donor country. This objective is best achieved by selling the most expensive equipment, requiring long-term reliance on service and spares from the exporting country and, preferably, involving technologies with standards that differ from those of competing vendors. This is not only economically inefficient but also unsupportive of efficiency and the development of locally based, low-cost energy sources, including renewables.

(8) *Transferring technical expertise.* Current staffing in most developing countries is entirely inadequate to build energy-efficient economies. Emphasis therefore needs to be placed on institution building and training to create this capability. Institutional twinning arrangements between industrialized and developing countries can facilitate the rapid transfer of expertise and efficient technologies and accelerate the development of renewable energy technologies.

REFERENCES AND BIBLIOGRAPHY

Baldwin, Sam *et al.*, 1985. 'Improved woodburning cookstoves: signs of success', *Ambio*, 14, 4–5.

Beg, Daud and Armstrong, J. R., 1989. 'Energy conservation in Pakistan: a unified approach', *Power Engineering Journal*, November.

Berkovski, Boris, 1991. 'Solar energy: strategic solution for a better environment', *Conference Proceedings, World Clean Energy Conference*, CMC, Geneva, 4–7, November.

Borrini, Grazia (ed.), 1990. *Lessons Learned in Community-Based Environmental Management: Proceedings of the 1990 Primary Environmental Care Workshop*, Istituto Superiore di Sanità, Directorate-General for Development Co-operation, Ministry of Foreign Affairs, Rome.

Brown, Lester *et al.*, 1991. *State of the World 1991.* (Worldwatch Institute), Earthscan, London.

Burley, William F., 1988. 'The Tropical Forestry Action Plan', in E. O. Wilson (ed.), *Biodiversity*, National Academy Press, Washington, DC.

Carpentieri, E., 1991. *An Assessment of Sustainable Bioenergy in Brazil: National Overview and Case Study for the Northeast*, PU/CEES Working Paper no. 119, Princeton University.

Cooper Weil, Diana *et al.*, 1990. *The Impact of Development Policies on Health.* WHO, Geneva.

Chandler, W. U. (ed.), 1990. *Carbon Emissions Control Strategies: Case Studies in International Cooperation*, Conservation Foundation, Washington, DC.

CMIE (Centre for Monitoring Indian Economy), 1988. *Current Energy Scene in India*, Economic Intelligence Service, Bombay, May.

CSE (Centre for Science and Environment), 1982. *The State of India's Environment – a Citizen's Report*, CSE, Delhi.

Escay J. R., 1990. *Summary Data Sheets of 1987 Power and Commercial Energy Statistics for 100 Developing Countries*, World Bank, Washington, DC.

Faiz, A., Sinha, K., Walsh, M. and Varma, A., 1990. *Automotive Air Pollution: Issues and Options for Developing Countries*, Infrastructure and Urban Development Department, World Bank, Washington, DC.

Far Eastern Economic Review, 1990. 'People powerless', 10 May.

Felix, Cutis S., 1990. *Assessment of US Trade and Investment Opportunities in Energy Efficiency Markets in India*, International Institute for Energy Conservation, Washington, DC, September.

Finance and Development, 1991. 'The Global Environment Facility', March.

Flannigan, Ted, 1991. Private communication.

Flavin, Christopher, 1986. *Electricity for a Developing World: New Directions*, Worldwatch Paper 70, Worldwatch Institute, Washington, DC, June.

Foley, Gerald, 1990. *Electricity for Rural People*, Panos Institute, London.

Ford, Andrew and Geinzer, Jay, 1990. 'Adding uncertainty to least cost planning', *Energy Policy*, May.

Frandsen, Sten, 1991. 'Wind energy development in light of the Danish experience', *Conference Proceedings, World Clean Energy Conference*, CMC, Geneva, 4–7 November.

Gadgil, Ashok, 1990. '*Bombay efficient lighting large-scale experiment*', unpublished note, Lawrence Berkeley Laboratory, Berkeley, Calif. April.

Geller, Howard, 1990. *Establishing an International Energy Efficiency Agency: A Response to the Threat of Global Change*, American Council for an Energy-Efficient Economy, November.

Gerard, David, 1991. Private communication, USAID Office of Energy, Arlington Va, February.

Gill, Laurie A., 1990. *The Implications of Current Trends in the Indian Energy Sector*. Environmental Defense Fund, New York, July.

Giminez, A., 1988. '*Transportation energy conservation activities in the Philippines*', paper for the conference on Energy Efficiency Strategies for Thailand, Pattaya, 4–6 March.

Goldemberg, Jose, Johansson, Thomas, Reddy, Amulya and Williams, Robert, 1987a. *Energy for a Sustainable World*, Wiley-Eastern, New York.

Goldemberg, Jose, Johansson, Thomas, Reddy, Amulya and Williams, Robert, 1987b. *Energy for Development*, World Resources Institute, Washington, DC., September.

Government of Australia, 1991. *Ecologically Sustainable Energy Process: Preliminary Results*, Government of Australia, Canberra, November.

Grubb, M. J., 1990. 'The Cinderella options: a study of modernized renewable energy technologies. Part 1-A technical assessment', *Energy Policy*, July–August.

Hall, D. O. and Rosillo-Calle, F., 1991. 'Biomass: a non-polluting source of energy', *Conference Proceedings, World Clean Energy Conference*, CMC, Geneva, 4–7 November.

Hanen, Ulf, 1990. 'Delinking of energy consumption and economic growth', *Energy Policy*, September.

Hardoy, Jorge E. and Satterthwaite, David, 1989. *Squatter Citizen: Life in the Urban Third World*, Earthscan, London.

Hardoy, Jorge E. and Satterthwaite, David, 1990. 'The future city', in Jorge E. Hardoy, Sandy Cairncross and David Satterthwaite (eds), *The Poor Die Young: Housing and Health in Third World Cities*, Earthscan, London.

Hirst, Eric and Brown, Marilyn, 1990. *Closing the Efficiency Gap: Barriers to Efficient Use of Energy*, Oak Ridge National Laboratory, Oak Ridge, Tenn., January.

Hohmeyer, O., 1988. *Social Costs of Energy Consumption*, Springer Verlag, Berlin.

Hohmeyer, O., 1991. Speech to the World Clean Energy Conference, Geneva, November.

Hunter, John M., Rey, Luis and Scott, David, 1983. 'Man-made lakes – Man-made diseases', *World Health Forum*, (WHO), 4.

Hurst, Christopher, 1990. 'Establishing new markets for mature energy equipment in developing countries: experience with windmills, hydro-powered mills and solar water heaters', *World Development*, 18.

IPCC, 1990. *Potential Impacts of Climate Change*, World Meteorological Organization and UNEP, Geneva.

Kats, Gregory, 1989. 'Global greenhouse warming: energy and development', in *Expert Seminar on Energy Technologies for Reducing Emissions of Greenhouse Gases: Collected Papers*, OECD and IEA, Paris, 12–14 April.

Kats, Gregory, 1991a. 'Slowing warming and sustaining development: the promise of energy efficiency', *Energy Policy*, January.

Kats, Gregory, 1991b. 'Hungary's energy options: models for Eastern Europe', *Energy Policy*, November.

Keepin, William and Kats, Gregory, 1988. 'Greenhouse warming: comparative assessment of two abatement strategies', *Energy Policy*, December.

Kolar, Stanislav, 1991. 'Energy and energy conservation in Eastern Europe: two scenarios for the future', unpublished paper, Battelle Memorial Institute.

Kosmo, Mark, 1987. *Money to Burn? The High Cost of Energy Subsidies*, World Resources Institute, Washington, DC.

Krause, Florentine, Bach, Wilfred and Kooney, John, 1990. *Energy Policy in the Greenhouse*, Earthscan, London.

Larson, E.D. *et al.*, 1989. 'Biomass gasification for gas turbine power generation', in T. Johansson *et al.*, (eds), *Electricity*, Lund University Press, Lund, Sweden.

Leach, Gerald, 1989. 'Africa', paper for International Workshop on 'A Little Breathing Space', Budapest, April.

Leach, Gerald and Mearns, Robin, 1988. *Beyond the Woodfuel Crisis: People, Land and Trees in Africa*, Earthscan, London.

Levine, Mark D., Gadgil, Ashok, Meyers, Stephen, Sathaye, Jayant, Stafurik, Jack and Wilbanks, Tom, 1991. *Energy Efficiency, Developing Nations, and Eastern Europe*, report to the US Working Group on Global Energy Efficiency, June.

McGowan, Francis, 1991. 'Controlling the greenhouse effect', *Energy Policy*, March.

Markandya, A. and Ayres, R. U., 1991. *'Barriers facing the achievement of ecologically sound industrial development'*, paper for the International Conference on Ecologically Sustainable Industrial Development, Denmark, 14–18 October.

Mills, David, 1991. 'Clean solar heat for homes, factories and electric power utilities', *Conference Proceedings, World Clean Energy Conference*, CMC, Geneva, 4–7 November.

Munasinghe, Mohan, 1990. *Electric Power Economics*, Butterworths, London.

Ogden, Joan M. and Williams, Robert H., 1989. *Solar Hydrogen: Moving Beyond Fossil Fuels*, World Resources Institute, Washington, DC, October.

Openshaw, Keith and Feinstein, Charles, 1989. *Fuelwood Stumpage: Financing Renewable Energy For the World's Other Half*, working paper, World Bank, Washington, DC, September.

OTA (Office of Technology Assessment), 1991. *Energy in Developing Countries*, US Government Printing Office, Washington, DC.

Pachauri, R. K. and Suri, Vivek, 1990. 'Contribution to greenhouse gases through large scale use of fossil fuels and bio-fuels', *Energy Environment Monitor*, March.

Peters, Robert, 1988. 'The effect of global climatic change on natural communities', in E. O. Wilson (ed.), *Biodiversity*, National Academy Press, Washington, DC.

Phillips, Michael, 1990a. *Energy Conservation Activities in Latin America and the Caribbean*, International Institute for Energy Conservation, Washington, DC, June.

Phillips, Michael, 1990b. *Energy Conservation Activities in Asia*, International Institute for Energy Conservation, Washington, DC, September.

Phillips, Michael, 1991. *The Least-Cost Energy Path for Developing Countries*, International Institute for Energy Conservation, Washington, DC, September.

Pretty, Jules N. and Scoones, Ian, 1989. *Rapid Rural Appraisal for Economics: Exploring Incentives for Tree Management in Sudan*, IIED, London.

Rader, N. *et al.*, 1989. *Power Surge: The Status and Near-Term Potential of Renewable Energy Technologies*, Public Citizen, Washington, DC.

Reddy, Amulya *et al.*, 1990a. *A Development-Focused End-Use-Oriented Energy Scenario for Karnataka: Part 2 – Electricity*, Department of Management Studies, Indian Institute of Science, Bangalore, April.

Reddy, Amulya *et al.*, 1990b. 'Comparative costs of electricity conservation', *Economic and Political Weekly*, 2 June.

SADCC (Southern African Development Co-ordination Conference), 1988. *Electricity in Rural Development. Vol. 1: Recommendations and Follow-Up Actions*, presented by the Technical and Administrative Unit at SADCC Energy Sector Seminar on Rural Electrification, Malawi.

Sargent, Caroline, 1990. *The Khun Song Plantation Project*, IIED, London, April.

Sarin, Madhu, 1989. 'Improved stoves, women and domestic energy', paper for the Nordic Seminar on Domestic Energy in Developing Countries, Lund Centre for Habitat Studies, Lund, Sweden.

Sathaye, Jayant and Ketoff, Andrea, 1990. 'CO_2 emissions from major developing countries: better understanding of the role of energy in the long term', *Energy Journal*, 12, 1.

Sathaye, J., Kethoff A., Schipper, L. and Lele, S., 1989. *An End-Use Approach to Developing Long-Term Energy Demand Scenarios for Developing Countries*, Lawrence Berkeley Laboratory, Berkeley, Calif., February.

Smith D. V. *et al.*, 1983. 'Report of the regional electrification survey to the Asian Development Bank', draft, Asian Development Bank, Manila.

Terrado, Ernesto, Mendis, Matthew and Fitzgerald, Kevin, 1989. *Impact of Lower Oil Prices on Renewable Energy Technologies*, working paper, World Bank, Washington, DC, February.

UNEP, 1986. *The State of the Environment: Environment and Health*, UNEP, Nairobi, June.

United Nations, 1989. *General Assembly Resolution 44/228* (establishing UNCED), United Nations, New York, December.

USAID, 1988. *Power Shortages in Developing Countries: Magnitude, Impacts, Solutions and the Role of the Private Sector*, USAID, Washington, DC.

US DOE (US Department of Energy), 1990. *The Potential of Renewable Energy: An Interlaboratory White Paper*, US DOE, Washington, DC, March.

WCED, 1987. *Our Common Future* (Brundtland Report), Oxford University Press, Oxford.

Williams, Robert H., 1988. *'Are runaway energy capital costs a constraint on development?'*, paper for the International Seminar on the New Era in the World Economy, São Paulo, 31 August – 2 September.

Williams, Robert H., 1989. *Invited Testimony before the Subcommittee of Foreign Operations of the Appropriations Committee of the US House of Representatives*, February.

Winter, C. J. *et al.*, 1990. 'Hydrogen as an energy carrier: what is known? What do we need to learn?', *International Journal of Hydrogen Energy*, 15, 2.

World Bank, 1990. *Funding for the Global Environment: The Global Environment Facility*, discussion paper, World Bank, Washington, DC, November.

10 Financing Sustainable Development

Johan Holmberg

INTRODUCTION

The debate on sustainable development that has emerged since the 1987 Brundtland Report (WCED, 1987) has given a new rationale to calls for additional North–South financial resource flows. A significant increase in concessional finance for developing countries will be essential, it is said, if these countries are to address their sustainable development needs.

The matter was coming to a head in the preparations for the 1992 UN Conference on Environment and Development. The preparatory process for UNCED had given clear evidence that developing countries saw 'new and additional' financial resources to support sustainable development in the South as a main aim of the conference. While sympathetic to a varying degree with a need for some additionality, Northern countries were equivocating and studiously avoiding commitments. The successful outcome of UNCED, billed as the largest summit meeting ever,[1] hinged in large measure on resolution of this issue, the complexity of which so far had exceeded the negotiating abilities of the international community of nations.

This chapter explores the viability of the claims for additional financial resource flows for sustainable development in the South and examines those mechanisms for raising revenue in the North to finance such flows that would in themselves contribute to sustainability objectives. The chapter begins with an overview of current North–South financial resource flows, followed by a summary of existing estimates of additional flows to finance sustainable development in the South. An assessment is made of the need for additional resources and the foreseeable difficulties in raising and also in spending them. The potential role of trade is mentioned, and there is a discussion of the use of economic incentive mechanisms for environmental management to raise financial resources. The chapter concludes on the note that financing sustainable development must mean meeting the twin objectives of raising funds and improving environmental management.

CURRENT TRENDS IN NORTH–SOUTH FINANCIAL RESOURCE FLOWS

During the 1980s, financial resource flows in real terms to developing countries declined sharply, as illustrated by Table 10.1.

Table 10.1: Total real net financial resource flows (from all sources, 1988 prices and exchange rates)

Year	US$ billion
1981	201.9
1985	128.3
1989 (prel.)	111.5

Source: OECD (1990, table 3-1).

The reduction in total flows has been caused mainly by reductions of private bank lending, which declined from 38.1 per cent of the total in 1981 to 7.2 per cent in 1989, and of export credits from OECD countries. As a result, official development assistance (ODA), or foreign aid, has grown in importance from 26.8 per cent of total flows in 1981 to 48.1 per cent in 1989. Foreign direct investment and other private flows have increased during the decade, as have grants from non-governmental organizations. These trends are summarized in Table 10.2.

The table shows ODA from all sources, including donors in Eastern Europe, OPEC countries and some developing countries. Total ODA from the countries in the OECD Development Assistance Committee (DAC) declined in 1989 to US$46.7 billion from US$48.1 billion the previous year. There was a modest upward move in DAC countries' ODA in real terms during the 1980s, at 1988 prices and exchange rates, from US$41.4 billion on average during 1980–5 to US$47.3 billion in 1989. However, ODA as a share of GNP for DAC member states combined declined from 0.35 per cent on average during 1975–80 to 0.33 per cent in 1989. In 1989 seven DAC members improved their ODA/GNP ratios, but the ratios for ten others worsened. During the 1980s, the Scandinavian countries and the Netherlands consistently

Table 10.2: Total net financial resource flows to developing countries

	Current US$ billion			*Percentage of total*		
	1981	*1985*	*1989*	*1981*	*1985*	*1989*
Official dev. finance (ODF)	45.5	48.9	69.0	33.1	58.0	62.5 (I)
of which:						
ODA	36.8	37.3	53.1	26.8	44.2	48.1
Other ODF	8.7	11.6	15.9	6.3	13.8	14.4
Export credits	17.6	4.0	1.2	12.8	4.7	1.1 (II)
Private flows	74.3	31.4	40.2	54.1	37.2	36.4 (III)
of which:						
Direct inv.	17.2	6.6	22.0	12.5	7.8	19.9
Bank lending	52.3	15.2	8.0	38.1	18.0	7.2
Other private flows	2.8	6.7	6.0	2.0	7.9	5.4
Grants by NGOs	2.0	2.9	4.2	1.5	3.4	3.8
Total flows (I+II+III)	137.4	84.3	110.4	100.0	100.0	100.0

Source: ibid.

maintained ODA above the target of 0.7 per cent of GNP established by the United Nations in 1970. Among other large donors, Canada roughly maintained its ODA/GNP ratio during the decade, and France, Germany and Japan increased their ratios, while the USA and the UK decreased theirs; the current level of the USA, 0.15 per cent, is the lowest of all DAC member countries (ibid., table 2).

In the view of DAC, there may in future years be substantial increases in ODA from large donors like Japan and France. While no firm ODA projections are possible, given the uncertainties in future aid prospects for some of the larger donors, DAC expects ODA to 'continue to show a modest upward move in real terms over the next few years' (ibid.).

ODA is the principal form of resource transfer to the poorest countries. In 1989, it accounted for nearly two-thirds of new resource flows to low-income countries and four-fifths to the poorest countries. In sub-Saharan Africa, net flows of ODA were on average 8 per cent of recipient GNP, but for selected countries the dependency on foreign aid was much higher; for example, for the Sahelian countries as a group, ODA during 1980–9 was equivalent to 17.8 per cent of GNP. For Ethiopia, the corresponding figure was 15.8 per cent; for Somalia, it was as high as 46.0 per cent, and in the extreme case of Mozambique, 76.1 per cent (ibid., table 37).

The reduction in international private bank lending to developing countries can in part be explained by the weakening of the financial situation of banks in the USA and in Japan due to rising interest rates and over-investment during the 1980s in a gradually collapsing real-estate market. At the end of the 1980s, German banks became increasingly preoccupied with the consequences of absorbing formerly East German industry and began to decrease their lending overseas. Further, the ratio of market capitalization to assets for all international banks was set at 8 per cent by the so-called Basle Accord, forcing banks to cut down on new lending as they struggled to raise capital (World Bank, 1991a).

Direct foreign investment (DFI) by OECD countries increased from US$7 billion in 1985 to US$25 billion in 1988. While there was a modest decrease in 1989, DFI is likely to increase in coming years as a consequence of the 'globalization' of business and in response to economic policy reforms in developing countries. For example, there are recent signs of increasing private capital flows into Latin America, where stock markets are appreciating, prices of secondary market debt climbing, and private investment increasing. However, DFI is likely to remain focused, as in the past, on middle-income countries with relatively developed infrastructure. Just twenty developing countries accounted for about 90 per cent of total DFI during the 1980s, with 39 per cent going to Central America (including Caribbean offshore centres), 34 per cent to Asia, 8 per cent to South America and only 4 per cent to sub-Saharan Africa (OECD, 1990; tables 3-2 and 3-3).

Other private flows include emerging securities markets (mainly Asian), which in the DAC statistics are given as US$4 billion in 1988 and increasing in 1989. However, the scope of the global equity market can have much greater importance for developing countries, with one estimate giving the potential total flow of new equity from all of the capital-exporting countries into emerging markets at about US$100 billion within some five years (Gill, 1989). This is a market where institutional investors, like pension funds and mutual funds, are likely to become more active. However, these investors look for countries with political stability, steady economic growth and strong national institutions and will therefore on the whole not be interested in the poorest countries.

Behind some of the above trends lies, of course, the huge debt overhang which in 1990 was equivalent to over US$1.3 trillion for all developing countries. Severely indebted countries have difficulties in attracting private flows of all kinds, and indeed of official export credits. Despite various initiatives, like the Brady plan and several different

Despite various initiatives, like the Brady plan and several different debt-equity schemes, the total debt burden on developing countries continued to worsen through the 1980s, creating particular difficulties for the 46 countries defined by the World Bank as severely indebted (of which 26 are also low-income countries with a per capita income of no more than US$610). Interest and dividends paid by developing countries were US$86.4 billion in 1981, US$95.6 billion in 1985 and US$107.7 billion in 1989. This almost cancels out the net financial flows, as illustrated in Table 10.3, showing net financial resource flows (Table 10.1) minus payments of interest and dividend by developing countries.

Table 10.3: Aggregate net financial transfers to developing countries (current US$ billion)

	Average 1980–2	1985	1987	1988	1989
All developing countries	46	–11	15	8	3
Memo items:					
Sub-Saharan Africa	11	8	16	14	14
Least developed countries	10	10	13	13	13

Source: OECD (1990, table 16).

The high US trade and fiscal deficits raising US interest rates, the cheaper American dollar and the availability of good investment opportunities in the USA have combined to attract massive capital inflows especially from the industrialized countries. Much of the world's capital formation during the 1980s was thus absorbed by the USA, reducing the availability of external resources for developing countries that need them most (Jun, 1990). An illustration is the real interest rate – that is, the interest base rate after deduction of the inflation rate – which is at historically high levels. In the UK the real interest rate during 1986–90 was on average 6.7 per cent, while it was negative (–1.7 per cent) during 1976–80 and 2.9 per cent during 1966–70.

Capital flight has exacerbated these problems. Citing estimates from the Bank of England, Jun (1990) states that accumulated capital flight during 1975–87 for seven highly indebted developing countries (Argentina, Brazil, Chile, Mexico, Peru, Philippines and Venezuela) amounted to US$150 billion.

In summary, during the 1980s there was a decline in North–South financial resource flows. There are signs that some private flows may countries with comparatively stable policies and strong institutions. The low-income developing countries will very likely continue to depend on ODA for their development finance. High international interest rates together with only modest growth of international financial flows to developing countries in coming years could slow development. This could be exacerbated by a broadened development agenda placing issues of sustainability in focus.

ESTIMATES OF ADDITIONAL RESOURCES FOR SUSTAINABLE DEVELOPMENT

Commission reports and research studies

Already at the time of the 1972 UN Conference on the Human Environment in Stockholm, governments accepted the need for additional funding to support specific types of action to protect the environment. The 1992 UN conference is set to place the environment firmly in the mainstream of development on the strength of the thesis that protection of the environment *and* development are essentially inseparable and two sides of the same coin. A number of reports suggest that sustainable development will require large sources of new financing, and that developing countries, in particular, will need a significant increase in financial support.

WCED pointed in 1987 at a need to increase financial resource flows for new multilateral efforts and action programmes for environmental protection and sustainable development (WCED, 1987). However, it did not pronounce itself on the size of requisite additional flows, suggesting a need to look for new approaches and new sources of revenue.

In 1988 the Worldwatch Institute attempted some rough calculations of the additional expenditure that would be required to meet certain targets it deemed essential for global sustainable development by the year 2000. The targets included slowing population growth, protecting topsoil on cropland, reforesting the Earth, raising energy efficiency, developing renewable energy and retiring the debt of developing countries. The institute estimated that the additional expenditure required to achieve sustainable development on a global basis would be US$46 billion in 1990 rising to US$145 billion in 1994 and eventually stabilizing at about US$150 million in 2000. About half of this expenditure would be recurrent cost (for example, for family planning) that in most poor countries would call for ODA, while the remainder would be recoverable investment cost (for example, for improved energy efficiency). The study stressed that these estimates were rough, 'bounded by wide margins of uncertainty' and intended to 'stimulate thinking about what it will take to put the world on a sustainable path' (Brown *et al.*, 1988).

The Worldwatch Institute estimates were later cited in an authoritative article by Jim MacNeill, the former secretary general of WCED and a principal author of the Brundtland Report (MacNeill, 1989). MacNeill's article by turn was quoted in a recent paper prepared at the World Resources Institute (Thacher, 1991).

In 1989 the Dutch government commissioned the consulting firm McKinsey & Co. to carry out a study on the international funding mechanisms required to accompany the necessary policy measures to stabilize emissions of greenhouse gases. The study suggested that 'for industrialized countries a target of minus 30 per cent net man-made greenhouse gas emissions, to be achieved by the year 2000 relative to 1986, would constitute a challenging but realistic goal' (McKinsey & Co., 1990). This would require some US$20 to 30 billion annually in additional international flows of funds, assuming use of the lowest-cost measures available.

That estimate included US$150 to 200 million per year for substitution of CFCs in developing countries, a theoretical maximum of US$10 to 15 billion per year for forest management funding to initiate afforestation and reduce deforestation in the tropics and a similar amount for funding of fossil-fuel energy conservation. The study focused on the global issues only and had no mandate to look into the other sides to sustainability raised by the Worldwatch Institute, like debt reduction, rehabilitation of eroded cropland and stabilization of population growth.

The UN International Fund for Agricultural Development has in a recent policy document highlighted the need for additional finance to cushion the negative fiscal effects for developing countries of expanded programmes in marginal, degraded areas. Even where the economic rationale for an increased focus on such areas can be demonstrated, the fiscal impact may often be negative since programme costs are often difficult to recover. As IFAD points out: 'the shift in lending towards more marginal areas raises concern about the ability and willingness of governments to sustain non-recoverable activities, the rationale for which lies in the realm of intergenerational equity' (IFAD, 1991). This would be support for a need for more concessional ODA for protection of the environment in such areas, where often the poorest population groups are found.

The World Resources Institute in 1989 prepared a report suggesting new initiatives to address unmet conservation financing needs in the developing world. The report indicated that while these needs 'are difficult to gauge precisely, there are indications that as much as US$20 to 50 billion per annum will be needed over the next decade' (World Resources Institute, 1989). The report does not specify what those indications are but departs from this premise to discuss comprehensive institutional initiatives.

The UN World Institute for Development Economics Research (WIDER) went further in a recent report. On the basis of studies undertaken by the institute, it suggested that to achieve what it called 'socially necessary growth' to reduce unemployment to manageable levels within a ten-year time horizon and reach basic needs goals in areas like health, education and poverty alleviation, together with an improvement in income distribution, additional net capital inflows to developing countries would have to increase immediately by US$40 billion rising to US$60 billion by the year 2000. Adding the expenditure required to alleviate past environmental damage and to support environmental protection for the future would raise additional net capital inflows to developing countries by another US$20 billion per year in the early 1990s rising to US$80 in the year 2000. On this basis, the additional demand for finance for sustainable development by developing countries was estimated at US$60 billion per year in the early 1990s, rising to US$115 billion in 1995 and US$140 billion in 2000 (Jayawardena, 1991).

Some Northern government views

Some donor governments have expressed themselves in favour of additional aid flows to the South to meet incremental costs for protection of the environment. Norway in 1989 proposed that Northern countries allocate 0.1 per cent of their GNP to a fund to help finance transitory measures in developing countries to arrest greenhouse gas emissions.

To date, this proposal has not found favour among other major donors, although some of them in the abstract have recognized a need for additional flows. For example, the policy document on foreign aid of the Dutch government from 1990 stressed that 'an international debate on the importance of genuinely additional funds must be launched' (Government of the Netherlands, 1991). A study by the Nordic governments noted that 'an increase in traditional development assistance seems to be necessary to enable the developing countries, especially the least developed among them, to take measures to deal with the poverty-related acute threats to the environment and the natural resource base' (Nordic UN Project, 1991).

In its 1991 budget submission to Parliament, the Swedish government stated that 'it is evident that increased transfers of financial resources and of technology from rich to poor countries are necessary if developing countries are to implement effective measures for sustainable development'. It went on to specify that increased financial transfers are of two kinds, mutually supportive:

- increases in traditional ODA, particularly to the least developed countries, to mitigate the threats against the environment that arise out of persistent poverty;
- international financial transfers to enable developing countries to participate in programmes to resolve the global environmental problems.

While avoiding any estimates of the size of additional transfers, it suggested that donor countries should meet requisite needs by raising their ODA volumes to the United Nations' 0.7 per cent target (Government of Sweden, 1991a).

New approaches to funding environmental action

Rapidly growing concern about global environmental problems in the late 1980s added a sense of urgency to the debate on additional financial flows. Following the exceptionally dry and hot years at the end of the decade, there was increasing public and political support in the North for the notion, still to be conclusively proven scientifically, that the world may be fast warming up, and that the consequences for all humanity would be so disastrous that action to avoid this must be taken even if there are still margins for uncertainty. Further, there was increasing recognition that some of the global problems, like damage to the ozone layer, were scientifically well understood and could be attended to, that all nations shared a responsibility to resolve these global problems, but that it was incumbent on the rich countries to pay the incremental costs incurred by developing countries to allow them to reduce their present and, mainly, future contribution to global environmental problems.

As a result of this thinking, which evolved over only a few years, the contracting parties to the Montreal Protocol on CFCs at a meeting in London in 1990 reached agreement to raise US$160 million over three years to assist developing countries to phase out CFCs and develop substitute products to protect the ozone layer.

The Global Environment Facility (GEF) was established in November 1990 to address the need for additionality to protect the global commons with the specific objectives of protecting the ozone layer, limiting emissions of greenhouse gases, protecting biodiversity and reducing pollution of international waters. GEF is operated over an initial three-year trial period by the World Bank with participation by UNDP and UNEP to provide concessional additional funding for investment projects and related activities and with a financing target of about US$1.4 billion.[2]

The intention was that contributions to GEF were to be additional to existing aid flows and on grant or highly concessional terms, 'because of the nature of the activities considered' (World Bank, 1991b). It was felt that the global environmental problems could not be tackled by diversion of existing ODA flows since they did add a new set of issues to the development agenda. In fact, several of the donor countries' contributions to GEF have come from existing aid budgets, thus reducing the intended element of additionality.

THE CASE FOR ADDITIONAL FLOWS: AN ASSESSMENT

The debate in the UNCED preparatory process

As pointed out in the declaration from the 'Stockholm Initiative' from April 1991, estimates of required additional North–South flows are all tiny when related to the current level of military expenditure of almost US$1,000 billion per year. Based on calculations by the Stockholm International Peace Research Institute, the potential 'peace dividend' in the North can be estimated at around US$100 billion per year, possibly rising to US$200 to 300 billion per year by the year 2000. Even after allowance for adjustment costs, as military forces are reduced and hardware is scrapped, the declaration suggests that there should be ample room for a peace dividend for increased international co-operation and proposes an annual target of US$30 to 40 billion for this purpose.[3]

To examine the viability of this and other proposals for additional North–South flows, it is instructive to refer to the debate on financial resources at the third meeting of the UNCED preparatory committee in Geneva in August and September 1991. That debate illustrated how divided the North and the South are on this issue, and what some of the Northern attitudes are. As a basis for the debate, the UNCED secretariat had submitted a paper referring to the aforementioned

WIDER study and to the estimates mentioned therein and summarized above.

The South, represented by Ghana as chairman of the G-77 group of developing countries, and with support from China, tabled a motion calling for 'new and additional funding', stressing that there can be 'no reallocation of existing multilateral or bilateral financial flows for development purposes'. Each international convention should be accompanied by a special fund, and in addition there should be a separate so-called Green Fund for the promotion of sustainable development (in addition to the existing GEF). Governance of funding mechanisms should be 'transparent, democratic in nature, with an equal voice for all parties', shorthand for saying that these mechanisms should not be administered by the World Bank. The motion borrowed language from the Beijing Ministerial Declaration on Environment and Development, adopted in June 1991 on the basis of a meeting in Beijing of representatives from forty-one developing countries (Government of China, 1991).

On the other side of the argument, the US delegation underlined that 'this is not a time for rhetorical posturing about ODA targets'. In the US view, 'existing resources and institutions can and must be more fully and more effectively utilized' to meet the needs for environmentally sound development. The US delegation stated that the potential role of private sector investment should be exploited more fully, 'in which case much additionality would ensue'. Further, it said that GEF is only now getting under way and should be the main financial mechanism for any additional flows, although a case could be made for making GEF operations more transparent.

The Nordic countries and the European Community, as represented by the Netherlands, came close to the US view. While sympathetic to a need for additional financial resources, these countries felt that any such resources should be mobilized by donor countries at least meeting the United Nations goal of ODA of 0.7 per cent of GNP.[4] They rejected the proliferation of funding sources that would result from attaching a special fund to each convention. Having recently participated in the establishment of GEF, they thought that more experience should be gained from this mechanism before others were created.

The North–South negotiating positions were clear: while the South set out to maximize 'additionality' for the environment, conveniently avoiding the very thesis of UNCED, namely that protection of the environment and development are inseparable, the North was equivocating and avoiding commitment. Developing countries see the global environmental issues (climate change, biodiversity, deforestation) as the donors' agenda. In return for signing up to the global concerns, these countries expected further ODA for their own agenda (sustainable development, poverty alleviation, and so on) on a national level. In essence theirs was therefore a compensatory argument rather than one based on perceived needs.

However, behind this posturing was the reality that financial transfers to the most needy countries are almost netted out by debt service payments (Table 10.3), that current income disparities and future development prospects differ considerably between Third World countries and that the sustainable development agenda doubtless will require some additional expenditure. Despite all the recent debate about this agenda there was little apparent readiness in the donor community to significantly increase resource flows to the South. The explanation lies in the political paradigm currently prevailing in the North (and, increasingly, in the world).

Foreign aid and domestic politics in the North

The political legacy of the 1980s has been a shift to the right of the entire spectrum of political debate, nationally as well as internationally. This is, of course, well known and much in current evidence, illustrated, *inter alia*, by the demise of communism and indeed of the Soviet Union. Although the extent of this political right turn and its manifestations obviously varies between countries, it is hardly hazardous to generalize that this has meant increased emphasis on market-based solutions, deregulation and privatization of public sector services, and the near impossibility for governments to raise taxes to maintain, let alone expand, such services. As a consequence, public systems in areas like education, health and transport are now underfunded and suffering declining quality and coverage, particularly in countries like the USA and the UK where the political right turn has been most dramatic.[5]

This political paradigm shift has also meant the spread of a 'survival of the fittest' mentality in the labour market, which in turn has allowed income disparities to widen and tolerated growing social problems. These problems are now manifest in many parts of the North and include increasing absolute poverty, homelessness and rising crime. They have been deepened but not created by the ongoing economic recession.

The consequence of these developments has been inward-looking political agendas in many Northern countries. When ordinary citizens are affected by declining education and health services, as well as growing urban decay and social unrest, international co-operation and solidarity with the poor countries move down the political agenda. The peace dividend is being dissolved by a combination of domestic needs and tax cuts. In the USA, there is talk about a new isolationism, as 'Bush's critics left and right demand a scaling back of overseas involvement' (*Time* magazine, 1991).

There has in some countries been a backlash against foreign aid, which increasingly has come to be associated with inefficiency, corruption, central planning, capital flight, environmental destruction and cronyism between aid administrations and local élites. Critics point at the aid dependency of African nations and note that the African crisis has deepened despite increasing aid flows, suggesting that African nations should be left to the vagaries of the international market-place and export themselves out of their crisis.[6]

The recent developments in Eastern Europe have monopolized much of the debate on international co-operation, if not yet a major share of flows. However, that could change if Eastern Europe is increasingly afflicted by political uncertainty and economic chaos, and there is a danger of developing countries being 'crowded out' from the development debate and aid considerations. According to a World Bank estimate in December 1991, demands for funds (of all types, including aid) from the Gulf, the former Soviet Union and Eastern Europe would amount to about US$100 billion per year, adding one percentage point to the already high real interest rates (World Bank, 1991c).

The response of governments has been to maintain aid at current levels, at best at rough parity with the prevailing GNP/ODA ratio. While some large donors may increase their ratios in future years, as noted above, on the whole this is not a propitious time to be talking about greatly increased North–South flows. The political support for this notion is simply not at hand in the majority of the DAC countries. If increased poverty is tolerated at home, it is tolerated abroad as well, particularly in remote lands.

Nevertheless, it is necessary to place these developments into a proper perspective. With time there may well be a backlash against the current political paradigm. The political weight of environmental issues will probably increase in the North as the impact of global problems accumulates, and there may well be support for increased aid flows. There is no question that the economies of the North could with ease sustain the additional aid flows suggested as necessary for sustainable development in the South. But it is necessary to define this additionality in realistic and achievable terms.

301

The feasibility of additionality

Even if the political will for additional resource flows were present, there are some critical questions that need to be addressed. *First*, there is the nature of existing estimates of the size of such flows. They are little more than back-of-the-envelope calculations intended to illustrate orders of magnitude in order to provoke debate; indeed, some have been supplied with that explicit objective. The problem with such estimates in an area where no 'hard' research findings are available, and by the nature of things possibly cannot be, is that they tend to acquire a life of their own and be cited by other authors without all the original reservations being provided as well. In the absence of reliable research, donor representatives with a critical disposition a priori are bound to be underwhelmed by the arguments given.

Evidently, discussing additionality in the abstract is like fishing in the dark, pending the cost calculations of the UNCED action programme to be carried out by the conference secretariat by March 1992. However, the dynamic of the UNCED process is such that the resultant cost estimates may well be large and consequently dismissed as unrealistic by the North.

Second, the existing estimates imply that *all* development in the South is sustainable development, and that *all* ODA increases would be conducive to sustainable development. But this is clearly not the case. The recent history of development in the Third World provides many examples of aid projects that were manifestly pernicious not only to the environment but to development *per se*. For example, aid-financed subsidies of productive investment in industry and agriculture have distorted local incentive structures and created inefficient enterprises that have both added to pollution and been impediments to economic growth. Likewise, food aid has often contributed to depressing local food prices and thus been a disincentive to local production. While those lessons have on the whole been taken on board by aid donors and recipients,[7] there still remains a sizeable portion of current North–South flows that is used for purposes that are not consistent with sustainable development. At a guess, that portion would correspond to at least one-quarter of current ODA, possibly more. Ideally, that portion should be deployed differently before additional resources are made available.

However, defining sustainable development in the narrow sense with a focus only on protection of the environment and poverty alleviation is problematic. For example, aid agencies like the British ODA or the Swedish SIDA devote 6 to 7 per cent of their disbursements to renewable resource development, and perhaps 20 to 25 per cent to meeting poverty-oriented basic needs. However, these areas overlap, and available data do not allow a definition of what precise portion of aid meets sustainability criteria. It is not possible to make the case that poverty can be alleviated without infrastructural development and growth-generating import support, although some projects in those areas may not be sustainable. Development then becomes a proxy, however unsatisfactory, for sustainable development, until aid agencies are able to ascertain that all their disbursements are for purposes conducive to sustainability. The point to note here is that some of the scarce resources used to promote development are not deployed sustainably and should be shifted to other uses.

Third, there is the issue of absorptive capacity in developing countries. For obvious reasons it is in the poorest countries, where the need for additional external finance is greatest, that the difficulties of efficiently absorbing existing ODA flows are also greatest, let alone large additional infusions. Table 10.4 shows how African countries over the period 1985–8 on average were able to absorb only 84 per cent of ODA commitments.

Table 10.4: Commitments and disbursements to sub-Saharan Africa, all types of ODA and all donors (US$ billion at 1988 prices and exchange rates)

	1985	1986	1987	1988
Commitments	16.6	17.3	18.5	18.8
Disbursements	15.0	14.8	14.4	15.0
Per cent	90	86	78	80 (av. 84)

Source: OECD (1990, tables 38 and 39).

Further, limitations on absorptive capacity in the least developed countries are most keenly felt in areas directly relevant to sustainable development: poverty alleviation, meeting basic needs, rural development and biodiversity conservation. Because of institutional and personnel constraints, in aid agencies and recipient countries alike, it is more difficult to raise ODA disbursements in these areas than it is, for example, to increase import support programmes that simply provide foreign exchange for necessary imports without regard to their end use or indeed to their sustainability.

Low absorptive capacity is not in itself an argument against increasing ODA. There is considerable scope for improvements in aid programming procedures, for example by substituting project aid for more flexible programme aid. But the main impetus for change in this regard would be an improved economic policy framework in recipient countries, as in the recent experiences from Latin America illustrated above, preferably coupled with international action on debt and on trade restrictions. However, low absorptive capacity *is* an argument for proceeding cautiously with calls for precipitous increases in ODA volumes.

The previous chapters in this book do not support the thesis that sustainable development necessarily requires large additional infusions of external finance. On the contrary, the approaches that are advocated are, on the whole, locally based, participatory and low cost. For example, large savings in ODA would ensue if more emphasis were placed on energy conservation and less on expansion of power generating capacity, as argued in Chapter 9. Local resource management, as advocated by Chapters 4 and 8, is certainly not very demanding in terms of foreign aid.

So what is left of the case for additionality? On balance, there is doubtless a need for *some* additionality, but on a more modest scale than suggested by available estimates and by arguments in the UNCED debate. Over a billion people live in absolute poverty, and much remains to be done to meet basic needs in developing countries. The prospects for addressing such needs are improving with an end to superpower tensions and the concomitant relaxation of security in large parts of the world, coupled with sustained economic policy changes conducive to accelerated growth in many countries. Further, global environmental issues will in coming years grow rapidly in scope and complexity and for their solution require international agreements, or bargains, that will have to involve additional financial resource flows.

Quantification of achievable future additionality would be hazardous and subject to all sorts of imponderables. The best that can be hoped for at this time, given Northern political attitudes, is likely to be a more rapid rate of increase in real ODA to developing countries than in the 1980s – that is, a rate faster than that of increase in donor countries' GNP. This should work together with consistent provision of funds by donors to address global environmental issues, notably through GEF, *additional* to ODA, and resumption of private flows to the poorest countries, particularly in sub-Saharan Africa, at a rate corresponding to implementation of economic policy reform. This would not allow for any comprehensive solution to Third World debt, nor would it provide for aid to Eastern Europe.

POTENTIAL SOURCES OF ADDITIONAL FINANCE

What is sustainable development finance?

The conclusion of the foregoing is that the context for financing sustainable development during the 1990s will be constrained. It will therefore be necessary to take a fresh look at potential sources of finance, including those that in the UNCED preparatory process have been called 'new and innovative', and to set priorities. But it is useful first to specify what we mean by sustainable development finance.

This book deals with a vision of a sustainable future world, a vision that is considered attainable on the strength of current evidence. On that basis, it is suggested that sustainable development finance means three things.

First, it will mean an element of *automaticity*, an aspect of development finance proposed as early as 1979 by the British economist Barbara Ward and subsequently repeated in the WCED report of 1987 (Ward, 1988 [1979]). What this suggests is that in an increasingly interdependent world where rich and poor countries alike share responsibility for management of the planet, but where endowments of financial and other resources differ greatly, sustainable development in the poor countries cannot in the long run continue to depend on increased voluntary contributions, in effect on charity, from the rich. Moves must therefore begin to be made towards the same kind of resource transfers that occur, with automaticity, in a domestic economy, as the rich are taxed to transfer part of national income to the less fortunate.

Automatic transfer mechanisms were considered and rejected by governments in the 1970s; in 1977, the UN General Assembly approved the principle of automatic resource transfers, but it was never implemented by governments. Proposals for, for example, international sales taxes on certain widely traded products or tolls on international journeys raise issues of how any such revenue would be collected and equitably distributed between nations. Any approach involving elements of automatic resource transfers would have to respect the ultimate sovereignty of donor governments.

Second, it is suggested that sustainable development finance be raised by *economic activity* that is sustained by the size and growth of the economies of the countries where finance is to be raised. To a degree, this is what is now happening with ODA linked to donor country GNP. However, this linkage is a target only, a target that some countries, as we have seen, choose to set aside. The objective here should be to raise funds increasingly for protection of the environment, domestically and internationally, through charges or taxes on production and trade and to a decreasing extent directly on income gained by individuals and institutions.

Third, sustainable development finance should contribute to sustainability in its own right by being generated from revenue raised from *charges on pollutants and polluting behaviour*. When linked with the second criterion, this means that revenue to support sustainable development, again both domestically and internationally, should be raised from charges on the products and processes that now contribute to making development unsustainable. It would also mean that unsustainable development in the North would pay for sustainable development in the South, a neat symmetry that would certainly be consistent with the calls made in the UNCED preparatory process for more equitable development, economically as well as environmentally.

If funds raised in this manner could be used, initially, to finance costs of tackling global environmental problems and, eventually, also to finance ODA, with a mechanism for control by the countries where the bulk of the funds would be raised (that is, the North), then a framework for sustainable development finance would be established. That would take time. In the meantime, it is necessary to look at all possible sources of finance.

Overview of new and existing sources of finance

Potential sources of finance for sustainable development in the South would essentially fall into five categories:

- improved management of existing resources;
- debt relief;
- trade and private investment;
- new sources of finance;
- economic incentive mechanisms for environmental management.

A complete and exhaustive review of all conceivable sources of finance would be outside the scope of this chapter. The following discussion will focus on those of most direct relevance to public policy-makers concerned with sustainable development.

Improved management of existing resources
It should be evident that all efforts to improve management and use of existing resources should be exhausted before calls are made for additional flows. There would appear to be considerable scope to make better use of existing ODA and also to raise more financial resources from domestic sources in developing countries.

As the World Bank has recently pointed out, the efficiency with which *foreign aid* is used matters to development; improvements in both quality and quantity of aid are needed; and efficiency in the use of aid depends on the policies of aid donors and recipients alike (World Bank, 1991a). There are two basic problems with donor countries' policy that cause aid efficiency to be less than it could be. One is that donors often use foreign aid as an active instrument of foreign policy, sometimes reducing and increasing aid allocations in response to actions and statements by the recipient government, sometimes not being forceful enough in asking for necessary policy changes and sometimes even tolerating abuse of aid funds in the broader interest of maintaining good political relations. The other problem is that, as aid budgets increasingly have come under siege, it has become more difficult for governments to keep at bay the various domestic constituents who wish to avail themselves of aid money to further their own ends and not necessarily to eradicate poverty.

Foreign aid could be provided on more concessionary terms than at present and be better targeted on the poorest countries, on poor groups in those countries and on basic needs for those groups. For example, no more than an average of 36.1 per cent of all ODA from the DAC countries was untied in 1988 – that is, freely available for worldwide procurement, the economically most efficient form of resource transfer. Some donor countries tie most of their bilateral aid. Of the larger DAC donors, Italy in 1988 provided only 8.1 per cent untied bilateral aid, the UK 9.8 per cent and the USA 18.1 per cent (OECD, 1990, table 6). In 1989, only 24 per cent of aid from the DAC countries was destined for the least developed countries, a percentage that was the same in 1981–2 (ibid., table 42). Basic needs for poor groups, like primary education and health services, receive only about 10 per cent of bilateral ODA.[8]

An area of particular concern is technical assistance, notably in the form of foreign experts, which in 1989 absorbed US$10.6 billion or 23 per cent of bilateral ODA from DAC countries. This is often donor-driven and frequently, although by no means always, expensive and of doubtful quality. Despite the unquestioned progress made in training in Third World countries during the 1980s, the number of bilateral experts and volunteers rose from 68,700 in 1980 to 79,000 in 1987. It has been estimated in Kenya that 40 per cent of foreign aid to that country is used for expatriate salaries and benefits, non-Kenyan consultants and training programmes in donor countries.[9]

On the *recipient side*, there is considerable scope in many cases for mobilizing financial resources locally to reduce foreign aid dependency.

Economic reforms will very likely reduce capital flight abroad. Reducing economic inefficiency in the public sector, including para-statal enterprises (nationalized industries), is often a major component in structural adjustment programmes. Options for charging for public services often need to be explored more fully, although the revenue effect is not always very significant, for example some 5 per cent of health sector operating costs in developing countries (UNDP, 1991). Restructuring taxation from charges on trade to taxes on consumption and income could facilitate both resource mobilization and economic growth. A strengthened financial system, both informal and formal, would have an important role to play in mobilizing private savings for investment. Then, of course, there is the potential for saving financial resources from military spending. Third World military spending declined from US$173 billion in 1987 to US$146 billion in 1989, a result partly of the end of the Iran–Iraq war but partly of reductions elsewhere too. However, military expenditure still remains on average about 5 per cent of GDP in developing countries, a sum that in many countries would be enough to double government spending on infrastructure or on health and education (UNDP, 1991; World Bank, 1991a).

One of the main lessons learned from development in the 1980s is that the aid recipient country's policy framework makes a difference for the sustainability of development and for the efficiency of aid use. In the 1990s, with increasing scarcity of ODA relative to needs, there are likely to be increasing calls by donors for recipient country policies conducive to sustainability. By the same token, donors are likely to increasingly question the existence of large military budgets, often used primarily for purposes of internal security, in countries requesting increased aid. This could mean an increase in conditionality – that is, the provision of increased flows of ODA only in return for development policies seen to be supportive of sustainable development.

Debt relief

Public and private debt relief could become a significant source of finance by providing relief from onerous obligations. It is evident that countries that are required to pay half or more of their export revenue to service their debt can never derive enough benefit from trade to achieve sustained economic growth and will remain dependent on foreign aid. Sustainable development in the highly indebted countries will require a comprehensive solution to the debt crisis. While success in this area to date has eluded the creditor community of nations and institutions, the recent write-off of 50 per cent of the debts of Poland and of Egypt illustrates that this is largely a matter of political commitment in major donor countries.

A plethora of proposals exist for tackling both the private and public debt of developing countries, and the purpose here is not to revisit them. However, two points need to be made. First, there is a need to underline that cancellation of debt requires real resources on the part of creditors, and that such resources therefore need to be provided as part of any 'additionality' required for sustainable development. Second, any debt relief must be provided with attention to sustainability objectives. Debt-for-nature swaps are examples of attempted non-fungibility – that is, attempts to force the recipient country to spend money on projects conducive to sustainability. But since money is more fungible than commonly believed, there will be 'leakages' and resources mobilized for other purposes not necessarily related to protection of the environment. This relates back to the issue of conditionality mentioned above.

In the UNCED preparatory process, the need to include the debt issue has been raised by developing countries' representatives, but this has largely been ignored by Northern countries, on the ground that 'UNCED cannot deal with everything'. Yet debt relief in poor countries is a requirement for sustainable development, and the linkage between the two is very evident.

Foreign trade and private investment
Foreign trade is another issue that is not explicitly debated in the UNCED preparatory process, yet could also serve as a source of finance for sustainable development. The relationship between natural resource dependence and income is well established; most of the poorest countries depend heavily on natural resources for employment and economic growth. Typically, poor countries supply primary commodities for processing in middle- or high-income countries. During the 1980s, world commodity prices declined persistently; for example, real prices of non-fuel commodities declined by 40 per cent during 1980–8. Industrialized countries benefited from changes in terms of trade, while developing countries, on the whole, were adversely affected. As long as this situation persists, developing and indebted countries are forced increasingly to consume their natural resources just to service their debt and gain a minimum of export revenue, and sustainable development will remain beyond reach.

Some of the industrialized countries, which champion the use of market-based solutions to development, are in practice introducing a number of protective measures such as quotas, subsidies, voluntary export restraints and anti-dumping measures that discriminate against developing countries' exports and world trade. This is largely the result of increased world market competition and the inability of GATT to control non-tariff barriers. For example, during 1966–86, the share of imports affected by non-tariff measures increased by 160 per cent for the European Community. UNCTAD estimated in 1986 that elimination of all trade restrictions by industrialized countries would lead to an increase in exports by developing countries of more than 10 per cent, which for 1988 would be equivalent to US$54 billion, roughly corresponding to total ODA in that year (German Bundestag, 1990). Action by developing countries to reform their trade policies must be met by equal efforts by industrialized countries to reduce protection as a prerequisite to sustainable development.

To encourage direct foreign investment, incentives for overseas corporations to invest in environmentally benign technology in developing countries should be explored. As mentioned above, this is likely to be comparatively more relevant to middle-income developing countries. Nevertheless, with the introduction of economic reform also in the poorest countries, some of these will be increasingly able to attract foreign capital. Many of the barriers to acquisition of technology currently lie in these countries themselves, for example policies and laws that do not provide adequate protection of foreign technology developers (Markandya and Ayres, 1991).

With the growing consumer awareness of environmental issues, there have lately appeared a small but increasing number of 'green' investment funds, primarily interested in equity investments. The major premise of these funds is that the worldwide environmental industry, by one such fund estimated as having an annual turnover of US$170 to 250 billion, has considerable future growth potential and therefore presents an attractive investment opportunity.[10] While these funds typically will invest in industrialized countries, many of them are open to investment in developing countries also, provided that issues of market volatility, currency fluctuations, repatriation restrictions and other potential pitfalls characterizing emerging capital markets can be contained.

New sources of finance

With the prospect of a scarcity of finance for sustainable development, proposals have been made in conjunction with UNCED for 'new and innovative' sources of finance, some of which will be briefly summarized here. Some of them were raised already in the 1970s and are not new at all. The political climate was not ripe then, and it may not be ripe now either. But the debate is gaining momentum, and its pace is likely to accelerate as global environmental problems continue to worsen. For example, a proposal that appeared fanciful at first, the early ideas about a global fund to support measures to limit global warming, rapidly materialized in the shape of GEF.

One idea that dates back to the 1970s is to charge for the use of the global commons. There could potentially be revenue from sea-bed resources, ocean fishing and use of the high seas for shipping and use of the atmosphere for air transport and for communications. Another idea that has been floated in UNCED relates to the use of 'Earth stamps' for postage. The difficulties arising out of such proposals are mainly institutional, as it is unclear how such revenue would be administered and equitably used for development and environmental protection.

Many of the above-mentioned present or potential sources of finance for sustainable development may well hold less promise than, on the face of it, they appear to have. The difficulties in raising ODA efficiency have been dealt with at some length in view of the increasing importance of foreign aid for the poorest countries. While easy to point out, these difficulties arise out of structural features of foreign aid and are unlikely to go away. The debt crisis is still looking for a solution, but that is not for lack of effort. Powerful and well-entrenched political interests in the industrialized countries mitigate against improving world terms of trade in favour of developing countries. Private investment in support of sustainable development may well increase in importance but will hardly provide requisite capital for the poorest countries in the short term. All of these sources hold potential and may well increase available financial resources on the margin, but the prospects are uncertain and essentially hinge on presently unforeseeable political developments. We will therefore now turn to other instruments with apparently more powerful potential not only to raise revenue but also to manage the environment.

ECONOMIC INCENTIVE MECHANISMS

Overview

Most approaches to pollution control involve direct regulation of the quantity of pollution allowed by individual sources or the control technology most sources use. This tends to be costly and increasingly ineffective as pollution sources multiply. The principal alternative approach would be to use market forces in the form of economic incentives to reduce pollution. Incentive mechanisms incorporate the 'polluter pays' principle, adopted by OECD as early as 1972 but not yet widely applied in practice. Under this regime, polluters pay a financial penalty for higher levels of pollution and pay a lesser penalty, or receive an award, for lower pollution levels (Anderson, Hofmann and Rusin, 1990).

Incentive systems for environmental management can be classified in a number of ways but usually include (1) taxes and charges, (2) subsidies, (3) deposit-refund systems, (4) market creation and (5) financial enforcement incentives (OECD, 1989). The following discussion will be concerned with two specific sets of incentive systems only: carbon taxes and tradeable emission permits.

Carbon taxes

The idea of carbon tax gained widespread attention only as recently as 1989 when the European Community examined the idea of introducing a tax on carbon to raise funds for energy research (Grubb, 1989). The concept is straightforward: by introducing a tax on the carbon content of fossil fuels, the consumption of energy based on carbon is discouraged and the economic viability of alternative or renewable sources of energy is enhanced.

A carbon tax is attractive from several perspectives. It represents a mechanism for coming to grips with emissions of carbon dioxide, the major greenhouse gas,[11] that is economically efficient and does not distort markets. By applying the 'polluter pays' principle, it places the cost of emissions of carbon where it belongs, in the industrialized countries and on users of fossil-fuel-based technology. It would be easy to administer if collected where fossil fuels initially enter the economy: at the dock in the case of imports, at the mine or wellhead in the case of domestic production. It is a regressive tax in Northern countries, although there always remains the possibility of redistributing part of the tax revenue to compensate poorer households. But in developing countries the tax is more likely to be progressive, since consumers of fossil-fuel-based energy there are mostly the more affluent. For these and other reasons some economists argue in favour of replacing conventional income taxes with energy (carbon) taxes (Box 10.1).

A carbon tax could generate very significant additional revenue. A study in the USA has estimated the effects from a carbon tax phased in over a ten-year period, beginning at US$10 per ton of carbon in 1991 and rising to US$100 per ton in 2000 (in 1988 dollars). A tax of this magnitude was estimated to reduce US carbon dioxide emissions back to 1988 levels by the year 2000. When fully phased in, the tax would be equivalent to US$60.50 per ton of coal, US$12.99 per barrel of oil and

---

Box 10.1: The case for carbon taxes

The basic idea is to eventually shift a considerable part of the tax burden from labour, value added and capital to energy resources and pollution. Taxation of labour and capital will be reduced approximately by the amount of energy, resource and pollution taxes, so that the average tax burden is not increased. It can be assumed that energy taxes are rather easier and cheaper to administer and more difficult to evade than most of the present taxes.

Source: Weizsäcker (1989), as quoted in Grubb (1989).

US$1.63 per thousand cubic feet of natural gas. Additional revenue from the tax to the US Treasury was estimated to be about US$12 billion in 1991 rising to US$110 to 120 billion in 2000 (again in 1988 dollars). The tax would have effects on the US economy limited to a loss of 1 to 2 per cent of GNP annually during the decade. It would stimulate energy efficient production and development of renewable energy technology (CBO, 1990).

A 1989 study suggested that the revenue-earning potential of carbon taxes be used to generate capital for sustainable development in the South. By applying a carbon tax equivalent to a 10 per cent charge on coal in all OECD countries, some US$25 billion could be generated in annual revenue. However, as the study points out, much of that revenue would very likely be offset by reductions in other taxes, by tax credits to polluters making requisite environmental investments to mitigate their behaviour and by competing uses for the net revenues. Nevertheless, the study concludes, 'several billion' should remain for conservation purposes (World Resources Institute, 1989).

Carbon taxes have not yet been widely introduced, but some countries (for example, Finland, Sweden and the Netherlands) have them. International agreement on carbon taxes would be an important step towards curbing greenhouse gas emissions, and it would appear that this is an idea whose time has arrived. In September 1991, after two years of debate, the European Commission agreed on a proposal for an energy tax, starting in 1993 with US$3 per barrel of oil and rising by US$1 per year to a level of US$10 in the year 2000. The objective would be to stabilize carbon dioxide emissions at 1990 levels by the end of the century. Under the plan, the tax would be offset by tax cuts in other areas. While this measure thus has environmental management objectives, it also has potential for raising additional revenue arising from the efficiency gains in production and energy use.

Marketable carbon emission permits

There is growing experience with another market-based approach, namely that of marketable permits to emit carbon (or other pollutants). Such a system can take a variety of forms. Probably permits or quotas for emissions would be allocated to governments and then sold or leased between countries without any need for central direction. Unused permits would be sold by low-level greenhouse-gas-emitting countries, normally the developing countries, to high-level emitters, the industrialized countries, to generate revenue for sustainable development.

To be practical, a system of marketable permits would have to resolve the issue of allocation of shares. If permits were allocated in proportion to current emissions, countries with the highest level of pollution would be rewarded. Allocation in proportion to GNP opens up questions on definitions of GNP and international comparability; besides, countries with high GNP will be among the highest polluters. A typical Southern view would be to allocate to countries tradeable quotas in proportion to their populations (Agarwal and Narain, 1991; Parikh *et al.*, 1991). Recognition of equal worldwide per capita entitlements of carbon emissions would have forceful practical and moral arguments in its favour. However, this might well be unworkable in view of the very large level of income transfer implied by such a system and could, besides, fly in the face of efforts to raise awareness of the need to reduce world population. An alternative approach might therefore be to allocate entitlements on the basis of adult population only (Grubb, 1989).

Potentially, a system of marketable emission permits could yield significant revenue to developing countries; one estimate talks about US$100 to 150 billion annually. It would be economically efficient relative to the costs of operating a scheme of direct regulations. Initially, it could be introduced partially and on the basis of targets for reductions in emissions that could be partly regional and partly based on level of development. Such trading, it has been suggested, could be the precursor of global trading arrangements (Markandya, 1991).

A system of marketable emission permits would very likely require some international agency to define the market, provide incentives to comply and adjudicate disputes in cases of emissions in excess of permit levels. There would be problems to be overcome to avoid hoarding of permits by wealthy actors in the market. Practical experience from permits markets, mostly from the USA, indicates that efficiency is lost where it has not been possible to establish truly competitive markets that remain 'thin', with few actors. Marketable permits are more likely to work when they are simple and unambiguously defined, and when monitoring and enforcement costs are low. It is not yet clear what institutional arrangements would be required to bring this about on a global scale.

Economic incentive systems: an appraisal

Much of the current debate on sustainable development centres on the need for current polluting behaviour, and consequently lifestyles, to change, mainly but not exclusively in the North. By acting directly on consumers' underlying motives, economic incentive mechanisms seem to be the most effective instrument to bring about such change. In a sustainable future world, the use of such mechanisms will be much more widespread than today, raising the cost of polluting practices and products relative to other comparable alternatives.

However, the impact on revenue of economic incentive mechanisms, while potentially large, is ambiguous and subject to all sorts of claims. Why would Northern governments, if subject to the kind of fiscal constraints discussed above, want to use revenue from these sources for purposes of sustainable development in the South and not to meet pressing needs on the domestic agenda? Further, treasuries in Northern countries are likely to object to the notion of hypothecation of tax revenue – that is, earmarking of revenue for a specific purpose – in view of the negative impact this would have on fiscal discipline.[12]

In the North, it is possible to set up a partial balance sheet with, on the liability side, unmet domestic *and* international needs for sustainable development and compensatory conventional tax reductions and, on the asset side, revenue from environmental taxes and the peace dividend from reduced military spending. If future costs of sustainable development increase, the tax revenue base has to expand. The future potential for such expansion lies in taxes on environmental 'bads'.

'Green' taxes are said to be revenue-neutral and primarily an instrument to manage the environment. Yet they do have an undeniable potential for broadening the tax revenue base. Besides being in themselves instruments for raising tax revenue, they are more conducive to economic growth than conventional taxes on income. Without resorting to hypothecation, the increasingly widespread application of such taxes will make it more difficult for governments to argue against increased use of public funds for sustainable development, including ODA. In the end, it would be difficult for governments not to yield to the logic that fiscal instruments to improve the national environment should be used also for raising revenue to finance improvements of the international environment, as these same governments are arguing that the two are increasingly interrelated.

Even under international agreements (such as the one now contemplated by the European Commission), 'green' taxes would be raised by governments, not by any international body. There would appear to be little present prospect of any international machinery that would levy and dispense international charges, for example on the global commons as mentioned above. However, there would very likely be scope for expanding and replicating facilities similar to GEF where voting powers are proportional to contributions. One way of doing this might be to attach to the regional development banks facilities similar to GEF.

Such a proposal would perhaps be invidious to developing countries, but the overall financial resource shortage would probably override their objections. However, with time, the distinction between global and national environmental problems, never very clear in the first place, will diminish. At the same time, the ability of the international development banks, and other aid agencies, to provide support only for sustainable projects will improve. Judging from the evolution that has taken place during the past decade on this subject, it would not be rash to predict that by the end of the current decade the bulk of development finance will be for sustainable development.

CONCLUSIONS

There is justification for the argument that sustainable development in developing countries will require *some* additional North–South resource flows. The additionality that can realistically be available, and that can usefully be absorbed, is much less than sometimes assumed. Nevertheless, availability of capital may be a constraint on sustainable development in the South in coming years.

There are possibilities of freeing financial resources through more efficient use of existing aid, through using domestic sources in developing countries, through reductions of debt and through fewer restrictions on foreign trade. Various economic incentive mechanisms offer a potential for increased revenue to be used for sustainable development. There is an increasing receptivity to the application of such mechanisms for purposes of environmental management. What is suggested here is that the use of these mechanisms for the additional purpose of raising funds for sustainable development be considered by industrialized countries.

The issues involved are complex; the research in these areas is only just emerging; and governments still lack the political will to commit themselves either to 'green' taxes on a wide scale or to significantly increased ODA. Still, the debate is moving and is gaining momentum because of UNCED. It would be no mean achievement if at UNCED countries could agree on a schedule of work to begin to look in earnest at mechanisms that would meet the twin objectives of raising finance for sustainable development while, at the same time, reducing pollution levels by application of the 'polluter pays' principle, thus contributing doubly to sustainable development, in the North and in the South. Such mechanisms would feature prominently in a future sustainable world.

NOTES

I am indebted to Anil Markandya and Koy Thomson for comments on drafts of this chapter.

1 By decision by the UN General Assembly, heads of state will represent their governments at the event in Rio, Brazil, in June 1992, making UNCED easily the largest summit meeting ever held.

2 The target for the size of GEF has been set at SDR 1 billion, equivalent to US$1.37 billion, for the Global Environment Trust Fund. In addition, the facility operates the Ozone Layer Trust Fund resulting from the Montreal Protocol. Other trust funds could be added later.

3 The Stockholm Initiative was an attempt to tie up the work of the four commissions at work during the 1980s (the Brandt Commission, the Palme Commission, the World Commission on Environment and Development and the South Commission). It was a gathering of past and present world leaders in Stockholm in April 1991 (Government of Sweden, 1991b).

4 Not surprisingly, these countries all exceed this target.

5 In mid-1991, several US states were said to face bankruptcy, with, for example, Connecticut having a budget deficit of more than a third of its total US$7 billion budget, having already closed its parks and laid off almost 40 per cent of state workers. New York City has long been in a similar situation and in 1991 was forced to adopt budgetary measures that would reduce street lighting and the size of the police force, despite rising crime on the streets. In the UK, a series of riots in September 1991 underscored the effects of neglect of urban public services as a consequence of declining local council tax revenue. In both countries, poverty increased and income disparities widened during the 1980s.

6 While improvements can doubtless be made in the design and implementation of aid programmes, this particular critique overestimates the role that aid can play and underestimates the importance of recipient countries' policies on the efficiency of aid. It is not clear how African nations could possibly export themselves out of their crisis, given their lack of productive infrastructure, adverse terms of trade and debt service obligations.

Interestingly, much of the criticism of foreign aid comes from a constituency that argues that aid should increasingly be tied to procurement in the donor country, a feature that is generally considered to reduce aid efficiency. For a comprehensive analysis of foreign aid, see Cassen (1986).

7 ODA from the DAC countries for 'industry and other production' decreased from 11.5 per cent of total commitments in 1975–6 to 5.8 per cent in 1987–8, while food aid decreased from 12.7 per cent in 1975–6 to 5.4 per cent in 1987–8 (OECD, 1990, table 10).

8 Estimate derived from ibid., table 29.

9 On this subject, see ibid., tables 33–5, Cohen (1991) and Forss *et al.*, (1988).

10 One of the largest Scandinavian banks estimates this market at 1 to 2 per cent of of the gross world product, which was roughly US$20 trillion in 1990, an estimate very close to that of the cited US 'green' investment fund.

11 Carbon dioxide, CO_2, is estimated to contribute 57 per cent of the heat-trapping potential of the major greenhouse gases.

12 If it were to be done for one purpose, it could presumably be done for other purposes as well, and in the end fiscal management would be impossible. The retort to that, of course, is that the link between fiscal revenue and expenditure for particular purposes is being made by politicians all the time.

REFERENCES AND BIBLIOGRAPHY

Agarwal, Anil and Narain, Sunita, 1991. *Global Warming in an Unequal World: A Case of Environmental Colonialism*, Centre for Science and Environment, New Delhi.

Anderson, Robert C., Hofmann, Lisa A. and Rusin, Michael, 1990. *The Use of Economic Incentive Mechanisms in Environmental Management*, Research Paper no. 051, American Petroleum Institute, Washington, DC, June.

Brown, Lester R. *et al.*, 1988. *State of the World 1988* (Worldwatch Institute), Norton, New York.

Cassen, Robert and associates, 1986. *Does Aid Work?*, Clarendon Press, Oxford.

CBO (Congressional Budget Office), 1990. *Carbon Charges as a Response to Global Warming: The Effects of Taxing Fossil Fuels*, Congress of the United States, Washington, DC, August.

Cohen, John M., 1991. *Expatriate Advisors in the Government of Kenya: Why They Are There and What Can Be Done about It*, Development Discussion Paper no. 376, Harvard University, Cambridge, Mass., June.

The Economist, 1991. 7 September.

Forss, Kim *et al.*, 1988. *The Effectiveness of Technical Assistance Personnel*, study commissioned by DANIDA, FINNIDA, NORAD and SIDA, Stockholm, March.

German Bundestag, 1990. *Protecting the Tropical Forests: 2nd Report of the Enquête Commission*, German Bundestag, Bonn.

Gill, David, 1989. *Global Investors, their Emerging Market Expectations, and Mexico's Opportunity*, Batterymarch Financial Management, Boston, Mass.

Government of China, 1991. 'Beijing ministerial declaration on environment and development', Ministerial Conference of Developing Countries on Environment and Development, Beijing, 18–19 June.

Government of the Netherlands, 1991. *A World of Difference: A New Framework for Development Co-operation in the 1990s*, policy document, Ministry of Foreign Affairs, The Hague.

Government of Sweden, 1991a. *Proposition 1990/91: 100, bilaga 5*, submission to the Swedish Parliament of budget proposals for 1991–2, Ministry for Foreign Affairs, Stockholm.

Government of Sweden, 1991b. *Common Responsibility in the 1990s – the Stockholm Initiative on Global Security and Governance, April 22 1991*, Prime Minister's Office, Stockholm.

Grubb, Michael, 1989. *The Greenhouse Effect: Negotiating Targets*, Royal Institute for International Affairs, London.

IFAD, 1991. *Progress Report on IFAD's Evolving Approaches to Environmentally Sustainable Rural Poverty Alleviation*, document for the fourteenth session of the Governing Council, IFAD, Rome, April.

Jayawardena, Lal, 1991. 'A global environmental compact for sustainable development: resource requirements and mechanisms', mimeo, World Institute for Development Economics Research of the UN University (WIDER), Helsinki, August.

Jun, Kwang W., 1990. 'Alternative means of resource mobilization for development during the 1990s', draft mimeo, World Bank, Washington, DC, May.

McKinsey & Co., 1990. *Protecting the Global Environment: Funding Mechanisms*, report prepared for the Ministerial Conference on Atmospheric Pollution and Climatic Change, Noordwijk, Netherlands, 6–7 November, 1989, McKinsey & Co., Amsterdam.

Markandya, Anil, 1991. 'Global warming: the economics of tradeable permits', in David Pearce (ed.), *Blueprint 2 – Greening the World Economy*, Earthscan, London.

MacNeill, Jim, 1989. 'Strategies for sustainable economic development', *Scientific American*, September.

Markandya, Anil and Ayres, R.U., 1991. 'Barriers facing the achievement of ecologically sound industrial development' (mimeo), paper for the International Conference on Ecologically Sustainable Industrial Development organized by UNIDO and the Government of Denmark, Copenhagen, 14–18 October.

Nordic UN Project, 1991. *The United Nations in Development: Reform Issues in the Economic and Social Fields, a Nordic Perspective*, Almqvist & Wiksell International, Stockholm.

OECD, 1989. *Economic Instruments for Environmental Protection*, OECD, Paris.

OECD, 1990. *Development Co-operation, 1990 Report*, OECD, Paris.

Parikh, Joyti *et al.*, 1991. *Consumption Patterns: The Driving Force of Environmental Stress*, Indira Gandhi Institute of Development Research, Bombay.

Thacher, Peter S., 1991. 'Background to institutional options for management of the global environment and commons', mimeo, World Resources Institute, Washington, DC, April.

Time magazine, 1991. 16 September.

UNCED, 1991. *Progress Report on Financial Resources*, A/CONF.151/PC/51, UNCED, Geneva, 5 July.

UNDP, 1991. *Human Development Report 1991*, Oxford University Press, Oxford.

UNFPA, 1991. *The State of World Population 1991*, UNFPA, New York.

Ward, Barbara, 1988. *Progress for a Small Planet*, Earthscan, London (first published in 1979).

WCED, 1987. *Our Common Future* (Brundtland Report) Oxford University Press, Oxford.

Weizsäcker, Ernst U., 1989. 'Global warming and environmental taxes', paper for the International Conference on Atmosphere, Climate and Man, Turin, January.

World Bank, 1989. *Sub-Saharan Africa: From Crisis to Sustainable Growth. A Long-Term Perspective Study*, World Bank, Washington, DC.

World Bank, 1991a. *World Development Report 1991*, Oxford University Press, Oxford.

World Bank, 1991b. 'Global Environment Facility (GEF)', document for executive directors' meeting, 14 March.

World Bank, 1991c. *World Debt Tables 1991–92*, vol. 1, World Bank, Washington, DC, December.

World Resources Institute, 1989. *Natural Endowments: Financing Resource Conservation for Development*, World Resources Institute, Washington, DC, September.

11 Living in a Sustainable World

John Rowley and Johan Holmberg

INTRODUCTION

'What should sustainable development sustain? It should be human life, not just trees. The environment should be measured in human terms.' The words are those of Mahbub ul Haq, the distinguished economist and architect of the *Human Development Report*, published by the United Nations Development Programme. He was commenting on what he sees as a loss of focus on people, especially in the industrialized world, in current consideration of environment and development (Box 11.1).

The same reasoning caused him to reflect that for the peoples of the developing countries the pressing environmental issues are not so much global warming as water and land. 'Polluted water', he pointed out, 'contributes to 90 per cent of all Third World diseases, and land degradation is the number one issue for peasant farmers' (UNDP, 1991). Though these observations appear to overlook the fact that rising seas and storm-surges triggered by climate change would probably impact most severely on the arid lands and crowded coastal regions of the developing world, they do make a salutary starting point for our final chapter. The purpose of this is to attempt to pull together some practical conclusions on how in these last years of the millennium we might begin to move more purposely towards the goal of a healthy planet inhabited by healthy people.

If we accept the argument of Goodland *et al.* (1991), quoted in Chapter 1, that we live in a 'full' world where the sink functions – that is, the ability of our environment, including the atmosphere and the oceans, to absorb the wastes humanity is generating – are being taxed to the limit, then we have increasingly to question our lifestyles. The notion of universal economic growth, the continual generation of more goods and services, will need to be examined. But more particularly, the concept of the full world has two principal aspects that intimately affect how we live on this planet. First, the rates of population growth must be slowed down, mainly in the developing countries. Secondly, the levels of consumption must be reduced, mainly in the industrialized countries.

Box 11.1: The environmental basis for health

Much of the growing volume of books, articles and reports about sustainable development still fails to reflect a concern for human needs; priority is given to the discussion of ecological sustainability with little or no mention of development (Mitlin, 1992). Most writings on sustainable development fail to mention the environmental problems which impact most on the health and livelihoods of the poor majority in developing countries.

A recent WHO report suggests that human welfare and health are central to the concern for sustainable development (WHO, 1992). The most immediate environmental problem world-wide is the scale of ill health and premature death arising from biological agents in the human environment – in water, food, air or soil. They cause or contribute to the premature deaths of millions of people (mostly infants and children) and to the ill health of hundreds of millions more. The problems are concentrated in the developing countries, where

- five million infants or children die every year from diarrhoeal diseases, largely as a result of contaminated food or water,
- two million people die from malaria each year and 267 million around the world are infected with the disease, and
- hundreds of millions suffer from debilitating intestinal parasitic burdens.

There are also serious environmental health problems shared by both developed and developing countries, including

- hundreds of millions of people who suffer from respiratory and other diseases caused or exacerbated by biological and chemical agents in the air – both indoors and outdoors, and
- hundreds of millions who are exposed to unnecessary chemical and physical hazards in their homes, workplaces or wider living environment, including 500,000 who die and tens of millions more who are injured in road accidents each year.

Health also depends on whether people can obtain resources: food, water, energy and the means to acquire shelter. Some 1.4–1.5 billion people lack the income or agricultural land to meet such basic needs. Hundreds of millions suffer from under-nutrition (including those who suffer seasonally or during times of drought).

This chapter will look at these two aspects of living in a sustainable world. The relationship between population and the environment is examined; some essential elements of population policy are cited; and a case is made for approaches to family planning similar to those presented earlier in the book under the banner of 'primary environmental care' (PEC; see Chapter 1) with an emphasis on the need for empowering women. A summary is given of major North/South consumption patterns, and some policy initiatives are suggested. In particular, it is argued that Northern countries need to evolve a new consumer ethic reinforced by the introduction of prices that fully reflect environmental costs and much more emphasis on the development of environmentally benign technology.

STABILIZING POPULATION: THE BIGGEST CHALLENGE

Population growth and the environment

One of the most confusing and contentious aspects of the population issue is the relative importance of population growth as a factor in sustainable development.

It is unfortunate, but understandable, that the debate about population has become polarized along ideological grounds. On the one side there are those motivated by lingering Malthusian fears of human populations swamping the Earth and swarming over national borders. On the other there are those who see such concerns as diverting attention from radical political, economic and social reforms. Yet others have religious or other fears over the issues of family planning and women's rights.

Because population is usually seen as a problem for developing countries – where 95 per cent of the projected 3.2 billion growth in numbers by 2025 is expected to take place – the contribution of developed countries' populations to environmental problems such as waste and pollution is sometimes overlooked. It has been calculated, for example, that the average Swiss pours 2,000 times more toxic waste into the environment than the average Sahelian farmer (Pradervand, 1991). If levels of waste and consumption do not change, the 57 million extra Northeners expected during the 1990s will pollute the Earth more than the extra 911 million Southerners (Harrison, 1992).

Fortunately, there is a growing consensus that taking up polar positions on population is not helpful. As long ago as 1984, at the International Population Conference in Mexico City, governments agreed that population and development problems should be tackled as closely interrelated ones (Rowley, 1984). In terms of environmental impact, *population* is now more clearly seen as a multiplier of the interaction between *consumption per person* and the *technologies* to supply that consumption and dispose of the waste (Ehrlich and Ehrlich, 1991). This relationship can be described by the model $I = P \times A \times T$, where I is environmental impact, P is population, A affluence (or per capita consumption), and T technology.

According to Barry Commoner, technology will often be the major actor in this equation. He has calculated, for example, that in measuring the causes of pollution from nitrates, cars and electricity in sixty-five developing countries, between 1970 and 1980, population was a less important factor than technology, though it was, nevertheless, responsible for between 24 and 31 per cent of the increase in pollution (Commoner, 1989). Others maintain that population is frequently a crucial factor. It has, for instance, been argued that population growth at 1.9 per cent a year from 1950 to 1985 was a major factor in the increase of global carbon dioxide emissions from 2,349 million tonnes to 6,793 million tonnes, an annual increase of 3.1 per cent (Harrison, 1992).

In the case of agriculture, increased population will frequently lead to new technologies which allow for greater productivity, without necessarily damaging the land. But in some situations new technology may not be affordable or easy to apply. One situation is where slash-and-burn farming is common. This is a form of rotational cultivation which can be highly sustainable if population density is low and if there is no pressure to produce crops for export. It is particularly suitable for tropical upland areas with low soil fertility. Unfortunately, in many regions of the world, increased population densities and competition for scarce forest resources have undermined the system. A huge influx of migrants into hills and mountains in Vietnam, Indonesia and the Philippines has shortened the rotational cycle and prevented forest regeneration (Rambo, 1990). Elsewhere, pioneering slash and burn, which clears plots of primary forest and uses them intensively until the fertility is destroyed, is also unsustainable. In large areas of Africa, increased use of land once allowed to lie fallow for several years has led directly to deforestation, loss of species, loss of soil fertility and increased erosion.

There is no doubt that population has had a major impact on deforestation in developing countries. In the fifteen years to 1986, forest and woodland shrank by 125 million hectares, while the farmed areas increased by 58.7 million hectares. A similar amount of land was used up by houses, factories and roads, while pasture increased by 7.9 million hectares (FAO, 1987). In the same period, population in developing countries grew by 2.2 per cent a year, perhaps accounting for some four-fifths of the loss of forest cover (Harrison, 1992). Along with the loss of trees has gone some of the protection against erosion, since not everywhere will adequate manure or compost have been applied to make up for the loss of organic content in the soil, nor action have been taken to compensate for loss of the holding action of roots on sloping land. And with the loss of trees goes loss of species.

But if population is an important factor in environmental degradation and the perpetuation of poverty, it is only one factor among many. Those who argue that unequal landholdings are a major factor in forcing poor people on to marginal land are quite right – especially in Latin America.

In countries such as Brazil and Guatemala, the unequal distribution of land is a more important cause of severe pressure on marginal land than an overall land shortage (Thiesenhusen, 1989). Poverty itself is a cause of much resource damage – forcing the poor and landless to move into forest lands, to use marginal land or to deplete inshore fisheries. Moreover, many of the pressures on developing countries' resources come from the developed world, which extracts massive amounts of hardwoods, cash crops, meat and minerals to feed its often wasteful appetites.

Poverty, low agricultural prices and appalling communications often prevent poor farmers from making the investments or applying the technologies which would enable them to increase yields to feed increased numbers. Some causes of poverty stretch back to bankers in Washington, London or Geneva, who hold the purse-strings on national debts, or to corrupt governments nearer home. Population, nevertheless, remains a fundamental factor in the environmental impact equation, whatever the level of consumption or technology.

Slowing population growth could, for example, play a major role in slowing carbon dioxide emissions from the developing countries, which on present trends will grow from 0.8 tons to 1.67 tons per person by 2025. Nafis Sadik, the Executive Director of the United Nations Population Fund, has pointed out that if the UN low population projection could be achieved, instead of the medium, this would reduce emissions in the year 2025 by 1.3 billion tonnes – enough to offset 84 per cent of present deforestation rates (Sadik, 1990). A summary of global population trends is provided in Box 11.2.

Slowing population growth is conceivably the biggest challenge facing

---

Box 11.2: Population: the facts

World population has more than doubled from 2.5 billion in 1950 to 5.4 billion today. The fundamental reason for this increase is the continuing fall in death rates, which has not been accompanied by an equivalent fall in birth rates.

According to the United Nations medium variant, world population will reach 10 billion by 2050 and level out at about 11.6 billion towards the end of the twenty-second century. This assumes that developing world fertility will be at replacement level of just over two children per woman by 2050. But even if that were achieved today world population would still grow to 8.4 billion before stabilizing. The medium-high projection puts population at 12.5 billion, the medium-low at 7.8 billion by the middle of the next century.

The rate of population growth peaked in the late 1960s and is now about 1.7 per cent. But the annual additions will peak some time towards the end of the decade at around 100 million and then slowly decline. Nearly all these additional people will live in the developing world, and it is projected that over 80 per cent of the increase in these countries up to the year 2025 will be in urban areas.

Around 37 per cent of people in developing countries are under 15 years of age, and as they reach sexual maturity their fertility will have a major impact on future population growth.

Fertility in the developed world is below replacement level of 2.0 to 2.1 births per woman. Only the momentum of unbalanced age distribution and immigration keeps population growing.

---

development planners in the Third World. The necessary policies are complex and slow acting, as those who have been attempting to include them in national conservation strategies have found. In Pakistan, where population has grown from 30 million to 114 million since 1950 and threatens to reach 200 million by 2010, it is now realized that the best hope is merely to delay the achievement of that total by six to ten years (Box 11.3). But if that can be done, the time can be used to ease the pressures on the cities and phase in other development and distributional strategies. And there is a chance that another fateful doubling to 400 million might be averted. Where population growth rates have been brought down sharply, as in Thailand or Korea, the benefits in per capita social investment and reduced pressure on the environment are already being felt.

The same might be said of China, though in that case there is widespread agreement that population has already grossly overshot the environmental carrying capacity of the country. According to Dr Qu Geping, Vice-Chairman of the Environmental Protection Commission

Box 11.3: Pakistan: a conservation strategy

Many countries have begun work on a national conservation strategy (NCS) based upon the model of the *World Conservation Strategy* published in 1980 and its successor *Caring for the Earth: A Strategy for Sustainability* (IUCN, UNEP and WWF, 1991). But few strategy documents have incorporated population factors as well as the Pakistani NCS, co-ordinated by the IUCN office in Karachi.

This recently completed report states that it may be possible for the country, with a present population of 114 million, to accommodate 200 million people – the number expected to live there around the year 2010 – by adopting the suggested sustainable development programmes. But, the report says:

> there is no possibility of accommodating the 400 million people projected to be living in this country by 2035–40 if existing trends in population growth continue. If this is allowed to occur, Pakistan will become an international charity case, like Haiti, Ethiopia, Sudan and Bangladesh – dependent on the goodwill of others, with no realistic opportunity to improve the lot of its people and no expectations other than a continuing decline in living standards for the vast bulk of them.
>
> (*NCS of Pakistan*, 1991)

The report then charts out three broad options available to policy-makers 'faced with this inexorable momentum of population growth'. The first of these is to continue on the current path with no overt political commitment to population planning and low levels of funding for a 'population welfare programme'. The result: not much slowing in the march to 200 million people by the year 2010.

The second option would involve firm political support for fertility reduction and for upgrading the status of women, aided by a multisectoral programme which significantly shifts funds to social sectors, such as education and health.

The third option would follow the second path but add on a policy to sustain the natural resource base. Key items in this policy would support out-migration from the fragile ecological areas such as uplands, range-lands and deserts, and retention of populations in the more robust canal-irrigated areas. This in turn would allow a sustainable rate of urbanization.

Such a policy, says the report, could give Pakistan an extra six to ten years before a population of 200 million is reached and would have 'enormous distributional and environmental consequences'. It would also increase the likelihood that food needs could be met in most regions of the country.

The *NCS of Pakistan* suggests setting specific targets for fertility reduction, which would bring average family size down from 6.5 children to half that over twenty years – 'an enormous but not impossible task'. It would like to see a return to the 1981 levels of population in the fragile ecological zones through out-migration – though it admits this will not be possible in rapidly growing regions such as Baluchistan where there is no tradition of emigration.

The report also suggests a target for population retention in the fertile irrigated areas of at least 40 per cent. One way to do this would be to make the villages more inviting to stay in – with better health facilities, better water supplies, a paved market road and a reliable source of electricity. In addition, it supports the idea of developing agriculture-based rural industries.

Whether Pakistan can develop the political will and administrative capacity to implement such a plan is open to question. However, integrated planning of this kind would be an essential first step towards a pattern of sustainable development in the country.

and Administrator of the National Environmental Protection Agency, studies show that, based upon China's natural resources and the level of its science and technology, the country's 9.6 million square kilometres can appropriately support about 700 million people. However, this limit is now exceeded by 400 million people and may be exceeded by 600 million by the end of the century. According to Dr Qu, 'a large number of our environmental problems result directly or indirectly from the pounding of population increase'. These include deforestation, grassland degradation, desert encroachment, water resource shortage and waste of mineral resources (Qu Geping, 1989). In fact, China's total cultivated area has fallen by 17 million hectares since 1957 and in nine provinces there is less than 0.067 ha per person, below what is necessary for self-sustaining agriculture. But the situation would have been much worse if China had not managed to bring its total fertility rate down from an average of 5.8 children in the 1970s to 2.4 children in the late 1980s (Ni Shaoxiang, 1989). The official policy of levelling out the population at 1.4 to 1.5 billion some time in the next century looks over-ambitious, but the nightmare of 2 billion people crowded on to a shrinking resource base has been averted.

Population planning: lessons from experience

One of the lessons from such examples is that action in countries with too rapid population growth needs to be taken urgently. Because policies take time to achieve results and population growth feeds on itself, it is imperative not to delay. But what policies should be pursued and how should they relate to other actions to conserve the environment, to tackle poverty and to sustain development? It is here that the lessons of successful population planning have much to offer. There need be no conflict, and there are potentially strong synergies, between what we now know must be done to slow population growth and what will also alleviate poverty, improve the lives of women and children and empower communities to act in their own interest.

The particular nexus of activities necessary to slow population growth rates was well described in the *State of the World's Children 1991* report by UNICEF (UNICEF, 1991). This argued that four broad factors work together to bring about the transition to lower birth rates: economic and social progress, improvements for women, family planning programmes and reduced infant and child deaths. These four factors act together 'in a cat's cradle of synergisms'. For example, 'women's advancement (and especially secondary education) makes family planning more likely; family planning reduces both child deaths and child births; slower population growth can assist economic progress; economic progress can lead to lower birth rates'. All these factors acting together will exert a far greater downward pressure on birth rates than any one of them acting alone. The link between the level of child deaths and the take-up of family planning is especially strong. Few countries have a rate of acceptance of family planning beyond 35 per cent of couples in the child-bearing age as long as under-5 mortality rates remain much above 100 per 1,000 births. It is equally uncommon to find under-5 mortality rates below 100 if family planning acceptance remains much below the 35 per cent mark.

'In the context of overall development', the report says,

> all of these basic factors in fertility decline – improvements in the lives of women, reduced child deaths, and the availability of family planning – are important *in themselves*. All of them make a direct contribution to improving the lives of millions of people; the fact they *also* make a strong synergistic contribution to solving the population problem, and that they can all be accomplished at a relatively modest cost, adds up to what should be an irresistible case for simultaneous action on all these fronts in the decade ahead.
>
> (ibid.)

In its 1992 report UNICEF stresses, particularly, the special benefits of 'the responsible planning of births' which it calls 'one of the most effective and least expensive ways of improving the quality of life on earth'. Indeed, it argues that family planning could bring more benefits to more people at less cost than any other single technology now available to mankind. It could save the lives of perhaps one-quarter to one-third of the 500,000 women who now die every year from causes related to pregnancy and giving birth. It could prevent many if not most of the more than 50,000 illegal abortions which are now performed on women *every single day* and which result in the deaths of 150,000 young women every year. In addition, it could not only save the lives of several million children each year – the majority of whom die from preventable 'high risk', badly spaced and timed births – but also significantly improve the nutritional health and quality of life of children throughout the developing world (UNICEF, 1992).

Equally pertinent is the importance of environmental improvements in the nexus of factors which interacting together can achieve a sustainable future. Safe, sufficient and affordable water supplies, sanitation, sustainable farming technologies, healthy low-cost housing, affordable sources of fuel whose use does not imply unhealthy levels of indoor air pollution: these are all part of a package of basic needs which will help child survival, improve living standards and create the conditions under which population policies and transition to the small family norm can be brought about.

That still leaves open the question of how, in the real world, these changes can be encouraged. In much of Africa and Latin America investments in social sectors such as health and education have been falling. In India some 250 million people live in extreme poverty (World Bank, 1990). In Mexico, per capita income fell by 9 per cent in the 1980s while the working population grew by 3 per cent every year. Overall income disparities between rich and poor countries are widening. In 1976, the countries classified by the World Bank as low income, the poorest countries, on average had a per capita income of only 2.4 per cent of the per capita income in countries defined as high income; in 1982, the figure was 2.2; and in 1988, it had fallen to 1.9.

This situation calls for fundamental changes in policies to bring about a fairer relationship between rich and poor – at a national as well as the international level. It calls for agreements and incentives to deal with the global environmental threats such as climate change and the loss of biodiversity. The political will must be found by governments to increase the priority given to social investments in people and in conservation. Issues of education, health and housing, of land reform, soil conservation, clean water and sanitation must come higher up the agenda. As will be argued below, a new morality of consumption has to be found. But the one essential investment will be in people themselves.

There is now plenty of evidence in this book and elsewhere that the empowerment of people to take as much charge as possible of their own environment and their own common needs is the only way forward to truly sustainable development. Empowerment, the active involvement of the beneficiaries of development in the design and implementation of activities intended to improve their welfare, has in preceding chapters been cited as an essential ingredient of primary environmental care. As shown below, there is plenty of evidence to suggest that empowerment, particularly of women, is equally important in bringing about successful family planning programmes. The remarkable work of IPPF's affiliate in Columbia, Profamilia, tapped a huge, previously unmet demand for family planning services in that country and has halved average family size in twenty years.

While in the North environmentally polluting consumption and technologies have led to what Pierre Pradervand has dubbed 'wealth-generated ecocide', the destruction of impoverished environments in the South constitutes 'ecocide by poverty'. In the North, the problem can be solved if government and people find the will to apply the available solutions. In the South, it will require a strategy of popular action among individuals and groups, supported by government, to develop the knowledge and faith to apply the synergistic solutions discussed above.

This does not mean that people's organizations have to be involved in activities which tackle simultaneously all the interventions needed to meet basic needs, achieve slow population growth and care for the environment. Sometimes planting trees and improving water supplies might form part of an approach aimed at increasing incomes and productivity. Family planning activities might be linked with other family concerns such as child weighing, maternal care, immunization and income-generating schemes.

Empowerment of women

There is one powerful link which naturally joins concerns with the local environment to reproductive, maternal and child health: women. In Korea, the link was made by the women's clubs of the Saemaul Movement which spread across the country, concerned first with family planning but then increasingly with environmental improvements and farming activities (Reditt, 1981). In India, the women in some 3,000 villages have developed integrated development projects concerned with exploring options beyond motherhood. This initiative, started by the Family Planning Association of India, has had remarkable results, improving levels of health, literacy, sanitation and environmental well-being. Smokeless stoves, biogas units and chicken farms have spread. More importantly, so have a plethora of action groups involving

---

Box 11.4: Women house builders in Costa Rica

Faced with a rapid growth of population, which if continued could take the present population of 3 million to 6.7 million by 2025, and massive immigration from neighbouring Nicaragua and El Salvador, Costa Rica faces severe environmental pressures. In particular, the pressure on land is fierce in the west-central plain, around the cities of San José and Heredia. Here, government policy has been to buy up and clear farmland and hand it over to squatters even before basic services have been installed. What houses it has built have been basic cement boxes in rows facing busy roads, with no communal facilities and often poor access to employment.

Now an alternative model is being pioneered by Costa Rica's principal women's organization, CEFEMINA, in partnership with a campaigning housing group called COPAN. Together they are empowering a committed group of local women to create their own communal settlement on the 118 hectare site of a former coffee plantation at Guarari.

Here the women are planning and building groups of houses around communal recreation areas and playgrounds for the children. They are restoring and extending the vegetation around a watershed at one end of the site. They are also planning schools and health services, planting gardens and medicinal plants and developing income-generating schemes. Special efforts are being made to protect the natural vegetation, and children are involved in campaigns to plant more trees. Each house in Guarari costs about US$2,500. To qualify for one, the head of household needs 900 hours of credits for work done on the site, all family members being allowed to add to the credits.

Committees of local residents manage every aspect of the work in Guarari, from rabbit breeding to education and health. This last is based upon CEFEMINA's concept of preventive health care, called 'living health', in which everyone takes part. Within this concept is included family planning, developed with the help of the Asociación Demográfica Costarricense (ADC), the local affiliate of the International Planned Parenthood Federation (IPPF). Introduced sensitively through group meetings, the programme has been very successful. Family size is already well below the national average, with commensurate reductions in child mortality and fewer abortions.

Source: Dennis (1989).

---

women, men and young people. The villages have come alive with new knowledge and new energy (Datta, 1991).

Elsewhere, as in Costa Rica, women have taken the lead in building a new type of environmentally friendly urban settlement (Box 11.4), a 'green lung' in place of a concrete prison. It is the sort of initiative which has been institutionalized in Sri Lanka, where the 'million houses programme' has now seen local people build a million and a half new houses with the help of small loans and some technical advice (Rowley, 1987). Even the poorest communities, as far apart as Burkina Faso in the Sahel and the delta islands of Bangladesh, have discovered the power of group action (*People*, 1991).

The Naam movement, based in Burkina Faso, is largely made up of women members grouped into an African federation which chooses projects with minimum outside assistance. At one village, Saminga in Burkina Faso, the women worked with five neighbouring communities to build a dam to trap and collect drinking and irrigation water. Making up, as they do, some 70 per cent of the adult village population, the women's leadership is vital. And as Pierre Pradervand discovered when he visited various Sahel projects where women had grouped together to improve their own environment, 'illiterate peasant women from some of the most remote areas of the world practically kidnap visitors to talk to them about family planning' (Pradervand, 1992).

In the Bangladesh case, women in storm-swept Hatia Island have broken through centuries of oppression to change the balance between the sexes and begin a process of co-operation with the men to tackle village problems (Box 11.5). One report described it as 'a peaceful revolution – a total transformation of poor people's sense of their own power, their ability to control their lives, rather than simply being the victims of the rich and powerful' (Harrison, 1991). Significantly, family planning has been enthusiastically adopted by the women of Hatia.

Agencies such as Oxfam, which helped to seed this last initiative, have developed the concept of primary environmental care to popularize such approaches. If it is to flourish and spread, it will need to be supported by open-minded networking between non-government organizations, not always known for their generosity in sharing territory. It will require the backing of governments and local officials, traditionally fearful of stirring up radical movements. It will require imagination to experiment in adapting successful projects under various local circumstances. It will need to be part of a broader policy of social investment in women and girls, in their education and health in particular, in family planning and in environmental conservation.

The participatory approaches will not always work. Even in the best of circumstances they will tend to be slow, time consuming and cumbersome. Often they are viewed with suspicion by government officials who fondly espouse them in their rhetoric. Sometimes the social structure of the population will be so inequitable that participatory approaches aimed at the poorest will be frustrated. Nevertheless, the evidence indicates that the approaches summarized here under the label of primary environmental care offer hope that the evil circle of poverty, population growth and environmental degradation can be broken.

Box 11.5: Banding together to end oppression in Bangladesh

Few women face greater difficulties than those in Bangladesh, where they are haggled over for dowries, married off as teenagers, often subject to violence and held within the strict limits of *purdah*. The situation in the delta region, subject to cyclones and flooding, is especially hard. As the struggle to make a living becomes more desperate, many wives are abandoned or divorced. Like widows, they are forced to fend for themselves, often shamed by having to work outside the *bari* or household area. Always poorly paid and often forced to beg, they struggle alongside their children to survive.

Yet in the delta island of Hatia, things have begun to change. Here, women have banded together to help themselves. Encouraged by the Dnip Unnayam Sagstha, or Island Development Society, a group of women have organized themselves despite the initial opposition of their husbands. Saving only two *thaka* a week (about 6 US cents), they were able to raise their first loan of 1,000 *thaka* from the development society. They started buying paddy, cooking it and reselling it at a profit. They paved the muddy road to the bazaar, managed to force a pay rise for domestic work and were able to mobilize a new concern among men and women in the community against violence. In the face of the women's successes, local men started their own development group and began to collaborate in an effort to avoid dowry payments by arranging marriages within the group, to discourage divorce and to encourage family meals where food is fairly shared and problems can be discussed.

Reporting on the groups on Hatia island, Harrison was struck by the fact that every one of the women he spoke to was using a modern method of contraception, obtained from the local health centre – something none of them were doing before the group was set up.

Source: Harrison (1991).

TOWARDS SUSTAINABLE CONSUMPTION IN THE NORTH

Current inequities in consumption and trends in pollution

With the growing recognition that the carrying capacity of the planet is being taxed to its limits, there is an urgent need not only to slow the rate of population growth but also to change present patterns of resource consumption. While the poor in developing countries often have little option but to consume natural resources unsustainably, their behaviour can only be addressed through accelerated economic development and the type of action discussed elsewhere in this book. However, global sustainability will ultimately be impossible unless major changes are brought about in the consumption patterns in Northern countries which are responsible for some of the most daunting global environmental problems confronting humanity. Gross disparities in resource consumption between North and South will have to be overcome, lest some countries become defensively isolationist while others slide into insecurity and conflict (IUCN, UNEP and WWF, 1991).

Table 11.1 draws on a report prepared by the Indira Gandhi Institute of Development Research in Bombay and summarizes the North/South inequities in consumption patterns. The table shows the North/South shares of total consumption, the average disparity ratio (ADR) in consumption levels, taking the ratio of per capita consumption levels of Northern and Southern countries, and the extreme disparity ratio (EDR), defined as the ratio between the richest and the poorest country, using the USA and India by way of illustration. It should be noted that the East European countries have been included among the Northern countries, while the newly industrialized countries of Asia are included among the Southern countries. The ADR is therefore smaller than the real disparities between, for example, the European countries and the low-income countries of Asia and Africa.

Table 11.1: Consumption of selected items, North/South

Item	Share (per cent)		ADR North/South	EDR North/South
	North	South		
Meat	64	36	6	52
Cereals	48	52	3	6
Round wood	46	54	1	6
Paper, etc.	81	19	14	115
Fertilizers	60	40	5	6
Iron and steel	80	20	13	22
Cars	92	8	24	320
Electricity	81	19	13	46
CO_2 emissions	70	30	8	27

Source: Parikh *et al.* (1991; data variously from 1987–89).

The Northern countries have 24 per cent of the world population, but their share in global consumption of the various commodities shown in the table ranges from 46 to 92 per cent. Overall, their per capita consumption is three to eight times higher than that of developing countries for items of basic needs (food, etc.) and more than twenty times higher for motor cars. Energy consumption as measured by carbon dioxide emissions is eight times higher.

The per capita consumption of cereals was 717 kg in the North and 247 kg in the South, giving an ADR of about 3 in 1988. As the Indian report points out, it should be perfectly possible to feed a world of some 8 billion people at the Northern consumption level. The European countries at present more or less feed themselves despite high population densities. As set out in Chapter 4, there are techniques available that are capable of sustaining the needed cereal production without undue ecological stress.

However, this is manifestly untrue for consumption of energy-intensive products and services. Northern countries generated the equivalent of 3.36 tons of carbon per capita in 1988 (5.4 tons in the USA). For a world population of 8 billion, the total annual gross atmospheric emissions would be 27 billion tons (or 43 billion tons at the US rate) compared to present gross emissions of 5.7 billion tons per year. The rate of carbon dioxide build-up in the atmosphere would thus be almost 5 times higher (7.5 times higher, if the US consumption rates are used) than it is today, and at present rates the world seems set for sustained global warming due to excessive energy consumption. Obviously, such increases would not be sustainable.

The world economy has experienced a rate of growth over the last few decades which is historically unprecedented. In 1990, the global output of goods and services totalled roughly US$20 trillion, an increase from US$15.5 trillion in 1980. During the 1980s, the world economy grew at an average rate of about 3 per cent per year. It is worth considering that the increase of US$4.5 trillion to the world product during the decade exceeded the entire world product in 1950. In other words, growth in global economic output during the 1980s was greater than during the thousands of years from the beginning of the human race until 1950 (Brown, 1991).

This rapid rate of economic growth and the resultant consumption increases are now posing formidable environmental challenges. Gus Speth of the World Resources Institute has summarized the dramatic changes in pollution as four long-term trends (Speth, 1991a):

(1) *From modest quantities to huge quantities.* As a result of human activity, annual global emissions of carbon dioxide have increased about tenfold in this century, while annual sulphur dioxide emissions

grew by an estimated 446 per cent globally. The quantities of solid waste in the USA alone have doubled over the past three decades, and hundreds of millions of tons of hazardous wastes are now generated annually. During the twentieth century, there have been vast increases in the quantities of pollutants imposed on a finite environment.

(2) *From gross insults to micro-toxicity.* Before the Second World War, concern with air and water pollution focused primarily on smoke and sewers, problems that are as old as urbanization itself. While these problems remain serious world-wide, they are no longer the major issues they once were in the Northern countries: for example, the killer fogs of London are a memory of the past. However, with the growth of the synthetic organic chemicals industry during the past fifty years tens of thousands of synthetic compounds have been introduced into the environment: pesticides, plastics, industrial chemicals, detergents, food additives and other commercially valuable products. Gradually, increasing numbers of these products are being identified as harmful to people or nature. 'Of the roughly 70,000 chemicals in trade today, as many as 35,000 are classed by the US Environmental Protection Agency and by OECD as definitely or potentially harmful to human health' (ibid.). Two associated problems relate to the rapid build-up of nuclear and other hazardous wastes.

(3) *From First World to Third World.* While the volume of pollutants generated by the First World still vastly exceeds that of the developing countries, the latter are catching up fast as they apply cheap and 'dirty' technology to further their economic growth. Some of the most dramatic and alarming examples of pollution can be found in Eastern Europe and in the developing countries. The unplanned urban growth typical of these countries is accompanied by increased traffic and energy consumption, undesirable industrial locations and, consequently, metal pollution. For example, the highest ambient levels of trace metals are now encountered in the urban areas of developing countries with cities like Hong Kong, Rio de Janeiro, Buenos Aires and Guatemala City having 0.15 to 2.4, 0.13 to 1.7, 0.3 to 3.9 and 0.24 to 2.9 micrograms per cubic metre of air respectively, much higher values than those generally reported in urban areas in Europe or North America (Nriagu, 1990). In India, an estimated 70 per cent of total surface waters are polluted, and only 217 out of a total of 3,119 towns and cities have even partial sewage treatment facilities (Speth, 1991a).

(4) *From local effects to global effects.* As late as the 1970s, air pollution was largely a local phenomenon and was treated as such by legislation

and remedial action in the North, with the result that many cities now have better air than they had then. In the same manner, most pollution was until only half a generation ago seen as a localized problem to be solved within a region, community or neighbourhood. Meanwhile, overall global use of fossil fuels, and emissions of traditional pollutants resulting from them, such as carbon dioxide and sulphur and nitrogen oxides, have continued to climb. As a result, a significant international environmental agenda emerged during the 1980s. There is mounting concern about global environmental problems, such as the greenhouse effect and damage to the ozone shield. Regionally, acid rain is becoming a major problem. This is the case in Europe and North America, and it is emerging as an important issue in parts of Asia and Latin America (ibid.).

Altering these four trends and putting resource consumption on a more equitable and sustainable footing is one of the greatest challenges of our time facing the North. This is so because changing these trends will profoundly affect human sensitivity and ingrained behaviour. All people, but particularly those in rich countries of the North, will need to alter their lifestyles now, 'for the sake of a decent standard of living for our contemporaries and a dignified future for our descendants' (IUCN, UNEP and WWF, 1991).

What is to be done?

To address the question of what needs to be done to change consumption patterns, the influential environment organizations IUCN, UNEP and WWF advocate the following priority actions in their strategy document (IUCN, UNEP and WWF, 1991):

(1) A combined approach to resource and population issues:
  - Increase awareness about the need to stabilize resource consumption and population.
  - Integrate resource consumption and population issues in national development policies and planning.
(2) Action to reduce excessive consumption and waste of resources:
  - Develop, test and adopt resource-efficient methods and technologies.
  - Tax energy and other resources in high-consumption countries.
  - Encourage 'green consumer' movements.
(3) Action to stabilize population:
  - Improve maternal and child health care.
  - Improve education for women and girls.[1]
  - Double family planning services.

Creating increased awareness about the linkages between population, wasteful consumption and environmental degradation is an important task for governments in rich and poor countries alike. However, in Northern countries this will only become effective if coupled with efforts to introduce what the strategy refers to as an 'ethic for living sustainably', a new morality of consumption, one that emphasizes that more is not necessarily better, and that accepts the notion of limited economic growth in the rich countries (see Chapter 1).

Tinbergen and Hueting have spelled out what this would mean in practice:

> In terms of national accounts, environmentally benign activities represent a smaller volume. Thus a bicycle-kilometre represents a smaller volume than a car-kilometre; a sweater a smaller volume than a hot room; an extra blanket a smaller volume than heating the whole house; beans a smaller volume than meat; and a holiday by train a smaller volume than holiday flights. This is mainly because the exhaustion of the environment and resources is not charged to national income as costs. If it were, the differences would become much smaller or nil.

They go on to say that saving the environment will certainly check production growth and probably lead to lower levels of national income, but that this 'analysis should arouse optimism rather than pessimism, because environmentally benign activities are remarkably cheap' (Tinbergen and Hueting, 1991).

So the task for the leaders in the North, mostly but by no means only the politicians, is to explain this to the public, make the need for this new morality credible and themselves lead by example. And this is where most of them fail. Their rhetoric still is far from matched by their actions and, indeed, by the mandates given to them by voters mostly concerned with the bread-and-butter issues of the day.

The *National Conservation Strategy of Pakistan*, described in Box 11.2, is a good example of the integration of policies relating to resource consumption, conservation and population into the national development planning process. What made the Pakistani experience so interesting is that it was a truly participatory effort that evolved after an extensive process of consultations touching all walks of life in the country. By contrast, the British government's White Paper on the Environment, *This Common Inheritance*, issued in 1990, was an attempt to reconcile consumption, pollution and natural resource use in the UK; but it was seen and received largely as a top-down political statement. As such, it was not embraced by environment NGOs or others potentially able to influence public opinion, which will reduce its impact.

The population issue (item 3 above) was covered in the first half of this chapter, where the point was made that the same participatory, low-cost approaches that have been found to work well in the context of the environment can also be the basis for successful family planning programmes. It was also argued that these programmes do best when they are part of a broader social development effort enhancing the status, health and education of women and girls. The only additional aspect to be underlined here is the need for more resources for family planning in the context of aid to the most needy countries. The United Nations Population Fund has estimated that to keep population growth to the UN medium variant, mentioned in Box 11.2, funding for population programmes would have to double by the end of this century. Today, US$4.5 billion is spent annually on family planning services in lower-income countries with US$0.7 billion as development assistance from the OECD countries. This figure should increase to US$9 billion by the year 2000, with half this amount coming from development assistance (UNFPA, 1991). This should be seen in the light of the overall need for better targeting of foreign aid on basic needs for poor groups mentioned in Chapter 10 above.

But to limit excessive resource consumption in the North, the two issues raised under item 2 are probably most important – alongside the new morality mentioned above. First, it will be necessary to embark on what Gus Speth has called 'a worldwide environmental revolution in technology' (Speth, 1991b). Governments in the North must begin to stimulate a rapid and drastic increase in the efficiency with which materials and energy are used. Second, this is only likely to happen if the right economic signals are given, if the costs of environmental degradation are internalized in the prices of goods and services, and if implicit subsidies of practices that degrade the environment are phased out. These two aspects must be seen as closely interrelated: the technological push will come only if the right economic incentives are present; and those incentives can be provided only if alternative technological options can be discerned.

Arguably, it is energy use that should be the focus of interest. As shown above, current patterns of energy use are plainly not sustainable and will become even less so as development accelerates in populous low-income countries (such as India). This is well known and much has been written on the potential role of renewable energy. But, again, the practice is far from the rhetoric. For example, in 1989, the member countries of the International Energy Agency (IEA) spent 74 per cent of their energy research budget on fossil fuels and nuclear energy, but only 7 per cent on renewable technologies and 5 per cent on conservation (Droste and Dogse, 1991). In the UK, the Department of Energy spent £24 million, more than ever, on research on renewables in 1991 but £113 million in 1990 on nuclear power research. Again in the UK, the government target for renewable energy generation is 1,000 MW in the year 2000, still only 2 per cent of Britain's total energy needs in that year and equivalent to the capacity of *one* modern coal-burning power station. Clearly, the proportions should be changed, with the desirable, non-polluting energy sources required in a future sustainable world receiving most, or at least a greatly increased share of, funds for research and development.

Barbier, Burgess and Pearce point out that we are at an important watershed for technological development, with several significant renewable technologies, such as photovoltaics and wind-power, beginning to achieve market penetration on a large scale. Once market penetration is assured, economies of scale and improved reliability of these technologies may lead to sustantial cost reductions at a rapid rate. However, market forces alone are unlikely to secure the 'optimal' rate of substitution, given current implicit subsidies of environmental costs of fossil fuels. It may therefore be necessary to impose taxes, like carbon taxes, to change relative prices in favour of renewables with a view to accelerating their adoption by consumers (Barbier, Burgess and Pearce, 1990; see also Chapter 9).

Economic incentives go to the heart of the behaviour of individual consumers. Comprehensive changes in polluting patterns of consumption in the North can only be brought about by governments willing to make active and innovative use of fiscal instruments. The first step in this direction should be to eliminate the current subsidies on consumption of forest resources, automotive transport, energy, water and pesticides, to mention just a few (see Chapter 9). This would help to get what Speth calls 'environmentally honest prices', that is, prices that incorporate full environmental costs (Speth, 1991b). The second step should be to impose taxes on various pollutants, such as fossil and nuclear fuels and the organic chemical compounds referred to earlier. Of particular importance in that context would be a carbon tax, a tax equivalent to the carbon content in fossil fuels, with a view to improving the efficiency in use of such fuels. Environmental user fees, charges on uses of common property resources (like lakes and rivers) and tax credits to reward environmentally benign behaviour (like improved insulation of houses) would be other examples of fiscal instruments available to governments.

In the North, there is an increasing willingness to begin to consider introduction of carbon taxes, at least within the European Community (see Chapter 10). However, this move needs to be accelerated and given much more emphasis in energy *and* fiscal policies than is currently the case. There is a strong logic to the notion that to raise public revenue the things that need to be reduced, like pollution and environmentally destructive behaviour, should be taxed rather than what needs to be increased, like employment and income (Goodland *et al.*, 1991).

To summarize, a policy framework conducive to sustained reduction of profligate consumption in the North would need three central elements: (1) an ethic or morality that encapsulates the philosophy of limited economic growth; (2) greatly increased efforts to develop environmentally benign technology, primarily but not exclusively in the energy sector; and (3) 'getting the prices right' by internalizing environmental costs and making innovative use of fiscal instruments to that end.

All of this is well known. But it needs to be said again that, in the absence of greatly increased efforts by concerned policy-makers and by others able to influence public opinion in Northern countries, the prospect of a sustainable future may remain elusive. There remains a wide gap between what the governments in these countries say they are willing to do to improve their environment and reality. For example, as mentioned in Chapter 1, the commitment by the European Community and Japan to reduce greenhouse gas emissions is far from enough to stabilize concentrations of such gases in the atmosphere. In the UK, the government is committed to a reduction of carbon dioxide emissions to 1990 levels by 2005. But its Department of Transport's 1989 national road traffic forecasts predict that car mileage will increase by 66 per cent until 2005. This means that, even if all other sectors freeze their emissions at present levels, carbon dioxide production in the UK would still be 10 per cent higher in 2005 as a result of the growth in road traffic alone (Greenpeace, 1991). Again in the UK, the government claims to be 'in the forefront of action to protect the ozone layer', but ten of the thirty-nine English county councils still have no CFC recycling facilities, and only a minute proportion of CFCs available are being recovered (Friends of the Earth, 1991).

Since the UN conference on the environment in Stockholm in 1972 there has been very substantial progress in environmental awareness and also in changing consumer behaviour in the Northern countries. Environmentalism has moved from the fringe to the mainstream of political debate. Nobody seriously disputes the issues it raises. Increasing consumer awareness of the need for change is making industry adjust its ways. Governments are pursuing green improvements, albeit with varying sincerity and success.

What is at issue is whether these changes are all happening fast enough to avert some of the looming global catastrophies. In the run-up to the 1992 UN conference governments in the rich countries were avoiding serious commitment to action that would help to put the world on a sustainable development path. Sadly, it is difficult to avoid the conclusion that there will be no significant change in current consumption patterns until the effects of global warming and ozone layer depletion really start to bite in the North. Not until the ordinary man in the street is affected, has close relatives afflicted by skin cancer due to increased ultraviolet radiation or experienced economic dislocation because of climate change, not until then is it likely that we will see Northern governments introduce the policies that may save this small planet.

CONCLUSIONS

The environmental impact of human activities depends both on the number of people and on the resource consumption level of each individual. The Earth can only absorb such impact up to a certain level – its carrying capacity – and there is growing consensus that this level is being approached at accelerating rates. Urgent action is therefore required to reduce the rates of growth of human numbers, mainly in the South, and also to reduce or eliminate patterns of consumption, mainly in the North, all of which contribute to global environmental problems.

There is evidence that successful approaches to family planning can be built on the low-cost, participatory approaches to primary health care and environmental conservation that earlier in this book have been called primary environmental care. However, emphasis must be placed on the empowerment of women in the context of family planning interventions, and on the enhancement of women's status, health, education and income-earning potential. There will also be a need to greatly increase – some say to double by the end of the decade – expenditure on family planning services and to increase manifold the use of foreign aid for this purpose in the poorest countries.

Profligate consumption in the North is one of the main reasons for current global environmental problems. Efforts to change the behaviour of consumers in the industrialized countries in an environmentally benign way have begun but have not nearly gone far enough if, for example, the risks of global warming are to be averted. To achieve this, more concerted efforts are required in three areas by political leaders and others able to influence public opinion: the evolution of a 'green' consumer ethic or morality; a technological revolution doubling the efforts to develop more environmentally benign technologies; and full-cost environmental pricing providing the requisite economic incentives for technological change.

NOTES

1 This item is mentioned in Chapter 3 of *Caring for the Earth* (IUCN, UNEP and WWF, 1991) in the context of 'action to reduce gender disparities, and ensure that women are enabled to play a full part in the process of national development'.

REFERENCES AND BIBLIOGRAPHY

Barbier, Edward B., Burgess, Joanne C. and Pearce, David W., 1990. *Slowing Global Warming: Options for Greenhouse Gas Substitution*, Discussion Paper 90-05, London Environment Economics Centre, London, October.

Brown, Lester R., 1991. 'The new world order', in Lester R. Brown, *et al.*, *State of the World 1991*, (Worldwatch Institute), Earthscan, London.

Commoner, Barry, 1989. 'Rapid population growth and environmental stress', in *Consequences of Rapid Population Growth in Developing Countries*, proceedings of UN expert group meeting, August 1988, ESA/P/WP.110, United Nations, New York.

Datta, Bishakha, 1991. 'Focussing on women in Karnataka', *People* (IPPF, London), 18, 2.

Dennis, Frances, 1989. 'Women build homes and health in Costa Rica', *Earthwatch*, (IPPF, UNFPA and IUCN, London), 37.

Droste, Bernd von and Dogse, Peter, 1991. 'Sustainable development – the role of investment', in Robert Goodland *et al.* (eds), *Environmentally Sustainable Economic Development: Building on Brundtland*, UNESCO, Paris.

Ehrlich, Paul R. and Ehrlich, Anne H., 1991. *The Population Explosion*, Hutchinson, London.

FAO, 1987. *Production Year Book*, FAO, Rome.

Friends of the Earth, 1991. *Disinheriting the Earth*, Friends of the Earth, London.

Goodland, Robert, Daly, Herman, El Serafy, Salah and Drost, Bernd von (eds), 1991. *Environmentally Sustainable Economics Development: Building on Brundtland*, UNESCO, Paris.

Greenpeace, 1991. *This Common Incompetence*, Greenpeace, London.

Harrison, Paul, 1991. 'Living dangerously', *People* (IPPF, London), 18, 3.

Harrison, Paul, 1992. *The Third Revolution*, I. B. Tauris and St Martin's Press, London.

IUCN, UNEP and WWF, 1991. *Caring for the Earth – a Strategy for Sustainable Living*, Earthscan, London.

McNamara, Robert, 1991. 'A blueprint for Africa', *People* (IPPF, London), 18, 1. Full text of speech to African Leadership Forum, June 1990, from World Bank, Washington, DC.

Mitlin, Diana, 1992. 'Sustainable development: a guide to the literature', *Environment and Urbanization*, 4, 1, April.

National Conservation Strategy of Pakistan, 1991. National Planning Commission in collaboration with the IUCN, Islamabad. See also *Earthwatch* (IPPF, UNFPA and IUCN, London), 40, 1990.

Ni Shaoxiang, 1989. 'Population pressures on resources and the environment', *Earthwatch* (IPPF, UNFPA and IUCN, London), 34.

Nriagu, Jerome O., 1990. 'Global metal pollution – poisoning the biosphere?', *Environment*, 32, 7, September.

Parikh, Jyoti *et al.*, 1991. *Consumption Patterns – the Driving Force of Environmental Stress*, Indira Gandhi Institute of Development Research, Bombay, October.

People, (IPPF, London), 1991. 18, 2–3.

Pradervand, Pierre, 1991. 'The interaction of population and natural resources', background document for Social Services Division, IUCN, Gland, Switzerland.

Pradervand, Pierre, 1992 (forthcoming). 'The salt of the Earth', *People and the Planet* (IPPF, UNFPA and IUCN, London), 1, 1.

Qu Geping, 1989. 'Over the limit', *Earthwatch*, (IPPF, UNFPA and IUCN, London), 34.

Rambo, Terry, 1990. 'Slash-and-burn farmers: victims or villains?', *Earthwatch*, (IPPF, UNFPA and IUCN, London), 39.

Reditt, Jacqueline, 1981. 'Quietly weaving a new social fabric', *People* (IPPF, London), 8, 3.

Rowley, John, 1984. 'A watershed of ideas', *People*, (IPPF, London), 11, 4.

Rowley, John, 1987. 'Helping people to build a million houses', *People* (IPPF, London), 14, 1.

Sadik, Nafis, 1990. *The State of World Population 1990*, UNFPA, New York.

Speth, James Gustave, 1991a. 'Environmentally unsustainable consumption patterns: is there a way out?', (mimeo), background paper for the UNCED secretariat, World Resources Institute, Washington, DC.

Speth, James Gustave, 1991b. 'On the road to Rio and to sustainability: addressing the real problems', (mimeo), paper for the Malente Symposium IX, World Resources Institute, Washington, DC.

Thiesenhusen, W. C. (ed.), 1989. *Searching for Agricultural Reform in Latin America*, Unwin Hyman, Boston, Mass.

Tinbergen, Jan, and Hueting, Roefie, 1991. 'GNP and market prices – wrong signals for sustainable economic success that mask environmental destruction', in Robert Goodland, *et al.* (eds), *Environmentally Sustainable Economic Development: Building on Brundtland*, UNESCO, Paris.

345

UNDP, 1991. *Human Development Report*, Oxford University Press.

UNFPA, 1991. *Population Issues – Briefing Kit*, UNFPA, New York.

UNICEF, 1991. *The State of the World's Children*, UNICEF, New York.

UNICEF, 1992. *The State of the World's Children*, UNICEF, New York.

Werner, Louis, 1991. 'Crossing the Rio Grande', *People* (IPPF, London), 18, 4.

WHO, 1992. *Our Planet, Our Health.* Report by the WHO Commission on Health and the Environment, WHO, Geneva.

World Bank, 1990. *World Development Report 1990*, Oxford University Press, Oxford.

Index